2004

W9-BNP-067

Marketing For Dummies
2nd Edition

Cheat Sheet

Seven Principles of Brilliant Sales and Marketing

Whatever you sell and whatever the size of your business, these simple and universal practices can help you market more effectively:

- **Never miss an opportunity to present yourself well.** Everything from your clothing and business card to the envelope in which you send a bill must work toward your marketing goals.

- **Spend at least ten minutes a day marketing your company.** So many people don't do marketing routinely — and then complain that they don't have enough customers or revenues.

- **Know what you want to get out of your marketing before you write the first check.** You can lose your focus all too easily and invest in useless activities. In a field as complex and multifaceted as marketing, have a simple, clear objective in sight at all times.

- **Know what makes you special to customers and prospects,** so that you can remind them of your strengths in every marketing communication. They buy from you for this reason alone.

- **Experiment.** Great businesses are built on great marketing formulas, and you have to arrive at those formulas through trial and error.

- **Sort out the people who don't want what you sell** and eliminate them from your marketing right away. Wasting time and effort on the wrong prospects is the single biggest cause of inefficiency in sales and marketing.

- **If your plan looks complicated, you aren't done with it yet.** The best marketing is blindingly simple. You want to aim for a one-page marketing plan, because you may actually be able to implement it!

Ten Ways to Spend Less on Marketing

Because marketing is a creative activity, you can always find new and better ways to make an impact and attract sales, even on a small budget. Here are some ideas that help you maximize your impact while minimizing your budget:

- **Make your communications more visually striking** by including images of people and using creative, dynamic layouts. This visual style gets more reader attention than any letter, brochure, or ad you generate, making it more effective and efficient for you.

- **Improve the appearance of your logo.** Most logos are boring, but great companies always have great logos. Wonder which came first?

- **Buy visibility on the Google and Yahoo! search engines.** This is inexpensive enough to work for local as well as global markets.

- **Release a survey** or host an interesting event to generate publicity.

- **Send out a press release** to your local media once every quarter or whenever you have valuable news to release, updating them on events in your business. Getting local news coverage isn't that hard, and it often attracts new business.

- **Find something simple and inexpensive to offer** along with your most popular product or service in order to pick up add-on sales.

- **Give out coupons to encourage prospects to try your product or service,** so that its qualities become obvious to them. Don't, however, give away price-cutting coupons or discounts for no good reason — think of other ways to increase sales appeal.

- **Offer (or improve) a guarantee,** one with no small print. If you have a good product or service, stand behind it!

- **Vow to never lose a customer.** Whenever you have a customer who's upset or at risk, find out why and win him back.

- **Figure out where you lose the most prospects or potential customers** and then concentrate your marketing at this point to convert more of them into customers.

For Dummies: Bestselling Book Series for Beginners

Marketing For Dummies, 2nd Edition

Cheat Sheet

Five Ways to Harness Marketing Energy

Marketing can do amazing things for a business if the process is creative and innovative. Here are some simple techniques to add creative energy to all your marketing efforts:

- **Brainstorming:** Think of 100 new ideas for marketing your business, and then use the best 10.
- **Analogies:** Think of things that your product is similar to and tell the customer (or potential customer) why.
- **Pass-along:** Write a simple idea for sales or marketing on a piece of paper or in an e-mail, and then pass that idea along to someone else with the instruction that he or she should add to it or list another idea. Keep circulating it until your coworkers or friends have helped you generate a long list of ideas and options to choose from.
- **Question assumptions:** Make a list of stupid questions and take the time to ask people what they think. "Why do you have to have branches to be in the banking business?" is a good example of a "stupid" question that may lead to a breakthrough marketing concept.
- **Rewriting:** Good old editing and rewriting can lead you to better marketing communications — it opens more creative doors than any other technique. Take a copy of a brochure and make yourself come up with five new headlines or titles that you can use for the cover of it. I'll bet you come up with at least one that's much more striking and interesting than the existing one. And you may realize that you can redo that brochure to make it more effective. Go ahead and try it.

Nine Rules for Avoiding Business Trouble

A dangerous area of marketing arises when people try to bypass regulations that ensure fair pricing, safety, and honest advertising. Such regulations are quite strong in the United States and Canada and have parallels in many other countries, as well.

- Always make sure your pricing is fair to customers and competitors (because unfair competitive practices are usually illegal).
- Always offer goods or services equal to or better than your competitors', never worse.
- Always clarify the limits of warranties for services or goods.
- Always provide full warnings and details about your product's content and source on labels.
- Always follow an open and honest policy with the media.
- Never say anything deceptive or misleading in ads or other communications.
- Don't limit access to special deals (legally, you have to allow everyone to take advantage of special deals, not just your best customers).
- Never distribute products that can do significant harm to anyone.
- Never discuss prices with competitors (that's called *price fixing,* and people go to jail for it!).

Wiley, the Wiley Publishing logo, For Dummies, the Dummies Man logo, the For Dummies Bestselling Book Series logo and all related trade dress are trademarks or registered trademarks of John Wiley & Sons, Inc. and/or its affiliates. All other trademarks are property of their respective owners.

For Dummies: Bestselling Book Series for Beginners

Marketing

FOR

DUMMIES®

2ND EDITION

Marketing
FOR
DUMMIES®
2ND EDITION

by Alexander Hiam, MBA

WILEY

Wiley Publishing, Inc.

Marketing For Dummies®, 2nd Edition

Published by
Wiley Publishing, Inc.
111 River St.
Hoboken, NJ 07030-5774
www.wiley.com

WILEY

About the Author

Alex Hiam is a consultant, corporate trainer, and public speaker with 20 years of experience in marketing, sales, and corporate communications. He is the director of Insights, which includes a division called Insights for Marketing that offers a wide range of services for supporting and training in sales, customer service, planning, and management. His firm is also active in developing the next generation of leaders in the workplace through its Insights for Training & Development arm. Alex has an MBA in marketing and strategic planning from the Haas School at U.C. Berkeley and an undergraduate degree from Harvard. He has worked as a marketing manager for both smaller high-tech firms and a *Fortune* 100 company, and did a stint as a professor of marketing at the business school at U. Mass Amherst.

Alex is the co-author of the best-seller, *The Portable MBA in Marketing* (Wiley), as well as *The Vest-Pocket CEO* and numerous other books and training programs. He has consulted to a wide range of companies and not-for-profit and government agencies, from General Motors and Volvo to HeathEast and the U.S. Army (a fuller list of clients is posted at www.insightsformarketing.com).

Alex is also the author of a companion volume to this book, the *Marketing Kit For Dummies* (Wiley), which includes more detailed coverage of many of the hands-on topics involved in creating great advertising, direct mail letters, Web sites, publicity campaigns, and marketing plans. On the CD that comes with the *Marketing Kit For Dummies,* you'll find forms, checklists, and templates that may be of use to you. Also, Alex maintains an extensive Web site of resources that he organized to support each of the chapters in this book.

Publisher's Acknowledgments

We're proud of this book; please send us your comments through our Dummies online registration form located at www.dummies.com/register/.

Some of the people who helped bring this book to market include the following:

Acquisitions, Editorial, and Media Development

Project Editor: Tere Drenth

(Previous Edition: Jennifer Ehrlich)

Acquisitions Editors: Norm Crampton, Holly Gastineau-Grimes, Stacy Kennedy

Copy Editor: Laura K. Miller

General Reviewer: Celia Rocks

Editorial Manager: Michelle Hacker

Editorial Assistant: Elizabeth Rea

Cartoons: Rich Tennant, (www.the5thwave.com)

Production

Project Coordinator: Adrienne Martinez

Layout and Graphics: Andrea Dahl, Denny Hager, Heather Ryan

Proofreaders: Laura Albert, Andy Hollandbeck, Carl William Pierce, Brian H. Walls, TECHBOOKS Production Services

Indexer: TECHBOOKS Production Services

Special Help: Jennifer Bingham

Publishing and Editorial for Consumer Dummies

Diane Graves Steele, Vice President and Publisher, Consumer Dummies

Joyce Pepple, Acquisitions Director, Consumer Dummies

Kristin A. Cocks, Product Development Director, Consumer Dummies

Michael Spring, Vice President and Publisher, Travel

Brice Gosnell, Associate Publisher, Travel

Kelly Regan, Editorial Director, Travel

Publishing for Technology Dummies

Andy Cummings, Vice President and Publisher, Dummies Technology/General User

Composition Services

Gerry Fahey, Vice President of Production Services

Debbie Stailey, Director of Composition Services

Contents at a Glance

Table of Contents

Introduction

· ·

Marketing is the most important thing that you can do in business today, even if your job title doesn't have the word *marketing* in it. Marketing, in all its varied forms, focuses on attracting customers, getting them to buy, and making sure that they're happy enough with their purchase that they come back for more. What could be more important? Ever try to run a business without customers?

This book is the second edition of *Marketing For Dummies*. Since I researched and wrote the first edition, I've benefited from the experiences and questions of hundreds of thousands of readers. In that time, I also wrote the companion to this book, *Marketing Kit For Dummies*. Now, in this book, I'm excited to see how many improvements and additions I can make this time around. In addition to updating, I've added a great many more tips and quick-action ideas to help the busy reader find solutions and take actions that can produce an impact on sales and profits quickly.

About This Book

I wrote this book to help you do that critical job of marketing as well as you possibly can. I wrote with a variety of marketers in mind, including small business owners and entrepreneurs who wear the marketing and sales hat along with several other hats. I also wrote for managers and staffers of larger organizations who work on plans, programs, product launches, ad campaigns, printed materials, Web sites, and other elements of their organization's outreach to customers and prospects.

I kept in mind that some of my readers market consumer products, others sell to businesses, and some market physical products, while others offer services. The different types of business have many important distinctions, but good marketing techniques can work wonders anywhere.

Marketing can be a great deal of fun — it is, after all, the most creative area of most businesses. In the long run, however, marketing is all about the bottom line. So, although I had fun writing this book, and I think you can enjoy using it, I take the subject matter very seriously. Any task that brings you to this book is vitally important, and I want to make sure that the advice you get here helps you perform especially well.

Conventions Used in This Book

I refer to any organized, coordinated use of sales, advertising, publicity, customer service, the Web, direct mail, or any other efforts to contact and influence customers as your *marketing program.* I want you to have a marketing program. Creating a program means avoiding random or disconnected activities. It also means thinking about how everything interlinks and contributes to achieving your marketing goals. Whether you work in a large organization or own a small business, you need a coherent, well-thought-out marketing program!

I refer to whoever buys what you sell as the *customer.* This customer can be a person, a household, a business, a government agency, a school, or even a voter. I still call them your customers, and the rules of sound marketing still apply to them. (Some of my first-edition readers applied the principles of marketing to the challenge of attracting new members for their church congregation — thus proving just how broadly you can productively apply the techniques!)

I refer to what you sell or offer to customers as your *product,* whether it's a good, service, idea, or even a person (such as a political candidate or a celebrity). Your product can be animate or inanimate, tangible or intangible. Many of my readers sell services. But if you offer it, it's a product in marketing jargon, and using just one term for whatever the reader wants to sell saves us all a lot of time and wasted printer's ink.

I also treat person-to-person sales as one of the many possible activities under the marketing umbrella. You need to integrate selling, which is its own highly sophisticated and involved field, into the broader range of activities designed to help bring about sales and satisfy customers. I address ways of managing sales better as part of my overall efforts to make all your marketing activities more effective.

Foolish Assumptions

I assume that you're reasonably intelligent (not a foolish assumption, given what I know about my past readers). You need to be clever, caring, and persistent to do marketing well. But, although I believe you're intelligent, I assume that you don't have all the technical knowledge that you may need to do great marketing, so I explain each technique as clearly as I can.

I also assume that you're willing to try new ideas in order to improve sales results and grow your organization. Marketing is challenging and requires an open mind and a willingness to experiment and try new ideas and techniques.

I must also assume that you're willing and able to switch from being imaginative and creative one moment to being analytical and rigorous the next. Marketing has to take both approaches. Sometimes, I ask you to run the numbers and do sales projections. Other times, I ask you to dream up a clever way to catch a reader's eye and communicate a benefit to them. These demands pull you in opposite directions. If you can assemble a team of varied people, some of them numbers oriented and some of them artistic, you can cover all the marketing bases more easily. But if you have a small business, you may be all you have, and you need to wear each hat in turn. At least you never get bored as you tackle the varied challenges of marketing!

Finally, I assume that you have an active interest in generating new sales and maximizing the satisfaction of existing customers. This sales orientation needs to underlie everything you do in marketing. Keep in mind that the broader purpose on every page of this book is to try to help you make more and better sales happen!

How This Book Is Organized

This book is organized into parts that I describe in the following sections. Check out the Table of Contents for more information on the topics of the chapters within each part.

Part 1: Designing a Great Marketing Program

Military strategists know that great battles must be won first in the general's tent, with carefully considered plans and accurate maps, before the general commits any troops to action on the field of battle. In marketing, you don't have any lives at stake, but you may hold the future success of your organization in your hands! I advocate just as careful an approach to analysis and planning as if you were a general preparing on the eve of battle. In Chapter 1, I show you how to make sure that you have an efficient, effective program (meaning a coordinated set of marketing activities). In Chapter 2, I also show you how to base your program on strong, aggressive strategies that maximize your chances of sales and success. And in Chapter 3, I help you write your strategies and tactics down in a plan of action that you can be reasonably confident will actually work.

Part II: Leveraging Your Marketing Skills

Great marketing requires a wide range of special skills. If you don't already have all of them, this part shores up any gaps and helps you take advantage of specialized tools and techniques.

In Chapter 4, I cover an essential marketing skill: how to find out what you need to know in order to develop better strategies and design better ads and other elements of the marketing program. Where can you find the best customers? What do they respond to? What is the competition up to? Imagining, communicating, and researching make up the power skills of great marketers, and I want to make their benefits available to you!

Chapter 5 shares that most precious and hard-to-capture of marketing skills: the marketing imagination. When marketers can bottle up a little of this magic and work it into their marketing programs, good things begin to happen. Chapter 6 addresses another fundamental marketing skill: communicating with customers. Good ideas plus clear, interesting communications add up to better marketing.

Part III: Advertising for Fun and Profit

Advertising is the traditional cornerstone of marketing. Firms combined advertisements with sales calls back in the early days of marketing, and great things happened to their revenues. In this part, I show you how to create compelling, effective ads, brochures, and fliers on paper — the traditional medium of marketing. You can run full-page, color ads in national magazines if you have a big budget, or you can place small, cheap black-and-whites in a local newspaper — and either one may prove effective with the right creativity and design. Everyone can access radio and TV these days, too, regardless of budget, if you know how to use these media economically and well. However, you may also want to use perhaps the simplest — and most powerful — form of advertising: the simple sign; from signs on buildings, vehicles, and doors to posters at airports and billboards on roadways. You can put advertising to good use in your business in so many different ways.

Part IV: Finding Powerful Alternatives to Advertising

Many marketers are discovering the power of publicity and discovering how to help the media cover their stories and to get more exposure at far less cost than if they had advertised. Special events also provide you with a powerful alternative or supplement to ad campaigns and can bring you high-quality sales leads. Also take a good look at how you use (or can begin using) direct mail, the Web, and other options for bringing in prospects and closing high-quality sales.

Part V: Selling Great Products to Anyone, Anytime, Anywhere

The classic marketing program has five components (the 5 Ps), but much of what marketers do (and what is covered throughout Parts I through IV) falls into the fourth P: promotion. In this part, I'm going to go deeper into the other Ps: product design and branding, pricing and discounting to create incentives for purchase, the aggressive use of distribution strategies to place your product in front of consumers when and where they are most likely to buy, and selling and servicing customers. I want to draw your attention to the all-important product and make sure yours is naturally brilliant enough to shine out and beckon customers to you. I also encourage you to examine your distribution, sales, and service, because these can make or break a marketing program (and a business), too.

Part VI: The Part of Tens

The Part of Tens is a traditional element of *For Dummies* books, and it communicates brief but essential tips that didn't fit easily into the other parts. I recommend that you look at this part whenever you need insights or ideas because it encapsulates much of the essential philosophy and strategies of good marketing practice. And reading this part also helps you avoid some of the dead ends and traps that await the unwary marketer.

Icons Used in This Book

Look for these symbols to help you find valuable stuff throughout the text:

This icon flags specific advice that you can try out in your marketing program right away. The icon uses a dollar sign for the filament of the light bulb because the acid test of any great idea in business rests in whether it can make you some money.

Sometimes, you need the right perspective on a problem to reach success, so this icon also flags brief discussions of how to think about the task at hand. Often, a basic principle of marketing pops up at this icon to help you handle important decisions.

All marketing is real-world marketing, but this icon means that you can find an actual example of something that worked (or didn't work) in the real world for another marketer.

In marketing, lone rangers don't last long. Successful marketers use a great many supporting services and often bring in graphic artists, ad agencies, research firms, package designers, retail display designers, publicists, and many other specialists. You can't do it all. Sometimes, the best advice I can give you is to pick up your phone and make a call. And this icon marks a spot where I give you leads and contacts.

You can easily run into trouble in marketing because so many mines are just waiting for you to step on them. That's why I've marked them all with this symbol.

When I want to remind you of essential or critical information you need to know in order to succeed, I mark it with this icon. Don't forget!

Where to Go from Here

If you read only one chapter in one business book this year, please make it Chapter 1 of this book. I've made this chapter stand alone as a powerful way to audit your marketing and upgrade or enhance the things that you do to make profitable sales. I've packed the rest of the book with good tips and techniques, and it all deserves attention. But whatever else you do or don't get around to, read the first chapter with a pen and action-list at hand!

Or maybe you have a pressing need in one of the more specific areas covered by the book. If fixing your Web site is the top item on your to-do list, go to Chapter 10 first. If you need to increase the effectiveness of your sales force, try Chapter 17, instead. Or are you working on a letter to customers? Then Chapters 6 and 13 on marketing communications and direct mail can really help out your project. Whatever you're doing, I have a hunch that this book has a chapter or two to help you out. So don't let me slow you down. Get going! It's never too early (or too late) to do a little marketing.

Part I
Designing a Great Marketing Program

The 5th Wave   By Rich Tennant

"That's very innovative of the Girl Scouts, but I'm just not interested in buying a box of Girl Scout Cigars."

In this part . . .

*J*ohn W. Teets, as chairman of the Greyhound Corporation, supposedly advised his people that management's job is to see the company not as it is, but as it can be. Helping you recognize that vision is the purpose of this part. Whatever your current business or service is and does, this part helps you imagine and plan what it may best become in the next quarter and year. How do you do that?

You need, first, to understand your marketing program — the integrated ways in which you reach out to motivate customers and win their loyal support. Next, I highly recommend that you come to grips with the big strategy questions in a marketer's life — who are we and what makes us so special that our sales and profits deserve to grow? Finally, I also recommend that you write down your big-picture insights to help organize and simplify later decisions about the details of marketing. A plan, even a simple one-page plan, can help you a lot as you make marketing decisions throughout the coming year.

Chapter 1

Maximizing Your Marketing Program

*I*n case you think a program sounds too formal for you, think again. All organized, planned, and focused marketing or sales activities are (in marketing lingo, at least), *programs*. Without the structure of an organized program, marketing efforts are inefficient and uncoordinated. If you don't know whether you have a marketing program, then you probably have an inefficient one that you can improve dramatically before the end of this chapter. And if you do have a defined marketing program, this chapter can help you increase its impact.

A marketing program ought to be based on a *marketing strategy,* which is the big-picture idea driving your success. The program shows all the coordinated activities that together make up the tactics. In other words, your program is the way you want to implement your strategy. And if you want to make both strategy and program clear, write them both up in a *marketing plan.* But you don't have to get fully into the technicalities of strategies and plans right now, because in this chapter, I go over lots of simpler, quicker things you can do to leverage your marketing activities.

Knowing Your Customer

The first and most important principle of marketing is: Know your customer. When you understand how customers think and what they like, you can find appropriate and appealing ways to communicate with them about the product or service you want them to buy.

Make 7-Up yours!

Imagine this scene: A group of teenage boys is sitting around, talking and laughing. One of them makes a joking insult to another, and the second one shoots back the phrase, "Make seven." Everyone bursts out laughing. What just happened, and what in the world does it have to do with marketing?

For further insight into this scene, you may also need to know that one of the teenagers is wearing a T-shirt that says "Make 7" on the front, and on the back, "Up Yours!" The phrase **up yours** is a rather coarse insult, and the T-shirt represents a play on the phrase "Make 7-Up Yours." For those in the know, the "Make 7" from the front of the shirt can replace the traditional insult on the back of the T-shirt.

Not laughing yet? Chances are, you're not in the 12- to 24-year-old demographic group that the Make 7-Up Yours! ad campaign targeted. It was used to increase the appeal of the beverage to a contemporary teen audience in the United States, and it worked. The brand won the interest of teens and young adults with this campaign, especially males in this age group. And they happen to be heavy consumers of sodas, so they can increase sales and market share if they like a brand.

You need to understand your customer on two levels: the rational, functional dimension of making a purchase decision, and the irrational, emotional dimension. Every purchase, whether of a soda, a software program, a consulting service, a book, or a manufacturing part, has both rational and emotional elements. So to truly know your customer, you must explore two questions:

- ✔ **How do they feel about your product?** Does it make them feel good? Do they like its personality? Do they like how it makes them feel about themselves?

- ✔ **What do they think about your product?** Do they understand it? Do they think its features and benefits are superior to the competition and can meet their needs? Do they feel that your product is a good value given its benefits and costs?

Sometimes, one of these dimensions dominates for the customer you want to sell to. In other instances they're equally important. Which is true of your customers? You need to take one of the three following approaches:

- ✔ **Informational approach:** The approach you use if your customers buy in a rational manner. This is the case for many business-to-business marketers. It involves showing the product and talking about its benefits. Comparisons to worse alternatives are a great idea when using an informational approach. Use this approach when you think buyers are going to make a careful, thoughtful, informed purchase decision or when you have strong evidence in favor of their buying *your* product or service instead of others.

✔ **Emotional approach:** This approach pushes emotional instead of rational buttons. For example, a marketer of virus-scanning software may try to scare computer users by asking them in a headline, "What would it cost you if a virus destroyed everything on your computer right now?" That emotional appeal can be much more powerful than a pile of statistics about the frequency and type of viruses on the Web. Use an emotional approach when your customers have strong feelings you can tap into and relate to your product or service, or when you think people are going to make an impulse decision.

✔ **Balanced mix:** This approach uses a combination of informational and emotional appeals. It is what I would choose to sell anti-virus software, and many other products, because it engages both the rational and emotional sides of the buyer's mind. For example, after a scare-tactic (emotional) headline asking what would happen if a virus destroyed everything on your computer, I would follow up with a few statistics such as, "One out of every ten computer users suffers a catastrophic virus attack each year." The facts reinforce the nervous feelings the headline evoked, helping move the prospect toward purchase.

Decide which of these three approaches to use, and use it consistently in all your communications. And when in doubt, use the balanced mix to hedge your bets.

Getting focused

You begin to organize and focus your marketing program when you define as clearly as possible who you're targeting with your marketing. Your marketing may include sales, service, product design and packaging, all marketing and media communications, and anything else that helps win loyal customers. A marketing program can encompass tens to hundreds of contributing elements, so you need a clear focus to keep them all on target. Remember that your target is a clearly defined customer.

To help you focus, write a detailed description of this customer, as if you were developing their character for use in a novel or screenplay you plan to write. (The plot of this story is, of course, that the character falls in love — with your product.)

You further increase your focus when you decide whether your target customers prefer marketing that takes a rational, information-based approach, an emotional, personality-based approach, or a balanced mix of the two. By simply being clear about whom to target and whether to market to them in an informational or emotional manner, you have taken a great leap in providing a clear focus. You know whom to target, and you have an important clue as to how to target them and communicate with them in every element of your program.

Another aspect of your customer focus is whether you want to emphasize attracting new customers, or retaining and growing existing customers. One or the other may need to dominate your marketing program, or perhaps you need to balance the two. Marketing to new prospects is usually a different sort of challenge from communicating with and satisfying existing customers, so knowing what is most important helps you to improve the effectiveness of your marketing.

As a marketer, you face a great many decisions and details. Marketing tends to be fragmented, so that marketing efforts spring up with every good idea or customer demand, rather like rabbits. In most organizations, hundreds of marketing rabbits are running around, each one in a slightly different direction from any other. Focus gets every element of your marketing program moving in the right direction.

Finding out why customers like you

In marketing, always think about what you do well, and make sure you build on your strengths in everything you do.

You can't be all things to all customers. You can't be the best on every rational and emotional dimension. If you try to meet the competition on their ground, you remain in second place. So now I want you to clearly and succinctly define (notes, please!) what your special strength or advantage is. Start your sentence like this: "My product (or service) is special because . . ."

Your answer to that question reflects whatever the special brilliance of your product or business is. I'm borrowing this term from Celia Rocks, a marketing agency director who developed a concept called *brilliance marketing* and who works with marketers to identify their most fundamental strengths before trying to do any advertising, sales, publicity, or other marketing. Then she makes sure that everything they say and do is based on their strengths.

Use this strength-based marketing method to add an additional degree of focus to your marketing program. Take a minute to think about what makes your firm or product special, and why customers have been attracted to the light of your brilliance in the past. Then make sure your program amplifies and reflects your light and never loses sight of it.

For example, if you're known for good customer service, make sure to train, recognize, and reward good service in your employees, and to emphasize good service in all communications with your customers and prospects. A photo of a friendly, helpful employee ought to be featured in your advertising, brochures, sales sheets, or Web page, because friendliness personifies your special brilliance in customer service. You can also quote customer testimonials that praise your service. And you may want to offer a satisfaction guarantee of some sort too. Focus on your strength in all that you do, and your marketing program becomes more profitable.

Figuring out the best way to find customers

I periodically survey managers of successful businesses to ask them about their marketing practices. And the first and most revealing question I ask is, "What is the best way to attract customers?" Now, the interesting thing about this question is that the answer differs for every successful business. So, you need to answer this question yourself; you can't look the answer up in a book.

Take a look at the following list to see some of the most common answers — things that businesses often say are most effective at bringing them customers:

- ✔ **Referrals:** Customers sell the product (see coverage of word of mouth in Chapter 11 for how to stimulate them).

- ✔ **Trade shows and professional association meetings:** Contacts sell the product (see Chapter 12).

- ✔ **Sales calls:** Salespeople sell the product (see Chapter 17).

- ✔ **TV, radio, or print ads:** Advertising sells the product (see the chapters in Part III).

- ✔ **Product demonstrations, trial coupons, or distribution of free samples:** Product sells itself (see Chapters 14 and 15).

- ✔ **Web sites and newsletters:** Internet information sells the product (see Chapter 10).

- ✔ **Placement and appearance of buildings/stores:** Location sells the product (see Chapter 16).

As the preceding list indicates, each business has a different optimal formula for attracting customers. However, in every case, successful businesses report that one or two methods work best. Their programs are therefore dominated by one or two effective ways of attracting customers. They put one-third to two-thirds of their marketing resources into the top ways of attracting customers, and then use other marketing methods to support and leverage their most effective method. And they don't spend any time or money on marketing activities inconsistent with their best method and that rob resources from it.

So, you need to find the one best way to attract customers to your business. If you already know, you may not be focusing your marketing program around it fully. So you need to make another action note and answer another question: What is your best way to attract customers, and how can you focus your marketing program to take fuller advantage of it?

When you answer this question, you're taking yet another important step toward a highly focused marketing program that leverages your resources as much as possible. Your marketing program can probably be divided into three lists of activities:

  ✔ Works best

  ✔ Helpful

  ✔ Doesn't work

If you reorganize last year's budget into these categories, you may well find that your spending isn't concentrated near the top of your list. If not, then you can try to move your focus and spending up. I call this the *marketing pyramid,* and in workshops, I challenge marketers to try to move their spending up the pyramid so that their marketing resources are concentrated near the top. What does your marketing pyramid look like? Can you move up it by shifting resources and investments to higher-pulling marketing activities?

Defining Your Marketing Program

Peter Drucker, one of few justly famous management gurus, has defined marketing as the whole firm, taken from the customer's point of view. This definition is powerful, because it reminds you that your view from the inside is likely to be very different from the customer's view. And who cares what you see? The success of any business comes down to what customers do, and they can only act based on what they see. That's why marketing and advertising gurus often say, "Perception is everything." You must find ways to listen to your customers and to understand their perceptions of your firm and offerings, because your customers (not you) need to define your marketing program.

This section requires you to think about and write down some ideas, so get out a pencil and some paper to jot down notes while you're reading.

Finding your influence points

From the customer's point of view, identify the components of your marketing program. (The components include everything and anything that the customer sees, hears, talks to, uses, or otherwise interacts with.) Each customer interaction, exposure, or contact is an influence point where good marketing can help build customer interest and loyalty.

I want to warn you that, if you have a marketing plan or budget already, it probably doesn't reflect this customer perspective accurately. For example, in many firms, the marketing department is separate from product development, yet customers interact with your products so, to them, this is a key component of the marketing program.

Similarly, some of the people who sell your product may not be in your plan or even on your company's payroll. A salesperson in the field, a distributor, a wholesaler, or anyone else who sells, delivers, represents, repairs, or services your product is on the marketing front lines from the customer's perspective. All these people may be seen to represent or even be the product, from the customer's point of view. Are they all representing your firm and product properly — with the focus and professionalism you want in your marketing program? Are they available when and where needed? Are they likeable? Is their presentation and personality consistent with your strategy for your marketing program? If not, you must find ways to improve their impact on the customer, even though you may not have formal authority over them.

Analyzing your five Ps

In marketing, the only things that really matter are points of contact between the customer and your communications, products, and people. These interactions with you constitute the marketing program, from the customer's point of view. I call them influence points, and I find that most of them aren't itemized in a firm's marketing budget or plan.

When does your customer interact with your people, your product, or information about your people and product? Take a few minutes to make up your master list of influence points, which will form the basis of a more extensive and accurate marketing program and plan. To help you do this, I suggest you use the five Ps of marketing: product, price, placement, promotion, and people. Now think about your influence points using these five Ps.

Product

What aspects of the product itself are important — have an influence on customer perception and purchase intentions? Include tangible features and intangibles like personality, look and feel, and also packaging. Remember that first impressions are important for initial purchase, but that performance of the product over time is more important for repurchase and referrals. (And remember that by *product,* marketers mean whatever it is you offer your customers, whether physical and tangible or intangible and more service oriented.)

List the aspects (both rational features and emotional impressions) of your product that influence customer perception.

Price

What does it cost the customer to obtain and use your product? The list price is often an important element of the customer's perception of price, but it isn't the only one. Discounts and special offers are part of the list of price-based influence points too. And don't forget any extra costs the customer may have to incur, like the cost of switching from another product to yours. This can really affect the customer's perception of how attractive your product is. (If you can find ways to make it easier/cheaper to switch from the competitor's product to yours, you may be able to charge more for your product and still make more sales.)

List the aspects of price that influence customer perception.

Placement

When and where is your product available to customers? Place is a big influence, because most of the time, customers aren't actively shopping for your product. Nobody runs around all day every day looking for what you want to sell her. When someone wants something, she is most strongly influenced by what is available to her. Getting the place and timing right is a big part of success in marketing and often very difficult. When and where do you currently make your product available to customers?

List the aspects of placement (in both time and space) that influence accessibility of your product.

Promotion

This fourth P incorporates any and all ways you choose to communicate to customers. Do you advertise? Send mailings? Hand out brochures? What about the visibility of signs on buildings or vehicles? Do distributors or other marketing partners also communicate with your customer? If so, include their promotional materials and methods because they help shape the customer's perception too. And what about other routine elements of customer communication, like bills? They're a part of the impression your marketing communications make too.

List all the ways you have to promote your offering by communicating with customers and prospects.

People

Almost all businesses offer a variety of human contacts to customers and prospective customers, including salespeople, receptionists, service and support personnel, collections, and sometimes shipping, billing, repair, or other personnel, too. All these points of human contact are important parts of the marketing program, even though they may not all be working well to help keep your program focused and effective right now.

List all the points of human contact that may be important to the success of your program.

Adding to your list

You need to find efficient, effective ways to positively influence customer perception. You want to use elements of your marketing program to motivate customers to buy and use your product (service, firm, whatever). The list of your current influence points for each of your five Ps is just a starting point on your journey to an optimal marketing program. Now ask yourself what else can be added. Think about each of the five Ps and try to add more possible influence points. Look to competitors or successful marketers from outside your product category and industry for some fresh ideas. The longer your list of possibilities, the more likely you are to find really good things to include in your marketing program.

For example, Guthy-Renker prints up brochures describing its Rodan & Fields Proactivity Solution acne mediation and has them stuffed in bags at Staples during the fall back-to-school shopping season. Teenagers shop for their school supplies at Staples, and they're big users of acne mediations. These medications are traditionally sold via expensive TV advertising, but Guthy-Renker finds the shopping bag stuffers are a powerful supplementary way to influence customers to choose their brand over others.

Can you think of one or more new ways to reach and influence your customers and prospects in each of the five Ps? If so, add them to your list as possibilities for your next marketing program.

Determining what works best for each P

Within each of the five Ps of marketing, one or two things have the biggest impact and give you the most improvement for your effort. Make your best guess or do some research to find out what works best.

Observe the results from different activities in an experimental way and then focus on those activities that produce the biggest results. Or you can ask customers or industry experts their opinion to find out what elements of each of the five Ps have the biggest impact on your customers and their purchase decisions. Should you concentrate your resources on a bigger presence at industry trade shows, or build up your Web site? Should you use print advertising or hire a publicist to get editorial coverage? Depends on what works best for you program, customers, and industry.

Deciding which P is most important

Ask yourself which of the five Ps needs to be most important in your marketing program. If you've already identified what customers like about you (for example, your marketing brilliance or a distinct point of difference from competitors), this may point you toward one of the five Ps.

The company that sells the quality of its service, for example, obviously needs to emphasize people in its marketing program and business plan. In contrast, the company whose products are technically superior needs to make sure its marketing investments focus on maintaining the product edge.

Don't be tempted to make price the main focus of your marketing program. Many marketers emphasize discounts and low prices to attract customers. But price is a dangerous emphasis for any marketing program; you're buying customers instead of winning them. And that is a very, very hard way to make a profit in business. So unless you actually have a sustainable cost advantage (a rare thing in business), don't allow low prices or coupons and discounts to dominate your marketing program. Price reasonably, use discounts and price-off coupons sparingly, and look for other things to focus on in your marketing program.

Are Parts of Your Program Uncontrolled?

I want to give you a simple example to show how hard it is to control all the influence points in a marketing program, for a company whose marketing I recently evaluated. American Marine is a Singapore-based manufacturer of high-quality, attractive Grand Banks motor yachts. Their products are handsome, rugged, and seaworthy, and customers have an almost fanatical love of and loyalty to the product. (In other words, the product sells itself, if you can just find people who have enough money to buy it.) This manufacturer showcases the product in its well-designed, full-color brochures and product sheets, with both attractive color photos of the boats and detailed specifications and floor plans. (The company recognizes that customers have both informational and emotional elements in their purchase decision, and it covers both bases well in its printed materials.)

However, Grand Banks yachts are sold through regional distributors, who occasionally fail to maintain the same high standards when they add their own cover letter or other printed materials to the manufacturer's marketing materials. Recently, I was asked to evaluate a regional distributor's presentation, so I requested information over the Internet. In response, I received a plain, low-quality brown envelope with a boring, black-ink cover letter lacking any picture or logo-type drawing of the product. Hidden beneath this unimpressive packaging and form letter were the truly impressive corporate brochures about the product. The product in this case costs (for a used boat) a half million dollars or more, and a new one can cost more than a million. To make a sale like that, you need to put some extra care and effort into making sure everything you show the prospect is sophisticated and impressive.

I see communication problems like this all too often with my clients. The Grand Banks mailing would have been much more effective if the entire package were done to the high standards set by the corporate marketing materials and the product itself. My recommendation was that both envelope and cover letter ought to:

✔ Demonstrate high-quality design and materials to represent the fine craftsmanship of the product.

✔ Show the product, because the product makes the sale in this case.

Little details can and do make all the difference in closing a sale! Does your marketing program display this kind of inconsistency and does it also miss opportunities to get the message across fully and well? If so, you can increase your program's effectiveness by eliminating these pockets of inconsistency to prevent out-of-control marketing. Given the reality that some of your influence points may be partially or fully uncontrolled right now, I want you to draw up a list of inconsistent and/or uncontrolled elements of your marketing program. I think you will find some in each of the five Ps of your program — these inconsistencies are common. And if you can make even one of them work better and more consistently with your overall program and its focus, you're improving the effectiveness of your marketing. Use Table 1-1.

Table 1-1	Focusing Your Marketing Program for Fun and Profit
Customer Focus	
Define your customers clearly: Who are they? Where and when do they want to buy?	
Are they new customers, existing customers, or a balanced mix of both?	
Understand what emotional elements make them buy: What personality should your brand have? How should customers feel about your product?	
Understand what functional elements make them buy: What features do they want and need? What information do they need to see in order to make their decision?	
Product Attraction	
What attracts customers to your product?	
What is your special brilliance that sets you apart in the marketplace?	
Do you reflect your brilliance through all your marketing efforts?	
Most Effective Methods	
What is the most effective thing you can do to attract customers?	
What is the most effective thing you can do to retain customers?	

(continued)

Table 1-1 *(continued)*	
Which of the five Ps (product, price, place, promotion, people) is most important in attracting and retaining customers?	
Controlling Points of Contact	
What are all the ways you can reach and influence customers?	
Are you using the best of these right now?	
Do you need to increase the focus and consistency of some of these points of contact with customers?	
What can you do to improve your control over all the elements that influence customer opinion of your product?	
Action Items	
Draw up a list of things you can do based on this analysis to maximize the effectiveness of your marketing program.	

Clarifying Your Marketing Expectations

When you make improvements to your marketing program, what kind of results can you expect? As a general rule of thumb, the percentage change in your program will at best correspond with the percentage change you see in sales. For example, if you only change 5 percent of your program from one year to the next, you can't expect to see more than a 5 percent increase in sales over whatever their natural base would be.

Projecting improvements above base sales

Base sales are what you can reasonably count on if you maintain the status quo in your marketing. If, for example, you have seen steady growth in sales of 3 to 6 percent per year (varying a bit with the economic cycle), then you may reasonably project sales growth of 4 percent next year, presuming everything else stays the same too. But things rarely do stay the same, so you may want to look for any threats from new competitors, changing technology, shifting customer needs, and so on, and be careful to adjust your natural base downward if you anticipate any such threats materializing next year. Your base, if you don't change your program, may even be a negative growth rate, because competitors and customers tend to change even if you don't.

After you have a good handle on what your base may be for a status quo sales projection, you can begin to adjust it upward to reflect any improvements you introduce. Be careful in doing this, however, because some of the improvements are fairly clearly linked to future sales, while others aren't. If you have tested or tried something already, then you have some real experience upon which to project its impact. If you're trying something that is quite new to you, be very cautious and conservative about your projections at first, until you have your own hard numbers and real-world experience to go on.

Planning to fail, figuring out why, and trying again

Start small with new ideas and methods in marketing so that you can afford to fail and gain knowledge from the experience, and then adjust and try again. Effective marketing formulas are usually developed through a combination of planning and experimentation, not just from planning alone. In marketing, you don't have to feel bad about making mistakes, as long as you recognize the mistakes and take away useful lessons.

When it comes to marketing, I'm a positive pessimist. My philosophy is, "What can go wrong, will go wrong . . . and we'll be fine!" I try to avoid being too heavily committed to any single plan or investment. I keep as much flexibility in my marketing programs as I can. For example, I don't buy ads too far in advance even though it would be cheaper, because if sales drop I don't want to be stuck with the financial commitment to a big ad campaign. And I favor monthly commissions for salespeople and distributors, because then their pay is variable with my sales and goes down if sales fall — so I don't have to be right about my sales projections.

Flexibility, cautious optimism, and contingency planning give you the knowledge that you can survive the worst. That way, you have the confidence to be a creative, innovative marketer and the courage to grow your business and optimize your marketing program. And you can afford to profit from your mistakes.

Don't expect to solve all your company's problems through your marketing program. If the product is flawed from the customer's perspective, the best thing you can do as a marketer is to present the evidence and encourage your company to improve the product. Marketing can't make a dog win a horse race, so don't let others in your company try to tell you otherwise.

Finding More Ways to Maximize Your Marketing Impact

I want to end this chapter by sharing my conviction that you can improve a marketing program and increase the sales and profits of your business in an infinite number of ways. You have looked at some of the most important ways to focus your marketing, but I want to encourage you to keep searching for more ideas and to implement as many good ideas as you can.

Here, for example, are some additional ways to maximize your marketing program:

- **Talk to some of your best customers.** Do they have any good ideas for you? (Ignore the ideas that are overly expensive, however. You can't count on even a good customer to worry about your bottom line.)

- **Thank customers for their business.** A friendly "Thank you" and a smile, a card or note, or a polite cover letter stuffed into the invoice envelope — all are ways to tell them you appreciate their business, and people tend to go where they're appreciated.

- **Change your marketing territory.** Are you spread too thin to be visible and effective? If so, narrow your focus to your core region or customer type. But if you have expansion potential, try broadening your reach bit by bit to grow your territory.

- **Get more referrals.** Spend time talking to and helping out folks who can send customers your way. And make sure you thank anyone who sends you a lead. Positive reinforcement increases the behavior.

- **Make your marketing more attractive (professional, creative, polished, clear, well written, well produced).** Often, marketing programs can pull better simply by upgrading the look and feel of all the marketing communications and other components. (Did you know that the best-dressed consultants get paid two to five times as much as the average in their fields?)

- **Smile to attract and retain business.** Make sure your people have a positive, caring attitude about customers. If they don't, their negativity is certainly losing you business. Don't let people work against your marketing program. Spend time making sure they understand that they can control the success of the program, and help them through training and good management so that they can take a positive, helpful, and productive approach to all customer interactions.

- **Offer a memorable experience for your customer or client.** Make sure that doing business with you is a pleasant, memorable experience. Plan to do something that makes it memorable (in a good way, please!).

✔ **Know what you want to be best at and invest in being the best.** Who needs you if you're ordinary or average? Success comes from being clearly, enticingly better at something than any other company or product. Even if it is only a small thing that makes you special, know what it is and make sure you keep polishing that brilliance. It is why you deserve the sale.

✔ **Try to cross-sell additional products (or related services) to your customer base.** Increasing the average size of a purchase or order is a great way to improve the effectiveness of your marketing program. But keep the cross-sell soft and natural. Don't sell junk that isn't clearly within your focus or to your customer's benefit.

✔ **Debrief customers who complain or who desert you.** Why were they unhappy? Could you have done something simple to retain them? (But ignore the customers who don't match your target customer profile, because you can't be all things to all people.)

Every time you put your marketing hat on, seek to make at least a small improvement in how marketing is done in your organization and for your customers.

Marketing programs need to constantly evolve and improve. Most fall far short of their full potential, which is why for every hundred businesses, only a few really succeed and grow. The others don't have the right marketing programs needed to maximize their success. Think big when it comes to marketing. You can always do something more to improve your effectiveness and maximize your results.

Chapter 2

Clarifying Your Marketing Strategy

Strategies are the big-picture insights that guide your marketing program and make sure all those activities add up to success. A good strategy gives a special kind of high-level direction and purpose to all you do. This chapter shows you how to take your focus to an even higher level, by centering your program around a single, core strategy that gives you an overarching goal. With a core marketing strategy, your program begins to fall into place naturally. Your strategy needs to be a hub around which all your marketing activities rotate.

Figure 2-1 shows how a strategy provides an organizing central point to a program of marketing activities. This example is for the gift shop at an art museum. Their strategic goal was to get museum visitors to come into the shop and make a substantial purchase. They developed a variety of tactics for their marketing program, each of which is clearly helpful in achieving the strategy. Make sure you too can draw a solid arrow from your chosen strategy to each of the activities on the rim. Try to explain in simple words how the activity helps implement your strategy and achieve your strategic goal. If the link to the big-picture strategy isn't clear, modify or eliminate the activity.

If you have more than one strategy, draw more than one wheel. But avoid too many or your resources get spread so thin you can't achieve *any* of your goals. Also, try to select strategies that have some synergy. The strategy wheels need to belong on the same wagon or they can't move you forward.

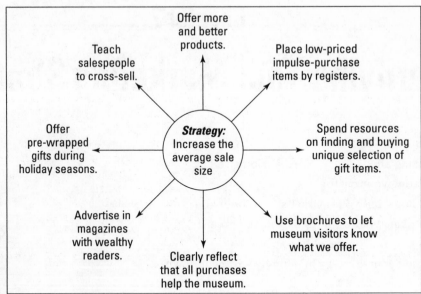

Figure 2-1:
A strategy
wheel for a
museum's
gift shop.

Expanding with a Market Expansion Strategy

Market expansion is the most common strategy in marketing. The idea is disarmingly simple. Just pick some new territory and head out into it. Oh, and don't come back until you've struck gold.

The market expansion strategy has two variants: You can expand your market by finding new customers for your current products (often this means going into new geographic territory to do so), or your can try to sell new products to your existing customers and market.

If you choose to adopt a market expansion strategy as your main focus — the hub of your marketing wheel — then make sure a majority of your marketing activity is working toward this goal. For example, if you seek publicity, make sure most of it is about your new product or in your new market, not about the old. It may take all your resources to effectively expand your market. And the faster you get through the transition and achieve your growth goal, the better, because extra costs are associated with the transition.

Risk increases if you experiment with new products — defined as anything you're not accustomed to making and marketing. And so you should discount your first year's sales projections for a new market by some factor to reflect the degree of risk. A good general rule is to cut back the sales projection by 20 to 50 percent, depending upon your judgment of how new and risky the product is to you and your team.

Expanding sales within your territory

Training Leaders of San Francisco is expanding its market without expanding its geographic territory. Its expansion plans are based on increasing the range of employee training programs it offers. Focusing on training supervisors and managers of California businesses, the company recently added courses on employee motivation, conflict handling, and other topics in order to increase its potential market and grow its sales. With a longer product line, Training Leaders can make more frequent and varied sales to the large employers it targets in its region. And its sales goals can be increased to reflect its market expansion strategy. But by how much? It depends not only on the increase in its potential market due to its product expansion, but also on the strategic risks of growing its market. The biggest risk is that clients don't like the new courses as much as the old. The company needs to make sure it maintains its high standards and continues to wow its customers as it adds services.

Risk also increases if you enter any new market — defined as new kinds of customers at any stage of your distribution channel. You should discount those sales projections by 20 to 50 percent if you're entering a new market to reflect your lack of familiarity with the customers.

What if you're introducing a new product into a new market? *Startup firms* often run both these risks at once, and need to discount sales projections even further to reflect this risk. Sometimes a market expansion strategy is so risky that you really should not count on any revenues in the first year. Better to be conservative and last long enough to figure out how to correctly handle the marketing than to over-promise and have the program die before it succeeds.

Specializing with a Market Segmentation Strategy

A *market segmentation strategy* is a specialization strategy in which you target and cater to (specialize in) just one narrow type or group of customer. If you're in the consulting business, you can specialize in for-profit businesses, or you can specialize in not-for-profits. You can even design and market your services to individuals — as, for example, a career development consultant does. Each of these types of customer represents a subgroup, or segment, of the larger consulting industry. And you can drill down even further to define smaller segments if you want. You can specialize in consulting to the health-care industry, or to manufacturers of boxes and packaging, or to start-up firms in the high tech sector. Certain consultants use each of these strategies to narrow down their markets.

The advantage of a segmentation strategy is that it allows you to tailor your product and your entire marketing effort to a clearly defined group with uniform, specific characteristics. For example, the consulting firm that targets only the health-care industry knows that prospective clients can be found at a handful of health-care industry conferences and that they have certain common concerns around which consulting services can be focused. Many smaller consulting firms target a narrowly defined market segment in order to compete against larger, but less specialized, consulting firms.

Specializing to outdo the competition

Use the segmentation strategy if you think your business can be more profitable by specializing in a more narrowly defined segment than you do now. This strategy works well when you face too many competitors in your broader market and you can't seem to carve out a stable, profitable customer base of your own. Also use the specialization strategy if it takes better advantage of things you're good at. It goes along well with the idea of focusing better, based on your unique qualities or special brilliance (see Chapter 1).

Adding a segment to expand your market

If you're running out of customers and market and need to expand (see the "Expanding with a Market Expansion Strategy" section earlier in this chapter), one way to do it is to decide to target a new segment. For example, the consultant specializing in coaching executives in the health-care industry could decide to start offering a similar service to not-for-profits. A different approach and marketing program may be needed, because the two industries are different in many ways and have only partial overlap (some hospitals are not-for-profits, but many not-for-profits are not hospitals). By specializing in two segments instead of just one, the consulting firm may be able to grow its total sales significantly.

Developing a Market Share Strategy

Another common and powerful strategy is to increase your market share through your marketing activities. In essence, this means taking some business from your competitors. *Market share* is, very simply, your sales as a percentage of total sales for your product category in your market (or in your market segment if you use a segmentation strategy too). If you sell $2 million worth of shark teeth and the world market totals $20 million per year, then your share of the global shark tooth market is 10 percent. It's that simple. Or is it?

Choosing a unit

What unit should you measure sales in? Dollars, units, pesos, containers, or grams are fine, as long as you use the same unit throughout. You can calculate your share of the North American market for fine hardwoods in board feet sold, so long as both your sales and industry sales are measured in board feet sold, and dollar sales or tons aren't mixed into the equation by mistake. Just pick whatever seems to make sense for your product and the information you have access to.

For example, if you import fine English teas to the U.S. market and wholesale them to grocery stores and specialty shops, you can look up U.S. tea wholesalers at www.census.gov (where the latest U.S. census data is posted) and find out that there are 98 other tea wholesalers with a total of $3.886 million in annual sales. If your sales are $525,000, then your market share is 0.525 ÷ 3.886 or 13.5 percent.

Alternatively, you may estimate that three quarters of the wholesalers handle low-cost, inexpensive teas and don't compete directly with you, in which case you can calculate your market share of the quarter of total sales that are similar specialty teas: 0.525 ÷ (0.25 × 3.886) or 54 percent — a much larger share based on a narrower definition of the market. Which is right?

Defining the total market

What is your product category? This may be the most important strategic question you ever ask or answer. If you sell specialty teas, are you competing with the mass-market brands like Lipton, or not? Should you count their sales in your market share calculations and try to win sales from them?

Ask your customers. Are they choosing among all the tea options, or just some of them? What matters is *customer perception:* how the customer sees the category. So watch them or ask them to find out what their purchase options are (see Chapter 4 if you want to conduct a formal study). Get a feel for how they view their choices. Then include all the likely or close choices in your definition of the market. With specialty teas, you may find that a majority of consumers do sometimes drink the cheaper mass-market brands too. And you may also find that you must as a wholesaler fight for grocery shelf space and room on restaurant menus against the mass-market brands. So you probably do need to use total market sales as your base, not just specialty sales.

On the other hand, you do compete more closely against other specialty teas, so you may want to track this smaller market share number also, and set a secondary goal for it. A wholesale tea importer's strategic goals may therefore look something like this:

✔ Increase dollar sales of our products to U.S. end consumers of tea from 13.5 percent to 15 percent.

✔ Protect our share of the specialty tea market by keeping it at 54 percent or higher.

✔ Differentiate ourselves even more from Lipton, Tetley, and other mass-market tea brands by emphasizing what makes our tea special to avoid having to compete directly against much larger marketers.

How can these two market share goals be achieved? For starters, a wholesaler needs retail shelf space, so you may need to push to win a larger share of shelf space from retailers. And to earn the right to this shelf space, you may need to do some consumer advertising or publicity, provide the stores with good point-of-purchase displays or signs, improve your product packaging, or do other things to help ensure that consumers take a stronger interest in buying your products.

This plan needs to revolve around the goal of increasing share by 1½ percentage points. Each point of share is worth roughly $40,000 in annual sales (one percent of the total sales in the market), so a plan that involved spending, say, an extra $25,000 to win a 1.5 percent share gain can provide an extra $60,000 if it works. But will it work? To be cautious, the marketer may want to discount this projection of $60,000 in additional sales by a risk factor of, say, 25 percent, which cuts it back to a projected gain of $45,000.

Then consider timing. Remember that the plan can't achieve the full gain in the first month of the year. A sales projection starting at the current level of sales in month one and ramping up to the projected increase by, say, the sixth month, may be reasonable. Dividing $45,000 by 12 to find the monthly value of the risk-discounted 1.5 share point increase gives you $3,750 in extra monthly sales for the sixth month and beyond. Lower increases apply to earlier months when the program is just starting to kick in. But the marketing expenses tend to be concentrated in the early months, reflecting the need to invest in advance in order to grow your market share.

Researching the market share strategy

To calculate market share, you need to estimate the total sales in your market. Doing so requires some research on your part. (Sorry, you can't avoid the research.) While you're at it, why not try to get some historical data — the sales in your market for the past five or ten years, for example? This information allows you to look at the growth rate of your market — which is an indicator of its future potential for you and your competitors.

Such data is most easily obtained from industry trade associations or from marketing research firms, many of which track sales by year in different product categories. Other sources of data on market size and trends are available from your friendly research librarian, who (at any major city or college library) can direct you to sources such as *Standard and Poor's Industry Surveys*, *Directory of U.S. and Canadian Marketing Surveys and Services,* and the trade magazines for the industry of your choice (that generally cover industry size and trends at least once a year). Trade magazines are often the best source for the business-to-business marketer.

Such data is now increasingly available on the Web, too. For keyword searches, enter the name of your product combined with **sales figures** or **market size** and see what you can find. Sites with marketing information abound. Try www. demographics.com for articles from *American Demographics* — one may cover your industry or target customers.

I also recommend *Sales & Marketing Management,* especially for consumer-products marketers. For a modest subscription or single-issue price, you can get more data than you care to crunch on what is called *Merchandise Line Sales* for all the United States, and also by individual metropolitan areas (along with a ranking of metro areas by size). And now they post much of their Survey of Buying Power data (some of it for a fee) at www.salesand marketing.com, so you can do online studies of every state, metro market, county, and major city in the United States. You can find population data, effective buying income, and retail sales data there.

Knowing your competitors

Perhaps the most important research you can do for the market share strategy, however, is to simply study your closest and/or most successful competitors. What do they do well? How do they take business from you now? What new initiatives are they trying this year? The better you understand them, the more easily you can take customers away from them. Talk to customers, suppliers, distributors, and anyone else with good knowledge of their practices, and gather any online information about them from their Web sites. Also collect their marketing materials and brochures, and keep track of any information you come across on how they market. For example, if they're picking up good business by having a booth at a trade show you don't attend, then consider getting a booth next time to make sure you're able to compete against them there.

Using the napkin method for estimating market share

Take a look at this simple method for estimating market size and share that you can sketch on the back of a napkin if you haven't the time or money for fancier approaches:

1. **Estimate the number of customers in your market (how many people in your country are likely to buy toothpaste, how many businesses in your city buy consulting services).**

2. **Estimate how much each buys a year, on average (six tubes, fifteen hours of consulting service).**

   You can check your sales records, or ask some people what they do, to improve this estimate.

3. **Now, just multiply the two figures together to get the total size of the annual market, and then divide your unit sales into it to get your share.**

Setting market share goals

Market share gives you a simple way of comparing your progress to your competitors from period to period. If your share drops, you're losing. If your share grows, you're winning. It's that simple. And so most marketing programs are based at least partly on a *strategic market share goal,* such as: "Increase share from 5 percent to 7 percent by introducing a product upgrade and increasing our use of trial-stimulating special offers." And the *post mortem* on last year's program should always be based on an examination of what market share change accompanied it. (If you don't already do routine post mortems, or careful analyses of what happened and why it differed from your plans, you should.) If the past period's program doubled your market share, seriously consider replicating it. But if share stayed the same or fell, you're ready for something new. So whether you make share gain the focus of your program or not, at least keep it in mind and try not to lose any share.

Should you invest in growing your share?

In addition to its use as a benchmark, market share may also give you insights into the realities of your potential success. Well, at least into the future profitability of your product and business. Many experts believe that market share is a good long-term predictor of profitability, arguing that market share leaders are more profitable and successful than other competitors. This belief is taken so seriously in some companies that low-share brands are dropped so as to focus spending on those brands with a chance at category leadership.

If this theory is correct, then you need to build market share aggressively. I favor share-growth strategies myself, because some good studies are showing that high-share businesses have higher returns on investment on average. The Strategic Planning Institute (a consulting firm in Cambridge, Massachusetts) has extensive data on market share and financial returns in its PIMS (Profit Impact of Marketing Study) database. I like their database because it looks at *business units* (divisions or subsidiaries in a single market) rather than whole companies, so it is more marketing oriented. And those business units with higher market shares have higher pretax ROIs (or *returns on investment;* the percentage yield or the amount earned as a percent of the amount invested). The relationship is roughly as shown in Table 2-1.

Table 2-1	**Profiting from Market Share**
Market Share (Percent)	*ROI (Percent)*
Less than 7	10
7 to 15	16
15 to 23	21
23 to 38	23
38 or more	33

Also impressive is some PIMS data suggesting that a gain in market share seems to lead to a corresponding gain in ROI (although the ROI gain is a half to a quarter as large on a percentage basis). You can visit pimsonline.com for more details of their research on effective marketing strategies.

Oh, by the way, I must warn you that loss of share leads to loss of ROI. So a good strategy for many plans is to defend existing market share. You can accomplish this by keeping your brand's image well polished, by innovating to keep your product fresh, and by designing good marketing programs in general. So I generally advise marketers to defend leading shares, and to try to grow their low shares into leading positions. For example, if you're a strong third-place finisher in the share race, you should probably consider investing in a growth effort in order to leapfrog the number two player and get within striking distance on the number one slot.

Mycomputer.com analyzed use of Web browsers in the year 2000 to find out who had what market share. Microsoft was way out front (where they like to be) with 81 percent of people using versions of Internet Explorer. Netscape followed far behind at 16 percent, and America Online had just .3 percent. Since then, as the share data caused me to predict in the first edition of this book, Microsoft's lead has grown and it has been the only one of the three to make good profits from the product.

But not all studies say the same thing about market share. If you're a small firm with a narrow market niche, trying to grow your share by expanding aggressively can get you in trouble. Balance share growth with the need to avoid excessive risks.

Revising Your Strategy over the Life of the Product Category

Every *product category* — the general grouping of competitive products to which your product belongs (be it merchandise or a service), has a limited life. At least in theory — and usually in all-too-real reality — some new type of product comes along to displace the old. The result is a never-ending cycle of birth, growth, and decline, fueled by the endless inventiveness of competing businesses. Categories of products arise, spread through the marketplace, then decline as replacements arise and begin their own life cycles. Marketing works differently depending on where in its life cycle your product is. In this section, I show you a practical version of the life-cycle model that helps you choose the most applicable of three powerful marketing strategies.

To use the life-cycle model, you must look at the long-term trend in the over-all market, as indicated by the sales of your brand and its major competitors.

Interpreting and predicting market growth

Over a long period of time, sales (in dollars, units, or as a share of the potential market) will

✔ Follow a sigmoid growth curve (like a stretched-out, right-leaning S, or sigma, in shape).

Having trouble visualizing that? See the bottom half of Figure 2-2 for a picture of this life-cycle curve. Because of this characteristic pattern, products generally go through a series of four life-cycle stages.

✔ Level off to grow at the rate that the customer base grows.

✔ Fall off when a replacement product enters the market.

The introduction phase

Sales start slowly because a new product concept takes time to gain momentum and catch on. That makes the introductory phase of the life cycle a tough one for marketers. You have to educate consumers about the advantages of the new product. And the more unfamiliar the product is, the more change the product demands from users, and the longer this introductory phase takes. In introduction, marketers emphasize coaching prospective new customers about their exciting new product. They worry less about competition than about converting the dubious to their cause.

The growth phase

After a while — often after 10 to 20 percent of the potential market is reached — the idea gains momentum. The life cycle enters its growth stage. Consumers accept the product, and begin to adopt it in greater numbers. Growth rates shoot upward. Unfortunately, the obvious success of the new product attracts more competitors — the number of competing products always grows during the growth phase, so the market leaders generally lose market share. But still, the rapid growth usually enriches all viable competitors and everybody is happy. In this phase of the life cycle, marketers jockey for position by trying to maximize their share of distribution and of consumption, hoping to emerge in maturity as one of the leaders.

Stimulating a second childhood

Sometimes markets seem to have matured and then are revived with a new growth phase by creative marketers. Low financing, heavy promotion, and the introduction of interesting SUVs, light trucks, and sports cars have helped create a new growth phase in the U.S. auto market. In recent years, the number of cars has increased to the point that there are significantly more cars than drivers in the United States. The old ceiling to the market was assumed to be the number of drivers, but now auto marketers are selling individual drivers multiple cars for different purposes.

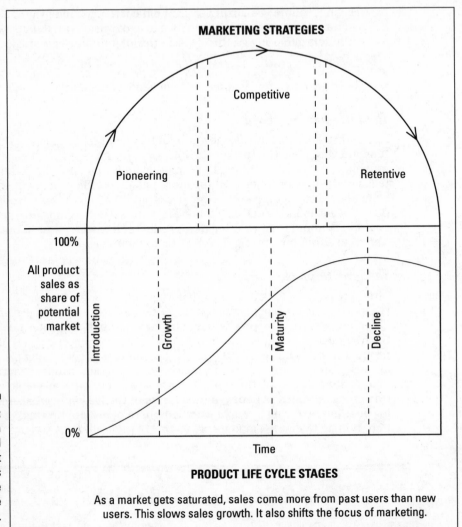

Figure 2-2:
Growth
rates and
market
conditions
over the
product life
cycles.

As a market gets saturated, sales come more from past users than new users. This slows sales growth. It also shifts the focus of marketing.

The maturity phase

A sad thing happens to end the growth-stage party: Marketers begin to run out of market. After most able-bodied people who like to skate have bought their first pair of in-line roller skates, for example, the nature of the roller skate market has to change. Now you can't get rich just by spreading the good news about this new product. You have to wait until people are ready to replace their old skates, and then you have to fight tooth-and-nail with competitors to make the sale. At best, you keep most of your old customers and pick up a share of the new people who have thoughtfully managed to be born and grow up with a proclivity for roller-skating. The days of heady growth are over because your market is becoming *saturated,* meaning that most potential customers have already found out about and started using the product. In-line roller skates reached this point a few years ago. The cellphone market will reach it within the next few years.

When a market is saturated, you can no longer grow just by finding new customers. Your ambitions are limited by the rate at which customers replace the product and your ability to steal customers from your competitors. Competitive, share-oriented marketing is the way to go, and you should focus on refining your points of difference from competitors and communicating them clearly to customers.

The death phase

Finally, the product life-cycle model says, people stop replacing their old products with similar new ones because something even better has come along. Who buys new LP records now that the same music is available on CDs? Most products eventually enter a decline stage in which sales fall, profits evaporate, and most of the competitors exit. Sometimes you can make good money by hanging on to serve the die-hard loyals, but often this stage is a waste of time. Best to make hay while the sun shines and then switch your product line into some hot new growth markets.

Reincarnation: Life after the death phase

Some marketers — perhaps those who believe in reincarnation — refuse to give up. They think a dose of imagination and some clever marketing can revive a dying product. And sometimes they're right. Take the case of baking soda, a simple compound used by the pinch to make muffins, cakes, and other homemade delectables that the modern consumer hasn't time to bake.

Arm & Hammer, which has the largest baking soda market share in North America, watched its sales decline for years. Then some creative marketers at the company discovered something strange: Some customers — not many, but at least a few — bought huge amounts of the stuff. Boxes and boxes. What for? Further

research revealed that some people used baking soda for things other than baking. Brushing their teeth. Cleaning their rugs. Deodorizing their refrigerators and kitty litter boxes. Dabbing on their underarms in place of deodorant. Amazing what people do with the stuff.

And so Arm & Hammer went back to an introduction-phase marketing strategy. They started educating the public about all these neat uses for baking soda. And the product rose from its deathbed to record-growing sales again. Voilá. Life after death. (Old LPs are also having a reincarnation now, thanks to their use in scratching, a form of music that can only be made using old-fashioned LPs on turntables.)

Choosing your life-cycle strategy

In the upper half of Figure 2-2 is the advertiser's version of the life cycle with its helpful emphasis on what to do to win sales. I have redrawn it slightly (usually the model looks like a half of a wagon wheel) to make it tie into the product life-cycle drawing. Put the two together, and you have that finest of combinations: situation diagnosis plus practical prescription.

The advertising life-cycle model says that products go through three stages, each requiring a different marketing strategy: *pioneering* (use it when the majority of prospects are unfamiliar with the product), *competitive* (use it when the majority of prospects have tried at least one competitor's product), and *retentive* (use it when attracting new customers costs more than keeping old customers). And by tying these to the life-cycle model, you can choose the right strategy based on the current growth rate trend in your market. Table 2-2 shows the strategic objectives of each of these stages.

Table 2-2	What to Do in Each Product Stage	
Pioneering	*Competitive*	*Retentive*
Educate consumers	Build brand equity	Retain customers
Encourage trial usage	Position against competitors	Build relationships with customers
Build the distribution channel	Capture a leading market share	Improve quality
Segment market to better serve specific needs	Improve service	Upgrade product

Everything about your marketing program follows from these simple strategies. And you can tell when you need them by looking at where you are in your product's life cycle. That makes your strategic thinking fairly simple.

For example, if you're marketing a radical new product that has just begun to experience accelerating sales, then you know you're moving from the introduction to the growth stage of the product life cycle. Table 2-2 indicates that a pioneering strategy should apply. And the table tells you that you need to educate consumers about the new product, encourage them to try it, and make sure that the product is widely distributed. Now you have a clear strategic mandate as you move on to define your marketing program.

How should you price this pioneering product — high or low? Well, price should be low enough to keep from discouraging new customers, so the high end of the price range may be a mistake. On the other hand, no mandate exists to compete head-to-head on price (that would be more appropriate to the competitive strategy later on). So the best time to use low prices is probably in special offers to stimulate trial. In fact, perhaps free samples are appropriate now, especially if coupled with a moderately high list price.

And your advertising? It certainly needs to be informative; showing potential consumers how to benefit from the product. Similarly, you know you need to encourage distributors to stock and push the product, so special offers to the trade and a strong sales effort (through your own salespeople or through reps or distributors) should get a fair share of your marketing budget.

All these conclusions are fairly obvious — if you stay focused on the strategic guidelines in the model. And that is the beauty of strategy — it makes the details of your tactics so much clearer and simpler.

Designing a Positioning Strategy

A positioning strategy takes a psychological approach to marketing. It focuses on getting customers or prospects to see your product in a favorable light. The positioning goal you articulate for this kind of strategy is the position your product holds in the customer's mind.

When you go to the trouble of thinking through your positioning statement, you have — a positioning statement. So what? You can't use it to sell products. But you can use it to design all your marketing communications. Everything you do in your marketing program, from the product or service's packaging to its advertising and publicity, should work to convince customers of the points your positioning statement contains. So put the statement up over your desk and refer to it to make sure that you communicate the right information and feelings to get the point across and help customers think about your product in the right way.

For example, you may decide to emphasize speed and reliability whenever advertising a courier service. You may even make a grid or positioning map with one axis representing a range from low to high speed and the other from low to high reliability, and then stake out the quadrant where both are as high as your goal, as Figure 2-3 shows.

Figure 2-3:
A positioning map for a delivery service.

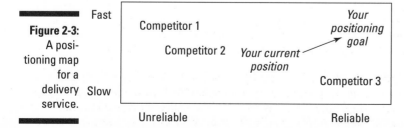

Here are some of the more common options for a positioning strategy:

- ✔ **You may position against a competitor.** "Our interest rates are lower than Citibank's." (This tactic is a natural in a mature product category, where the competitive strategy applies.)

- ✔ **You may emphasize a distinctive benefit.** "The only peanut butter with no harmful transfats." (This positioning strategy can be combined with a pioneering strategy or a competitive one.)

- ✔ **You can affiliate yourself with something the customer values.** "The toothpaste most often recommended by dentists." (Doing so allows some of the virtues of this other thing to rub off on your brand.) A celebrity endorser, an image of a happy family playing on the beach, a richly appointed manor house set in beautiful gardens, a friendly giant: All have been used to position products favorably in consumers' minds.

You can write down your positioning strategy in big print and post it above your desk to make sure that you actually stay focused on its execution. Handing out copies of your positioning statement to your ad agency, distributor, publicist, salespeople, and anyone else who works on or in your marketing program also pays off.

Writing a positioning statement is pretty easy. First you must decide:

- ✔ What type of customer you target
- ✔ What you do for that customer
- ✔ How you do it
- ✔ Why you do it better than competitors

Next, you should fill in the following with your own words:

- ✔ Our product offers the following benefit:
- ✔ To the following customers (describe target segment):
- ✔ Our product is better than competitors in the following manner:
- ✔ We can prove we're the best because of (evidence/differences):

Considering Other Core Strategies

Are there other winning marketing strategies? Certainly. In fact, strategy, like everything in marketing, is only limited by your imagination and initiative. If you can think of a better approach to strategy, go for it. This section goes over a few examples of other strategies that marketers have proven to be effective in recent years. Perhaps one of them may work for you.

Simplicity marketing

I love the new gas pumps that allow you to swipe your own credit card. It's so simple and quick. This is an example of a simplicity strategy. Use this strategy in your business to position yourself as simpler, easier to understand, and easier to use or work with than the competition. So-called simplicity positioning is a new opportunity according to research firm Datamonitor. They predict that people are going to be increasingly attracted to simple brands that are easy to buy and use. In fact, their studies indicate that many customers are willing to pay a premium in order to avoid complexity and make purchase decisions simply and quickly. Can this approach be useful to customers in your market? Look for technologies or processes that can make your customers' lives simpler and easier.

Quality strategies

Most marketers grossly underrate quality. All else being anywhere near equal, a majority of customers choose the higher-quality option. But be careful to find out what your customers think quality means. They may have a different view from you. And also be careful to integrate your quality-based marketing messages with a genuine commitment to quality in all aspects of your business.

You can't just say you're better than the competition; you really have to deliver. But if customers see you as superior on even one dimension of quality — then by all means emphasize this in your marketing. Quote customer testimonials praising your quality, describe your commitment to quality in your marketing materials, and make trial usage easy for prospective customers, so that they can experience your quality, too. And also make sure your pricing is consistent with a high-quality image. Don't focus on advertising deep discounts, as these signal cheapness, not quality.

Reminder strategies

A reminder strategy is good when you think people would buy your product if they thought of it — but may not without a reminder. A lot of routine purchases benefit from this strategy (Got milk?).

Point-of-purchase marketing (POP) is often an effective way to implement the reminder strategy. Point-of-purchase marketing simply means doing whatever advertising is necessary to sway the consumer your way at the time and place of their purchase. For retail products, this often means a clever in-store display or sign to remind the consumer.

Precise International (of Orangeberg, New York) uses this strategy to market its Wenger Swiss Army Knife product line in jewelry and knife stores. Working with Phoenix Display and Packaging Corp. (of Wilmington, Delaware), Precise International creates a variety of countertop and floor display cases that feature giant models of the distinctive red pocketknife with its white cross logo. Although the pocketknife market has been mature for decades, if not centuries, Wenger has a strong brand identity that allows it to maintain a large and profitable share of the market simply by reminding consumers of its product. Often consumers walking past one of these POP displays realize that a Swiss Army Knife is the perfect gift — for someone else or even for themselves.

Writing Down Your Strategy

What is your marketing strategy? Is it a pure version of one of the strategies reviewed in this chapter, or is it a variant or even a combination of more than one of them? Whatever it is, take some time to write it down clearly and thoughtfully. Put it in summary form in a single sentence. (If you must, add some bullet points to explain it in more detail.)

Looking at an example

For example, here is what one company's market strategy looks like:

Our strategy is to maximize the quality of our security alarm products and services through good engineering and to grow our share of a competitive market by communicating our superior quality to high-end customers.

What you have here is a nice, clear statement of strategy. Now you know what the big-picture game plan is and can set to work designing good products and packaging, friendly services, and impressive ads that communicate your quality to consumers.

Dusting it off and reading it, for goodness sake

Is your strategy obvious in all you do? When you adopt a specific marketing strategy, you must actually read it from time to time and check that you're following it. I'm often amazed at the lack of relationship between companies' strategies and their actions.

For example, take the case of an auto component manufacturer emphasizing efficiencies as a way to win contracts from the big automakers. Efficiencies include quicker order turnaround, computer systems to manage orders and inventories better, and substitutable component parts to simplify repairs. Companies like Ford or Toyota want to buy from suppliers who make good component parts quickly, reliably, and cheaply. But this particular firm isn't consistent in communicating its efficiency strategy to its customer base. It purchased very handsome full-color brochures illustrating its marvelous efficiency. However, it hired an inexpensive direct-mail service to send these brochures to its entire customer list. The result was that many of the labels had errors in them, and the envelopes used were so light and cheap that many of them tore during mailing. The impression made was a poor one, and quite inconsistent with the intended strategy.

After you develop a marketing strategy, be sure to follow it. You may need to write it down and post it so that you (and others) can't forget it. In fact, I highly recommend that you do some formal planning to figure out exactly how you will implement your strategy in all aspects of your marketing program. And I show you how to develop a plan as painlessly as is possible in Chapter 3.

Chapter 3

Writing a Marketing Plan

*Y*ou don't have to write a marketing plan to use this book or even to bene-fit from this chapter. But you may want to, because it's not as hard as you may think, and, most important, a good plan increases the odds of suc-cess. In fact, most of the really successful businesses I know — small or large, new or old — write a careful marketing plan at least once a year.

Marketing combines lots of activities and expenditures in the hope of gener-ating or increasing sales. You won't see those sales numbers rise without a coherent plan linking a strategy based on the strengths of your position to a *marketing program* (set of sales and marketing activities) that can convince targeted customers to purchase. Marketing can get out of control or confused in a hurry unless you have a plan. Every successful business needs a market-ing plan. (Yes, even if you're in a small or start-up business. In fact, especially if you are. You don't have the resources to waste on unplanned or ineffective marketing.)

Identifying Some Planning Rules and Tips

Marketing plans vary significantly in format and outline from company to company, but all have core components covering

▶ **Your current position** in terms of your product, customers, competi-tion, and broader trends in your market.

- ✔ **For established businesses, what results you got in the previous period** in terms of sales, market share, and possibly also in terms of profits, customer satisfaction, or other measures of customer attitude and perception. You may want to include measures of customer retention, size and frequency of purchase, or other indicators of customer behavior, if you think them important to your new plan.

- ✔ **Your strategy.** The big picture that will help you get improved results.

- ✔ **The details of your program.** All your company's specific activities, grouped by area or type, with explanations of how these activities fit the company's strategy and reflect the current situation.

- ✔ **The numbers,** including sales projections and costs. Consider whether knowing these additional numbers would help your business: market share projections, sales to your biggest customers or distributors, costs and returns from any special offers you plan to use, sales projections and commissions by territory, or whatever helps you quantify your specific marketing activities.

- ✔ **Your *learning plans*.** If you have a new business or new product, or if you're experimenting with a new or risky marketing activity, you want to set up a plan for how to test the waters or experiment on a small scale first. You need to determine what positive results you want to see before committing to a higher level. Wisdom is knowing what you don't know — and planning how to figure it out.

Leaving wiggle room in your plan

If you're a start-up, you should really consider a step-wise plan with a time-line and alternatives or options in case of problems. The more unfamiliar the waters, the more flexibility and caution your plan needs. Make flexibility your first objective for the plan if you're writing a marketing plan for the first time. You want to avoid large advance purchases of media space or time, use short runs of marketing materials at the copy shop over cheaper off-set printing of large inventories, and so on. (I cover details such as these in Parts III and IV.) Optimizing your plan for flexibility means preserving your choice and avoiding commitments of resources. Spending in small increments allows you to change the plan as you go.

Maximizing efficiencies

If your business has done this all before and your plan builds on years of experience, you can more safely favor *economies of scale* over flexibility. (It is cheaper and more efficient to advertise, for example, if you do it on a large scale, because you get deeper discounts on design of ads and purchase of ad space or time.) If you know a media investment is likely to produce leads or sales, go ahead and buy media in larger chunks to get good rates. And don't be as cautious about testing mailing lists with small-scale mailings of a few hundred pieces. A good in-house list supplemented by 20 percent or fewer newly purchased names probably warrants a major mailing without as much emphasis on advance testing. Adjust your plan to favor economies of scale if you feel confident that you can make sound judgments in advance.

But always leave yourself at least a *little* wiggle room. Reality never reflects your plans and projections 100 percent of the time. Aim for an 80 percent match in marketing, and plan accordingly.

Understanding the Do's and Don'ts of Planning

Total up your costs fully and carefully. Marketing programs end up like leaky boats very easily. Each activity seems worthy at the time, but too many of them fail to produce a positive return — ending up like holes in the bottom of your boat: Too many of those holes, and the water starts rising. The following sections share some of the common ways marketers lose money (so that you can try to avoid them), plus one effective strategy for not wasting cash.

Don't ignore the details

You build good plans from details like customer-by-customer, item-by-item, or territory-by-territory sales projections. Generalizing about an entire market is hard. Your sales and cost projections are easier to get right if you break them down to their smallest natural units (like individual territory sales or customer orders), do estimates for each of these small units, and then add those estimates up to get your totals.

Don't imitate the competitors

Even though everyone seems to market their products in a certain way, you don't have to imitate them. High-performing plans clearly point out what aspects of the marketing program are conventional and why — and these plans also include some original, innovative, or unique elements to help differentiate your company from and outperform the competition. Your business is unique, so make your plan reflect your special talents or advantages. (See the excellent book *Brilliance Marketing Management* by Celia Rocks if you haven't yet found what makes you special in the market.)

Don't feel confined by last period's budget and plan

Repeat or improve the best-performing elements of the past plans, but cut back on any elements that didn't produce high returns. Every plan includes some activities and spending that aren't necessary and can be cut out (or reworked) when you do it all over again next year. Be ruthless with any underperforming elements of last year's plan! (If you're starting a new business, at least this is one problem you don't have to worry about. Yet.)

Don't engage in unnecessary spending

Always think it through and run the numbers before signing a contract or writing a check. Many of the people and businesses you deal with to execute your marketing activities are salespeople themselves. Their goal is to get *you* to buy their ad space or time, to use their design or printing services, or spend money on fancy Web sites. They want your marketing money. They don't care as much as you do whether you get a good return or not. You have to keep them on a tight financial rein.

Do break down your plan into simple sub-plans

If all your marketing activities are consistent and clearly of one kind, a single plan is fine. But what if you sell services (like consulting or repair) and also products? You may find that you need to work up one plan for selling products (perhaps this plan aims at finding new customers) and another plan for convincing product buyers to also use your services. The general rule is that if the plan seems too complicated, divide and conquer! Then total everything up to get the big picture — overall projections and budgets.

If you have 50 products in five different product categories, writing your plan becomes much easier if you come up with 50 sales projections for each product and five separate promotional plans for each category of product. (Believe it or not: This method sounds harder but really is much simpler.) I've included some methods to break down your planning, making it easier and simpler to do:

- ✔ Analyze, plan, and budget sales activities by sales territory and region (or by major customer if you're a business-to-business marketer with a handful of dominant companies as your clients).

- ✔ Project revenues and promotions by individual product and by industry (if you sell into more than one).

✔ Plan your advertising and other promotions by product line or other broad product category, as promotions often have a generalized effect on the products within the category.

✔ Plan and budget publicity for your company as a whole. Only budget and plan publicity for an individual product if you introduce it or modify it in some way that may attract media attention.

✔ Plan and budget for brochures, Web sites, and other informational materials. Be sure to remain focused in your subject choices: One brochure per topic. Multipurpose brochures or sites never work well. If a Web site sells cleaning products to building maintenance professionals, don't also plan for it to broker gardening and lawn-mowing services to suburban homeowners. Different products and customers need separate plans.

Remember that every type of marketing activity in your plan has a natural and appropriate level of breakdown. Find the right level, and your planning will be simpler and easier to do.

Writing a Powerful Executive Summary

An executive summary is a one-page plan. This wonderful document conveys essential information about your company's planned year of programs and activities in a couple hundred well-chosen words or less. If you ever get confused or disoriented in the rough-and-tumble play of sales and marketing, this clear, one-page summary can guide you back to the correct strategic path. A good executive summary keeps everyone on the same page. It's a powerful advertisement for your program, communicating the purpose and essential activities of your plan in such a compelling manner that everyone who reads it eagerly leaps into action and does the right things to make your vision come true.

Draft the executive summary early in the year as a guide to your thinking and planning. But revise it often, and finish it after finishing all the other sections, because it needs to summarize them.

Help yourself (and your readers, if others in your company are going to be involved in approving or implementing the plan) by giving an overview of what's the same and what's different in this plan, compared to the previous period's plan. Draft a short paragraph covering these two topics.

Summarize the main points of your plan and make clear whether the plan is

✔ **Efficiency oriented:** Say that your plan introduces a large number of specific improvements in how you market your product.

✔ **Effectiveness oriented:** Say that your plan identifies a major opportunity or problem and adopts a new strategy to respond to it.

Make sure that you summarize the bottom-line results — what your projected revenues will be (by product or product line, unless you have too many to list on one page) and what the costs are. Also show how these figures differ from last year's figures. Keep the whole summary under one page in length if you possibly can.

If you have too many products to keep the summary under one page in length, you can list them by product line. But a better option is to do more than one plan. You probably haven't clearly thought out any plan that can't be summarized in a page. I've worked with many businesses in which marketing prepares a separate plan for each product. Divide and conquer.

Clarifying and Quantifying Your Objectives

Objectives are the quantified, measurable versions of your strategies. For example, if your strategy involves raising the quality of service and opening a new territory in order to grow your sales and market share, you need to think through how you'll do all that and set a percentage increase goal for sales and a new, higher goal for market share. These numbers become your objectives. They flow from your thinking about strategies and tactics, but put them up near the front of your plan to help others quickly understand what you're saying.

What objectives do you want your plan to help you accomplish? Will the plan increase sales by 25 percent, reposition a product to make it more appealing to upscale buyers, introduce a direct marketing function via the Internet, or launch a new product? Maybe the plan will combine several products into a single family brand and build awareness of this brand through print and radio advertising, which will gain market share from several competitors and cut the costs of marketing by eliminating inefficiencies in coupon processing, media buying, and sales force management. Address these sorts of topics in the objectives section of the plan. These points give the plan its focus.

If you write clear, compelling objectives, you'll never get too confused about what to write in other sections — when in doubt, you can always look back at these objectives and remind yourself what you're trying to accomplish and why.

Try to write this part of the plan early, but keep in mind that you'll rewrite it often as you gather more information and do more thinking. Objectives are such a key foundation for the rest of the plan that you can't ever stop thinking about them. However, for all their importance, they don't need a lot of words. A half page to two pages, at most. (Paradoxically, I have to tell you more about these short upfront sections than about the longer, detail-oriented sections in the back because planners find the short sections more conceptually challenging.)

Every plan should include (along with more unique or situation-specific variables) the objective of reinforcing the brand image at every point of contact with prospective or current customers. Ad agency Howard, Merrell & Partners (from Raleigh, North Carolina) emphasizes this objective for all its clients. In its own marketing materials, the agency often talks about reinforcing brand values at all points of human contact. And I guarantee that an audit of all your communications at every point of human contact will reveal many places where you don't achieve this objective as fully or consistently as you can, so put this objective in every marketing plan and aspire to achieve it more fully every year.

Preparing a Situation Analysis

The context is different for every marketing plan. A *situation analysis* examines the context, looking at trends, customer preferences, competitor strengths and weaknesses, and anything else that may impact sales. The question your situation analysis must answer is, "What's happening?" The answer to this question can take many forms, so I can't give you an easy formula for preparing the situation analysis. You should analyze the most important market changes to your company — these changes can be the sources of problems or opportunities. (See Chapter 4 for formal research techniques and sources.)

But what most important changes have occurred since you last examined the situation? The answer depends on the situation. See the difficulty? Yet somehow you have to gain enough insight into what's happening to see the problems and opportunities clearly.

Seeing trends more clearly than others do

In fact, your goal is to see the changes more clearly than the competition. Why? Because if your situation analysis isn't as accurate as the competition's, you'll lose market share to them. If your analysis is about the same as your competition's, then you may hold even. Only if your situation analysis is better than the other guy's can you gain market share on the competition.

What you want from your situation analysis is

✔ **Information parity:** When you know as much as your leading competitors know. If you don't do enough research and analysis, your competitors will have an information advantage. Therefore, you need to gain enough insight to put you on a level playing field with your competitors.

(That includes knowing about any major plans they may have. Collect rumors about new products, new people, and so on. At a minimum, do a weekly search on a Web-based search engine for any news about them.)

✔ **Information advantage in specific areas:** Insight into the market that your competitors don't have. Information advantage puts you on the uphill side of an uneven playing field. That's an awfully good place from which to design and launch a marketing program or advertising campaign. Look for new fashions, new technologies, new ways to segment the market — anything that you can use to change the rules of the game even slightly in your favor.

Most marketing plans and planners don't think about their situation analysis this way. I'm telling you one of my best-kept secrets because I don't want you to waste time on the typical *pro forma* situation analysis, in which the marketer rounds up the usual suspects and parades dull information in front of them without gaining an advantage from it. That approach, although common, does nothing to make the plan a winner. If all you wanted to do was the minimum, then I don't think you'd have bothered to buy this book in the first place.

Using a structured approach to competitor analysis

What kinds of information can you collect about your competitors? It varies significantly, so I can't give you a pat formula. You can certainly gather and analyze examples of their marketing communications. You may have (or be able to gather) some customer opinions from surveys or informal chats. You can group the information you get from customers into useful lists, like figuring out the three most appealing and least appealing things about each competitor. You can also probably get some information about how they distribute and sell, where they are (and aren't) located or distributed, who their key decision-makers are, who their biggest and/or most loyal customers are, and even (perhaps) how much they sell. Gather any available data on all-important competitors and organize the information into a table for easy analysis.

Building a competitor analysis table

Here's an example of a format for a generic Competitor Analysis Table. Make entries on the following rows in columns labeled for Competitor #1, Competitor #2, Competitor #3 and so on:

✔ **Company:** Describe how the market perceives it and its key product.

✔ **Key personnel:** Who are the managers, and how many employees do they have in total?

✔ **Financial:** Who owns it, how strong is its *cash position* (does it have spending power or is it struggling to pay its bills), what were its sales in the last two years?

✔ **Sales, distribution, and pricing:** Describe its primary sales channel, discount/pricing structure, and market share estimate.

✔ **Product/service analysis:** What are the strengths and weaknesses of its product or service?

✔ **Scaled assessment of product/service:** Explore relevant subjects like market acceptance, quality of packaging, ads, and so on. Assign a score of between 1 and 5 (with 5 being the strongest) for each characteristic you evaluate. Then sum the scores for each competitor's row to see which seems strongest, overall.

✔ **Comparing yourself to competitor ratings:** If you rate yourself on these attributes, too, how do you compare? Are you stronger? If not, you can include increasing your competitive strength as one of your plan's strategic objectives.

JIAN's Marketing Builder® software has an Excel template for writing a competitor analysis table. I helped JIAN design the program, and last time I checked, this software was only $50. You may want to pick it up if you have to write a detailed plan in a hurry. (No, I don't get royalties if you purchase it — this recommendation isn't self-serving. And because this software is a useful tool, I put a link to it on my Web site, www.insightsformarketing.com.)

Explaining Your Marketing Strategy

Many plans use this section to get specific about the objectives by explaining how your company will accomplish them. Some writers find this task easy, although others keep getting confused about the distinction between an objective and a strategy. The objective simply states something your business hopes to accomplish in the next year. The strategy emphasizes the big-picture approach to accomplishing that objective, giving some good pointers as to what road you'll take.

An objective sounds like this:

> Solidify our leadership of the home PC market by increasing market share by 2 points. A strategy sounds like this: Introduce hot new products and promote our brand name with an emphasis on high quality components, in order to increase our market share by 2 points.

Combining strategies and objectives

Some people view the difference between objectives and strategies as a pretty fine line. If you're comfortable with the distinction, write a separate *Strategy* section. If not, combine this section with the objectives section and title it *Objectives and Strategies*; what you call the points doesn't matter, as long as they're good. For more details about how to develop and define marketing strategies, see Chapter 2.

Your strategies accomplish your objectives through the tactics (the five Ps) of your marketing plan. (See Chapter 1 for a discussion of the five Ps.) The plan explains how your tactics use your strategies to accomplish your objectives.

Giving your strategy common sense

This advice is tough to realize. Unlike a mathematical formula or a spreadsheet column, you don't have a simple method to check a marketing strategy to make sure that it really adds up. But you can subject a marketing strategy to common sense and make sure that it has no obvious flaws.

Strategy fails to reflect limitations in your resources

Don't pull a Napoleon. If you're currently the tenth-largest competitor, don't write a plan to become the number one largest by the end of the year simply based on designing all your ads and mailings to claim you're the best. Make sure that your strategy is reasonable. Would the average person agree that your strategy sounds attainable with a little hard work? (If you're not sure, find some average people and ask them.) And do you have enough resources to execute the strategy in the available time?

Strategy demands huge changes in customer behavior

You can move people and businesses only so far with a marketing program. If you plan to get employers to give their employees every other Friday off so those employees can attend special workshops your firm sponsors, well, I hope you have a backup plan. Employers don't give employees a lot of extra time off, no matter how compelling your sales pitch or brochure may be. I've found out, as an executive in the training industry, I need to adjust my firm's products and services so they fit into the training time employers are willing to spare. Otherwise, no marketing program can succeed. The same is true of consumer marketing. You simply cannot change strongly held public attitudes without awfully good new evidence. For example, see the "Saving the grapefruit" sidebar later in this chapter about a new campaign designed to make consumers think of grapefruit as hip and trendy. I'm betting that strategy is unrealistic.

Saving the grapefruit

Imagine you're the leading producer of grapefruits in Florida. Are you happy? No. The product category is entering decline and sales have fallen for the past five years. Your strategic choices are clear: Either you start planting orange trees, or you do something to revive grapefruit sales.

The typical grapefruit eater is elderly. Consumers see the fruit, according to research commissioned by the Florida Department of Citrus, as an old person's breakfast item. It has a grandma-used-to-eat-it image that hurts sales, and people in a hurry find dealing with the fruit a hassle. You have to cut it and dig out each bite. But that need not doom this fruit to the old folks' home. Take the lobster, for example. It's even harder to eat, but extremely popular. So with the right remake of its image, can't the grapefruit become popular again?

At time of writing, the grapefruit growers are trying to revive sales with a new ad campaign. The ads attempt to position grapefruit juice as a hip alternative beverage for health-conscious women in their 20s and 30s. Marketers have real difficulty dictating what *cool* is. To help give grapefruit juice a cool image, they're placing ads in magazines that they think the hip women read. They're also introducing new alcoholic mixed drinks that use grapefruit juice — using venues like alternative film festivals to do so. When marketing cool, you need to win over the *opinion leaders,* the people who start trends. These people tend to do cool things like go to film festivals, and the marketers hope that these consumers will go home and spread the drink to their friends, automatically making the drink hip and new.

Still, it's a risky strategy. Coolness is the most fickle and fleeting of brand images. I have a hunch that over the next few years, the plan will bomb. To my marketing eye, a fresh-alternative-for-the-bored-consumer strategy is more realistic and sustainable for the poor old grapefruit than trying to make it youthful and hip.

But only time will tell. Am I right or not? You be the judge.

A competitor is already doing the strategy

This assumption is a surprisingly common error. To avoid it, include a summary of each competitor's strategy in the *Strategy* section of your plan. Add a note explaining how yours differs from each of them. If you're marketing a computer installation and repair service in the Los Angeles area, you really need to know how your strategy differs from the multiple competitors also trying to secure big corporate contracts in that area. Do you specialize in certain types of equipment that others don't? Do you emphasize speed of repair service? Are you the only vendor who distributes and supports CAD/CAM equipment from a leading maker? You need a distinctive strategy to power your plan. You don't want to be a me-too competitor.

Strategy requires you to know too much that you don't already know

I can't use some brilliant strategies for my business because they would require me to do too many things I don't know anything about. For example, there is a growing need for computer skills training, but my firm doesn't have experience developing, selling, or delivering computer courses. I can write a grand plan describing how we'll capture 10 percent of the computer training market in the Northeastern United States next year, but I probably can't execute it. Strategies that involve doing a lot of things you have little or no expertise in are really start-up strategies, not marketing strategies. If you want to put a minority of your resources into trying to start a new business unit, go ahead. But don't put your entire marketing plan at risk by basing it on a strategy that takes you into unfamiliar waters.

Summarizing Your Marketing Program

A *marketing program* (see Chapter 1) is the combination of marketing activities you use to influence a targeted group of customers to purchase a specific product or line of products. A marketing program starts, in my view, with an analysis of your *influence points* (see Chapter 2) — in other words, how your organization can influence customer purchases. And the program ends with some decisions about how to use these influence points. Usually you can come up with tactics in all five of the marketing Ps: product, price, placement (or distribution), promotions, and people.

I suggest that you prioritize by picking a few primary influence points — ones that will dominate your program for the coming planning period. This approach concentrates your resources, giving you more leverage at certain points of influence. Make the choice carefully; try to pick no more than three main activities to take the lead in your program. Use the (usually many) other influence points in secondary roles to support your primary points. Now you begin to develop specific plans for each, consulting later chapters in this book as needed to clarify how to use your various program components.

Say that you're considering using print ads in trade magazines to let retail store buyers know about your hot new line of products and the in-store display options you have for them. That's great, but now you need to get specific. You need to pick some magazines. (Call their ad departments for details on their demographics and their prices — see Chapter 7 for how.) You also need to decide how many of what sort of ads you'll run, and then price out this advertising program.

Do the same analysis for each of the items on your list of program components. Work your way through the details until you have an initial cost figure for what you want to do with each component. Total these costs and see if the end result seems realistic. Is the total cost too big a share of your projected sales? Or (if you're in a larger business), is your estimate higher than the boss says the budget can go? If so, adjust and try again. After a while, you get a budget that looks acceptable on the bottom line and also makes sense from a practical perspective.

A spreadsheet greatly helps this process. Just build formulas that add the costs to reach subtotals and a grand total, and then subtract the grand total from the projected sales figure to get a bottom line for your program. Figure 3-1 shows the format for a very simple spreadsheet that gives a quick and accurate marketing program overview for a small business. In this figure, you can see what a program looks like for a company that wholesales products to gift shops around the United States. This company uses personal selling, tele-marketing, and print advertising as its primary program components. It also budgets some money in this period to finish developing and begin introducing a new line of products.

Overview of Program to Target Retail Store Buyers	
Program Components	**Direct Marketing Costs ($)**
Primary influence points:	
– Sales calls	$450,700
– Telemarketing	276,000
– Ads in trade magazines	1,255,000
– New product line development	171,500
	Subtotal: $2,153,200
Secondary influence points:	
– Quantity discounts	$70,000
– Point-of-purchase displays	125,000
– New Web page with online catalog	12,600
– Printed catalog	52,000
– Publicity	18,700
– Booth at annual trade show	22,250
– Redesign packaging	9,275
	Subtotal: $309,825
Projected Sales from This Program	$23,250,000
Minus Total Program Costs	– 2,463,025
Net Sales from This Marketing Program	**$20,786,975**

Figure 3-1:
A program budget, prepared on a spreadsheet.

This company's secondary components don't use much of the marketing budget when compared to the primary components (which use 87 percent of the total budget). But the secondary components are important, too. A new Web page is expected to handle a majority of customer inquiries and act as a virtual catalog, permitting the company to cut way back on its catalog printing and mailing costs. Also, the company plans to introduce a new line of floor displays for use at point of purchase by selected retailers. Marketers expect this display unit, combined with improved see-through packaging, to increase turnover of the company's products in retail stores.

If your marketing plan covers multiple groups of customers, you need to include multiple spreadsheets (such as the one in Figure 3-1) because each group of customers may need a different marketing program.

For example, the company whose wholesale marketing program you see in Figure 3-1 sells to gift stores — that's the purpose of that program. But they also do some business with stationery stores. And even though the same salespeople call on both, each of these customers has different products and promotions. They buy from different catalogs. They don't use the same kinds of displays. They read different trade magazines. Consequently, the company has to develop a separate marketing program for each, allocating any overlapping expenses appropriately. (For example, if you make two-thirds of your sales calls to gift stores, then the sales calls expense for the gift store program should be two-thirds of the total sales budget.)

Exploring Your Program's Details

In this part of your plan, you need to explain the details of how you plan to use each component in your marketing program. Devote a section to each component, which means that this part of your plan may be quite lengthy (give it as many pages as you need to lay out the necessary facts). The more of your thinking you get on paper, the easier implementing the plan will be later — as will rewriting the plan next year.

Although this portion is the lengthiest art of your plan, I'm not going to cover it in depth here. You can find details about how to use specific components of a marketing program, from product positioning to Web pages to pricing, in Chapters 7 through 17 of this book.

At a minimum, this part of the plan should have sections covering the *five Ps* — the product, pricing, *placement* (or distribution), *promotion* (how you communicate with and persuade customers), and people (salespeople, customer service staff, distributors, and so on). But more likely, you'll want to break these categories down into more specific areas. You can even get as detailed as this book does, having a section corresponding to each of Chapters 7 to 17, for example.

Don't bother going into detail in your marketing plan on program components that you cannot alter. Sometimes, the person writing the marketing plan can't change pricing policy, order up a new product line, or dictate a shift in distribution strategy. Explore your boundaries and even try to stretch them, but you need to admit they exist or your plan can't be practical. If you can only control promotion, then this section of the plan should concentrate on the ways that you'll promote the product. In which case, never mind the other Ps. Acknowledge in writing any issues or challenges you have to cope with, given that you can't change other factors. Now write a plan that does everything you can reasonably do given your constraints. (A section called *Constraints* ought to go into the Situation Analysis if your company has such constraints.)

Managing Your Marketing Program

The main purpose of the management section of the plan is simply to make sure that enough warm bodies are in the right places at the right times to get the work done. The management section summarizes the main activities that you, your employees, or your employer must perform in order to implement your marketing program. The section then assigns these activities to individuals, justifying the assignments by considering issues such as an individual's capabilities, capacities, and how the company will supervise and control that individual.

Sometimes this section gets more sophisticated by addressing management issues, like how to make the sales force more productive or whether to decentralize the marketing function. If you have salespeople or distributors, develop plans for organizing, motivating, tracking and controlling them. Also develop a plan for them to use in generating, allocating, and tracking sales leads. Start these subsections by describing the current approach, and do a strengths/weaknesses analysis of that approach, using input from the salespeople, reps, or distributors in question. End by describing any incremental changes/improvements you can think to make.

But make sure that you've run your ideas by the people in question *first* and gotten their input. Don't surprise your salespeople, sales reps, or distributors with new systems or methods. If you do, they'll probably resist the changes, and sales will slow down. So schmooze and share, persuade and propose, maximizing their feeling of involvement in the planning process. People execute sales plans well only if they understand and believe in those plans.

Projecting Expenses and Revenues

Now you need to put on your accounting and project management hats. (Neither fits very well, perhaps, but try to bear them for a day or two.) You need these hats to

- ✔ Estimate future sales, in units and dollars, for each product in your plan.

- ✔ Justify these estimates and, if they're hard to justify, create worst-case versions, too.

- ✔ Draw a timeline showing when your program incurs costs and performs program activities. (Doing so helps with the preceding section and also gets you prepared for the unpleasant task of designing a monthly marketing budget.)

- ✔ Write a monthly marketing budget that lists all the estimated costs of your programs for each month of the coming year and breaks down sales by product or territory and by month.

If you're a start-up or small business, I highly recommend doing all your projections on a *cash basis*. In other words, put the payment for your year's supply of brochures in the month in which the printer wants the money, instead of allocating that cost across 12 months. Also factor in the wait time for collecting your sales revenues. If collections take 30 days, show money coming in during December from November's sales, and don't count any December sales for this year's plan. A cash basis may upset accountants, who like to do things on an accrual basis — see *Accounting For Dummies,* 2nd Edition, by John A. Tracy (Wiley) if you don't know what that means — but cash-based accounting keeps small businesses alive. You want a positive cash balance (or at least to break even) on the bottom line during every month of your plan.

If your cash-based projection shows a loss some months, fiddle with the plan to eliminate that loss (or arrange to borrow money to cover the gap). Sometimes a careful cash-flow analysis of a plan leads to changes in underlying strategy. One business-to-business marketer I worked with adopted as its primary marketing objective the goal of getting more customers to pay with credit cards instead of on invoices. The company's business customers cooperated, and average collection time shortened from 45 days to under 10, greatly improving the cash flow and thus the spending power and profitability of the business.

Several helpful techniques are available for projecting sales, such as buildup forecasts, indicator forecasts, and time-period forecasts. Choose the most appropriate technique for your business based on the reviews in this section. If you're feeling nervous, just use the technique that gives you the most conservative projection. Here's a common way to play it safe: Use several of the techniques and average their results.

Buildup forecasts

These predictions go from the specific to the general, or from the bottom up. If you have sales reps or salespeople, have each one project the next period's sales for her territories and justify her projections based on what changes in the situation she anticipates. Then aggregate all the sales force's forecasts to obtain an overall figure.

If you have few enough customers that you can project per-customer purchases, build up your forecast this way. You may want to work from reasonable estimates of the amount of sales you can expect from each store carrying your products or from each thousand catalogs mailed. Whatever the basic building blocks of your program, start with an estimate for each element and then add these estimates up.

Indicator forecasts

This method links your forecast to economic indicators that ought to vary with sales. For example, if you're in the construction business, you find that past sales for your industry correlate with *GDP* (gross domestic product, or national output) growth. So you can adjust your sales forecast up or down depending upon whether experts expect the economy to grow rapidly or slowly in the next year.

Multiple scenario forecasts

You base these forecasts on what-if stories. They start with a straight-line forecast in which you assume that your sales will grow by the same percentage next year as they did last year. Then you make up what-if stories and project their impact on your plan to create a variety of alternative projections.

You may try the following scenarios if they're relevant to your situation:

- ✔ What if a competitor introduces a technological breakthrough?
- ✔ What if your company acquires a competitor?
- ✔ What if Congress deregulates/regulates your industry?
- ✔ What if a leading competitor fails?
- ✔ What if your company has financial problems and has to lay off some of your sales and marketing people?
- ✔ What if your company doubles its ad spending?

For each scenario, think about how customer demand may change. Also consider how your marketing program would need to change in order to best suit the situation. Then make an appropriate sales projection. For example, if a competitor introduced a technological breakthrough, you may guess that your sales would fall 25 percent short of your straight-line projection.

The trouble with multiple scenario analysis is that . . . well, it gives you multiple scenarios. Your boss (if you have one) wants a single sales projection, a one-liner at the top of your marketing budget. One way to turn all those options into one number or series of numbers is to just pick the option that seems most likely to you. That's not very satisfying if you aren't at all sure which, if any, will come true. So another method involves taking all the options that seem even remotely possible, assigning each a probability of occurring in the next year, multiplying each by its probability, and then averaging them all to get a single number.

For example, the Cautious Scenario projection estimates $5 million, and the Optimistic Scenario projection estimates $10 million. The probability of Cautious Scenario occurring is 15 percent, and the probability of Optimistic Scenario occurring is 85 percent. So you find the sales projection with this formula: $[(\$5,000,000 \times 0.15) + (\$10,000,000 \times 0.85)] \div 2 = \$4,630,000$.

Time period projections

To use this method, work by week or month, estimating the size of sales in each time period, and then add these estimates for the entire year. This approach helps you when your program or the market isn't constant across the entire year. Ski resorts use this method because they get certain types of revenues only at certain times of the year. And marketers who plan to introduce new products during the year or to use heavy advertising in one or two *pulses* (concentrated time periods) also use this method because their sales go up significantly during those periods. Entrepreneurs, small businesses, and any others on a tight cash-flow leash need to use this method because you get a good idea of what cash will be flowing in by week or month. An annual sales figure doesn't tell you enough about when the money comes in to know whether you'll be short of cash in specific periods during the year.

Creating Your Controls

This section is the last and shortest of your plan — but in many ways, it's the most important. This section allows you and others to track performance.

Identify some performance benchmarks and state them clearly in the plan. For example:

✔ All sales territories should be using the new catalogs and sales scripts by June 1.

✔ Revenues should grow to $75,000 per month by the end of the first quarter if the promotional campaign works according to plan.

These statements give you (and, unfortunately, your employers or investors) easy ways to monitor performance as you implement the marketing plan. Without them, nobody has control over the plan; nobody can tell whether or how well the plan is working. With these statements, you can identify unexpected results or delays quickly — in time for appropriate responses if you have designed these controls properly.

A recent survey by the research firm, The Aelera Corporation, concluded that only 61 percent of marketing programs are effective. That's just a little more than half. Those odds aren't very good, so use plenty of controls and track your marketing activities on a weekly basis, if you can. Look for deviations from the plan and take action early to correct or improve the plan. Good controls allow you to make it into that minority of marketers who can look back at the end of the year and actually rate their plan a success.

Using Planning Templates and Aids

Referring to model plans can help you in this process. Unfortunately, most companies don't release their plans — they rightly view them as trade secrets. Fortunately, a few authors have compiled plans or portions of them, and you can find some good published materials to work from.

You can look at sample marketing plans and templates in several different books. These texts show you alternative outlines for plans, and they also include budgets and revenue projections in many formats — one of which may suit your needs pretty closely:

✔ *The Vest-Pocket Marketer* by Alex Hiam (yours truly!), published by Prentice Hall

✔ *The Marketing Kit For Dummies*, by Yours Truly (Wiley), which includes a cool five-minute marketing plan worksheet, if you're the impatient sort

✔ *How to Really Create a Successful Marketing Plan* by David Gumpert, published by *Inc.* magazine

✔ *The Marketing Plan* by William Cohen, published by John Wiley & Sons

You can probably order any of these books from your local bookstore, or you can go to www.insightsformarketing.com for these and other relevant resources, including planning software.

Part II
Leveraging Your Marketing Skills

The 5th Wave   By Rich Tennant

In this part . . .

Albert Einstein once said that imagination is more important than knowledge. But still, knowledge can be useful, too. In Part II, I help you ground your marketing efforts in both. I share ways of increasing your knowledge of your customers, competitors, and market, and I also help you turn your imagination into profitable marketing ideas and actions.

Several basic skill sets underlie everything else you do in marketing. Great marketing demands skills in analysis, so I show you how to do some simple market research in this part. But great marketing also requires creativity and imagination, and I devote an entire chapter to helping you dip into this free and easy-to-leverage asset of your business. A little imagination can increase the return on a marketing or advertising effort by a factor of ten, so please make sure that you tap into the power of your marketing imagination!

The third essential skill is communications, the key to almost every aspect of marketing. In this section of the book, I help you translate the insights from your research and creativity into really powerful marketing communications, no matter which of the many media you choose to communicate through (which I talk about in later sections of this book).

Chapter 4

Researching Your Customers, Competitors, and Industry

*I*n this chapter, I help you better understand your customers and competitors, and in the process, better understand yourself, too. What makes your offering better or worse than that of your competitors? That question, and more like it, can help you clarify your strategy, make more accurate sales projections, and decide what to emphasize (visually or verbally) in your marketing program (advertising, sales presentations, discussions with the media, Web site, and so on). A little research can go a long way toward improving the effectiveness of your marketing.

One percent of companies do 90 percent of the market research. Big businesses hire research firms to do extensive customer surveys and to run discussion groups with customers. The marketers then sit down to 50-page reports filled with tables and charts before making any decisions. I don't recommend this traditional approach, because you probably have far less time and money, let alone patience, that this approach demands.

Instead, I help you adopt an inquisitive approach by sharing relatively simple and efficient ways of learning about customers and competitors. As a marketer, you need to ask questions and seek useful answers, something you can do on any budget.

Knowing When and Why You Do Research

Large companies do so much research, in part, to cover the marketer's you-know-what if the marketing campaign subsequently fails. That's a bad reason to waste time and money doing endless surveys and focus groups. (A *focus group,* by the way, is a group of potential or actual customers who sit around a table discussing your product while a trained moderator guides their conversation and hidden video cameras immortalize their every gesture and phrase.) More than half of all marketing research spending really just builds the case for pursuing strategies the marketers planned to do anyway. Don't waste your time on that.

What are good reasons to do research? Basically, if you can get a better idea or make a better decision after conducting marketing research, then research is worth your while. Also, sometimes research helps you explore your identity to improve the way you position yourself in the market (see Chapter 2 for an explanation of marketing strategies). I can't think of any other reasons to bother with research, can you?

Researching to find better ideas

Information can stimulate the imagination, suggest fresh strategies, or help you recognize great business opportunities. So always keep one ear open for interesting, surprising, or inspiring facts. Don't spend much money on this kind of research. You never really know if you're going to get any useful information from this research — most of it just goes in one ear and out the other without suggesting anything new and clever. But take subscriptions to a diverse range of publications and make a point of talking to people of all sorts, both in your industry and beyond it, to keep you in the flow of new ideas and facts. Also, ask other people for their ideas.

Every marketer should carry an idea notebook in pocket or purse and make a point of collecting a few contributions from people every day. This habit gets you asking salespeople, employees, customers, and strangers on the subway for their ideas and suggestions. You never know when a suggestion may prove valuable. Lee Iacocca kept an idea notebook in his early days as a marketing guy in the auto industry — and out of those jottings came the idea for the Ford Mustang!

Researching to make better decisions

Do you have any situations that you want more information about before making a decision? Then take a moment to define the situation clearly and list the options you think are feasible. Choosing the winning ad design, making a more accurate sales projection, or figuring out what new services your customers want — these situations provide examples of important decisions that research can help you make. Table 4-1 shows what your notes may look like.

Table 4-1	Analyzing the Information Needs of a Decision		
Decision	**Information Needs**	**Possible Sources**	**Findings**
Choose between print ads in industry magazines and e-mail advertisements to purchased lists.	How many actual prospects can print ads reach?	Magazines' ad sales people can tell us.	Three leading magazines in our industry reach 90 per cent of good customers, but half of these are not in our geographic region. May not be worth it?
	What are the comparable costs per prospect reached through these different methods?	Just need to get the budget numbers and number of people reached and divide available money by number of people.	E-mail is a third the price in our market.
	Can we find out what the average response rates are for both magazine ads and e-mailings?	Nobody is willing to tell us, or they don't know. May try calling a friend in a big ad agency; they may have done a study or something.	Friend says response rates vary wildly, and she thinks the most important thing is how relevant the customer finds the ad, not the medium used.

(continued)

Table 4-1 *(continued)*

Decision	Information Needs	Possible Sources	Findings
	Have any of our competitors switched from print to e-mail successfully?	Can probably get distributors to tell us this. Will call several and quiz them.	No, but some companies in similar industries have done this successfully.

Conclusions?

Seems like we'll spend less and be more targeted if we design special e-mails and send them only to prospects in our region. Don't buy magazine ad space for now; we can experiment with e-mail, instead. But we need to make sure the ads we send are relevant and seem important, or people just delete them without reading them.

Researching to understand love and hate

The reactions to your product or service determine your success and your product's fate. If you collect a rating of all the descriptive features of your product from customers, many of those ratings will prove quite ordinary. A bank branch offers checking, savings, and money market accounts. So what? Every bank does. But a few of the features of that bank may be notably exceptional — for better or for worse. If the teller windows often have long lines at lunch when people rush out to do their banking, that notable negative stands out in customers' minds. They remember those lines and tell others about them. Long lines at lunch may lead customers to switch banks and drive away other potential customers through bad word of mouth.

Similarly, on the positive side of the ledger, if that bank branch has very friendly tellers and a beautifully decorated lobby with free gourmet coffee on a side table for its customers, this notable warmth and friendliness sticks in customers' minds, building loyalty and encouraging them to recruit new customers through word of mouth.

To scoot or not to scoot

Here's a great example of the brilliance curve at work. Have you heard about the new high-tech Segway Human Scooter? It has all sorts of computerized gyroscopes, or something, so that it balances and moves with each subtle tilt of your body, even though it has just two wheels next to your two feet. In its first year or two, the press covered its wonderful abilities — its brilliance — and sales grew as a result. Then it dropped out of the headlines for a while, only to reemerge when manufacturers announced a recall.

The problem? When its batteries run low, it can become unstable, leading to nasty spills (President Bush fell off one — how's that for bad publicity?). No doubt this product has many ordinary aspects, but only the features that are the outliers on its brilliance curve get our attention — the things that customers consider notably good and bad about it. Obviously, the marketers need to move aggressively to eliminate the problems and then refocus their publicity efforts on the positive story of how amazing the product's performance can be.

If you gather customer ratings, you can draw a graph of all the features of your product, rated from negative through neutral to positive. You find most features cluster in the middle of the resulting bell curve, failing to differentiate you from the competition. A few features stick out on the left as notably negative — and you have to fix those features fast! Other features, hopefully, stand out on the right as notably positive. You need to nurture and expand upon these features, and don't forget to boast shamelessly about them in all your marketing communications.

Do some research to understand your own *brilliance curve* (as I call it) by asking customers to rank you on a laundry list of descriptors for your business/product/service. The scale ranges from 1 to 10 (to get a good spread), with the following labels:

1	2	3	4	5	6	7	8	9	10
Very bad		Bad		Average		Good		Very good	

For example, the list of items to rate in a bank may include checking accounts (average), savings accounts (average), speed of service (bad), and friendliness of tellers (very good), along with many other things you'd need to put on the list in order to describe the bank, in detail. Getting customers to fill in a survey sheet is important enough that I'd consider offering them a reward for doing so. You can waive the fees on their checking account for the rest of the year if they mail in a completed form. Or (if you don't mind honest feedback) you can ask them to fill in a rating form while standing in that long line!

Adopting an inquisitive spirit

An inquisitive spirit is at the heart of good marketing research. And it's free — you don't have to have PandG's research budget to take advantage of it! Ask yourself why customers do what they do; what caused a change in your market; where those customers you lose end up going. Almost any question works as a starting point. The first — and most important — step in any research effort is to ask a penetrating question. Let me give you an interesting example.

Do you know the Whiskas brand of cat food? Maybe, but maybe not — Whiskas trails better-known brands and is ranked #6 in U.S. cat food sales. What can be done to give it more appeal? To counter this problem, Whiskas marketers developed an innovative series of TV ads to help it gain share. These ads don't portray pet cats like children or as silly clowns. Breaking with these older advertising traditions, the ads portray cats as the semiwild animals they are, stalking prey, sneaking around, and generally being catlike. Where did this innovative advertising idea come from? From people who keep cats — or do I mean humans who are kept by cats?

When people talk about their cats and what they like about those furry felines, the wildness and independence of cats often comes up. Cats are like little lions. Cat owners feel that cats haven't "sold out" the way dogs have. Such comments gave the marketers of Whiskas the insight that overly cute, personified portrayals of cats don't jive with the cat-lover's image of his cat.

The Whiskas ads reflect this important insight, and Whiskas marketers reached this insight by taking time to observe and listen to cat owners with an open mind and a fresh ear. If you haven't gone out and spent some time really trying to understand your customers lately, then maybe you ought to. What are you doing tomorrow? Oh dear, don't tell me. You're too busy to listen to your customers? Hmm. Maybe you need to rethink your priorities.

One end of this scale represents the features customers think you do brilliantly. The other end represents the features you need some work on (to put it nicely!). If you want to get fancy, you can also ask some customers to rate the importance of each item on the list to them, personally. If you're lucky, your brilliant areas are important to them and your bad areas aren't. But most likely, you need to clean up those worst-on-the-list features to make them average, at least (so they don't become what every customer remembers and talks about). And you definitely need to focus on leveraging the high-rated items. Talk them up in marketing and invest even more in them to maximize their attractiveness.

Planning Your Research

Research should start with a careful analysis of the decisions you must make. For example, say you're in charge of a 2-year-old software product that small businesses use to develop their marketing plans. As the product manager, what key decisions should you be making? The following are the most likely:

- ✔ Should we launch an upgrade or keep selling the current version?
- ✔ Is our current marketing program sufficiently effective, or should we redesign it?
- ✔ Is the product positioned properly, or do we need to change its image?

So before you do any research, you need to think hard about those decisions. Specifically, you need to

- ✔ Decide what realistic options you have for each decision.
- ✔ Assess your level of uncertainty and risk for each decision.

Then, for any uncertain or risky decisions, you need to pose questions whose answers should help you reduce the risk and uncertainty of the decision. And now, with these questions in hand, you're ready to begin your research!

When you work through this thinking process, you often find that you don't actually need research. For example, maybe your boss has already decided to invest in an upgrade of the software product you manage, so researching the decision has no point. Wrong or right, you can't realistically change that decision.

But some questions make it through the screening process and turn out to be good candidates for research. For these research points, you need to pose a series of questions that have the potential to reduce your decision-making uncertainty or to reveal new and exciting options for you as a decision-maker.

For example, take the question, "Is the product positioned properly, or do we need to change its image?" To find out whether repositioning your product makes sense, you may ask how people currently perceive the product's quality and performance, how they view the product compared to the leading competitors, and what the product's personality is. If you know the answers to all these questions, you're far better able to make a good decision.

That's why you must start by defining your marketing decisions very carefully. Until you know what decisions you must make, marketing research has little point. See Figure 4-1 for a flowchart of the research process.

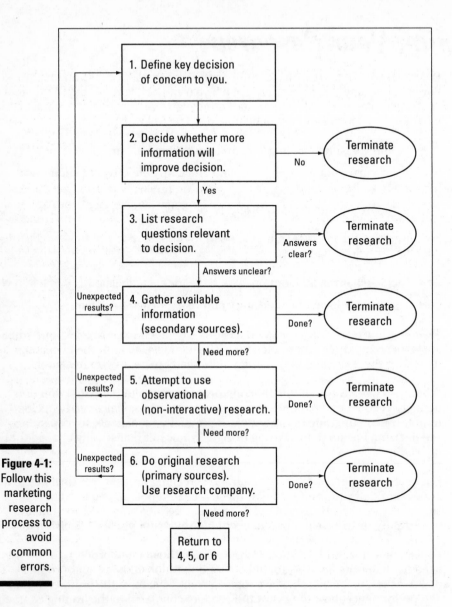

Figure 4-1:
Follow this
marketing
research
process to
avoid
common
errors.

Doing Original Research

Primary research gathers data from people in answers to questions. In general, this type of research gathers data by observing people to see how they behave or by asking them for verbal or written answers to questions.

Observing your customers

Years ago, managers from the Boston Aquarium wanted to find out which attractions were most popular. They hired a researcher to develop a survey, but the researcher told them not to bother. Instead, he suggested they examine the floors for wear and for tracks on wet days. The evidence pointed clearly to certain attractions as most popular. The floors in front of those attractions had the most wear. And damp paths led to the attractions that visitors preferred to go to first.

Consumers are all around you — shopping for, buying, and using products. Observing consumers, and finding something new and of value from doing so, is not hard. And even *business-to-business marketers* (who sell to other businesses instead of end-consumers) can find plenty of evidence about their customers at a glance. The number and direction of a company's trucks on various roads can tell you where their business is heaviest and lightest, for example. Despite all the opportunities to observe, most marketers are guilty of Sherlock Holmes' accusation that "You have not observed, and yet you have seen." Observation is the most underrated of all research methods.

Find a way to observe one of your customers as she uses one of your products. I want you to observe, not just watch. Bring along a pad and pencil, and take care to notice the little things. What does the customer do, in what order, and how long does she spend doing it? What does she say, if anything? Does she look happy? Frustrated? Disinterested? Does anything go wrong? Does anything go right — is she surprised with how well the product performs? Take detailed notes and then think about them. I guarantee that you end up gaining at least one insight into how to improve your product.

Asking people questions

Survey research methods are the bread and butter of the marketing research industry, and for a good reason. You can often gain something of value just by asking people what they think. The survey methods do have their shortcomings. Customers don't always know what they think or how they behave. And even when they do, getting them to tell you can be quite costly. Nonetheless, every marketer finds good uses for survey research on occasion. (For gory details of how to write a customer questionnaire, see the example I've posted on the Web page that supports this book at www.insightsformarketing.com, under the topic "Improving a Questionnaire.")

If your product makes customers happy, those customers come back. If not, adios. And because recruiting new customers costs anywhere from 4 to 20 times as much as retaining old ones (depending upon your industry), you can't afford to lose customers. Which means you can't afford to dissatisfy them. So every marketer needs to measure and set goals for customer satisfaction.

If you work for one of the two-thirds majority of businesses that doesn't increase its customers' satisfaction each year, you need to get cracking. And the best whip to crack is a customer satisfaction measure that portrays your company or product in a realistic light (you can measure with survey questions or with the rate of customer complaints; the best measures combine multiple sources of data into an overall index). After this measure gets reported to everyone on a regular basis, your company has to look hard at customer satisfaction.

Many such measures fluff up customer satisfaction to conceal problems. In bigger companies, I sometimes see people pressuring customers to give them good ratings because they're afraid of getting in trouble. For example, if you buy a new car, you may get a call from the dealer a few days later, asking you to rate the dealer's service high when a research firm calls you the next day. This sort of tactic is like evaluating the comfort of a mattress by spreading a soft comforter over it and then seeing if it looks level. The best measures put some weight on the mattress. The more stress you induce, the more meaningful the response!

Also watch out for over-general questions or ratings. Any measure based on a survey that asks customers to "rate your overall satisfaction with our company on a 1-to-10 scale" isn't much use. What does an average score of 8.76 mean? Sure, that's pretty high. But are customers satisfied? You didn't really ask them. And even worse, you didn't ask them if they're more satisfied with you than they used to be. Or if they're less satisfied with competitors than with you. I favor asking a series of more specific questions, such as "was it convenient and easy to do business with us?"

Customer satisfaction changes with each new interaction between customer and product. Keeping up with customer opinion is a never-ending race, and you need to make sure that you're measuring where you stand relative to those shifting customer expectations and competitor performances.

Your customer satisfaction has to be high, relative to both customer expectations and competitors' ratings, before that customer satisfaction has much of an effect on customer retention rates. Make sure that you ask tough questions to find out whether you're below or above customers' current standards. You can ask customers revealing questions, similar to the following list:

1. **Which company (or product) is the best right now?**

   (Give a long list with instructions to circle one, and give a write-in blank labeled *Other* as the final choice.)

2. **Rate [your product] compared to its competitors:**

Far worse			Same		Far better	
1	2	3	4	5	6	7

3. Rate [your product] compared to your expectations for it:

Far worse			Same		Far better	
1	2	3	4	5	6	7

You can get helpful customer responses by breaking down customer satisfaction into its contributing elements. (Focus groups or informal chats with customers can help you come up with your list of contributing elements.) For example, you can ask the following questions about an overnight letter carrier:

1. Rate Flash Deliveries compared to its competitors on speed of delivery.

Far worse			Same		Far better	
1	2	3	4	5	6	7

2. Rate Flash Deliveries compared to its competitors on reliability.

Far worse			Same		Far better	
1	2	3	4	5	6	7

3. Rate Flash Deliveries compared to its competitors on ease of use.

Far worse			Same		Far better	
1	2	3	4	5	6	7

4. Rate Flash Deliveries compared to its competitors on friendliness.

Far worse			Same		Far better	
1	2	3	4	5	6	7

When doing research, you can too easily lose sight of the end-of-process goal — customer satisfaction. Sure, you may need to find out about a lot of other issues in order to design your marketing program or diagnose a problem. But none of what you find out matters unless it boils down to increased customer satisfaction in the long run. Whatever else you decide to research, make sure you keep one eye on customer satisfaction. It's the ultimate reality test of any marketing program!

A Marketer's Dozen Ways to Get Ideas for Low-Cost Research

You don't have to spend a quarter of a million dollars researching ideas for a new ad campaign (or anything else). Instead, focus on ways of gaining insight or checking your assumptions using free and inexpensive research methods.

If you decide you want to actually go spend tens of thousands of dollars on research, go ahead: Plenty of firms are ready to take your money and produce big reports in exchange (and the big New York and London ad agencies do good-but-expensive research for their clients, too).

But how can you do useful research without a lot of time, money, and staff to waste? This section shares 14 ideas to get you off on the right foot.

Comparing your approach to that of your competitors

When you compare your marketing approach to competitors, you easily find out what customers like best. Make a list of the things that your competitors do differently than you. Does one of them price higher? Does another one give away free samples? Do some of them offer money-back guarantees? Make a list of at least five points of difference between your business and its major competitors based on an analysis of marketing practices. Now ask ten of your best customers to review this list and tell you what they prefer — your way or one of the alternatives. Keep a tally. And ask them why. You may find that all your customers vote in favor of doing something differently than the way you do it now.

Creating a customer profile

Take photographs of people you characterize as your typical customers. Post these pictures on a bulletin board and add any facts or information you can collect about those customers, too. This board becomes your customer database. Whenever you aren't sure what to do about any marketing decision, you can sit down in front of the bulletin board and use it to help you tune into your customers and what they do and don't like. For example, make sure the art and wording you use in a letter or ad is appropriate to the customer on your board. Will they like it, or is the style wrong for them?

Entertaining customers to get their input

Invite good customers to a lunch or dinner, or hold a Customer Appreciation event. Entertaining your customers puts you in contact with them in a relaxed setting where they're happy to chat and share their views. Use these occasions to ask them for suggestions and reactions. Bounce a new product idea off of them or find out what features they'd most like to see improved. Your customers can provide an expert panel for your informal research, and you just have to provide the food!

Using e-mail to do one-question surveys

If you market to businesses, you probably have e-mail addresses for many of your customers. Try e-mailing 20 or more of them for a quick opinion on a question. Result? Instant survey! If a clear majority of them say they prefer using a corporate credit card to being invoiced because the card is more convenient, well, you've just gotten a useful research result that may help you revise your approach.

Surfing government databases

Many countries gather and post extensive data on individuals, households, and businesses, broken down into a variety of categories. In the United States, you can find out how many people earn above a certain amount of money a year and live in a specific city or state — useful if you're trying to figure out how big the regional market may be for a luxury product. Similarly, you can find out how many businesses operate in your industry and what their sales are in a specific city or state — useful if you're trying to decide whether that city has a market big enough to warrant your moving into it. (I show you some specific examples and Web addresses for gathering useful data from the U.S. government in the "Using Free Data" section later in this chapter.)

Watching people use your product

Be nosey. Find ways to observe people as they shop for and consume your product or service. What do they do? What do they like? What, if anything, goes wrong? What do they dislike? You can gain insight into what your consumers care about, how they feel, and what they like by observing them in action. Being a marketing voyeur provides you a most useful and interesting way to do research — at no charge. And if you're in a retail business, be (or ask someone else to be) a *secret shopper* by going in and acting like an ordinary customer to see how you're treated and get a feel for what you do and don't like.

Establishing a trend report

E-mail salespeople, distributors, customer service staff, repair staff, or friendly customers once a month, asking them for a quick list of any important trends they see in the market. You flatter people by letting them know that you value their opinion, and e-mail makes giving that opinion especially easy for them. A trend report gives you a quick indication of a change in buying patterns, a new competitive move or threat, and any other changes that your marketing may need to respond to. Print out and file these reports from the field and go back over them every now and then for a long-term view of the effectiveness of your marketing strategies, too.

Analyzing competitors' ads and brochures

Clip and collect marketing materials (brochures, ads, Web pages, and so on) from competitors and analyze them, using a *claims table.* Open up a spreadsheet (or draw a blank table on a piece of paper or poster board) and label the columns of this new table, one for each competitor. Label each row with a feature, benefit, or claim. Enter key phrases or words from an ad in the appropriate cell. Include the most prominent or emphasized claims per competitor (put one to three claims per competitor). When filled in, this table shows you, at a glance, what territory each competitor stakes out and how it does the staking. One may claim it's the most efficient, another the most helpful, and so on.

Compare your own claims with those of competitors. Are you impressive by comparison, or does a more dominant and impressive competitor's claims overshadow you? Do your claims stand out as unique, or are you a me-too marketer without clear points of difference? The claims table helps you see yourself as customers do — through the lens of your marketing materials and in comparison to your competitors. Using this table often delivers uncomfortable moments of truth that force you to rethink and improve your marketing approach. (But be careful to base your claims on genuine strengths, not just advertising fluff, by understanding what makes you brilliant — see the following section.)

Researching your "brilliance"

Perhaps the most important element of any marketing plan or strategy is clearly recognizing what makes you especially good and appealing to customers (I talk more about this in Chapter 2). Your positive uniqueness is your *brilliance* (according to the new discipline of brilliance marketing, which you can find more about on the Web site for this book — www.insightsfor marketing.com). To research your brilliance, find the simplest way to ask ten good customers this simple but powerful question: "What is the best thing about our [fill in the name of your product or service], from your perspective?" (Or you can do the more detailed "brilliance curve" survey I describe in the "Researching to understand love and hate" section earlier in this chapter.)

The answers to this question usually focus on one or, at most, a few features or aspects of your business. Finding out how your customers identify your brilliance proves a great help to your marketing strategy. After you know what you do best, you can focus on telling the story about that best whenever you advertise, do publicity, or communicate with your market in any way. You can also concentrate your spending and improvement efforts on the things customers like most about you. Investing in your strengths (versus your competitors' strengths or your weaknesses) tends to grow your sales and profits most quickly and efficiently.

Probing your own customer records

Most marketers fail to "mine" their own databases for all the useful information those databases may contain. A good way to tap into this free data (because you already own it!) — study your own customers with the goal of identifying three common traits that make them different or special.

A computer store I'm a customer of went through their records and realized that their customers are

- More likely to be self-employed or entrepreneurs than the average person
- More sophisticated users of computers than most people
- Big spenders who care more about quality and service than the absolute cheapest price

This store revised its marketing goal to find more people who share these three qualities. What qualities do your customers have that make them special, and that would make a good profile for you to use in pursuing more customers like them?

Surveying your own customers

You can gather input from your own customers in a variety of easy ways because your customers interact with your employees or firm. You can put a stamped postcard in shipments, statements, product packages, or other communications with your customers. Include three or fewer simple, non-biased survey questions, such as, "Are you satisfied with this purchase? no = 1 2 3 4 5 = yes." Also leave a few lines for comments, in case they have something they want to tell you. You generally get low response rates with any such effort, but that's okay. If someone has something to tell you, they let you hear about it. And even a 5 percent response gives you a steady stream of input you wouldn't otherwise have.

Testing your marketing materials

Whether you're looking at a letter, broadcast fax, catalog, Web page, tear sheet, press release, or ad, you can improve that material's effectiveness by asking for reviews by a few customers, distributors, or others with knowledge of your business. Do they like the material? Do they like it a lot? If they're only luke-warm about it, then you know you need to edit or improve it before spending the money to publish and distribute it.

Customer reviewers can tell you quickly whether you have real attention-getting wow-power in any marketing communication. Big companies do elabo-rate, expensive tests of ads' readability and pulling power, but you can get a pretty good idea for much less money. Just ask a half-dozen people to review a new marketing material while it's still in draft form. An even simpler (and very effective) technique? Make a list of possible headlines for an ad on a piece of paper and ask potential customers (or anyone in the industry whom you can talk into helping) to check the one they like best. You may be surprised by the results.

Interviewing defectors

You can easily overlook another gold mine — company records of past cus-tomers. Figure out what types of customers defect, when, and why. If you can't pinpoint why a customer abandoned you (from a complaint or a note from the salesperson, for example), try to contact the lost customer and ask him directly.

Tracking these lost customers down and getting them on the phone or set-ting up an appointment with them may prove difficult. Don't give up! Your lost customers hold the key to a valuable piece of information: What you do wrong that can drive customers away. Talk to enough of them, and you see a pattern emerge. Probably three-fourths of them left you for the same reason (which can be pricing, poor service, inconvenient hours, and so on — that's for you to find out).

When your research reveals the most common reason for customers to defect, do something about that reason. Plug that hole and you lose fewer customers down it. And keeping those customers means you don't have to waste valuable marketing resources replacing customers. You can keep the old ones and grow every time you add a new one.

Asking your kids

Seriously! Your children, or any kids on hand that you can get to think about your market for a few minutes, probably have a unique and more contemporary view than you. Ask them simple questions like "What will the next big thing be in [name your product or service here]?" Think about using this great question to ask kids: "What's cool and what's not cool this year?" They know, and you don't. In any consumer marketing, you need to make sure that you're cool and your competitors aren't. Because kids lead the trends in modern society, why not ask them what those trends are? Even in business-to-business and industrial markets, kids and their sense of what's happening in society can be helpful — often giving you early indicators of shifts in demand that may have an impact all the way up the line, from consumers to the businesses that ultimately serve them.

Using Free Data

The world is overflowing with data, and some of that data can give you just what you need to get started on your research project. So before you buy a report or hire a research firm, dig around for some free (or at least cheap) stuff.

Of course, you generally get what you pay for when it comes to free data. For example, I visited the United States Census Bureau's home page on the World Wide Web at www.census.gov to see whether I could get detailed census data on households in several Massachusetts counties. Yes, you can buy their data at a modest price, on paper or computer disk, but you have to play phone tag for a day and then wait endlessly for delivery. Or you can go to one of many private vendors that analyze and update the census data and happily sell customized reports to you — for a lot more money.

Sometimes free data is old or lacking in detail, and you need to decide whether it's good enough for your purposes or not. Often, it is — if you just want to know, for example, which neighboring counties are large enough to support your household cleaning service; then who cares if you use census data from a few years ago? You don't need 100-percent accuracy; you're just looking for general indications of market size. Even if you do need more accuracy and detail, the free stuff can get you started by narrowing down your focus and helping you form some good hypothetical answers to test later.

Free data generally falls into a category known as *secondary data* — meaning already collected or published by someone else — so you get it second hand.

Often, the best source of free or almost-free data is your national government. Many governments collect copious data on economic activity, population size, and trends within their borders. In the United States, the Census Bureau is the best general source of data on how many of what sorts of people and households live where. And the Department of Commerce has endless data on what sorts of businesses do how much of what, where.

Government databases

If you want to use the Web to explore useful data compiled and posted by various agencies of the U.S. government, go to www.census.gov, the main gateway into U.S. census data on households and businesses. You should also know www.census.gov/epcd/www/econ97.html, the current address for U.S. data from the economic census (which goes out to five million businesses every five years) and the Survey of Business Owners.

A while ago, I needed to figure out where to focus a new sales initiative in a city my firm had not sold to before. I went to: http://factfinder.census. gov/home/saff/main.html?_lang=enand_ts=, where I clicked on Data Sets and pulled up a quick report on the Springfield, Massachusetts, metropolitan statistical area in order to find out which industries have the biggest numbers of employees. Why do I care about that? Because my firm does employee training in the workplace, so big numbers of employees gives a good indicator of market potential. Within seconds, I had a table on my screen showing number of establishments (businesses) and total number of employees, organized by industry. From the information in that table, I saw the top five industries in Springfield, ranked by number of employees (see Table 4-2).

Table 4-2	Top Five Industries in Springfield, Massachusetts		
NAICS Industry	**Number of Establishments**	**Number of Employees**	**Average Employees per Establishment**
Manufacturing	962	38,854	40
Retail Trade	2,446	31,552	12
Finance/Insurance	734	20,802	28
Accommodation and Food Services	1,256	18,364	15
Health Care and Social Assistance	1,029	15,681	15

I added the last column myself, dividing the number of employees by the number of establishments. Small employers don't usually buy outside training materials and services and bigger ones do. From this analysis, based on free census data, I can make a reasonable guess that I can find good prospects (large employers with a lot of employees to train) in two of these industries: manufacturing and finance/insurance. These industries have a lot of establishments in the area, and they have a higher average number of employees, too.

Obviously, my study of this market wasn't done after I checked out the Springfield statistical information, but I had a good beginning — and all for free in a moment on the Web. Next, I may turn to other free and easy sources of secondary data: local chambers of commerce for names of the largest employers in my two target industries, and a local phone book or directory assistance for contact numbers. A Google.com key-term search for **Springfield, MA chamber of commerce** didn't turn up a Web page for the chamber, but I did find various sites listing the names and phone numbers of a half-dozen chambers in that metropolitan area (including chambers in nearby towns and cities). Well, sometimes you have to abandon the Web and fall back on the good old telephone. By calling the half-dozen chambers I found, I talked to several intelligent staffers, asking them for the names of the largest health care and manufacturing employers in the area.

In this way, I drilled down to specific names and addresses of several dozen prospective companies to sell employee training to in that market. And I got this information within 15 minutes of posing the question, thanks to the power of secondary research on the Web and the telephone. All that was left to develop the market was to find out more about these companies (again, the Web proved a good place to start because they all had Web sites). And I also networked to find people who worked at some of these businesses, people I then I called to ask about details. A third source I used was a search of articles about the companies in the local media. By the time I began my sales process by calling and setting up appointments, I had gathered a lot of free information to help me know which companies to call, who to ask for, and what to talk about. You can usually focus a sales effort using such free and (relatively) easy secondary research.

Media data

If you're doing any advertising, ask the magazine, newspaper, Web server, or radio station you buy advertising from to give you information about their customer base, giving you a bit about the people exposed to your ads. They can help you make sure you reach an appropriate audience, and they can give you some exposure numbers that you can then use to calculate the effectiveness of your advertising.

I buy placement of some key-term listings on the Google and Yahoo! search engines for my corporate training firm, Insights for Training and Development. Along with the good exposure they provide, these search engines also make available a detailed report of how people accessing these search engines used my key-term listings. I can (for free) find out from Google that in the past week,

2,045 people searched for the term *"leadership style,"* and that my listing ranked 7, on average, in the results those searchers got — meaning it appeared as the seventh listing on their page. Of these 2,045 people doing a search for the term, 135 of them read my message and clicked through to my site, where the company sells training materials and assessments that help supervisors and managers find out more about good leadership.

If I look at my own site's reports, I can see that about one in a hundred such clicks turns into an immediate order (usually from a company's training department). What if I want more orders? Well, I can calculate that I'm now getting a 135/2045 or 6.6-percent click-through from my Google listing. If I get that rate up to 13 percent, I can double the number of prospects coming to my site from Google and probably see the number of orders from those prospects double, too. And that's just what we did, increasing our bid per click (or amount we pay Google; see Chapter 10) slightly in order to get a placement in the top three or four spots. We also fiddled with the wording of our message to make sure the consumer clearly understood what we sold. Clicks went up with each of these changes, and so did sales. And we got the data we used for this research and planning entirely free.

Demographics!

I have to add that exclamation point to the word "demographics," or nobody pays any attention to it. *Demographics* — statistics about a population — seem kind of boring to most people. Yet trends in the ethnic makeup of your market, its average age, or its educational levels provide you with very good clues as to how your marketing ought to change. For example, the populations of the United States, Canada, most European countries, and Japan are aging. What does that mean to marketers?

Nothing at first glance. So what if the average person is a year or two older today than the average a decade ago? You can still target products to people of different ages and ignore the long-term demographic trend.

Older Americans share a common set of values and attitudes that makes targeting them with marketing messages easier. They have common needs — for example, they need easier-to-read packaging and easier-to-use controls. And they have a great deal of disposable income because elders hold the majority of the wealth in most societies. As the population ages, this already attractive marketing segment grows faster than others. (See the book *Defining Markets Defining Moments* by Geoffrey E. Meredith, Charles D. Schewe, and Janice Karlovich [Wiley] for a good overview of U.S. consumer groups by age.)

You can find this sort of opportunity easily when you pay close attention to demographic data and other secondary sources of information. Yet many marketers ignore these inexpensive sources of data and overlook important changes in their markets as a result.

Chapter 5

Engaging Your Marketing Imagination

*W*hen the designers at clothing company Hugo Boss introduced an expensive line of men's jeans, they specified a rich, saturated black dye to give these pants a deep black appearance that wouldn't fade easily. The pants looked great. One problem, though. Some customers complained that the black dye bled onto other clothing in the wash or even (when the pants were new) onto the wearer's skin in wet weather. Hugo Boss could have chosen the easy route and sewn a warning label into the product so as to be able to repel any damage claims.

But that's not a very good solution, is it? If you design a handsome pair of jeans and price them fairly high, give them an attractive silver brand plaque on the waistband, and distribute them in upscale stores, everything you're doing signals quality and sophistication — *except* that irritating little warning that the pants may ruin your other clothes or furniture. A warning label of the traditional kind detracts from the image of the product, and marketers always want to avoid anything that puts their product in a bad light.

So instead of hiding the warning away on a cheap label inside the pants, Hugo Boss's marketers created an attractive black mini-pamphlet containing several pages of well-written, appealing information about the product. Designers gave this little booklet a sophisticated matte-plastic cover sheet both to protect it and give it an even more interesting look. Stores attached this booklet to the outside of the jeans with a matching loop of soft, thick plastic cord. The black cover bears the brand name, reversed in attractive white block letters. Inside the booklet, the consumer finds "Care Instructions: Dark Denim," describing the special qualities of the material. With a little creativity, the marketers took what may have been a detraction and recast it as an interesting point of distinction. Instead of hiding the nature of the fabric, they showcased it. The pamphlet tells the buyer that Hugo Boss is proud of the dark color — talking about the "natural beauty" of the material and its "absolute authenticity."

This story illustrates one of the infinite number of ways in which good marketing depends on creativity. Marketers must always seek new approaches and reject assumptions and limitations. There's always a better way. And if things aren't going your way — sales are slow, the boss rejects your proposals, customers complain about service, or your mailings don't get a good response — then remember to take some time out for creativity. The right creative idea at the right moment can turn the marketing tide your way.

Turning the Tide with Creativity

In marketing, progress is the direct result of creativity. Creativity is, in fact, the most fundamental and powerful of all the marketing skills. But do you profit from it as much as you could?

Have you changed your marketing lately?

Do a quick marketing creativity audit right now. Respond to each of the situations in Table 5-1 as honestly as you can, circling 1 if your answer is "rarely," 5 if your answer is "frequently," and the numbers in between if your answer is somewhere between "rarely" and "frequently."

Table 5-1	Marketing Creativity Audit
Marketing Creativity Actions	*Rating (1=rarely; 5=frequently)*
We make improvements to the selection, design, packaging, or appearance of our product(s).	1 2 3 4 5
We experiment with prices, discounts, and special offers to achieve our marketing goals.	1 2 3 4 5
We find new ways to bring our product(s) to customers, making buying or using the product(s) more convenient or easier for them.	1 2 3 4 5
We update and improve our brand image or the ways we communicate that brand image.	1 2 3 4 5

Marketing Creativity Actions	Rating (1=rarely; 5=frequently)
We try creative new ways of communicating with customers and prospects.	1 2 3 4 5
We improve the look and feel of our sales or marketing materials.	1 2 3 4 5
We listen to customer complaints or objections, and we find creative ways to turn those complaints into our next business opportunities.	1 2 3 4 5
We change our marketing message.	1 2 3 4 5
We reach out to new types of customers to try to expand or improve our customer base.	1 2 3 4 5
We share creative ideas and have freewheeling discussions with all those people who are involved in marketing our product(s).	1 2 3 4 5

Add up all the numbers you circled to get a score between 10 and 50. Find where your score falls in the range following this paragraph to find out what your Marketing Creativity Score means. Depending on your answers, you can rate your marketing creativity as very low, low, medium, or high. You need to be at least in the medium range, if not at the high end, to gain any benefits from creativity.

- 10–19 = very low
- 20–29 = low
- 30–39 = medium
- 40–50 = high

As this audit points out, don't leave anything alone in marketing. If you can identify any unchanging elements of your sales, service, advertising, mailings, or anything else that touches the customer, you have just found your next marketing project, detailed in the following section.

Changing (almost) everything

The smartest thing to do when you have a stunning, timeless, classic success in marketing is to leave it alone. But how many of those kinds of concepts can you think of? An orange paper box of Arm and Hammer baking soda. The IBM logo. A Porsche sports car. A Swiss Army Knife. The Energizer Bunny. But I can't easily add many more items to the list in the preceding section. And I'm willing to bet your ad campaign doesn't necessarily fit here. So if you're not changing many of the aspects of your marketing program, I have to ask you a really tough question. Why not? The Stolichnaya Vodka commercials, with their endless variation on the theme of showing an image of the bottle hidden in another image, is certainly a classic. Yet its concept is constant precisely because it can be executed in an endlessly creative variety of ways, so I'm not sure it really counts as unchanging.

The most common reason marketers give for not changing their technique is that it takes too much effort. Nobody got around to thinking about it. And, as I bet you already guessed, I don't consider that much of a reason to leave things alone.

So now you should mess with everything. In fact, why not make a quick list of the aspects of your marketing program that nobody has looked at or tried to improve for the last few years? Jot down three to six things that you tend to take for granted. You've just made your creative to-do list. The remaining sections in this chapter can help you come up with creative improvements for the items on that list.

Harnessing your creativity

The scarcity of great creative work in marketing tells you something about creativity: Really useful creativity is hard to do well. You need real insight and effort to achieve the sort of inspiration that I'm talking about.

For example, take the award-winning design that Drissi Advertising in Los Angeles, California, did for a point-of-purchase cardboard display that promoted the release of a children's movie called *The Indian in the Cupboard* in video stores. This movie was based on a book about a boy who has a magic cupboard that has the power to bring toy characters — including a plastic figure of a Native American — to life. Drissi Advertising could have chosen many exciting scenes from the movie to illustrate in their point-of-purchase display. Instead, they decided to communicate the wonder of the magical cupboard itself. But how to show the power this cupboard possesses? They could have done the obvious and shown the cupboard's exterior, much as it appears from the outside to anyone seeing it for the first time.

But Drissi Advertising got really creative. They turned the image around and put the viewer *in* the box, looking out past a startled Indian, through a gigantic keyhole, and into the eye of an enormous child who peeks through that keyhole. The cardboard display folds to help create the illusion that the viewer is inside the box. And they printed the whole display on such a large scale that the viewer feels small compared to the big keyhole and giant boy looking in. The power of the display's visual image needs little copy to work — simply a banner headline across the top that says, "Unlock The Secret," and the name of the movie at the bottom.

Great creative thinking! As a result, marketing for this film received good responses from retailers, who put up the display in record numbers, and consumers, who bought the movie in good numbers. Creative marketing makes your product or business stand head and shoulders above the rest. But you can't do this kind of marketing unless you have great ideas.

Are you working on the marketing for a start-up? If so, you still have to make that to-do list, except that you get to backseat drive for the established leaders in your new market. What do other marketers ignore or fail to change and improve? Do they keep using the same sales pitches or techniques? Always mail the same kinds of catalogs to the same lists on the same schedule throughout the year (in which case, why not send yours two weeks sooner in a larger, more attractive format?). Or perhaps the industry you're entering always uses the Web to support its sales but not as its lead marketing medium. Whatever the constants, list them now. That list shows you the assumptions that you, an outsider and entrepreneur, must question if you really want to become the next industry leader.

Applying Your Creativity

Advertising — whether in print, TV, radio, outdoors, at point of purchase, or elsewhere — is a key area of application for creativity. If you work in the advertising industry, or use advertising in your marketing, you're dependent on creativity for your success. Why? Because if your ads just say what you want people to remember, people won't pay any attention to those ads. Too many other ads compete for their attention. Only the most creative ones cut through the clutter, attract attention, and make a permanent mark on consumer attitudes.

Think of the role of creativity in advertising as a vehicle for building relationships between your brand and your prospects. I find this a particularly powerful way to think about advertising's role in marketing — and you can make this role possible with the addition of creativity to your ads. Marketers use creativity to add something special and unique, to accentuate a brand's differences in order to help that brand stand out in the consumers' eyes.

IBM's laptops no doubt have some technical features that make them unique, more or less. But a lot of other companies make good laptops, too. So how do you make IBM's stand out? One headline from a print ad for IBM laptops emphasizes its portability — but that's hardly unique — so marketers added a special personality to the brand by putting the message this way: "It's what Shakespeare would have used on a flight to the coast."

The ad could have shown a businessman working on a laptop, with the header: "It's what the smart manager takes on a business trip." But the copywriter's creativity led to a more compelling statement and vision. (Imagine how you'd illustrate the resulting headline — have any fun ideas?) And this creative headline expresses hidden insight into the customer's need — something that goes back to the core product concept. The whole idea of a personal computer is to help the user do better work, so why not the best work?

If Shakespeare were alive today, wouldn't he demand the best writing tools available? So should today's consumer. That's the creative concept behind this successful ad. The ad was judged successful because it:

- ✔ Attracted attention to itself
- ✔ Was memorable
- ✔ Helped convey a positive perception of the product

Writing a creative brief

Advertising benefits from the use of a *creative brief,* an information platform on which to do your creative thinking. A creative brief lays out the basic purpose and focus of the ad, and provides some supporting information that provides helpful grist for your creative mill. Sometimes people think that the creative brief answers the journalists' basic questions: Who, what, when, where, why, and how?

Leading advertising agencies, like Leo Burnett, design the creative brief like this:

- ✔ **Objective statement:** What the advertising is supposed to accomplish. Make the goals or objectives clear and specific — and one objective is easier to accomplish than many. The objective statement also includes a brief description of whom you're aiming the ad at because this target group's actions determine if you accomplish an objective.

- ✔ **Support statement:** The product's promise and the supporting evidence to back up that promise. You use this point to build the underlying argument for the persuasive part of your ad. The support statement can be based on logic and fact, or on an intuitive, emotional appeal — either way, you need to include a basis of solid support.

- ✔ **Tone or character statement:** A distinct character, feel, or personality. You choose whether the statement should accentuate the brand's long-term identity or put forth a unique tone for the ad itself that dominates the brand's image. The choice generally flows from your objectives. A local retailer's objective may be to pull in a lot of shoppers for a special Labor Day sale. The retailer should give his event a strong identity, so she'd want to define an appropriate tone for her ad. In contrast, a national marketer of a new health-food line of sodas should build brand identity, so his creative brief should focus on defining that brand identity in words (or verbal images).

The following shows an example of a creative brief for a new coffee shop's local advertising:

- **Objective:** To bring people who work in nearby businesses into the store to try our coffee and pastries.

- **Support:** Features special coffees from a roasting company that's famous in other locations but has not been available in this area until now. Also offers excellent Danish pastries and croissants, baked on the premises by a French pastry chef.

- **Tone:** A sophisticated, gourmet tone is appropriate, but also warm and inviting. Those who appreciate the finest in life prefer to go to this shop. And those people go to this shop to meet like-minded sophisticates who also appreciate the best the world has to offer.

Applying the creative brief

After you fill in the three sections of the creative brief to your satisfaction, you're ready to start brainstorming or using any other creativity tools you care to try (see the "Generating Rich Ideas" section later in this chapter). The creative brief gives you a clear focus and some good working materials as you apply your creativity to developing a great ad or other promotional piece.

The creative brief is useful for any marketing communication, or for any situation in which you must design something creative to communicate and persuade.

Think about the task of designing a new booth for a trade show. If you write a creative brief first, you have to define what the booth should accomplish and what sort of customers you want to aim the booth at (the objective statement demands that you make these decisions). You also have to review (and maybe do some creative thinking about) the evidence available to support your company's claims to fame. What may make you stand out among exhibitors at a trade show? If you aren't sure, then use the demands of the support statement to do some research and creative thinking. Make sure that you have your evidence at hand so that your ideas for booth design can communicate this evidence effectively. Finally, you have to define the tone of your booth, or think about your company's overall image and how the booth can reflect that image in its tone. The tone or character statement requires this step.

As this example illustrates, the creative brief forces you to do some helpful foundational thinking about the booth before you actually start designing it. As a result, you've made your designs more focused and objective-driven than they would be otherwise.

Creativity in product development

I cover new product development and the improvement of old products in Chapter 14, but I'll mention one aspect of product development that's relevant to this discussion — how to manage a product development team so that it's optimally creative and effective. First, you need to put together the right team. That generally means a *diverse* team, one that includes the full range of knowledge that may be relevant. You need to include different functions, from sales and marketing to manufacturing and engineering, in the creative process. Why? Because they all have different knowledge bases that help generate good ideas. You need to bring them in eventually anyway, so why not now?

In midsize and larger companies, forcing closer interaction between research, business planning, marketing, and technical staff — as General Foods does — is essential. That company (which generates several new products every year) uses a variety of conference-type events, training, and cross-functional teams to mix up its people and help them make those unobvious connections between their different knowledge bases.

Creativity and brand image

One of the most important things you can do in marketing is create a strong, appealing brand image. Creativity is the key to doing just that. As you saw in the section "Writing a creative brief" earlier in this chapter, advertising communicates the all-important brand image or personality to the consumer. Sometimes advertising focuses on that image — and, by doing so, provides a common focus for all other design decisions, from product design to packaging to special events and other marketing communications. A strong brand identity, or personality, can become a living entity, something that the marketer creates and gives to the world. Brand development takes creativity to its farthest extreme by creating new forms of life.

Generating Rich Ideas

Okay, time to be creative. Ready, set, go. Come up with any good ideas yet? No? Okay, try again. Now do you have some good ideas? What? No?

If you can't be creative at will, don't be alarmed. Most people face this problem, whether in or out of the marketing field. Artists practice creativity every day, but people in business generally don't. As a result, most people have remarkably few creative ideas in a day, or even in a year. (How many creative ideas did you come up with and propose on the job over the last year?)

So when there's a need to be creative in marketing, many people find that they require some help. How do you act creative? What's involved in generating unusually creative ideas?

First, you must give yourself permission to be creative in your work. Creativity requires you to let the mind's engine sit in idle. You can't be creative if you're busy returning e-mails or phone calls, or rushing to finish your paperwork for the day. If the hands are busy, the mind is distracted from creativity, and your imagination may not be able to work. So, for starters, I must ask you to budget time for creativity. How much time? Well, if creativity is the most powerful and profitable of the marketing skills, how often do you think you should use it? One hour a month? One hour a week? One hour a day? One day a week? You have to figure out exactly how much creativity time you need based on what your product or company demands. I don't know how much creativity your business needs or how many opportunities you may capture by being innovative, but I do know that you need to commit some time and effort to using your imagination when you're at work.

Creativity isn't a science; it's a habit — a loose collection of flaky behaviors. Like soaking up information, questioning the problem, tossing ideas back and forth with an associate, and then setting the whole thing aside to incubate in the back of your mind while you do something else. So plan to work in different ways when you're doing your creativity. Set up a large flip chart and start listing crazy ideas for the next mailing. Ask someone to help you find 20 words that rhyme with your company or brand's name in the hope that this list may lead you to a clever idea for a new radio jingle. Cut out faces from ads in magazines to try to find one that expresses an appealing new personality that can represent your product, and find out how you can use that personality in packaging or on the Web.

In other words, open yourself up through new and different ways of working, asking questions, and exploring your marketing problems and opportunities.

Getting new ideas from simple activities

Here's a list of great activities for creative marketers. Try one or more of these approaches:

✔ **Seek ways to simplify.** Can you come up with a simpler way to explain your product or your business and its mission? Can you cut your two-page brochure down to ten words? Can you reduce the length of a headline in your print ad from eight words to one? Most marketing and advertising is too complicated and can be simplified. Creative insight can help simplify and clarify all aspects of your marketing. Simple is good because simple helps make your message bold, attracting attention and zapping the key idea into the customer's mind at once.

✔ **Think of a famous person from history and imagine that he or she is your spokesperson.** How would he change your packaging, advertising, Web site, and so on? For example, what would George Washington do to sell more of your product? Can you tie your brand into Washington in some way? Might General Washington's famous crossing of the Delaware River become a metaphor for competitors' customers who need to be led over to your new and better product? "Follow me, customers. Victory awaits us on the other side of the river, where the new XYZ Brand has set up a more comfortable camp for you!" Okay, it's a silly idea, but you'd be amazed how often great marketing starts with silly ideas.

✔ **Come up with ways to advertise or communicate to customers with really small messages.** Stamps? Stickers? One-second TV or radio commercials? Lapel pins? A miniature book that comes with a magnifying glass? See what else you can imagine. One of these ideas may actually prove useful for you.

✔ **Come up with ways to advertise or communicate to customers with really big messages.** Dirigibles, oversized billboards or murals, or a message in which each word appears on a separate sign, spread along a one-mile stretch of road? How about renting a large truck or bus and covering it with a marketing message or your brand name? Or maybe something simpler and zanier — like sponsoring a contest for who can bake and eat the largest cookie and then inviting the media to cover the event? Wait, I've got it! Why not make the largest alligator in the world into your mascot? Think big. You want to have a big impact, right?

✔ **Come up with interesting but inexpensive gifts you can give customers.** Everyone gets pens with the company name on them — that's boring. So try to think of some novel gift ideas. Items that make the customer say, "Wow!" or "Hey, that's cool, I can really use that."

✔ **Find new places to advertise.** Can you think of places to put messages to your customers that nobody in your industry has used before?

✔ **Think of at least ten ways to get a famous person to use your product.** Go ahead, give this one a try. Maybe you can come up with an idea good enough to actually pitch to the celebrity.

✔ **Cut out five stunningly beautiful, strange, or otherwise eye-catching pictures from an issue of *National Geographic* magazine.** Write a headline for each one that relates that picture to your product.

These activities spur you to engage your imagination in new and unusual ways. It's surprising how often a useful insight comes out of a half-hour spent pursuing a question like one of these. Great marketers generate their own creative questions all the time. These people have a creative itch and simply have to scratch it to be satisfied.

Group creativity

Being creative on your own is hard enough. But often in marketing, and work in general, you have to get a group or team of people to come up with some creative concepts. Good luck.

Most groups of people, when confined to a conference room for a morning, do little more than argue about stale old ideas. Or even worse, somebody suggests an absolutely terrible new idea, and the rest of the group jumps on it and insists the suggestion is great . . . thus eliminating the need for *them* to think. If you hope to get a group to actually be creative, you better use structured group processes. That means you have to talk the group into going along with an activity such as brainstorming. Sometimes the group resists at first, but be persistent. Ask them what they have to lose by generating ideas for a half-hour. I bet that after they try one brainstorming technique, they see how productive the group becomes and want to try more techniques.

I've included some of the best group creativity techniques later in this section. I know that all these techniques work — I've tried them often with a wide variety of groups, in marketing and in other disciplines, as well. I don't include some of the really silly techniques that are likely to fail or to make everybody laugh at you. I've tried too many of those techniques, as well, so you don't have to.

Note that these techniques generally produce a list of ideas. Hopefully a long and varied list. But still, just a list. So be sure to schedule some time for analyzing the list in order to identify the most promising ideas, and then develop those ideas into full-blown action plans.

Brainstorming

Brainstorming is a great way to increase the number and variety of ideas. The goal of brainstorming is to generate a very long list of crazy ideas, some of which may be surprisingly helpful. Brainstorming gets people to do *out-of-the-box thinking* — in which they generate unusual ideas beyond their normal thought patterns — if you push them to use brainstorming this way. Don't let your group just go through the motions of brainstorming. To really get in the spirit of it, they have to *free associate* — to allow their minds to wander from current ideas to whatever new ideas first pop up, no matter what the association between the old and new idea may be.

You may need to encourage your group by example. If you've stated the problem as "Think of new ideas for our trade show booth," you can brainstorm a half-dozen ideas to start with, just to illustrate what you're asking the group to do: a booth like a circus fun-house, a booth shaped like a giant cave, a booth in the form of one of your products, a booth decorated on the inside to look like an outdoor space complete with blue sky and white clouds overhead, a booth like the space shuttle launch pad featuring once-an-hour launches of a scale-model of the shuttle, a booth that revolves slowly, or a booth that offers free fresh-popped popcorn and fresh-baked cookies to visitors.

These ideas aren't likely to be adopted by the average company, but they do illustrate the spirit of brainstorming, which is to set aside your criticisms and have some fun generating ideas. The rules (which you must tell the group beforehand) are as follows:

✔ **Quantity, not quality.** Generate as many ideas as possible.

✔ **No member of the group can criticize another member's suggestion.** No idea is too wild to not write down, and you can even go as far as keeping a water gun on hand and squirting the naysayer.

✔ **No ownership of ideas.** Everyone builds off of each other's ideas.

Question brainstorming

Question brainstorming is another way to generate novel questions that can provoke your group into thinking more creatively. This technique follows the same rules as brainstorming, but you instruct the group to think of questions rather than ideas.

For example, if you need to develop a new trade show booth that draws more prospects, then the group may think of the following kinds of questions:

✔ Do bigger booths draw much better than smaller ones?

✔ Which booths drew the most people at the last trade show?

✔ Are all visitors equal, or do we want to draw only certain types of visitors?

✔ Will the offer of a resting place and free coffee do the trick?

After getting these questions from the group, you get the job of answering them and seeing how those answers can help you create a new and successful trade show booth.

Wishful thinking

Wishful thinking is a technique suggested by Hanley Norins of ad agency Young & Rubicam, and one that he has used to train employees in his Traveling Creative Workshop. The technique follows the basic rules of brainstorming, but with the requirement that all statements start with the words *I wish*.

The sort of statements you get from this activity often prove useful for developing advertising or other marketing communications. If you need to bring some focus to the list to make it more relevant to your marketing, just state a topic for people to make wishes about. For example, you can say, "Imagine that the Trade Show Fairy told you that all your wishes can come true — as long as they have to do with the company's booth for the next big trade show."

Analogies

Analogies are a great creativity device. You don't think I'm serious, I know, because the idea sounds so trivial. But I define creativity as making unobvious combinations of ideas. A good analogy is just that.

I saw a great example of an analogy in a drug company's print ad. The ad showed a painting of a person about to put a huge, old-fashioned key into a keyhole in the wall. The caption next to this illustration read: "Imagine 'intelligent' drugs that could tell sick cells from healthy ones, and then selectively destroy the targeted ones." Illustrations often use metaphors or analogies when trying to communicate a complex topic such as selective drug therapies.

To put analogies to work for you, ask your group to think of things similar to the subject or problem you're thinking about. At first, group members come up with conventional ideas. But they soon run out of these obvious answers, and they must create fresh analogies to continue. For example, you may ask a group to brainstorm analogies for your product as a source of inspiration for creating new advertisements about that product.

Advertisers for Nordic Track exercise equipment thought that a person's roll of stomach fat is like a flat tire on a car that needs to be changed. From this analogy sprang a winning headline: "Simple Instructions For Changing Your Spare Tire."

Pass-along

Pass-along is a simple game that helps a group break through its mental barriers to reach free association and collaborative thinking. People used to play this game just for fun, but who plays parlor games now that you have a TV room rather than a parlor? You can read the instructions here, in case you've never heard of the game:

> ✔ One person writes something about the topic in question on the top line of a sheet of paper and passes it to the next person, who writes a second line beneath the first.
>
> ✔ Go around the table or group as many times as you think necessary.

This game can be done with any number of people, from 3 to 20. Bigger groups need fewer cycles — in general, try to fill up a full page of lined paper. If people get into the spirit of the game, a line of thought emerges and dances on the page. Each previous phrase suggests something new until you have a lot of good ideas and many ways of thinking about your problem. Players keep revealing new aspects of the subject as they build on or add new dimensions to the lines above.

Say a team of marketing and salespeople meets to generate new product concepts for the product development department of a bank. Now, that sounds like a tough assignment — what can be new under the sun in banking? But you, the creative marketer, pick a subject and pass the paper around:

Subject: How can we make our customers' personal finances run better?

Pass-along ideas:

✔ Help them win the lottery.

✔ Help them save money by putting aside 1 percent each month.

✔ Help them save for their children's college tuition.

✔ Help them keep track of their finances.

✔ Give them a checkbook that balances itself.

✔ Notify them in advance of financial problems, like bouncing checks, so they can prevent those problems.

One idea leads to another. So even if the first idea isn't helpful, associating new ideas from the first one can produce useful thoughts. A bank probably can't get into the lottery ticket business (there must be a law against that). But after the members of this group thought along those lines, they came up with some practical ways of increasing their customers' wealth, like plans that can help them transfer money to savings automatically each month.

Nor can a checkbook balance itself — this task has to be performed by means other than magic. But what if a computer did the work? A bank can provide such a service if the customer is willing to bank over the Internet (electronically) so as to use the bank's computer, or use a checkbook program on her PC to track her account and generate checks and reports. Both technologies exist — why not combine one of them with a standard checking account service for those customers who like the idea of a checkbook that balances itself?

As this simple example illustrates, generating novel ideas doesn't take long, even in a mature industry like banking — as long as you use creativity techniques.

Managing the Creative Process

If you think of creativity as generating wild and crazy ideas, you're right — but only one fourth right. You have to do some open-minded thinking to come up with creative concepts. But to actually make any money from your creativity, you need to have a mix of activities that includes exploring for new ideas and developing the best of them into practical applications in your ads, products, sales presentations, or other marketing activities. In my creativity workshops, I show people how creativity needs to follow a four-step process to actually be of practical use in business:

1. Initiate.

In this step, you recognize a need or opportunity and ask questions that begin the creative process. For example, you may take a look at your brochure(s) and ask yourself if there isn't some way to use an illustration and a catchy headline to make the brochure more exciting and powerful. Or if you run a women's clothing store, you may recognize the need for a January sale to clear out fall and winter styles and make room for new spring fashions. Thoughts like these stimulate creative thinking and give it a practical focus. The creative brief that I discuss in the "Writing a creative brief" section earlier in this chapter is useful at the initiate stage.

2. Imagine.

In this stage of the creative process, you engage in the imaginative, wild-and-crazy thinking that taps into your artistic side. The brainstorming techniques I cover in the "Brainstorming" section earlier in this chapter are good for this stage; your goal is to see how many wild ideas your can generate.

3. Invent.

Now you need to get more practical. Take a critical look at all those wild ideas and choose one or a few that seem most promising. Work on them to see how to make them more practical and feasible for your application. For example, if you're working on a way to announce a 40 percent storewide discount at a women's clothing outlet, one of your creative ideas from Step 2 may have been "to have nude models stand in the window, waving to passersby to attract public attention to the sale." It's a bad idea, but it certainly is creative. Can you use it as raw material for inventing a good promotion? One store I know of did, by putting three full-sized mannequins in the window, each wearing only a poster board on a string around the neck. The first poster said "40%", the second one said "OFF," and the third said "EVERYTHING." It was an eye-catching display, and it communicated the message forcefully. But it took an inventor's persistence and practicality to translate a crazy idea into a good marketing communication.

4. Implement.

Finally, you need to complete the creative process by pursuing successful adoption or implementation of your new idea or design. You may have a great design for a new brochure, but you can't make money from it until you carefully select a printing method and find a way to distribute it to prospects. Or if you're designing a window display for a retail store, implementation may mean finding the right mannequins, signs, lighting, and so on, and setting up the display according to the creative concept or plan.

You may need different sets of talents to imagine wild ideas and to implement them in a practical way. In fact, each of the four steps in the creative process (initiating, imagining, inventing, and implementing) requires different types of behavior. Knowing this, you can discipline yourself to change your own style as you move through a round of creativity that follows the four steps of the creative process. Or you may want to tap into the different creative styles of multiple people in order to take advantage of people who are particularly well suited for one or another of the steps in the creative process. When I work on creative projects in marketing, I'm particularly good at bringing imagination to the project, so I usually try to team up with someone who complements me by being really good at implementation.

Harnessing All Creative Types

The imagining part of creativity is just one of the important steps. In marketing (and in business, in general) you have to actually do something with your creative ideas, and make those ideas work, to profit from your imagination. You must make a focused effort to invent practical ways to implement what you imagine. I call this process taking creativity to the bank.

The creative process includes four steps (see the preceding section) that rely on different types of behaviors. You may be especially suited to one or two of the steps, but probably not to all of them. I recommend you figure out which steps you are best and worst at, and then find people to help you fill your creative gaps. Read the following list of styles to see which suits your temperament best:

- ✔ **Entrepreneur:** The entrepreneur senses a need or problem and asks tough questions to initiate the creative process. ("Why do we do it this way? It seems so inefficient.") This style proves valuable in the first step of the creative process, the Initiate Step.

- ✔ **Artist:** The artist is highly imaginative and a free thinker. When given a focus for her imagination by the entrepreneur's initiating question, the artist can easily dream up many alternatives and fresh approaches from which to choose. ("We could do this, or this, or this, or . . . ") The artist comes to the fore in the second step of the creative process, the Imagine Step.

- ✔ **Inventor:** The inventor has a more practical sort of imagination and loves to develop and refine a single good idea until he makes it work. ("Let's see. If we adjust this, and add that, it will work much better.") The inventor is most productive in the third step of the creative process, the Invent Step.

> ✔ **Engineer:** The engineer's style is practical and businesslike, and engineers are particularly good at getting closure by taking an untested or rough invention the rest of the way and making it work smoothly and well. ("Great ideas, but let's come up with a firm plan and budget so we can get this thing started.") Engineers make sure the process reaches its essential fourth step, the Implement Step.

Whichever one of these creative roles most closely represents your approach to work, recognize that one role alone can't make good, creative marketing happen. Be prepared to adjust your style by wearing some of the other creative hats at times, or team up with others whose styles differ from your own. That way, you have the range of approaches that you need to combine in order to harness the power of creativity for all your marketing efforts.

I put a downloadable sample copy of the Creative Roles Analysis activity my firm publishes up on the www.insightsformarketing.com Web site so that you can use this activity to design more effective and productive creative teams. The CRA helps you make sure that you not only initiate, but also complete, the creative process often enough to keep your marketing innovative and new.

The case of the singing card

Consider the following example: The owners of a cleaning service felt that they were invisible to their customers because they entered offices at night to clean them when nobody was working. How to reach out and forge a more personal relationship? One idea they came up with was to collect information on the birthdays of their main contacts at these client companies and to leave them nice gifts or cards on the eve of their birthdays — to be discovered when they came in to work the next day.

Getting even more creative, they thought about giving their customers personalized singing cards, containing a message that says, "Because we aren't there during your workday to sing to you, we put our song into this card!"

A nice way to add a human touch, but imagining this idea and making it happen are two different things. They had to find a source of spring-operated musical chips they could put into a card. Then they worked with a designer at their local print shop to perfect the card and make sure it worked well (they found they needed a heavy paper to keep the music chip in place). Finally, they had to find out the birth dates of the individuals in their customer database and figure out which desk belonged to which customer. Getting this information took several weeks of subtle questioning and snooping around. In fact, it took two months and several hundred dollars to actually implement the idea, as simple as it was.

Chapter 6

Pumping Up Your Marketing Communications

In This Chapter

▶ Increasing your clarity and appeal

▶ Giving your brand a winning personality

▶ Using stopping power

▶ Using pull power

▶ Creating great writing

▶ Creating great visuals

-----

*Y*ou communicate constantly in marketing. In fact, most of what marketers do is actually communication of one sort or another. And if you can make that communication more effective, you can build sales and attract new or better customers. This chapter helps you pump up your marketing communications.

What's the difference between good and poor marketing communications? The single most important difference is *impact*. Good communications have the desired impact; poor communications don't. For example, I'm helping an educational institution improve its communications right now with the goal of making its name and strengths better known. Everything it does, from having a representative talk to the press to designing a brochure to sending out letters or revamping its Web site needs to make an impact and help the institution achieve its communication goal.

What goals do you have and how well are you achieving them right now? Think about that question as I show you some of the best ways to increase the impact of your marketing communications.

Establishing Your Communication Priorities

If you can communicate more effectively and persuasively than your competitors, then consider your marketing communications a success. If not, then you're throwing precious marketing dollars away, and you probably can't convince many people to buy your product.

Being clear about one thing . . .

Being noticed, having stopping power (see the "Stopping Power: Catching the Customer's Eye" section later in this chapter), grabbing attention — marketers need to remember these important priorities. And marketers also need to be persuasive — customers don't believe you're the best unless given darn good reason to do so. However, grabbing attention can distract you from the essential need to be clear in making your case. Often the most exciting and creative ads fail to actually make the sale because they're not simple and clear enough. A Burger King TV ad campaign boasted that Burger King's French fried potatoes had beaten McDonald's fries in a taste test. But consumers didn't pick up the nuances. They just noticed the mention of McDonald's fries, and rumor has it that sales went up at McDonald's instead of Burger King. Oops.

Clarity is the first job of the marketer. Creativity, excitement, and persuasion are actually secondary to clarity. Is that clear? Good!

Developing a recipe for good marketing communication

Communication goes on in many ways, at many points of influence — wherever you have some exposure to your markets. You need to craft a compelling message to send out through all those influence points. But how do you create a compelling marketing message?

1. **Position the product in your customers' minds.**

   You need the right positioning strategy as a foundation — along with products that follow through on the promises you make. A *positioning strategy* is a detailed (but readable) statement of how you want customers to think and feel about your product (or service). In other words, it describes how you're positioned in their minds and hearts. You can describe your positioning with attributes and adjectives (such as "fast," "helpful," or "sexy").

You can also describe your positioning with comparisons to competitors ("faster than a BMW") or metaphorical comparisons ("faster than a speeding bullet"). See Chapter 2 for details if you don't already have a clear positioning strategy taped to the wall above your desk.

2. **Craft a basic appeal, some motivating message that gets that positioning across.**

   Here is where you need to figure out what you can say that clearly conveys the gist of the positioning strategy. Take the basic statement of how you want people to think of your product and convert it into a message that may actually convince them. For example, if you want to introduce a new, healthier kind of pizza made only of organic and low-fat ingredients, your positioning statement may be, "healthier pizza that doesn't sacrifice taste." Okay, now craft the basic appeal that may convince others to see the pizza that way. Here's a possibility with appeal: "Instead of fighting to keep your kids from eating the unhealthy junk-food pizzas they love, why not give them healthy pizzas that are actually better tasting, too?"

3. **Find a creative big idea — something that packages your appeal in a message so compelling that people stop in their tracks.**

   The message should persuade them of your point or convince them to give your product or service a try. And it should do so creatively or else it will be boring and nobody will pay attention. For example, suppose you're marketing pizza whose basic positioning is "organic and low-fat, so it's healthy and it also tastes good." A basic appeal you want to use right now to convince people of that positioning strategy is to tell parents, "Instead of fighting to keep you kids from eating the unhealthy junk-food pizzas they love, why not give them healthy pizzas that are actually better tasting, too?" Now, what creative idea can you come up with to turn this appeal into a compelling communication? Here are some options:

   - Mother goes to pick-up window to get prescription for child and is shocked when the pharmacist reads the doctor's note, and then pulls a fresh-baked pizza out of a big oven, boxes it, hands it across the window, and says, "Give him as many pieces as he wants, day or night."

   - Kids stare longingly through the glass-fronted case of a candy store, in such a crowd that it's hard to even see what has drawn their attention. It turns out to be the newest flavor of the low-fat, organic pizza.

   - A journalist is interviewing swimmers on a remote tropical island where the average age is higher than anywhere else in the world. In response to the question, "What is the secret to your amazing health and longevity?" a tanned and fit grandmother says, "We don't do anything special, we just order out for pizza every night." She then dives off a cliff into a tropical pool of water. The pizza, of course, is from a little old mud hut with the logo of our brand over its door and a crowd of village children in the door, hands out, happily receiving slices of the magical pizza.

4. **Develop, edit, and simplify your creative idea until it's transparently clear and fits the medium you want to communicate it in.**

   Note that your choice of medium is partially determined by your message — and by the creative idea you select to get it across. To tell a story, you may choose television advertising if your budget is large. A streaming video version for your Web site or a radio ad version of the story will cut your costs compared to TV advertising (see Chapter 9). And to give you really low-cost options, you can have a cartoonist do a series of drawings in comic-strip format and turn them into a print ad, flier, or place them on your Web site.

These steps, when done well, create a compelling marketing message and communicate that message persuasively. The task is a difficult but a vital one — crafting the compelling message you need for all your marketing communications.

Deciding whether to appeal to logic or emotions

You face a choice in many marketing communications: Should you build your appeal and communication strategy around a strong claim, backed by irrefutable evidence? Or, in contrast, should you make an emotional appeal that feels right to the customer but lacks hard evidence?

You have to make this choice based on what you're marketing and who you're marketing it to because everyone makes decisions in both ways, depending on the situation. People usually make an emotional decision about who they want to marry, but they usually make rational decisions about what jobs to search for and which employment offers to accept. Similarly, in purchase decisions, sometimes the emotions prevail and sometimes the logical parts of our minds dominate.

To complicate matters even further, people are inconsistent about when they use which mode. Some people make highly emotional decisions about major purchases like cars and houses. Others approach the decision carefully and rationally, comparing statistics and running the numbers. Which camp do you fall into? If you've ever bought an automobile, try to recall why you bought it. If you say, "Because I liked it" or "Because I felt that it was a good car" or something similar, your emotions probably dominated your purchase decision. If, however, you say things like "Because it has good gas mileage and *Consumer Reports* rated it highly on safety and maintenance," then you made a logical or rational decision.

Each person tends toward one end or the other of this range — he makes decisions more rationally or more emotionally. And so you can pitch your marketing communications at the rational buyer or at the emotional buyer. You can even segment your market based on this difference, and design separate marketing programs for each!

Volkswagen decided to reposition itself in the American market as a fun-to-drive car for Generation Xers who are moving into parenting and responsible work roles but still feel an urge to express themselves as individuals. Volkswagen's approach was to emphasize the fun of driving their cars — and to convince consumers that their customers are special because of their love of driving and zest for life. This example presents a classic emotional appeal. The ads emphasize images over words and have a strongly intuitive appeal grounded in the values of Generation Xers. The advertisers tell you nothing factual about Volkswagen in those television ads, but you do get a strong emotional hit.

When you design your communications, I recommend you follow Volkswagen's lead and emphasize strongly one or the other way of thinking. When you waffle, trying to appeal to both sides of the brain at once, your message usually ends up weaker. Your job, as the communicator, is to get into the customer's head and sense which is the hotter button — the emotional or rational one.

So, which camp do your customers and prospects fall into right now? Make a note, and then be careful to develop all your marketing communications with this customer bias (toward either the rational argument or the emotional appeal) in mind.

Finding Four Easy Ways to Pump Up Your Appeal

You want to help people see what makes your product great. You want to get them to come into a store, send an e-mail, or make a phone call to buy it. But you can't just tell them that your product is great because they won't pay any attention. They've heard that one before. To start with, you need an appealing message. The message must sell itself!

What can you communicate that appeals to the consumer's basic motives and desires — and does so with enough strength to move him to action?

I must warn you that most appeals are ineffective. It is difficult to achieve the kind of impact you want as a marketer, so try one or more of the following strategies to improve the impact of your appeal:

✔ **Image strategy:** An *image strategy* shows people your product and its personality. It presents a good image of your brand, product, service, or business. For example, a day spa may develop a sophisticated logo and color scheme and work sophistication into everything, from its print ads and Web site to its decor, towels, bathrobes, and bottled water. What's your image? And do you communicate that image in an appealing way through all points of contact with your customers and prospects?

✔ **Information strategy:** An *information strategy* communicates facts that make you appealing. For example, a truck rental company may want to let prospects know how many of what kind of trucks it has available, in what good condition it keeps those trucks, and how reasonable it makes its terms of rental. The facts should make the sale. And if you know you're particularly strong in a certain area, then communicate the facts of your brilliance instead of wasting effort on more ordinary information. What information can you communicate that will appeal to customers and prospects?

✔ **Motivational strategy:** A *motivational strategy* builds a compelling argument or feeling that should lead prospects to take action and make a purchase. For example, a life insurance company may tell some stories about people who did have insurance and others who didn't, and what happened to their loved ones after they died. Prospects often experience strong emotional responses to these stories, so this approach should lead to new sales. What motivation can you provide that can move prospective customers to make a purchase now?

✔ **Demonstration strategy:** A *demonstration strategy* leverages the fundamental appeal of the product itself by simply making that product available to prospects. For some products, seeing is believing. AOL used this strategy effectively in its early years by simply mailing an access disk to prospects. When they used the free time it gave them on the Internet, many found that they liked the AOL server's interface and subscribed when their free time ran out. Sometimes marketing really is as easy as making the product available to people — like when a car dealership offers free test-drives of an exciting new model. Does your product have fundamental appeal that you can take advantage of by making it more accessible to prospects?

A good appeal may rely on only one of these strategies, or it can combine two, or even three, of them. But you certainly need to use at least one of these approaches when marketing your product or service.

What have you used in the past to communicate the appeal of your offering in a compelling manner? Did you use one of these strategies? Did you use it effectively? Can you add to the strength of your appeal or, even better, think of a new and more compelling way to appeal to people through your marketing communications?

Getting Personal: Giving Products Personality

Every automobile is given a personality by its marketers, and this personality is conveyed in everything including the name, design, color choices, sales materials, and advertising. You may not realize that the cars you see or drive have carefully crafted personalities, but these personalities help position each auto and help make it appealing to its intended buyers. For example, a Dodge Ram pickup truck has a tough, can-do, unfussy, masculine image. Its personality is forceful, rugged, and tough. Everyone who works on the marketing of a Dodge Ram has that personality description and tries to convey that personality consistently.

Giving your brand a personal identity, as if the brand were a living thing, can often help you create a lasting impression on the prospect. In fact, the best way to think about the task of building a brand's value is to imagine that you are bringing that brand to life. This tactic works especially well in conjunction with an emotional appeal because a compelling personality always attracts emotional buyers. But even if you use a logical appeal, I urge you to give your brand a supporting personality. Although a supporting personality isn't as decisive as an emotional appeal is, it still helps communicate with consumers and reminds them of your basic appeal. (If you're selling industrial design services to manufacturers, you can think of and present the brand as a careful, thoughtful engineer.)

Define your brand's personality clearly so that you can cultivate that personality whenever you communicate with customers and the outside world, in general. A richly scripted personality has the power to shine through all your marketing program's influence points, providing a consistent touchstone for all communications. If you know your brand well enough, you can communicate that intimacy to your customers.

Taking a page from fiction

How do you define a personality? Fiction writers call this task *character development,* and it ain't easy. But you can get a few tips about character development from good storytellers.

One device that works well in fiction or marketing: define a character's personality by his likes and dislikes. Sherlock Holmes, one of the most enduring fictional characters of all time, likes to smoke strong tobacco in his pipe when thinking about a problem and also plays the violin. He has a deep interest in aspects of science that have to do with crime, and he fills notebooks with clippings about famous criminals and their doings. But he has no interest in romance and no close friends but Dr. Watson, who helps him solve his cases. He is a cold, rational problem solver with a touch of artistic imagination (the latter inherited from Vermier, the Impressionist painter, who is a distant relative). All these facts about the man help create a characteristic image, one that publishers, game and toy makers, and movie producers have cashed in on for decades.

Similarly, you can draw up a list of traits or personality characteristics to associate with your brand or company name that adds up to a distinct personality. Jaguar ran an effective series of ads that associated fine old country houses and estates with their vehicles. If the Jaguar sedan were a woman, she would enjoy spending the weekend at her country estate — and, of course, would enjoy driving there in speed and comfort!

Another device I like to borrow from fiction involves writing a short event-based chapter about a character. Many authors give you a description of some actions or events in order to develop their characters. This description may appear within a chapter or as a freestanding chapter in a novel, for example, and it gives you a chance to get to know a main character well. You can do the same. (The opening mini-movie that comes before the title and credits of a James Bond movie establishes Bond's character in just a few minutes. That's the kind of writing I'm talking about.)

Say you're marketing Jaguar cars. You can write a brief story about how a Jaguar spends its weekend. Imagine the car as it drives through a rainstorm, winds along an old road beside a canal, and then turns up the long cobbled driveway to its grandfather's Edwardian-style farmhouse. What does the car sound like as it drives through that rainstorm? Does it whine? No. Does it roar? No, the sound is subtler. Smooth, but powerful. Perhaps its engine runs so quietly that the sound is lost in the timpani of raindrops on the hood and windshield — but the Jaguar can no doubt feel a faint, low humming down in its drive train.

With these sorts of thoughts, you can soon bang out a good description of this car's weekend trip. And as you work on this piece of fiction, you find a personality taking shape and form, new nuances emerging on the page with each bend of the road and scratch of the pen. (Hey, isn't copywriting fun? Why don't you try now?)

The preceding exercise has another valuable benefit for you and your brand. It helps you and other marketers achieve consistency in how you present the brand to customers. After you have developed a description of the brand's human personality, everyone can use this description as a guide by asking, whenever they do sales or marketing, whether their activities fit with that personality.

Asking your shrink

Psychologists have studied the puzzle of human personality for decades, sometimes even making a little progress. And so you can also draw insights from the field of psychology as you struggle to create and communicate a personality for your product.

In particular, I recommend the *trait perspective,* an approach used by psychologists in their research. The trait perspective seeks to understand the variation in human personalities by identifying the various traits that make up each individual personality. And you can give your brands a personality by describing their essential traits. The trait perspective helps you create a product personality because it focuses on describing, rather than explaining, human behavior. And marketers are pragmatists — you don't need to know why personalities develop, you just need to figure out what personality to give your products. That's a simple descriptive task. No need for a therapist. A sharp pencil gets the job done.

I like to use a *personality self-assessment instrument* — a fancy word for a survey-type form in which you select descriptions or adjectives that fit you, and then key out your *type* (or profile) from the answers. Only I use these questionnaires to describe my product, not me! You may have already used one of these instruments yourself because many companies use them to train, or even to screen, new employees.

One popular test is based on psychologist Carl Jung's personality types. The test uses 126 questions written by Isabel Myers and Katheryn Briggs (hence the name the *Myers-Briggs test.)* You can order a simplified version of the test, called Observations of Type Preference, from International LearningWorks (for their latest catalog, send to 1130 Main Avenue, Durango, CO 81301, or fax your inquiry to 970-259-7194). However, I prefer another product, called the Insight Inventory, because I find the personality profiles it produces particularly useful. Order it from HRD Press (Pelham, Massachusetts) by calling 413-253-3488, or by visiting trainingactivities.com. They offer a single copy of the instrument with a six-page interpretive guide for just $6.50 — all you may need for researching your brand's personality.

Stopping Power: Catching the Customer's Eye

Stopping power is the ability of an advertisement or other marketing communication to stop people in their tracks, to make them sit up and take notice.

Communications with stopping power generate "What did you say?" or "Did you see that?" responses. These communications generate a high level of attention — unlike most marketing communications, which simply do not have the ability to grab instant attention.

You can be sure that thousands of other marketing messages bombard your customer, along with your own. The high level of noise in the marketing environment means that most efforts to communicate fail. Most ads go unnoticed by most of the people they target.

Ask people to recall five ads they saw on television last night (if they watched TV last night, they probably saw many dozens). Watch their reactions. A puzzled look usually crosses their faces, as they try desperately to remember what they know they must have seen. Then they may say, "Oh, yeah. I saw that funny ad where this guy . . . " They may come up with several ads that way, if last night's crop of advertising was fairly good. And of these ads, they may remember the brands of one or two — but rarely all.

And if you do the same exercise, but ask about print ads in a magazine or newspaper or brochures or "junk mail" letters, you may well draw a complete blank. Many people don't recall even one ad in a magazine they read yesterday unless you actively prompt them. Or try asking about radio ads. Same problem.

This simple activity puts the importance of stopping power into perspective. Your ads need to have much more stopping power than most if you hope to get a significant number of people to remember and think about your product!

Principles of stopping power

According to Hanley Norins, who spent a lot of time training the staff at Young and Rubicam to make better ads, seven principles apply in making an ad or any marketing communication a real stopper. I've modified those principles through my own experience, coming up with the following list:

- **The ad must have intrinsic drama that appeals to everyone.** The ad should attract many people outside of the target audience. If kids like an ad aimed at adults or vice versa, that ad fulfills this principle.

- **The ad must demand participation from the audience.** The ad needs to draw people into some action, whether that action is calling a number, going to a store, laughing out loud, or just thinking about something. A stopper of an ad should never permit the audience to play a passive role.

- **The ad needs to force an emotional response.** This principle should hold true, even if you're making a rational appeal. The heart of the ad must still contain some basic human need, something about which people feel passionate.

✔ **The ad must stimulate curiosity.** The audience should want to know more. This desire gets them to stop and study the ad — and follow up with further information searches afterward.

✔ **The ad should surprise its audience.** A startling headline, an unexpected visual image, an unusual opening gambit in a sales presentation, or a weird display window in a store — all have the power to stop people by surprising them.

✔ **The ad must communicate expected information — in an *detcepxenu* way.** (*Hint:* Try reading that mystery word backward.) A creative twist, or a fresh way of saying or looking at something, makes the expected unexpected. You have to get the obvious information in: what the brand is, who it benefits, and how. But don't do so in an obvious way, or the communication doesn't reach out and grab attention and the audience just ignores your ad.

✔ **The ad may need to violate the rules and personality of the product category.** The product has to stand out. People notice things that violate expected patterns (and patterns certainly exist in marketing). So one way to do this is the make your ad distinctly different from what consumers have come to expect in your product's category. If you market office-cleaning services, for example, you no doubt buy Yellow Pages ads and make up fliers with your price list and a few client testimonials. Yawn! To complement these ordinary marketing efforts, send a sponge in the mail to prospective clients with your name and phone number on one side, and, on the other, the message, "Just in case you still insist on doing the cleaning without our help."

Although the preceding list was inspired by Hanley Norins, his book, *The Young and Rubicam Traveling Creative Workshop* (Prentice Hall), has a great deal more in it that you may find inspiring, too.

To make an ad that has drama, that surprises people, that violates the pattern, and that says the expected in an unexpected way — requires creativity. And so perhaps the most essential secret to stopping power is creativity. When you need to get those creative juices flowing, flip to Chapter 5.

Sex, anyone?

Advertising research reveals another secret of stopping power: sex. The header for this section illustrates the stopping power of sex. Even the word catches your eye. So to give an ad stopping power, just give it some sex appeal.

However, there's a hitch. (It figures.) The same research that shows sex-based ads have stopping power also shows that these same ads don't prove very effective by other measures. Brand recall — the ability of viewers to remember what product the ad advertised — is usually lower for sex-oriented ads than other ads. So although these ads do have stopping power, they don't seem to have any other benefits. They fail to turn that high initial attention into aware-ness or interest. They don't change attitudes about the product. In short, they sacrifice good communication for raw stopping power.

The only exception to the rule that sexy ads are bad communicators is when sex is relevant to the product. If you're marketing a lingerie store, running some print ads of scantily clad, attractive female models in the Sunday news-paper certainly makes sense. And those same lingerie-clad models could con-ceivably belong in an ad run in the same newspaper by a local auto dealer who wants to sell bright-red convertible sports cars, because the brand per-sonality of this product can include sexiness. But I'd leave sexy models out of ads for hardware stores, lawn-care services, or office supplies, because they have no obvious relevance.

David Ogilvy, the founder of Ogilvy and Mather, found out that sex doesn't always sell well the hard way. The first advertisement he produced featured an attractive, naked woman next to a cooking stove. He later admitted that the ad failed because the sexy woman had nothing to do with the appeal of the stove. He should have included a beautiful cake or a golden roast turkey, because they are actually relevant to the product.

Pull Power: Building Customer Traffic

Pull power is the ability of a marketing communication to draw people to a place or event. Smaller or local marketers usually concern themselves with pull power, instead of focusing on the national advertising concerns of *brand equity* (building the value of your brand) or positioning. After all, somebody has to actually *sell* a product at the ground level — in the local market, and customer by customer. And so, at this level, you just need to draw in those customers. Pull power is everything.

Pull power is the primary goal of all *local advertising*. (By local advertising, I mean advertising focused on a specific city or county — which includes almost half of all advertising in the United States.) Marketers use publicity, personal selling, direct mail, price-based promotions, and point-of-purchase spending to try to exercise effective pull power. Advertisers use more than half of all the money spent on all forms of marketing communications through all available influence points to pull consumers in.

My own firm puts much of its marketing budget into communications aimed at pulling shoppers to its Web site and toll-free telephone number. We send out personal letters or e-mails to our past customers every now and then with information about new products they may like — and, always, a link or address that can get them to our online order center. (We market our employee training services and products internationally, but using the Web, we can easily treat our customers as if they're local.)

Because of this pull orientation, local marketing communications are unique:

- ✔ Local communications tend to be part of a short-term effort, rather than a long-term campaign. Don't feel you have to do anything permanent. Short, powerful bursts usually have more pull power.

- ✔ You can do local communications on a shoestring budget — far smaller than the millions spent by national or multinational advertisers. Keep it simple!

- ✔ Local communications should generate customers in the store, make the phone ring, bring more folks to your Web site, or accomplish some other pull-oriented tactical goal. If your marketing communication isn't pulling, then pull it.

For maximum pull power, give people a strong reason to act. Tell consumers your location and that you have what they need. Ask them to come by, call, return a coupon, or visit your Web site. And keep inviting them, always in new and creative ways, so they never forget you.

Tightening Your Writing

Need great writing? Keep the writing direct. Keep the writing simple. Make it reach out and grab the reader!

Great writing is always clear. Much of marketing writing suffers from the following problems:

- ✔ It fails to come to the point.
- ✔ It uses passive sentences (where you can't tell who does what to whom).
- ✔ It employs sophisticated vocabulary without sufficient cause — meaning it uses big words needlessly.
- ✔ It uses difficult verb tenses instead of the present tense ("writing would have to communicate" rather than "writing communicates," for example).
- ✔ And as a result, typical writing bores or confuses its readers.

If you can find a novel way to make your point, do. Remember that you need originality and surprise if you want your writing to have stopping power. But above all else, make sure you write simply and clearly. When the customer relations manager at my firm, Insights for Training, decided to send our customers an announcement about new features on our Web site, we worked together on that e-mail for two weeks before sending it. At first, it was a full page long, with a lot of exciting (to us) information and graphics. But who reads a full-page e-mail? In the end, we boiled it down to two sentences that said, very simply, what the change was and why we thought they'd want to know. Clear and simple — and much more likely for potential consumers to actually read, understand, and act on. We weren't looking for a Pulitzer; we were just trying to communicate.

You can only get to the essence of a communication by writing, and then rewriting and rewriting. Keep reworking, keep rethinking, keep boiling your words down until you have something that penetrates to your point with startling clarity. (Nike's "Just Do It" is a strikingly simple and powerful statement of the brand's personality, isn't it?)

And then, after you make your point, shut up.

Creating Great Visuals

Before I get into how to use visuals, I want to point out that great photography has never been so available and affordable to marketers as it is now. The Web and digital imagery have combined to put millions of images at your fingertips, most of them priced in the $50 to $250 range, depending on how you use them. Take a look around sites like www.fotosearch.com, www.photodisc.com, www.indexstock.com, www.corbis.com, www.comstock.com, and www.weststock.com, all of which support keyword searches and can supply images in digital format for your use. You have no excuse for not using great photography in your marketing.

Pictures can truly be worth a thousand words. Imagine the following: A kid is playing tennis against a backboard when a dog runs up and steals the ball. The ball, bright yellow and fuzzy, overflows the dog's mouth as the camera zooms in to show the ball and mouth, filling the TV screen.

This visual image is simple. But it communicates a lot. Like how much fun kids, and dogs, have when playing with tennis balls. And the image offers drama — how does the kid feel when the dog takes his ball? How does the dog feel when he gets the ball? Most of all, the image reminds us that tennis is good fun for everyone, regardless of skill level, age, or even species!

The visual image I describe above is at the heart of a television spot promoting tennis from the U.S. Tennis Association. This spot illustrates the power of a good visual image or sequence of images to capture attention, tell an interesting story, and communicate a point. No words needed. And the spot also illustrates a key to successful visuals — a focus on one strong, relevant image. In this case, that image is the tennis ball, proudly framed in the dog's jaws. In your case, well, the image can be anything — as long as the image is (a) visually compelling, (b) easily recognizable, and (c) relevant to your appeal. (Is it?)

Importance of visual design

Let me first warn you that I can't show you how to be a good designer or artist in these few paragraphs. You need to work with artists to create effective visual imagery, unless you're an artist yourself. Gaining the technical skills and design sense to create something as simple as an illustrated brochure takes a long time, so imagine how long you would need to be able to perform more complex tasks, like a four-color print ad, a package design, or a television spot. But still, you may find yourself having to take on some of the design tasks in your marketing department or business. A catalog sheet, brochure, store window display, or other visual design may have to be done right now, without the budget for a creative agency or graphic designer. And the modern computer can put considerable design power into the amateur's hands.

If you have a Macintosh or PC running Quark Express and Photoshop software, with a high-quality scanner or a small budget for downloading images from stock photography vendors, you can play designer pretty effectively. My assistant, Stephanie, and I become the designers often when a project is too small to justify bringing in the pros. Heck, you can even lay out good ads or brochures using Microsoft Word on any PC. Off-the-shelf collections of photographic images from firms like Hemera can provide useable photographs at really cheap prices that you can drop into a Word page as jpeg files.

But, I must warn you that most of the homemade designing I see coming off of people's desktop computers and inkjet printers stinks. Sometimes these efforts waste the paper the homemade designs are printed on, insult the customer, and embarrass the profession of marketing. (We don't really think you're a dummy, that's just the catchy way the publishers give these book covers stopping power. So mind your marketing doesn't look stupid. Thank you!) Doing the design work yourself is now technically easy, but if you don't know much about design, you can get into trouble really quickly with the new technologies. You can find more information about designing-it-yourself in *Desktop Publishing and Design For Dummies,* by Roger C. Parker (Wiley). I also go into more design and writing details in my book, *Marketing Kit For Dummies* (Wiley) and on the site that supports these books, www.insightsformarketing.com.

Hierarchy in design

A good rule of thumb in designing anything visual — brochure, Web page, logo, ad, sign, package design, label, and so on — is to know what you want people to see first, second, and third.

They see the visually dominant aspect of the image first. This aspect needs appeal, to stop the prospects in their tracks and draw them closer so they look at the second and third aspects of the ad. The second thing they see should explain the basic appeal in a simple, clear way. And third, they should get some consistent, supporting evidence or feelings to back up what numbers one and two tell them. Now, with this hierarchy in mind, one image needs to be visually dominant. Not two images or ten images — one image. Have a focal point, or an entry point, for the eye.

What, may I ask, is the number one image or design element in your existing ads, brochures, or other visual communications? Does it clearly dominate, or do many elements compete for the top spot? Is the dominant visual element appealing and attractive enough to deserve this top spot? And does it clearly show how your product benefits the customer? In most cases, existing marketing communications fail this hierarchy test and need to be redesigned.

Here's a simple and powerful suggestion: Make a visual image of your product the most visible feature of your design. If you have a physical product, get a really, really great photo of it and place that in a dominant position in your ad, brochure, Web page, or other marketing device. If you provide an intangible service or process, give your service a visual identity by creating a really, really nice diagram, flowchart, picture of someone using or doing it, or a striking picture of something that can represent it (a rose can represent a dating service, for example).

Now place that product image as the biggest, most noticeable feature of your communication. In reality, a good picture is often worth a lot more than a thousand words.

See Chapter 7 for details on laying out print ads and brochures.

Part III
Advertising for Fun and Profit

The 5th Wave   By Rich Tennant

"How about this—'It's not just CRAP, it's Mel's CRAP'? Shoot! That's no good. I <u>hate</u> writing copy for this client."

In this part . . .

Many people quote Jerry Della Femina, the well-known advertising executive, as saying that advertising is the most fun you can have with your clothes on.

I'm not going to ask you to take your clothes off for this part of the book, but I am going to ask you to have some serious fun. Advertising needs to be creative and have that special spark to really work well.

In Part III, I outline the essentials of effective, eye-catching, mind-altering communications that can build your brand or reputation, attract great leads, or actually make a sale. The essence of great advertising communications remains the same across all the dozens of possible media — from the lowly business card or the simple brochure to the sophisticated print ad or local television spot ad.

And you have a lot of media choices — probably more than you realize — because you can always advertise in alternative ways, and advertising doesn't have to be as expensive as most people assume.

So, read on to find out how you can pump up your marketing communications and put advertising to better effect in your business. (By the way, this last sentence is a *call to action,* to use an ad copywriter's term that I discuss in Chapter 13. You always want to tell people what you expect them to do when you write an ad. Do you include a call to action in all your marketing communications?)

Chapter 7

Brochures, Print Ads, and Other Printed Materials

· ·

In This Chapter

▶ Recognizing the elements of printed advertising

▶ Understanding design and layout issues

▶ Designing with type

▶ Designing the simplest print product of all — brochures

▶ Placing and testing your print ad

· ·

Most marketers budget more for print advertising than any other type — the exception being the major national or multinational brands that market largely on television. But for most local and regional advertising, print probably provides the most flexible and effective all-around advertising medium.

Print advertising also integrates well with many other marketing media. You can use written brochures and other sales support materials (which have many design elements in common with print advertising) to support personal selling (see Chapter 12) or telemarketing (see Chapter 13). Similarly, a print ad in a magazine can generate leads for direct marketing (again, see Chapter 13). Print ads also work well to announce sales promotions or distribute coupons. (I cover the use of print ads for promotions in Chapter 15.)

And anyone with a basic computer and inkjet printer can now set up shop and create his or her own fliers, brochures, business cards, and ad layouts. In fact, Microsoft Word includes a number of excellent templates that simplify layout and allow you to bang out a new brochure or other printed marketing piece in as little as an hour. Print advertising and print-based marketing are the backbone of most marketing programs, even today in this high-tech world.

When designing anything in print, remember this: Your ad's purpose is to stimulate a sale. Think ahead to that goal. What will people see when they make that purchase? If your product sells in stores, create signs, packaging, displays, or coupons that echo the ad's theme and remind the buyer of that theme. If the sale occurs on your Web site, adjust the appearance of the site to be consistent with the ad. And if you make the sale in person, supply the salespeople or distributors with catalogs, order forms, PowerPoint presentations, or brochures (see the "Producing Brochures, Fliers, and More" section later in this chapter) that are consistent with your design, to remind them of the ad that began the sales process. Roll the ad's design forward to the point of purchase and beyond if you plan follow-up mailings, a mail-in warranty card, or other post-purchase contacts.

Designing Printed Marketing Materials

Many marketers start with their printed marketing materials (such as ads, brochures, or downloadable PDF-format product literature on their Web sites), and then work outward from there to incorporate the appeal and design concepts from their printed materials or ads into other forms of marketing. (A common look and feel should unite your print ads, brochures, and Web site, for example.)

Brochures, *tear sheets* (one-page, catalog-style descriptions of products), posters for outdoor advertising, direct mail letters, or catalogs all share the basic elements of good print advertising — good copy and visuals, plus eye-catching headlines. Therefore, all good marketers need mastery of print advertising as an essential part of their knowledge base. This section covers the essentials.

Dissecting the anatomy of printed materials

Before I can talk about how to create great printed marketing materials, I have to dissect an ad, brochure, tear sheet or similar printed marketing matter and identify its parts. Fortunately, you won't find anything gross or disgusting inside most printed marketing materials. Just parts. And each part has a special name:

- ✔ **Headline:** The large-print words that first attract the eye, usually at the top of the page.

- ✔ **Subhead:** The optional addition to the headline to provide more detail, also in large (but not quite as large) print.

- ✔ **Copy or body copy:** The main text, set in a readable size, like what printers use in the main text of a book or magazine.

- ✔ **Visual:** An illustration that makes a visual statement. This image may be the main focus of the ad or other printed material (especially when you've designed an ad to show readers your product), or it may be secondary to the copy. Such an image is also optional. After all, most classified ads use no visuals at all, yet classifieds are generally more effective than display ads for the simple reason that people make a point to look for classified ads (instead of making a point to avoid them, as many people do with displays)!

✔ **Caption:** Copy attached to the visual to explain or discuss that visual. You usually place a caption beneath the visual, but you can put it on any side or even within or on the visual.

✔ **Trademark:** A unique design that represents the brand or company (like Nike's swoosh). You should register trademarks — see Chapter 14.

✔ **Signature:** The company's trademarked version of its name. Often, advertisers use a logo design that features a brand name in a distinctive font and style. The signature is a written equivalent to the trademark's visual identity. Here is how a furniture maker called Heritage Colonial Furniture may do it:

H E R I T A G E
Colonial Furniture®

✔ **Slogan:** An optional element consisting of a (hopefully) short phrase evoking the spirit or personality of the brand. Timberland used a series of print ads in which the slogan "Boots, shoes, clothing, wind, water, earth and sky" appeared in the bottom left corner, just beneath the company's distinctive signature and logo — which marketers displayed on a rectangular patch of leather, like patches that appear on one of their products. As another example, a furniture maker called Heritage Colonial may use as its signature, "Bringing the elegance and quality of early antiques to the modern home."

Figure 7-1 shows each of these elements in a rough design for a print ad (a brochure's layout is a bit more complicated and is covered at the end of this chapter). I use generic terms in place of actual parts of an ad ("headline" for the headline, for example) so that you can easily see all the elements in action. This fairly simple palette for a print ad design allows you endless variation and creativity. You can say or show anything, and you can do so in many different ways. (And you can use this layout for a one-page marketing sheet to include in folders or as handouts at trade shows even if you aren't buying space to run the ad in a magazine or newspaper.)

Putting the parts together: Design and layout

Design refers to the look, feel, and style of your ad or other printed marketing materials. Design is an aesthetic concept and, thus, hard to put into precise terms. But design is vitally important: It has to take the basic appeal of your product and make that appeal work visually on paper (see Chapter 6 for details of how to develop appeal). Specifically, the design needs to overcome the marketer's constant problem: Nobody cares about your advertising. So the design must somehow reach out to readers, grab their attention, and hold it long enough to communicate the appeal of the product you're advertising and attach that appeal to the brand name in the readers' memories.

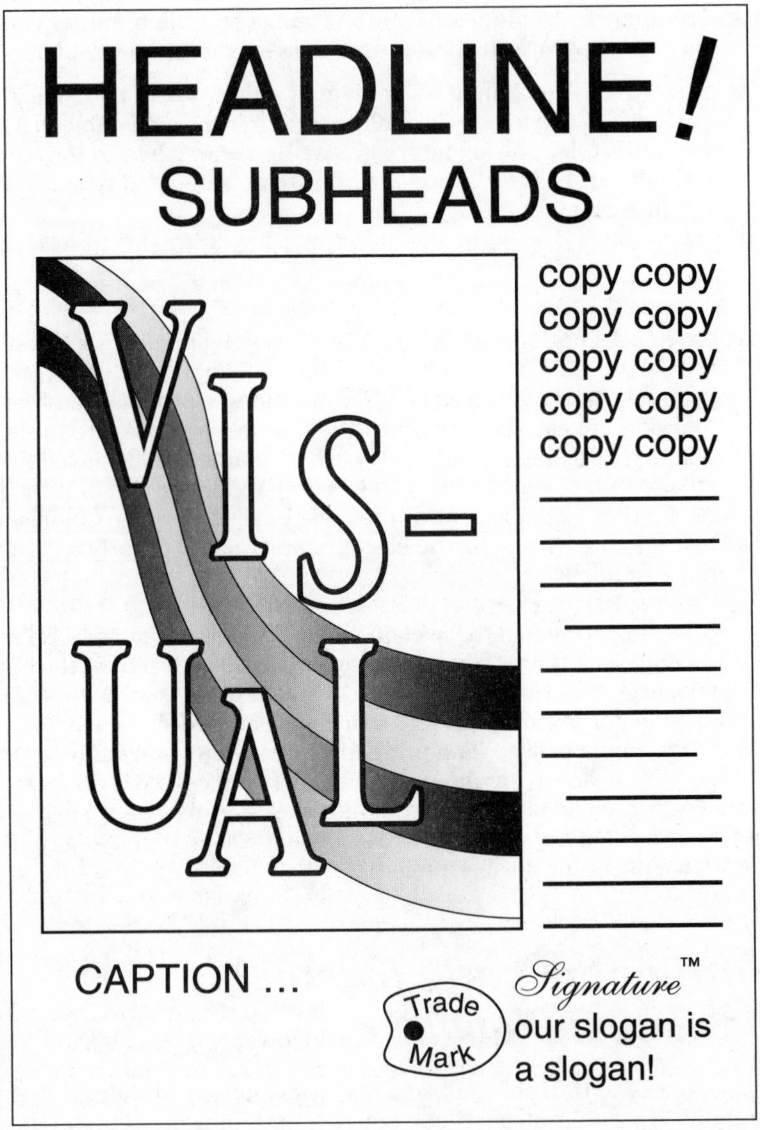

Figure 7-1:
The elements of a print ad.

A memorable photograph is often the easiest way to grab the reader. And if you don't have a better idea, use a photo of an interesting face or of a child, as long as you can make the image relevant in some way to your product. Also, beautiful nature scenes are good eye-catchers.

Great advertising has to rise off the page, reach out, and grab you by the eyeballs. In the cluttered world of modern print-based marketing, this design goal is the only one that really works! So I want you to tape up a bunch of ads from the same publication(s) yours will go in (or use samples of competitor brochures or catalog sheets or whatever exactly it is you will be designing in print). Put a draft of your design up along with these benchmarks. Step back — way back. Now, does yours grab the eye more than all the others? If not . . . back to the drawing board!

Understanding the stages in design

Designers often experiment with numerous layouts for their print ads or other printed materials before selecting one for formal development. I strongly recommend that you do the same — or insist that your designer or agency do the same. The more layouts you look at, the more likely you are to get an out-of-the-box idea that has eye-grabbing power. The rough sketches designers use to describe layout concepts are called *thumbnails*. They're usually small, quick sketches in pen or pencil — or, more recently, in design programs like Quark or PageMaker.

Designers then develop thumbnails with promise into *roughs,* full-size sketches with headlines and subheads drawn carefully enough to give the feel of a particular font and *style* (the appearance of the printed letters). Roughs also have sketches for the illustrations. The designers suggest body copy using lines (or nonsense characters, if the designer does the rough in a computer program).

Are you using an ad agency or design firm to develop your print ads or other printed marketing materials? Sometimes clients of ad agencies insist on seeing designs in the rough stage, to avoid the expense of having those designs developed more fully before presentation. I recommend that you ask to see rough versions of your designs, too, even if your agency hesitates to show you its work in unfinished form. After the agency realizes that you appreciate the design process and don't criticize the roughs simply because they're rough, you can give the agency more guidance and help during the design process.

After a rough passes muster, designers develop that rough into a *comp* (short for *comprehensive layout*). A comp should look pretty much like a final version of the design, although designers produce a comp on a one-time basis, so the comp may use paste-ups in place of the intended photos, color photocopies, typeset copy, and headlines. Designers used to assemble comps by hand, but now many designers and agencies do their comps on their computers. A high-end PC and color printer can produce something that looks almost like the final printed version of a four-color ad or other printed marketing material. Designers refer to a computer-made comp as a *full-color proof.*

A *dummy* is a form of comp that simulates the feel — as well as the look — of the final design. (Every design should have a feel or personality of its own, just as products should have a personality. Often you can create the best personality by simply carrying over the personality you've created for the product. Consistency helps.) Dummies are especially important for brochures or special inserts to magazines, where the designer often specifies special paper and folds. By doing a dummy comp, you can evaluate the feel of the design while you're evaluating its appearance.

Computer design

The modern, and more popular, way to get your preliminary design from the ad agency is to have them send the design over the Web in a desktop publishing program that the printing firm accepts. You can even do the color separations for four-color work on your PC and send those color separations, too. (Ask the printer for instructions to make sure that you submit the design in a format that the printer's system can use.) The printer then makes plates for printing the design straight from the file that you've e-mailed to them. *(Plates are metal or plastic sheets with your design on them — the printer applies the ink to the paper when the printing press does its thing.)*

Until recently, electronic submission to printing firms generally had to be done from an expensive and hard-to-master design program like Quark, but increasingly, printers are accepting Word files or PDF files generated by Acrobat (I prefer this route, because it reduces the chances of incompatibility problems). And if you're designing in a recent version of Word, you'll find that creating a PDF file can be done right out of your program, because Acrobat is now built in.

Mechanical versus electronic paste-up

The traditional way to submit a design to a printing firm is to generate what printers call *camera-ready art,* a version of the design suitable for the printer to photograph with a large-scale production camera in order to generate *color keys* (to convert colors to specific inks) and *films,* clear sheets for each layer of color to be printed. The designer used to produce this camera-ready art by making a *mechanical* or *paste-up,* in which the designer pastes typeset copy, visuals, and all the other elements of the design onto a foam-core board, using a hot wax machine.

A hot wax machine heats wax and spreads it on a roller so that the designer can roll a thin layer of warm wax onto the back of each element. The wax sticks each piece neatly to the board, allowing those pieces to be peeled off easily, in case you want to reposition anything.

We have one here at my office, and the other day I caught sight of the hot wax machine in the trash can. "Hey!" I objected, "Who threw the hot wax machine away?!" Everybody looked at me blankly. Younger than I am, my staff had no idea what the thing was and had never seen one in action. Well, I still like the old techniques, even if nobody else does. I took it out of the trash and hid it where none of my eager young employees can find it. (Just let them try to throw it away again . . . I'll throw their laptops away!)

Charrette, an art supply company, makes a cheap hand-held version of a hot wax machine called the Hand Waxer for people who only use this traditional method occasionally and don't want to spend the money on more sophisticated equipment. Ask your local art supply store to order the Hand Waxer for you, if you need one. (I sometimes use my Hand Waxer to do quick rough layouts using collaged materials I've cut out, thus avoiding the need to get everything scanned and into the computer until I know what I want to use.)

You can still work with a glue stick or hot wax and scissors to do rough layouts. But if you're quick and able on a computer and like to work in design and layout programs (such as Adobe PageMaker or QuarkXPress), you can do the same kind of creative rough designing simply by searching for images on the Web. (To find an image, try specifying an image search in Google, but remember not to use copyrighted images in your final design without permission or payment.) Copy the images onto your computer disk, and you can click and drag them into different programs and pages. Increasingly, this is how I do my rough design work today.

I recommend that you invest a bit of time and effort in honing these computer-based design techniques, too. Look up the latest *For Dummies* books on how to use PageMaker, QuarkXPress, Microsoft Publisher, or any other graphic design and layout program of your choice, or just work in Word, which is pretty impressive in its latest incarnations as a basic design program itself. Also take a look at the growing number of great-looking ad templates you can purchase on CD or via e-mail, and then adapt them in any of the common graphic design programs. As an example, see many options at www.stocklayouts.com.

Finding your font

A *font* is a particular design's attributes for the *characters* (letters, numbers, and symbols) used in printing your design. *Typeface* refers only to the distinctive design of the letters (Times New Roman, for example). Font, on the other hand, actually refers to one particular size and style of a typeface design (such as 10-point, bold, Times New Roman).

The right font for any job is the one that makes your text easily readable and that harmonizes with the overall design most effectively. For a headline, the font also needs to grab the reader's attention. The body copy doesn't have to grab attention in the same way — in fact, if it does, the copy often loses readability. For example, a *reverse font* (light or white on dark) may be just the thing for a bold headline, but if you use the reverse font in the body copy, too, nobody reads your copy. It's just too hard on the eye to read more than a line or two in reverse.

Choosing a typeface

What sort of typeface do you want? You have an amazing number of choices because designers have been developing typefaces for as long as printing presses have existed. (Just click Format⇨Font in Microsoft Word to see an assortment of the more popular typefaces.)

A clean, sparse design, with a lot of white space on the page and stark contrasts in the artwork, deserves the clean lines of a *sans serif typeface* — meaning one that doesn't have any decorative *serifs* (those little bars or flourishes at the ends of the main lines in a character). The most popular body-copy fonts without serifs are Helvetica, Univers, Optima, and Avant Garde. Figure 7-2 shows some fonts with and without serifs.

Figure 7-2: Fonts with and without serifs.

But a richly decorative, old-fashioned sort of design needs a more decorative and traditional serif typeface, like Century or Times New Roman. The most popular body-copy fonts with serifs include Garamond, Melior, Century, Times New Roman, and Caledonia.

Table 7-1 shows an assortment of typeface choices, in which you can compare the clean lines of Helvetica, Avant Garde, and Optima with the more decorative designs of Century, Garamond, and Times New Roman.

Table 7-1	Popular Fonts for Ads
Sans Serif	*Serif*
Helvetica	Century
Univers	Garamond
Optima	Melior
Avant Garde	Times New Roman

In tests, Helvetica and Century generally top the lists as most readable, so start with one of these typefaces for your body copy; only change the font if it doesn't seem to work. Also, research shows that people read lowercase letters about 13 percent faster than uppercase letters, so avoid long stretches of copy set in all caps. People also read most easily when letters are dark and contrast strongly with their background. Thus, black 14-point Helvetica on white is probably the most readable font specification for the body copy of an ad (or other printed marketing materials), even if the combination does seem dull to a sophisticated designer.

Generalizing about the best kind of headline typeface is no easy task because designers play around with headlines to a greater extent than they do with body copy. But as a general rule, you can use Helvetica for the headline when you use Century for the body, and vice versa. Or you can just use a bolder, larger version of the body copy font for your headline. You can also reverse a larger, bold version of your type onto a black background for the headline. Anything to make the headline grab the reader's attention, stand out from the body copy, and ultimately lead vision and curiosity into the body copy's text. (Remember to keep the headline readable. Nothing too fancy, please.)

Sometimes the designer combines body copy of a decorative typeface, one with serifs, like Times New Roman, with headers of a sans serif typeface, like Helvetica. The contrast between the clean lines of the large-sized header and the more decorative characters of the smaller body copy pleases the eye and tends to draw the reader from header to body copy. This book uses that technique. Compare the sans serif bold characters of this chapter's title with the more delicate and decorative characters in which the publishers set the text for a good example of this design concept in action.

Making style choices within the typeface

Any typeface gives the user many choices, and so selecting the typeface is just the beginning of the project when you design your print. How big should the characters be? Do you want to use the standard version of the typeface, a lighter version, a *bold* (or darker) version, or an *italic version* (one that leans to the right, like the letters spelling *italic version)?* Wow — what a hassle!

The process is easier than it sounds. Really! Just look at samples of some standard point sizes (12- and 14-point text for the body copy, for example, and 24-, 36-, and 48-point for the headlines). Many designers make their choice by eye, looking for an easy-to-read size that isn't so large that it causes the words or sentences to break up into too many fragments across the page — but not so small that it gives the reader too many words per line. Keep readability in mind as the goal.

Figure 7-3 shows a variety of size and style choices for the Helvetica typeface. As you can see, you have access to a wonderful range of options, even within this one popular design.

Figure 7-3:
Some of
the many
choices
that the
Helvetica
typeface
offers
designers.

Helvetica Light 14 point

Helvetica Italic 14 point

Helvetica Bold 14 point

Helvetica Regular 14 point

Helvetica Regular 24 point

Helvetica Regular Condensed 14 point

Helvetica Bold Outline 24 point

Keep in mind that you can change just about any aspect of type. You can alter the distance between lines — called the *leading* — or you can squeeze characters together or stretch them apart to make a word fit a space. Assume that anything is possible, and ask your printer, or consult the manual of your desktop publishing or word processing software, to find out how to make a change.

Now, having said that anything is possible, I want to warn you that your customers' eyes read type quite conservatively. Although most of us know little about the design of typefaces, we find traditional designs instinctively appealing. The spacing of characters and lines, the balance and flow of individual characters — all these familiar typeface considerations please the eye and makes reading easy and pleasurable. And so, although you should know that you can change anything and everything, you should also know that too many changes may reduce your design's readability. Figure 7-4 shows the same ad laid out twice — once in an eye-pleasing way and once in a disastrous way.

WHEN LIFE GIVES YOU LEMONS...

What should you do? Juggle them? Make lemonade? Open a farm stand? Or give up and go home to Momma?

WHO KNOWS? It's often hard to come to grips with pressing personal or career problems. Sometimes it's hardest to see your **own** problems clearly. Fortunately, JEN KNOWS. Jen Fredrics has twenty years of counseling experience, a master's in social work, and a busy practice in personal problem solving. Call her today to find out how to turn your problems into opportunities.

And next time, when life gives you lemons, you'll know just what to make. An appointment.

WHEN LIFE GIVES YOU LEMONS...

What should you do? Juggle them? Make lemonade? Open a farm stand? Or give up and go home to Momma?

WHO KNOWS? It's often hard to come to grips with pressing personal or career problems. Sometimes it's hardest to see your own problems clearly. Fortunately, JEN KNOWS. Jen Fredrics has twenty years of counseling experience, a master's in social work, and a busy practice in personal problem solving. Call her today to find out how to turn your problems into opportunities.

And next time, when life gives you lemons, you'll know just what to make. An appointment.

Figure 7-4: Which copy would you rather read?

Don't just play with type for the sake of playing (as the designer did in the left-hand version of the classified ad in Figure 7-4). Stick with popular fonts, in popular sizes, except where you have to solve a problem or you want to make a special point. The advent of desktop publishing has lead to a horrifying generation of advertisements in which dozens of fonts dance across the page, bolds and italics fight each other for attention, and the design of the words becomes a barrier to reading, rather than an aid.

Choosing a point size

When designers and printers talk about *font sizes,* they are referring to a traditional measure of the height of the letters (based on the highest and lowest parts of the biggest letters). One *point* equals about $1/72$ of an inch, so a 10-point type is $10/72$ of an inch high, at the most.

Personally, I don't really care — I've never measured a character with a ruler. I just know that if the letters seem too small for easy reading, then I need to bump the typeface up a couple of points. Ten-point type is too small for most body copy, but you may want to use that size if you have to squeeze several words into a small space. (But why do that? You're usually better off editing your body copy and then bumping up the font size to make it more readable!)

Your eye can't distinguish easily between fonts that are only one or two sizes apart, so you should specify a larger jump than that to distinguish between body copy and subhead, or subhead and headline.

Producing Brochures, Fliers, and More

You can get your print design out to the public in an easy and inexpensive way, using brochures, fliers, posters, and many other forms — your imagination is the only limit to what you can do with a good design for all your printed materials. Your word-processing or graphics software, a good inkjet or laser printer, and the help of your local photocopy or print shop (which also has folding machines) allows you to design and produce brochures quite easily, and also come up with many other forms of printed marketing materials. In this section, however, I focus largely on a basic brochure, because they're easy, a business staple, and effective at marketing your company.

You can also do smaller runs (100 or less) right from a color printer. Buy matte or glossy brochure paper designed for your brand of printer (HPs work well for this), and simply select the appropriate paper type in the print dialog box. Today's inexpensive inkjet printers can produce absolutely stunning brochures. But you have to fold these brochures yourself, and the ink cartridges aren't cheap. So you should print as needed rather than inventory a large number of brochures. Or try contacting your local copy shop. Kinko's and many other copy stores now accept e-mailed copies of files, and can produce short runs of your brochures, pamphlets, catalog sheets, or other printed materials on their color copiers right from your file.

Many brochures foolishly waste money because they don't accomplish any specific marketing goals; they just look pretty, at best. To avoid a pretty, but pointless, brochure that doesn't achieve a sales goal, make sure that you know

- Who will read the brochure
- How they will get the brochure
- What they should discover and do from reading the brochure

These three questions focus your brochure design and make it useful to your marketing.

Marketers often order a brochure without a clear idea of what purpose the brochure should serve. They just think a brochure is a good idea. "Oh, we need them to, you know, like, put in the envelope along with a letter, or, um, for our salespeople to keep in the trunks of their cars, like they do the other brochures. Or maybe we send some out to our mailing list. Or give them away at the next trade show."

With this many possibilities, the brochure can't be properly suited to any single use. The brochure becomes a dull, vague scrap of paper that just talks about the company or product but doesn't hit readers over the head with any particular appeal and call to action.

Listing your top three uses

Define up to three specific uses for the brochure. No more than three, though, because your design can't accomplish more than three purposes effectively. The most common and appropriate uses for a brochure are

- To act as a reference on the product, or technical details of the product, for prospects

- To support a personal selling effort by lending credibility and helping overcome objections (to find out more about sales, check out Chapter 17)

- To generate leads through a direct-mail campaign (I talk about direct-mail campaigns in Chapter 13)

Say you want to design a brochure that does all three of these tasks well. Start by designing the contents. What product and technical information must be included? Write the information down, or collect necessary illustrations, so that you have the *fact base* (the essential information to communicate) in front of you.

Writing about strengths and weaknesses

List the brilliance curve items related to sales (discussed in Chapter 4):

- The common sales objections or reasons prospects give for why they don't want to buy your product

- Customers' favorite reasons for buying or aspects of your product or business that customers like most

Organize your fact base to highlight these greatest strengths and overcome these biggest objections. The copy should read as if you're listening to their concerns and answering each with an appropriate response. You can write subheads like "Our Product Doesn't Need Service" so that salespeople or prospects can easily see how your facts (in copy and/or illustrations) overcome each specific objection and highlight all the major benefits.

Incorporating a clear, compelling appeal

Add some basic appeal (see Chapter 6), communicated in a punchy headline and a few dozen words of copy, along with an appropriate and eye-catching illustration. You need to include this appeal to help the brochure stand on its own as a marketing tool when the brochure is sent out to leads through the mail or passed on from a prospect or customer to one of his or her professional contacts.

The appeal needs to project a winning personality. It can be fun or serious, emotional or factual — but it must be appealing. The appeal is the bait that draws the prospect to your hook. Make sure your hook is well baited!

You have to include copy (and perhaps illustrations) designed specifically for each of those three purposes in "Listing your top three uses," earlier in the chapter. The appeal, with its enticing headline and compelling copy and visual, goes on the front of the brochure — or the outside when you fold it for mailing, or the central panel out of three if you fold a sheet twice. The subheads that structure the main copy respond to objections and highlight strengths on the inside pages. And you organize the fact base, needed for reference use, in the copy and illustrations beneath these subheads. If you don't know what each part of your brochure does, then you need to redesign it — otherwise, that brochure becomes a waste of time and money.

Figure 7-5 shows how you can lay out such a brochure, along with dimensions for text blocks or illustrations. Although you can lay out a brochure in many ways, I often prefer the format in Figure 7-5. It's simple and inexpensive because you print the brochure on a single sheet of legal-sized paper that you then fold three times. The brochure fits in a standard #10 or #12 envelope, or you can tape it together along the open fold and mail it on its own. This layout allows for some detail, but not enough to get you into any real trouble. Larger formats and multi-page pieces tend to fill up with the worst, wordiest copy, and nobody ever reads those pieces.

You can use the design shown in Figure 7-5 for direct mailings to generate sales leads, and you can also hand the brochure out or use it for reference in direct-selling situations. You can produce this brochure, using any popular desktop publishing software, and you can even print and fold it at the local photocopy shop (if you don't need the thousands of copies that make off-set printing cost-effective). To convert this design to an even simpler, cheaper format, use 8½-x-11-inch paper and eliminate the *return mailer* (the left-hand page on the front, the right-hand on the back, which can be returned with the blanks filled in to request information or accept a special offer). If you do remove the return mailer, however, be sure to include follow-up instructions and contact information on one of the inside pages!

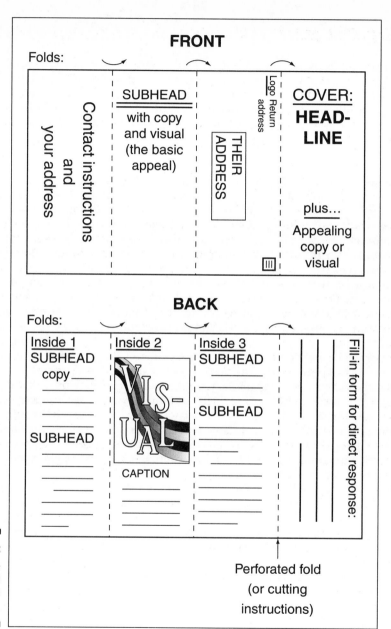

Figure 7-5:
A simple, multipurpose brochure layout.

Placing a Print Ad

This section covers a marketing specialty called *media buying,* with an emphasis on buying print ad space. Ad agencies and the marketing departments of big companies have specialists who do nothing but buy media, and some brokers specialize in it for mid-sized or smaller marketers. But if you're a smaller-scale marketer, you can easily figure out how to buy media space on your own.

Can you afford to advertise?

If you're marketing a small business, start by buying magazines or newspapers that you're sure your prospective customers read. Then look for the information in them that identifies the publisher and gives a phone number for advertisers to call. Call and request a *rate sheet* (a table listing the prices of ads by size of ad and also showing the discount rate per ad if you buy multiple ads instead of just a single one). If it's a magazine, also ask for the *schedule,* which tells you when ads for each issue need to be placed and what the topics of future issues will be. Alternatively, you can get information for advertisers on the Web sites of many publications.

After you've collected a selection of rate sheets from magazines or newspapers, take a hard look at the pricing. How expensive is the average ad (in the middle of the size range for each publication)? This may be a broad number. If a single ad costs 1/20th (5 percent) or more of your marketing budget for the entire year, throw the rate sheets away and forget about advertising in those publications. Your business is not currently operating on a large enough scale to be able to do this kind of advertising. You need dozens of ad placements at a minimum to make a good print ad campaign, so don't begin unless you can easily afford to keep going.

Instead of blowing that much money on a single ad, spread it over more economical forms of advertising and marketing, like brochures, mailings, and e-mails. If you operate on too small a scale or budget to afford advertising, try turning that ad design into a good flier and mailing it, instead. You can send it to 200 names and see what happens. That is a lot less risky and expensive than buying space in a magazine that goes to 200,000 names. Or you can search for smaller-circulation publications with a more local or specialized readership, where the rates may be much cheaper.

Finding inexpensive places to advertise

I went to the theater last night to see a local production of *The Wizard of Oz,* and I noticed that many local businesses purchased bought ad space in the program. What did this cost? Less than $100 for many of them. Compare that to an ad in a major magazine, which can cost $100,000. That's a big difference! My point is that, if buying ads in the best publications to reach your market is too expensive, you can always find smaller-circulation publications that charge less.

One great way to advertise for less is to take advantage of the tens of thousands of newsletters published by professional groups and interest groups. You can buy ad space in 10 or 20 such newsletters for far less money than buying one ad insertion in a big-city daily newspaper. But you may have to be creative and persistent, because opportunities to advertise in newsletters aren't as obvious as with larger and more professional publications.

One type of newsletter I like very much for small-budget advertising is the professional association's monthly newsletter. Professionals are people who have buying power, so even if you don't sell a product just for them, they may still respond to your ad. Some insurance agents have advertised successfully in newsletters that go to doctors, for example. And increasingly, such newsletters are published in Web versions in addition to — or even instead of — print versions. With a Web publication, you can take advantage of the larger reach of the Web with the lower price of a small publication.

Also be sure to explore local and small-town newspapers. You can find hundreds of newspapers and weeklies with *circulation* (readership) only in the tens of thousands, which means their rates for ads are one-fifth to one-tenth the price of a big-city newspaper (and even less expensive when compared to major national magazines). Of course, you don't reach as many people, either — advertising tends to be priced on a *cost per thousand readers* basis (the cost of buying that ad divided by the number of readers who read the publication, then multiplied by 1,000), so you generally get as much exposure as you're willing to pay for. But by buying ads in small-circulation publications, you avoid taking huge risks, and you minimize your investment. If an ad pays off, you can try running it in additional publications. But if it doesn't produce the results you want, you can afford to write off the cost without feeling too much pain.

Keep the scale of your print advertising (and indeed any advertising) at a level such that you can afford to run an ad that may produce zero sales. Although that's certainly not your goal, zero sales is always a possibility, and you want to base your buying decision on that possibility.

Selecting the ad size

What size ad should you buy? The answer depends in part on the design of your ad. Does the ad have a strong, simple visual or headline that catches the eye, even if it's only a third of a page in size? Or does the ad need to be displayed in a larger format to work well?

In addition to your (or your designer's) judgment about the specifics of your ad, also take into account some general statistics on what percentage of readers *notice* an ad based on its size. As you may expect, the rate goes up with size — bigger ads get more notice (all other things being equal), according to a study by Cahners Publishing Co. (see Table 7-2).

Table 7-2	Selecting the Right Size
Size of Ad	*Percent of Readers Noting Ad (Median)*
Fractional (part-of-page) Ads	24%
One-Page Ads	40%
Two-Page Spreads	55%

The bigger the ad, the bigger the impact. But also consider the fact that the percentage of readers noticing your ad doesn't go up *in proportion* to the increase in size. Doubling the size of your ad gives you something like a quarter more viewers, not twice as many. That's partly why the cost of a full-page ad isn't twice the cost of a half-page ad.

For example, a full-page four-color ad in *Health* magazine costs 59 percent more than a ½ page four-color ad. The same ad, run at full versus half size, probably attracts, at most, about a third more reader notices, meaning your cost per reader exposed to the ad is higher for that full-page ad than the half-page ad.

If you're pinching your pennies, a full-page ad is often your best choice. Even though a large ad costs more, it is sufficiently more noticeable than smaller sizes, which means you'll reach more readers and, thus, bring the cost per exposure down a bit. However, remember that a full-page ad is more economical, but it's also more risky, because you will have blown more money if the ad doesn't work. You may want to try testing a new design with a quarter-page, inexpensive ad, and if that pays off, buy a full-page ad the next time.

Testing and improving your print ad

Is anybody actually reading your ad? A *direct-response* ad, one that asks readers to take a measurable action like call, fax, or go to a store, gives you a clear indication of that ad's effectiveness within days of its first appearance. Say you expect to receive a lot of inquiries and orders over the telephone during the week the issue with your ad goes on sale. If you don't receive those calls, you know you have a problem. Now what?

Troubleshooting your ad

What if you want to know more about why that direct-response ad didn't get the desired level of response? Or what if you want to study an *indirect-response ad* — one that creates or strengthens an image or position in order to encourage sales? Much brand advertising is indirect, leaving it to the retailer or local office to close the sale. No phones ring, whether consumers liked the ad or not, so how do you know whether the ad worked?

To get this sort of information, you can go to a marketing research firm and have your ad tested for effectiveness. In fact, if you plan to spend more than $200,000 on print ads, you can probably consider the $20,000 or so needed to hire a research firm to pretest the ad money well spent. *Pretesting* means exposing people to the ad in a controlled setting and measuring their reactions to it.

To test an ad and see whether it's effective, use one of the free techniques in Chapter 4: You can assemble your own panel of customers and ask them to rate your ad and give you feedback about why they do or don't find that ad appealing. This feedback can give you good ideas for a new, improved version next time.

You can also tap into the large-scale studies of ad readership done routinely by some research firms. Just subscribe to the study, and the firm feeds you detailed data about how well each ad you publish works.

A number of commercial research services can give you additional information about how and to what extent people read your ad. Roper Starch Worldwide (www.roperasw.com or 212-599-0700) may be the best known of these services. If you sign up for its Starch Readership Service, the service asks consumers whether they noticed your ads in 150 different publications in the United States (and licensees of Roper Starch do similar readership studies in many other countries). Starch surveys 75,000 consumers each year, asking them about specific ads to find out to what extent consumers notice and read an ad, and to measure the level of interest the ad generated.

Say that the Starch data shows that readership of your ad falls a little lower than average and that, although many people note the ad, few read enough to get the point or even the brand name. Should you kill this ad and start over?

The answer depends on what's wrong with the ad. Starch data (or data from similar services or even a volunteer consumer panel) can help you find out because the Starch survey looks at individual elements of the ad, as well as the overall ad. You can find out how many people read the headline (or even the first versus second line of a two-line headline). Then you can see how many continued on to the first paragraph of the body copy, the photograph, or the logo and signature.

Sometimes you find a problem that can be fixed without starting from scratch. Maybe your headline and photo get high Starch scores, but the body copy flunks. You can try rewriting and shortening the copy, and you may also try changing the layout or your choice of fonts. Perhaps the body copy is in reverse font, which consumers find hard to read. Often, switching the text to dark letters on a white or light background raises the Starch score, without any other changes!

Or maybe you need to switch from a black-and-white or two-color visual to a four-color one. Sure, you have to pay more, but if the Starch scores go up enough, the resulting ad may yield a better return, despite its higher price. Cahners Publishing also reports from its studies that black-and-white ads and two-color ads attract the notice of about a third of readers, and four-color ads attract almost half of readers — 46 percent, to be precise. So as with size, more is better when it comes to colors. However, you need to run the numbers to see how the extra costs and extra readers affect your cost per thousand figure. As with all print ad decisions, you should be able to reduce the options to reasonable estimates of costs and returns and then pick the highest-yielding option.

Ad analysis for free?

Maybe you don't really need to spend good money on a research service to find out if your ads are working. Here are some alternatives:

✔ Run three variations on the ad and see which one generates the most calls or Web site visits (offering a discount based on a code number tells you which responses come from which ad).

✔ Do your own ad tests. Ask people to look at your ads for 20 seconds, and then quiz them about what they remember. If they missed much of the ad, you probably need to rewrite!

✔ Run the same ad (or very similar ones) in large and small formats and see which pulls in the largest number of consumers.

Any experiments you can run as you do your marketing gives you useful feedback about what's working and what isn't. Always think of ways to compare different options and see how those options perform when you advertise, giving you useful insight into ad effectiveness.

A brilliant example

Marketers generally assume that they have to work hard with colors and text to make their ads noticeable and persuasive. Statistically, they're right. But don't discount the power of imaginative design to simplify the task. You can do a simple two-color ad with very little text that actually works better than other, more elaborate ads.

Marketers printed a vertical half-page ad for Altoids ("the curiously strong mints" that come in a distinctive white metal tin with red trim around its edges) in only black and red, yet more than 90 percent of magazine readers noted that ad (according to a survey of the magazine's readers). The ad's 12 inches of height shows the figure of a person clad in a shiny silver suit and helmet, like the outfit a welder repairing a containment vessel at a nuclear power plant wears. A dark-tinted glass visor and full helmet totally conceal the figure's face and head. The figure's heavily gloved hands hold . . . a box of Altoids, slightly open, as if the figure plans to reach in and pop one into his mouth (don't ask me how).

The copy is strikingly simple. Across the bottom appears, in bright red, large, 3-D, outlined capitals, the product's name. Only the trademarked slogan (in white, outlined in black) appears beneath the name: "The curiously strong mints." That's all the copy, except for an Internet address (it's www.altoids. com in case you want to see what they do with readers who follow up on their ads). Two colors. Five words. A person in some kind of weird suit. This very simple, inexpensive ad built brand awareness and effectively created a quirky personality for the brand. Great print advertising doesn't have to be expensive, it just has to be clever.

Chapter 8

Billboards, Banners, Signs, and More

. . . .

In This Chapter

▶ Finding successful signs for your business

▶ Opting for bumper stickers, umbrellas, and shopping bags

▶ Using flags, banners, and awnings

▶ Designing billboards and other large signs

▶ Utilizing transit advertising

. . . .

*O*utdoor advertising refers to a wide variety of advertising. The most obvious (but not necessarily most important for you) are large (to very large!) signs and posters, including roadside billboards, but I also include signs, flags, and banners in this medium. Marketers also call the general outdoor advertising category *out-of-home* advertising.

All these methods try to communicate your message through public display of a poster, sign, or something of similar design requirements. That's why I incorporate signs, flags, banners, bumper stickers, transit advertising, and even T-shirts in this chapter, along with the traditional billboard formats. These media are more powerful than many marketers realize — some businesses succeed by using no other advertising, in fact. In this chapter, you find out how to design for and use *outdoor advertising* (the term I use to indicate outdoor signs and banners, plus related displays like posters and signs, which, just to keep you on your toes, can be displayed indoors as well as out).

Whenever you review your marketing program, stop to do an inventory of your signs, posters, T-shirts, and other outdoor ads. How many do you have displayed? Are they visible? Clear and appealing? Clean and in good repair? And then ask if you can find an easy way to increase the number and impact of these signs. When you need to make your brand identity and marketing messages visible, you can never do too much. The more the merrier!

Back to Basics: The Essential Sign

Here's a strange thing I discovered while writing this book: *Signs* (small, informational outdoor ads or notices) don't show up in the index or table of contents of most books on marketing. *Signs* are displays with brand or company names on them and sometimes a short marketing message or useful information for the customer, too. In my experience, every marketer and every marketing program needs to make good use of signs.

Signs are all over — if you're in an office right now, step to the nearest window and you can probably see a handful with ease. And signs are undeniably important. Even if they serve only to locate a store or office, they do a job that marketers need done. If your customers can't find you, you're out of business. So why do marketers — or at least those marketing experts who write the books — tend to ignore signs so completely?

You can't find a national or international set of standards for signs. You also can't find a major association to promote standards and champion best practices. When evaluating signs, I can't send you to the experts easily as I can with radio, TV, print, or other outdoor media. You'll probably end up working with a local sign manufacturer, and you and your designer have to specify size, materials, copy, and art. So why don't you take on the role of being the sign expert for your business, right now?

Many towns and cities regulate the display of signs in public places (you can usually get a list of the restrictions from local zoning boards). And if you rent retail or office space, your landlord may also have put some restrictions (or a *right of review*) into your lease. You should research these possible constraints before spending any money on design and construction of signs! If restrictions seem likely to cause trouble, you probably need to hire a lawyer to clarify your options or advocate for an exception before you start the design process. At the very least, talk to those who feel they have authority over your sign and seek their approval based on a sketch and plan before you spend any money having signs made or installed.

Consult your local or regional business telephone listings when you need to have a sign made. You should find several options. You may want to talk to a good design firm or experienced designer for a personal reference, too. And modern copy shops increasingly provide cheap high-tech solutions for smaller or temporary signs. (In the United States, Kinko's and FastSigns stores are helpful.)

To stand out next to those shiny, high-tech signs and project a quality image, have your sign designed and painted by an artist or consider hiring a cabinet-maker, stained glass artist, oil painter, or other arts and crafts professional. Most signs have little real art about them. So when a business hires an artist to carve its name and logo into a big piece of mahogany, the result is something truly special! Unusual and beautiful signs tell the world that your company is special, too. In fact, a really special sign, well displayed in a high-traffic area, has more power to build an image or pull in prospects than any other form of local advertising.

Everybody likes free advertising, and you can get great free exposures from signs. A magnetic sign on the side of a car or truck, like those you see on the cars of real estate agents, can reach thousands of people a day for free.

What your sign can do

Signs have limited ability to accomplish marketing goals — but perhaps not as limited as you think. You can use signs to help people find you — starting with a sign near the freeway exit and ending with signs marking the entrance to your store or parking lot.

It's amazing how many businesses make finding themselves difficult. My office in Amherst, Massachusetts, is near the main campus for University of Massachusetts at Amherst, the biggest college in the state and home to a top business school. Why do visitors often have to pull over in downtown Amherst and ask for directions to the campus? Well, no signs downtown point the way. Hmm. Maybe I should send a copy of this book to the president of the university with a bookmark stuck in this page.

Aside from their practical value (letting people know where you are), signs can and should promote your image and brand name. An attractive sign on your building or vehicle can spread the good word about your business or brand to all who pass by. Don't miss this brilliant opportunity to put your best foot forward in public.

By the way, about 25 percent of all commercial signs are in poor condition. Signs sit out in the weather, and when they fade, peel, or fall over, they give negative advertising for your business. Don't let your sign give the public the impression that you don't care enough to maintain your signs (they may even think you're going out of business!). Renew and religiously maintain your signs to get the maximum benefit from them.

Writing good signs

As a marketer, you need to master the strange art of writing for signs. Too often, the language marketers use on signs is ambiguous. The sign just doesn't say anything with enough precision to make its point clear.

All across the United States, you find millions of street signs that say *Ped Xing*. Who writes a sign using two made-up words? Only someone who wants to force the viewer to decipher their code. Ever notice that cars don't stop for people crossing? It's no wonder — the sign doesn't actually tell them what to do (lacks a call to action), doesn't give drivers a good reason to stop (lacks a benefit or cost), and doesn't even uses any words they know (lacks clarity). In marketing, you can't get away with such bad writing. To make the meaning crystal clear, a marketer can use something like: "Stop for People in Crosswalk" or "Let people cross the road." A smaller-print reminder of the fine for not stopping may add power to this clear call to action.

You may have to make the sign bigger to fit these words on it in a readable font. So be it. The form of the sign must follow its function. Before you approve any design, review the copy to make sure that the writing provides a model of clarity! *Try* misinterpreting the wording. Can you read the sign in a way that makes it seem to mean something you don't intend to say? And try thinking of questions the sign doesn't answer that seem obvious to you — remember that the consumer may not know the answers. For example, some people have a terrible sense of direction, so a sign on the side of a store leaves them confused about how to enter that store. Solution? Put an arrow and the instructions "Enter from Front" on the sign!

Marketers design some signs to convey substantial information — directions, for example, or details of a store's merchandise mix. Informational signs are often too brief or too lengthy. You should divide the copy and design into two sections, each with a separate purpose.

- ✔ **Have a header.** The first section is like the header in a print ad (see Chapter 7), and you design it to catch attention from afar and draw people to the sign. Given this purpose, brevity is key — and don't forget the essential large, catchy type and/or visuals.

- ✔ **Communicate essential information.** The second section of the sign needs to communicate the essential information accurately and in full. If the first section does its job, viewers walk right up to the sign to read the informational part, so you don't need to make that type as large and catchy. The consumer should be able to easily read and interpret the wording and type of the information, and this section needs to answer all likely viewer questions.

Most signs don't have these two distinct sections, and so they fail to accomplish either purpose very well. They neither draw people very strongly nor inform them fully. Unfortunately, most sign makers have a strong urge to make all the copy the same size. When pressed, the sign makers sometimes make the header twice as big as the rest of the copy. But going further than that seems to upset them. Well, to get a good sign, you may have to upset some people. As in many aspects of marketing, if you want above-average performance, you have to swim against the current.

Speaking of being unconventional, what about adding a beautiful photograph to your sign to give it more of the eye-catching appeal of a good print ad? Most sign printers/makers can include photographs now, but few marketers take advantage of this option.

Another problem — marketers write the copy on most signs in the most dumb-obvious manner. Tradition says that a sign, unlike any other marketing communication, must simply state the facts in a direct, unimaginative way. The dictionary should give "creative signs" as an example when it defines "oxymoron," because "creative" and "signs" tend to mix like oil and water.

One reason you don't see much creativity in signs? Most marketers assume people *read* signs. That's the conventional wisdom — that your customers and prospects automatically find and read your signs.

The average downtown street in the average city has more than five hundred signs per block. Try walking such a block and then listing all the signs you remember seeing. Some stand out, but most go unseen. And I bet you can't re-create the text of very many of those signs your eye bothered to linger on long enough to read. To avoid having your sign being lost in this sea of similar signs, you have to make yours stand out!

Whenever you find other marketers making dumb mistakes, you can turn their errors into your opportunities. And signs permit innovation in two interesting areas. You can innovate in the copy and artwork, just as you can in any print medium — from a magazine ad to a roadside billboard. But you can also innovate in the form of the sign itself. Experiment with materials, shapes, lighting, location, and ways of displaying signs to come up with some novel ideas that give your sign drawing power. Signs should be creative and fun! (So should all marketing, for that matter.)

Here are some of the many variations in form that you can take advantage of when designing a creative sign:

- ✔ Vinyl graphics and lettering (quick and inexpensive but accurate to your design)
- ✔ Hand-painted (personal look and feel)
- ✔ Wood (traditional look; routing or hand carving enhances the appeal)
- ✔ Metal (durable and accurate screening of art and copy, but not very pretty)
- ✔ Window lettering (hand-painted or with vinyl letters/graphics)
- ✔ Lighted boxes (in which lettering is back-lit; highly visible at night)
- ✔ Neon signs (Wow!)
- ✔ Magnetic signs (for your vehicles)

✔ Signs printed from an inkjet printer output, sent out from a local frame shop to be laminated on a display board with a plastic coating (This new form of framing is intended for indoor use, but I've seen some companies use it out of doors and it holds up surprisingly well. With it, you can make your own signs on your own printer.)

✔ Electronic displays (also known as *electronic message repeaters;* movement and longer messages, plus a high-tech feel, make these displays appropriate in some situations)

✔ Flat-panel TV screens (with shifting sign content and images or video) The price of these TVs has been coming down.

Small but Effective — From T-shirts to Shopping Bags

A broad definition of a sign may include any public display of your brand or marketing message. To me, a message on a T-shirt is just as legitimate as a message on a signboard. And it is often a lot easier and cheaper to make. The following sections share simple, small-scale ways to get your message across.

T-shirts, umbrellas, and bumper stickers, anyone?

In addition, don't forget that you can sometimes induce people to display your signs on their vehicles or bodies. (I cover T-shirts in the "Praising T-shirts" sidebar.) Your customers may think of a nice T-shirt as a premium item or gift for them, but you can see that T-shirt as a body billboard! It's nice that people are willing to go around with your advertising messages on their clothes (or even on their bodies — temporary tattoos are also a marketing option). Don't overlook this concept as a form of outdoor advertising. In fact, use it as much as you can. People happily display marketing messages if they like them.

Similarly, umbrellas (also available from premium companies — see Chapter 11) can broadcast your logo and name and a short slogan or headline — although only in especially wet or overly sunny weather.

Don't overlook bumper stickers and car-window stickers. If you make them clever or unique enough, people eagerly seek those stickers out to deface their nice new cars with them. Don't ask me why. But because people do, and because the cost of producing bumper stickers is cheap, why not come up with an appealing design and make stickers available in target markets as giveaways on store counters or as bill stuffers?

Praising T-shirts

Sometimes you just need a cheap T-shirt. My dresser has a drawer stuffed full of them, and many of those shirts have artwork that promotes a company or brand name. If you can make a T-shirt appropriate to your brand, then by all means use T-shirts as a premium item!

You can find even a good-quality T-shirt pretty cheaply, so you can easily implement the quality premium strategy with T-shirts. You achieve quality by making sure your T-shirts use a heavy, all-cotton fabric and sport a compelling design developed by a real designer.

Oh, and you need to use an experienced, quality-conscious silk-screener to put that fine design on those good T-shirts.

The poor selection of shirts available to T-shirt buyers through stores and other sources frustrates those buyers. A lack of exciting new designs, not a lack of drawer space, holds these customers back. So you just need to put a cool design on your T-shirt to get your target audience to want it. Customers can't get enough of this premium item — provided your design is fresh and good. No, I don't really want another cheap pen with some company's name on it. But I'm happy to get another good T-shirt. Heck, I may even pay you for it.

To find companies that provide customized T-shirts, try your local Yellow Pages for listings of silk-screening shops near you. (Although silk-screening shops screen onto many different materials and products, telephone directories generally list these shops under T-shirts.)

Commercial or brand-oriented bumper stickers are used by people who think the brand is so cool that it enhances the car — and this is a hard thing to achieve for some marketers. An alternative is to keep your brand identity small, and star an appealing message, instead. A clever joke, an inspiring quote, or something similar is appealing enough to get your message displayed. And for mugs, window stickers, and other premium items, the secret is to have a great visual design or other picture that people enjoy, or to offer a humorous cartoon.

You can even include a nice sticker in a direct-mail piece, where that sticker can do double duty — acting as an incentive to get people to retain and read the mailing and giving you cheap outdoor advertising when they display the sticker on their vehicles. (Contact local print shops, sign makers, or T-shirt silk-screeners; any of these businesses sometimes produce bumper stickers, too.)

It's in the bag

The big department stores believe in the importance of shopping bags as an advertising medium. But many other businesses fail to take advantage of the fact that shoppers carry bags around busy shopping malls and downtown areas, and also on subways, trains, and buses, giving any messages on the bags high exposure.

To use bags effectively, you need to make them far easier to read and far more interesting than the average brown paper or white plastic shopping bag. Remember, you're not just designing a bag — you're designing a form of outdoor advertising. So apply the same design principles. Come up with a *hook* — a striking image or attention-getting word or phrase that gets everyone looking at that bag. And try alternative colors or shapes. (By the way, most bag suppliers can customize their bags — check with suppliers in your local area. If no suppliers around you can, contact printers and silk-screeners. They can always handle bag orders for you, too.)

You can license the right to use a humorous cartoon from www.cartoonbank.com. Print that cartoon on a T-shirt or bag with the message "Brought to you by [your company]" and you won't believe how many people notice and appreciate it.

If you offer the biggest, strongest bag in a shopping area, you can be sure that shoppers stuff everyone else's bags into yours, giving your advertising message the maximum exposure. Sure, bigger, stronger bags cost more, which is why most stores offer wimpy bags that hurt your hands or rip open and spill their contents in the mud. But if you have an ad message you can get across with a bag, compare the cost of a better bag to other media. Pretty cheap, right? So why not go for it?

If you aren't in the retail business, you may think that this idea doesn't apply to you. Wrong! Plenty of store managers view bags as an irritating expense, rather than a marketing medium. Offer to supply them with better bags for free, in exchange for the right to print your message on the bags. Voilá! A new marketing medium for your program.

Discovering Flags, Banners, and Awnings

I have a theory that the first marketing or advertising by human beings took the form of a flag. It is still a simple but powerful way to communicate an identity or brand.

Outdoor messages on canvas or synthetic cloth make up an important part of many marketing programs. Think of a flag as a more dynamic kind of sign, and try to find ways to use them to build brand awareness, to make your location(s) more visible, or to get a marketing message displayed in more forms and places than you could otherwise. Also note that the costs of cloth-based forms of advertising can be surprisingly reasonable.

Flagging down your customers

The Metropolitan Museum of Art in New York City uses huge, brightly colored cloth banners to promote special shows. These banners make a wonderfully decorative contrast to the old gray stone of the building's facade, and they attract considerable attention from passersby on the busy street and sidewalks below.

A number of companies specialize in making custom-designed flags and banners. Of course, you see tacky paper banners — often produced by the local photocopy store — hanging in the windows of retail shops on occasion. But I'm not talking about those banners (because they probably don't help your image). I mean a huge, beautiful cloth flag flapping in the breeze. Or a bold 3-x-5-foot screen-printed flag suspended like a banner on an office or trade-show wall. Or a nylon table banner that turns the front and sides of a table into space for your marketing message. Or a street-wide banner, suspended from a wire cable, complete with air vents, tie-downs, and even sand pockets to keep the message readable in any weather.

Consider using a flag or banner as a sign for your store or business. So few marketers take advantage of this way to use a banner that it can help you stand out. A flag or banner is less static and dull than the typical metal or wood sign. Cloth moves, and even when it isn't moving, you know it has the potential for movement — giving the banner a bit of excitement. Also, flags or banners often seem decorative and festive. People associate flags and banners with special events because these decorations are traditionally used in that context, instead of for permanent display.

The smaller size and decorative nature of most flags and banners make them less offensive than other forms of outdoor advertising (especially those big billboards along freeways and in downtown areas that many people find annoying). In the United States, many communities and several states have created partial or full bans on billboards, but none have banned flags and banners. (Although zoning laws may require approval of your design. Check with your local town hall.) So if you find yourself in a community where you may encounter problems with public acceptance of a large billboard message, try a more low-key, decorative approach by using multiple flags and banners, instead. You need to find lower, nearer locations to display them because they're smaller than a billboard (I cover billboards in the "Posters and Billboards: Understanding Large Outdoor Ad Requirements" section later in this chapter). Check with a local realty firm to line up building owners willing to fly your flags. It's worth a try!

Flag companies give you all these options and more. These businesses regularly sew and screen large pieces of fabric, and they can also supply you with cables, poles, and other hardware you need to display flags and banners. In recent years, silk-screening technology and strong synthetic fibers have made flags and banners brighter and more permanent, expanding their uses in marketing. Check it out!

You can find a full line of stock and custom products available from the Arista Flag Corp. (www.aristaflag.com, 914-246-7700, or 800-382-4776). Ask for its custom flag and banner price list, which includes a lot of design ideas and specs, and also ask to see photos of effective banners from clients as diverse as Xerox, *The New Yorker,* the YMCA Summer Camp, and the Coca-Cola Concert Series.

Figure 8-1 illustrates the most common standard options and terminology of the flag and banner industry.

Canopies and awnings

If appropriate for your business, consider using an awning and canopy (most telephone directories list providers under the **awning and canopy** heading). For retailers, awnings and canopies often provide the boldest and most attractive form of roadside sign. Office sites may also find awnings and canopies valuable.

Awnings combine structural value with marketing value by shading the interior and can even extend the floor space of your store by capturing some of the sidewalk as transition space. An awning can perform all the functions a sign can, and more, and it can do so in a way that's highly visible but not intrusive. Yards and yards of awnings don't look as crass and commercial as huge signs because your eye accepts them as a structural part of the building. So you get the same amount of advertising as with a big sign without looking pushy.

Y-M-C-A

A YMCA Summer Camp banner is a great example of how to use the banner medium well. I'll give you a verbal picture of it: A series of silhouettes of kids playing take up the top two-thirds of this wider-than-it-is-tall banner — these simple visuals illustrate children playing basketball, jumping rope, playing baseball, swimming, and doing gymnastics. The bottom third contains the only copy, in big, clear capital letters: "YMCA" and its logo on one line, and

"Summer Camp" just below that line. With this minimal design, the banner conveys the brand name and tells us a lot about what the YMCA Summer Camp offers to whom. And the shiny cloth banner gives viewers the idea that the message must be something special and exciting. And because it's a banner, it can easily be displayed seasonally and then stored until the next spring sign-up period.

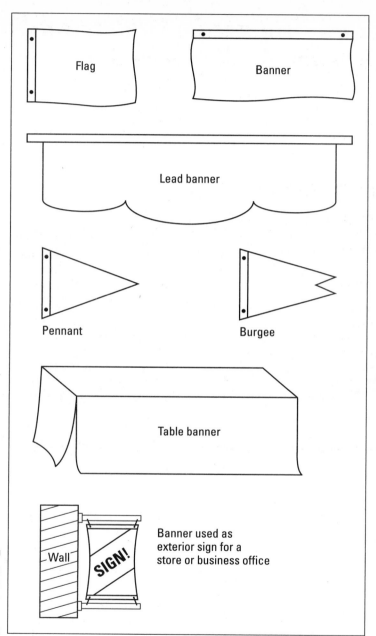

Flag

Banner

Lead banner

Pennant

Burgee

Table banner

Wall

SIGN!

Banner used as
exterior sign for a
store or business office

Figure 8-1:
Flag and
banner
options.

Posters and Billboards: Understanding Large Outdoor Ad Requirements

You view posters and billboards from a distance. Billboards along roads need to be readable from hundreds of feet away, which gives you a difficult design challenge.

Here's a simple exercise to help you understand the design requirements for a billboard. Draw a rectangular box on a sheet of blank paper, using a ruler as your guide. Make the box 2¼ inches wide and 1 inch high. That's the proportion of a standard outdoor *poster* (a large, printed advertisement posted on a signboard or building). Although a poster is much larger, that poster, from a distance, may look as small as that box on your sheet. (See Figure 8-2.) Now hold your paper (or Figure 8-2) at arm's length and think about what copy and artwork can fit in this space, while remaining readable to passersby at this distance. Not much, right? Be careful to limit your message to a few, bold words and images, or your poster becomes a mess that no one can read.

Figure 8-2:
From a distance, a large roadside poster looks no bigger than this image.

CAN YOU READ THIS
CAN YOU READ THIS
CAN YOU READ THIS
CAN YOU READ THIS
CAN YOU READ THIS

That's the problem with outdoor advertising, in general — viewers have to read the ad in a hurry, and often from a considerable distance. So the ad has to be simple. Yet people who travel the same road or sidewalk (or take the same elevator or ride the same bus route) view the same ad daily. So that ad has to combine lasting interest with great simplicity. That's tough!

Outdoor advertising is like print advertising, except that outdoor advertising must use far fewer words and far simpler images to make its point more economically and clearly — but, hopefully, with an entertaining hook. With all these constraints, you see the difficulty of designing effective outdoor ads. Make your message fun, beautiful, or at least important and clear, so that people don't resent having to see it often.

Deciding on formats for outdoor ads

You have several standard choices regarding the size of your outdoor ad and its distance from the average viewer.

- ✔ You can choose a standard *30-sheet poster* (although, with modern printing, they don't have to use 30 separate sheets anymore!). This billboard-sized ad measures 21 feet 7 inches wide by 9 feet 7 inches high.

- ✔ You can use a *bulletin,* a huge version of the poster that usually measures 48 feet wide by 14 feet high (these ads may be 10 x 30 feet or 10.6 x 30 feet in places). You can extend bulletins with extra panels on the bottom, sides, or top (see Figure 8-3 for details). A bulletin is four times as big as a 30-sheet poster, giving it incredible impact close up. Bulletins also make the text readable from a greater distance, so they work well along high-speed roads where the viewer isn't near your ad for long enough to read anything requiring close attention.

- ✔ You can also scale down for sidewalk-level viewing to the standard 11-x-5-foot *eight-sheet poster,* also called a *junior poster* in the industry. This poster is about a sixth the size of the standard 30-sheet poster. But when you place an eight-sheet poster closer to viewers than a standard-sized poster can be, it's sometimes even more effective than the bigger formats. Anyway, advertisers seem to think so; the format is growing in popularity.

- ✔ You can choose something oversized (and not standard) — a huge *spectacular,* a custom-made, often building-sized display such as those ads that grace Times Square in New York. These massive ads cost a bundle, and you should generally treat these ads as long-term, image-building investments.

  If you want to show your new pest control spray killing a giant cockroach, perhaps you should consider a giant can of the stuff on top of a building, timed to emit a puff of harmless spray once a minute in the face of a huge cockroach that is crawling up the outside of the building. Pretty? No. Attention-getting? Yes. Few rules apply to spectaculars — aside from the rules of gravity and engineering — so you can have some fun with this unusual form of outdoor advertising.

Figure 8-3 shows the proportions and relative sizes of the standard outdoor formats.

You can also explore the growing number of variations on these standards. Want your message displayed on the floor of a building lobby, on a kiosk at a mall, or alongside the notice boards at health and fitness centers? Or how about on signs surrounding the arenas and courts of athletic events? You can use all these options and more, by directly contacting the businesses that control such spaces or using one of a host of ad agencies and media-buying firms that can give you larger-scale access.

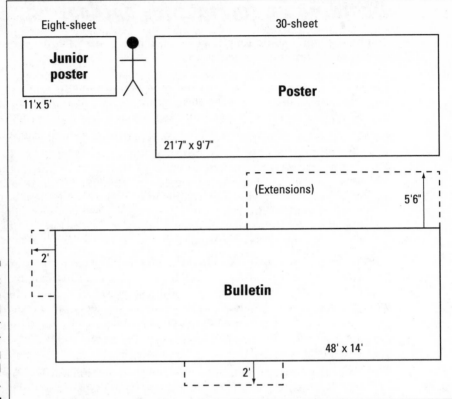

Figure 8-3:
Three
standard
sizes for
outdoor
advertising
in the United
States.

Maximizing the returns on outdoor advertising

The costs of outdoor advertising vary widely. But to give you some idea of what's involved, a bulletin along an expressway in the mid-sized city of Denver, Colorado, costs $3,815 per month to rent. If you rent a similar bulletin in the smaller, nearby city of Colorado Springs, where the freeway sees less traffic, it costs you $2,730 per month, according to Lamar Outdoor Advertising (www. lamarcolorado.com).

Given the high traffic rates on many expressways, you can get a pretty good buy for a billboard on a cost per thousand (CPM) viewers basis. For example, a Denver bulletin delivers about 34,100 exposures. You don't know the *reach* (number of viewers) versus *frequency* (how many times viewers see your ad), but the number generally ranges from 28 to 15 times per month in surveys (see www.cuposter.com). That reach works out to a price of $3,815 ÷ 34,100, or $0.11 per thousand exposures. Although prices vary — and I picked an especially cheap price to illustrate my point — outdoor advertising gives you cheap exposure, on a CPM basis.

A study from Simmons Market Research Bureau estimates the average U.S. 30-sheet poster reaches adults 18 years and older at a CPM of $1.43 per thousand. Although that's a far higher number than my quick estimate for that Denver billboard, it's still far cheaper than most other media. (Radio costs about twice that figure, and billboard costs are only a small fraction of TV and print costs!)

You can get statistics on billboards from *Out-of-Home Advertising Source,* published by SRDS in Des Plaines, Illinois (www.srds.com, 847-375-5000, or 800-851-7737). This annual publication covers the U.S. outdoor market for about $350, so unless you plan to do a fair amount of outdoor advertising, you may want to sweet-talk a local ad agency into looking up pricing in their copy, instead of buying your own.

Of course, the CPM figures I calculated and the average figure from Simmons give a serious market planner only the beginning point for cost estimates. You need to factor in your estimate of the percent of exposures that reach your target market This estimate may be small, given the numbers of people the ad can potentially reach (in which case the divisor in that CPM equation goes down and the price goes up). Simmons estimates, for example, that the average CPM for reaching female baby boomers aged 25-49 with a 30-sheet poster is $6.11 — more than four times as costly as when you don't care what sort of adults your poster reaches.

You need to consider the likelihood that those exposures lose value after the commuter has seen your billboard many days in a row. Do you get the same effect from the tenth viewing of a billboard as you do from the first or second? Will anyone even bother to look at the same billboard multiple times? Often not. In outdoor advertising, marketers talk about *reexamination rates,* the average number of times viewers bother to read the same outdoor ad. The best billboards have higher reexamination rates because people find them interesting enough to look at again and again.

Keep the limited message potential of outdoor advertising in mind. What you can communicate for that cheap price is pretty minimal, too.

Still, at those prices, outdoor advertising gives you a good buy. If you want cheap exposure for your brand name or to make consumers aware of a local product or service in a hurry, you can draw attention to your product by using the cheapest kind of advertising: outdoor ads. And in most urban markets, you can readily purchase enough outdoor advertising to (theoretically, at least) cover the entire market. The out-of-home advertising industry calls this practice a *100 showing,* meaning that you have enough billboards at viable locations to make exposing 100 percent of the people in that market to your message possible. (Similarly, a *50 showing* gives you a maximum of 50 percent coverage.)

As in print advertising in general, the costs vary based on ad size, as well as audience size. A bulletin costs about four times as much as the standard poster ad — reflecting the fact that a bulletin is about four times as big as a poster. A junior poster costs about a quarter of a poster ad, being about a sixth as large.

However, effectiveness does not vary with size in outdoor advertising as much as it does in standard print advertising for two reasons, each of them exploitable by savvy marketers:

✔ When you read a magazine, your distance from the ads remains (relatively) constant, regardless of the ad's size. But in outdoor ads, you generally place the smaller format ads closer to a flow of traffic than the larger ones. So a junior poster may be effectively as large and readable as a poster, in spite of its smaller size, because you place it down low and close to the road. Even if your junior poster isn't quite as impressive as a larger format billboard, it's still much more than a quarter as impressive because it's viewed from closer — so it's truly a bargain by comparison.

✔ Second, outdoor ads differ from print ads in magazines and newspapers in that the speed with which the viewer or reader notes the ad isn't constant for outdoor ads. You can assume that people flip through the pages of a magazine at the same rate, regardless of whether you buy a quarter-page or full-page spread. That's why the full-page spread catches the reader's eye more effectively — it stands out much better in that split second in which her eye scans the page before turning it.

Companies that sell outdoor advertising space operate on a similar premise. Those setting rates assume all traffic is equal because they often base these rates on *traffic counts* (number of vehicles per day — or day and night if you illuminate your poster— multiplied by the average occupancy of a vehicle). But a big difference exists between someone viewing a poster at 65 miles per hour on a freeway, someone viewing a poster at 45 miles per hour on a local road, and someone sitting next to a poster for ten minutes in the traffic jam leading to a toll booth or bridge. If you or your media buyer care enough to shop around (and possibly wait your turn) for locations with high- and low-speed traffic, you can get a billboard that a higher percentage of the people who pass by read more slowly and carefully!

Remember, not all outdoor advertising is equal. Location makes a huge difference in the effectiveness of your ad. And a smart shopper can find good locations that give a bigger bang for the buck than the average outdoor ad space. That's why some outdoor advertisers hoard good spaces, even committing to rent them for years at a time just to hold onto them.

Transit Advertising: Messages on the Move!

Transit advertising is any advertising in or on public transportation systems. These ads can appear in buses, taxis, commuter trains, and subway systems, along with airport, bus, train, and ferry terminals. Who knows? Maybe NASA will start renting ad space on the outside of its rockets some day.

The advertising industry classifies transit advertising as a form of outdoor advertising. This classification is misleading because you set up some transit ads indoors: ads at airport terminals, ads displayed within subway cars, and so on. Such confusion surrounding the term *outdoor* led to the development of the alternative term *out-of-home*. Out-of-home describes transit advertising better because transit advertising aims at people in transit rather than sitting in their homes.

Transit ads work well if you get the people in transit to take an interest in your product, from consumer products to business services. I've seen transit ads generate sales leads for local real estate agents and for international consulting firms. Yet few marketers make use of them. Consider being an innovator and trying transit ads, even if your competitors don't.

Standard options — the ones most easily available through media buying firms and ad agencies — include shelter panels, and bus and taxi exterior signs, and posters and back-lit signs in airports.

Shelter panels are 46-x-67-inch posters (in some cities — in others, different standards apply). These ads appear at bus-stop shelters. You can mount them behind a Lucite sheet to minimize the graffiti problem. In many cities, designers have back-lit some of the shelter panels for nighttime display. A one-month showing typically costs anywhere from $300 to $1,000, depending upon the city. You may need as many as 100 to 300 panels to achieve enough exposures to reach a 100-percent showing in a city, depending upon the city's size.

Bus signs come with well-accepted standards in North America — although some local bus services now offer the option of full-bus painting, as well. Here are the typical bus standards:

- ✔ **Large bus poster:** A 30-x-144-inch poster in a frame mounted on the side of the bus. This poster can be displayed on the street side or curbside (in the United States, the street side is generally the right-hand side). Sometimes called a *king-size ad*.

- ✔ **Medium bus poster:** A 30-x-88-inch poster, especially suited for the curbside of a bus. If you want to make sure that bus passengers and other pedestrians on the route see your poster, then the curbside is for you! Sometimes called a *queen-size ad*.

- **Small bus poster:** A 21-x-44-inch poster on the side of a bus, sometimes called a *traveling display.* If you have a simple message and a tight budget, this format may be big enough to give you the visibility you need.

- **Front and rear bus displays:** These ads measure 21 x 70 inches and give high visibility to drivers near the bus. A rear-end poster (or *tail-light ad*) gives great exposure to people in cars behind the bus. But if the bus exhaust is messy, your ad may not look so great after a few days. Check it out before buying.

- **Combinations:** Sometimes advertisers combine a front-end bus ad (or *headlighter*) with a curbside ad to maximize impact on pedestrians as they watch the bus go by. Add a shelter poster to the mix, and you have incredibly good coverage! Such combinations can be effective, especially if you think your ad may be challenging to read or you want to display two or three complementary ads to the same viewer.

If you are advertising in a European or other country, these North American standards may not apply. Outdoor ads, in general, and especially transit ads, aren't fully standardized in all countries. So check with the bus line, billboard owner, or whoever controls the ad space before you design your ad.

Airport advertising is a relatively new option but is taking off fast. If you want a relatively well-to-do audience with a rich mix of tourists and professional travelers, enquire about airport advertising options or visit brokers with Web information about transit advertising at sites such as www.metromarkcorp.com and www.travel-marketing.com, which overview options for U.S. airports and their equivalents in other countries (such as www.airport-advertising.co.uk).

You find one definite advantage in transit advertising — it typically delivers high frequency of viewer notices in a short period of time. Public transit vehicles generally travel the same routes over and over, and so almost everyone along the route sees an ad multiple times.

Keep this high frequency in mind when designing transit ads — you want to make sure that your ad doesn't become tedious or irritating upon repeated exposures. Avoid cheap humor and overly simplistic gimmicks.

Consider breaking the rule of outdoor advertising that says you have to make your design clear and simple. In transit advertising, you may be better off to layer the design so that you provide a clear, large-scale, simple message for first-time viewers — but also a more detailed design and message for repeat viewers to find within the poster. You can do something like hiding a Waldo-like character in your ads for people to find. Or including a riddle or puzzle for viewers to solve. You need to allow viewers to go deeper into the design over time each time they see it. This attraction should help keep the ad fresh and build viewer's interest in the ad and its message. You just need to use your imagination to figure out how to accomplish this goal for your business or product. Give it a try — if you succeed, your ad can draw all kinds of attention!

Does your company have its own vehicles on the road? If so, are you using them for outdoor advertising? Most marketers say either "no" or "sort of" when I ask them this question. Small, cheap, magnetic signs on the doors don't count. Nor does just a painted name on the door or side panel of a truck. If you pay for as much display space as even a standard-sized van offers, you probably hire a designer or agency and put great care into your message. And, in fact, you are paying for the exterior space on your vehicles; the cost just doesn't show up in the marketing budget. So why not cash in on this investment more fully by treating that truck or van as a serious advertising medium? Mount frames for bus-sized posters and display a professionally designed ad that you change monthly or weekly. Or hire a competent airbrush painter to do a more permanent, custom job on each vehicle.

When I say your own vehicles offer "free" advertising space, I'm not being entirely accurate. You do need to spend extra money cleaning your vehicles often so that the ads look good. As with all signs and outdoor ads, appearance is key — you need to clean and maintain those ads on a regular schedule. But when the ads are on your own vehicles, you can far more easily manage their appearance than with other outdoor advertising, when the ads may be spread across commercial outdoor or transit advertising space.

Chapter 9

Radio, Video, and TV

• •

In This Chapter

▶ Designing ads for radio

▶ Creating great video ads for little cash

▶ Using the emotional power of television

• •

Radio and television are well-established, extremely powerful marketing media, while video (especially if shot in digital format) is a hot new item for streaming-video messages on your Web site. Video also offers marketing messages on television screens and computers in your booth at a trade show.

The problem, traditionally, with radio and TV is that the costs associated with producing and broadcasting ads have been quite high, making these media too expensive for smaller marketers. I want to encourage you to be open-minded about radio, video, and TV, because new and easier ways to produce in these media are emerging all the time, along with a growing number of low-cost ways to broadcast your ads. Every year brings more radio and television channels, including cable TV, Web-based radio, and (soon) Web-based television options.

And even if you don't use these commercial media, you can quite possibly find more limited ways to share your ads with prospects. In fact, more and more marketers use CDs or Web sites that communicate in digital video, or with PowerPoint-type slides and radio-style voice-overs. Modern technology is making these media more flexible and affordable for all marketers.

Producing Ads for Radio

I have a set of tapes of old radio shows featuring that amateur sleuth known as The Shadow. My family and I have been listening to these classic radio dramas for years. Why are the old radio dramas so engaging? Because you can *see* the action so clearly as it unfolds. The script and sound effects (*SF* or *SFX* in radio lingo) create a string of powerful visual images in your mind as the story unfolds (note that the script tells you what supposedly makes the sound effects to make sure you can picture what's going on).

"Oh no, the giant black cat is coming toward us! My God, its eyes are glowing!" *(SF: Meeeowww. Snarl, snarl.)* "Help, it's backing me toward the edge of the roof of this ten-story building!" *(SF: Snarl, spit, snarl.)* "Look out Margo, you'll fall off!" *(SF: Sound of falling, with a woman's scream fading into distance.)*

You can see what's happening, can't you?

Conventional wisdom says you have only three elements to work with when you design for radio: words, sound effects, and music. And that's true in a literal sense, but you can't create a great radio ad unless you remember that you want to use those elements to generate *mental images* for the listener. And that means you can often perform the same basic plot on radio as on TV. Radio isn't really as limited as people think. People just rarely use radio to full advantage anymore, now that society's love affair with radio has been eclipsed by its love of TV and movies.

Favor direct over indirect action goals for radio ads. Sure, sometimes you want to use radio just to create brand awareness *(indirect-action advertising)*. But in general, the most effective radio ads call for direct action. Give out a Web address (if the listener can remember that address easily) or a toll-free number in the ad.

Put your brand name into your radio ad early and often, regardless of the story line. If you fail to generate the desired direct action, at least you build awareness and interest for the brand, which supports other points of contact in your marketing program. Radio is a great support medium, and not enough marketers use it that way. You may as well fill the vacuum with *your* marketing message!

Sound effects hazard ahead

I want to add a simple rule that can keep you out of trouble by helping you avoid confusion. Be sure that your script identifies all sound effects. Sound effects are wonderful and evocative, but in truth, many sound just about alike. Without context, rain on the roof can sound like bacon sizzling in a pan, a blowtorch cutting through the metal door of a bank vault, or even an alien spaceship starting up. So the script must identify that sound, either through direct reference ("Oh boy, I think that alien spaceship's motor is starting") or through context.

You can provide context with the script, the plot, or simply by other sound effects. The sounds of eggs cracking and hitting a hot pan, coffee percolating, and someone yawning all help to identify that sizzle as the breakfast bacon, rather than rain on the roof or that blowtorch cutting into a vault door.

Buying radio time

I often find myself urging marketers to try radio in place of their standard media choices. Why? Because, although local retailers frequently use radio for pull-oriented advertising, most other marketers overlook radio as a viable medium. Those advertisers don't realize how powerful radio can be — and they may not be aware of its incredible reach. In the United States, 95 percent of teenagers and adults listen to radio each week (according to Arbitron National Database), and 81 percent are listening on any given day. That's a lot of people. I bet your target audience is in there somewhere! (Also consider radio for all your publicity needs. You can find a lot of radio talk shows willing to invite you on as a guest if you pitch your expertise well and have a unique angle to discuss.)

Arbitron Inc. is the leading source of audited information about audience size and composition for television and radio stations in the United States and is also now providing information and assistance for those who want to purchase radio and video ad time on Webcasts. Visit Arbitron on the Web at www.arbitron.com if you're curious about its extensive operations. But as a marketer, you probably don't need to do business with them directly. The radio and TV stations or networks hire Arbitron to survey their audiences, and those stations or networks share the information with you and other potential advertisers for free.

Radio has a broader reach than that of other media in the United States (and many other nations, as well). Table 9-1 shows the daily reach figures for U.S. radio, TV, and newspapers.

Table 9-1	Reach Out and Touch Someone
Advertising Medium	*Daily Reach (Percentage of U.S. Population 18 Years Old and Over)*
Radio	81%
Television	76%
Newspapers	69%

Theoretically, radio can deliver a larger audience for your ads than print or TV can. Radio definitely gives you a good medium for broad reach goals.

You can also target radio advertising quite narrowly — both by type of audience and by geographic area. This fact helps make radio a very good buy. The general lack of appreciation for this medium also helps by keeping ad prices artificially low.

Radio ads are 77 percent cheaper than television ads and 86 percent cheaper than newspaper ads in the United States. And radio is generally cheaper in other countries, too. Radio programmers don't charge more for advertising slots partly because of the problem that people may not be paying any attention to the radio they have on in the background. But a well-designed ad can often capture their attention for a few seconds. Radio can be an awfully good buy, regardless of its differences from other media. (In Chapter 8, I talk about why outdoor advertising is also an incredibly good buy.)

Targeted advertising via radio

I like the fact that radio stations make a real effort to target specific audiences — after all, most advertisers try to do the same thing. You can get good data, both demographic and lifestyle- or attitude-oriented information, on radio audiences. And you can often find radio stations (or specific programs on those stations) that reach a well-defined audience, rich in those people you want to target, making radio an even better buy.

You can get details of audience characteristics for all U.S. radio stations from SRDS (Standard Rate and Date Service) in Des Plaines, Illinois (www.srds.com or 800-851-7737). A quarterly SRDS publication with daily electronic updates, *Radio Advertising Source* gives you enough information to plan most radio campaigns and handle buying radio ad slots. The publication offers details of how to buy radio time on the state, regional, or national levels for major campaigns. And SRDS can provide information in other formats and at other price levels, if you need it. A one-year subscription costs $467, so only people who really need this book should shell out the money for it. And if you work with radio, you're one of those people who needs it. (Alternatively, don't forget you can simply call any local station and ask for its audited report on its listeners, a document it gives a potential advertiser for free.)

And here's another option for radio advertising that you may not have considered. How about running ads over the internal broadcasting systems used in many stores? This opportunity gives you another great way to target a particular audience — for example, advertise your brand of tires at an automotive store. Marketers call this kind of ad *in-store audio advertising*. In-store audio advertising is an entirely different medium from a buying perspective because the store or a specialized service provider develops and controls the programming. As a result, most marketers don't know how to use in-store audio programming. But an ad agency may be able to help you gain access, and some specialized media-buying firms handle this kind of advertising, too. For example, 3M Media can book in-store audio advertising for you in a hundred different U.S. markets.

So remember: Don't overlook radio! It can give you better reach, better focus on your target market, and a lower cost per thousand exposures than any other medium. Like TV, radio can *show* as well as tell — you just have to use the listener's imagination to create visual images. And if you manage to create a really good script, I guarantee you can catch and hold audience attention.

Cheaper Ways to Use the Power of Video

If you're thinking of skipping this section, consider this: Video can cost $2,000 per minute to produce — or even $20,000 if you're making a sophisticated national TV ad. But it can also cost $100 a minute or less.

Do you have access to a good (emphasis on "good") hand-held digital video camera? Well, that (when combined with a high-quality microphone) is actually capable of producing effective video for your marketing, especially for use on the Web where low resolution video files are usually used, making camera quality less important. Many marketers don't realize that the limiting factor in inexpensive or homemade video is usually the sound quality, not the picture quality. So as long as you plug in a remote microphone and put it near anyone who is speaking, you can probably make usable video yourself.

Here are some tips if you decide to shoot video yourself:

- ✔ Write a simple, clear script, and time it before you bother to shoot any video.

- ✔ Clean up the background. Most amateur efforts to shoot video presentations or ads for marketing are plagued by stuff that shows up in the background. Eliminate trash cans, competitors' signs, and anything else unsightly.

- ✔ Use enough light, and try to have multiple light sources. A digital video camera is just a fancy camera, and it needs light to work. Normal indoor lighting is too dim for quality video. Instead, add more lights, including bright floodlights and open windows. And make sure light shines from both sides so that you fill the shadows. (Shadowed areas get darker in the video.)

- ✔ Shoot everything more than once. Editing is easy (well, easier) as a result of the many software programs you can use on your own PC to edit video. But editing is much easier if you have lots of footage to select from. When I shoot myself talking about a new product (for my Web site), I always repeat each short section several times. Then, in editing, I choose the version that came out best. That's how they make movie stars look good, and it can work well for you, too!

✔ You can produce radio ads or sound-only messages for your Web site using the same digital recording and editing capabilities as you use to do homemade digital video. The key is a quiet environment and a good microphone for recording. Or you can go into a production studio's sound booth and let the technicians there worry about the technical aspects.

✔ If you want actors, consider recruiting them locally and even asking people to volunteer. I hate to promote this idea, but if you can avoid paying union rates for your actors, you're better off; assuming you have a smaller company with a modest marketing budget. Paying union rates and residuals is appropriate for major or national campaigns but can be prohibitive for small marketers.

For information on editing and production, check out the many *For Dummies* books that help you better understand what's involved. Or hire a media production firm (I use MediaPro in San Francisco) that can do high-quality work at moderate rates. With plenty of smaller production firms around, try interviewing some in your area and getting samples of their work plus price quotes — you may find that by the time you master the software and come up to speed, you're spending as much doing your own work!

Designing Ads for TV

Television is much like theater. TV combines visual and verbal channels in real-time action, making it a remarkably rich medium. Yes, you have to make the writing as tight and compelling as good print copy, but the words must also sound good and must flow with the visuals to create drama or comedy.

TV ads must use great drama (whether funny or serious), condensed to a few seconds of memorable action. Think of a really powerful, moving, and memorable scene from a movie. How about (if you're a Bogart fan) the scene from *To Have and to Have Not,* in which Lauren Bacall tells Humphrey Bogart, as she slinks out of his hotel room, that all he has to do is whistle if he wants her back. It's one of the most well-known sequences in the movies.

These few seconds of drama seem to etch themselves into the memory of anyone who watches that film. Why? I don't know for sure. You can't really reduce great theater to a formula. A good script with just the right touch of just the right emotion. Great acting. Good camera work and a good set. The suspense of a developing relationship between two interesting characters. You don't need to achieve this level of artistry to make a good TV ad, but you certainly need to achieve a higher-than-average level to stand out. And if you can create truly great TV, your ad pays off in gold.

TV looks simple when you see it, but don't be fooled — it's not simple at all. Hire an experienced production company to help you do the ad, or do what many marketers do and hire a big ad agency (at big ad agency dollars) to design and supervise the production of your ad. This choice costs you, but at least you get quality work. Just remember that *you* ultimately decide whether the script has that star potential or is just another forgettable ad. Don't let the production company shoot until they have something as memorable as an old Bogart film (or at least close).

If you work for a smaller business and are used to shoestring marketing budgets, you may be shaking your head at my advice. You think you can do it yourself. Yes, I know you can go to a local cable station and shoot your own talking-head ads in its studio at little cost. But, boy, do those ads look cheap when shown on the local network affiliate right next to expensive ads from national advertisers. Why embarrass yourself in your own local market, and why waste even a little money on ads that don't work? If you're going to do TV, do it right. Either become expert yourself or hire an expert. Without high quality production, even the best design doesn't work. Why? Because people watch so much TV that they know the difference between good and bad ads — and they don't bother to watch anything but the best.

Simple video can look great in other contexts, like your Web site or a booth at a trade show, even if it wouldn't fly on television. (See the "Cheaper Ways to Use the Power of Video" section earlier in this chapter.)

Here's a bit of advice to balance the preceding warning. If you're on a shoestring budget, consider doing a self-made *spoof ad*. Make fun of one of the silly TV ad genres, like the one where an overenthusiastic salesman does a frantic 30-second sell. Because the whole point is to make a campy spoof, you don't want high production value. You can do this strategy on your own pretty easily, but you still need help from someone with experience in setting up shots and handling camera and lights.

Sometimes, film students at a nearby college are eager to help you produce your ad. To them, it's an opportunity to show they can do professional work. For you, it may be an opportunity to get near-professional work at very low prices. But make sure the terms are clear upfront. Both the students and their professors need to clarify (in writing) that you will own the resulting work and can use it in your marketing.

Getting emotional

TV differs from other media in the obvious way — by combining action, audio, and video — but these features make TV different in less obvious ways, as well. It is especially easy to evoke emotions in TV and video, just like traditional theater. When you plan to use TV as your marketing tool, always think about what emotion you want your audience to feel.

Select an emotional state that fits best with your appeal and the creative concept behind your ad. Then use the power of imagery to evoke that emotion. This strategy works whether your appeal is emotional or rational. Always use the emotional power of TV to prepare your audience to receive that appeal. Surprise. Excitement. Empathy. Anxiety. Skepticism. Thirst. Hunger. The protective instincts of the parent. You can create all these emotional states and more in your audience with a few seconds of TV. A good ad generates the right emotion to prime viewers for your appeal. The classic Prudential commercial ("Own a piece of the rock") is a strictly emotional appeal, designed to give us a feeling of permanence and dependability about the investment products the company pitches.

Some marketers measure their TV ads based on warmth. Research firms generally define warmth as the good feelings generated from thinking about love, family, or friendship. Although you may not need to go into the details of how researchers measure warmth, noting *why* people measure warmth can help you. Emotions, especially positive ones, make TV ad messages far more memorable. Many marketers don't realize the strength of this emotional effect because you can't pick the effect up in the standard measures of ad recall. In day-after recall tests, viewers recall emotional-appeal TV ads about as easily as rational-appeal ads. But in-depth studies of the effectiveness of each kind of ad tends to show that the more emotionally charged ads do a better job of etching the message and branding identity in viewers' minds.

So when you think TV advertising, think emotion. That's what TV can do — often better than any other media, because it can showcase the expressiveness of actors and faces — and emotion makes for highly effective advertising.

Look, Ma . . .

Be sure to take full advantage of TV's other great strength: its ability to show. You can demonstrate a product feature, show a product in use, and do a thousand other things just with your visuals.

Actually, in any ad medium, you want to show as well as tell. (Even in radio, you can create mental images to show the audience what you want them to see. I explain how in "Producing Ads for Radio" earlier in this chapter.) The visual and verbal modes reinforce each other. And some people in your audience think visually, although others favor a verbal message, so you have to cover both bases by using words and images in your advertising. But in TV, you have to adapt this rule: The TV ad should *show* and tell (note the emphasis on showing). Compare this with radio, where you show by telling. Or print, where the two modes balance each other out, so the rule becomes simply to show and tell.

TV ad designers rough out their ideas in a visually oriented script, using quick sketches to indicate how the ad will look, because of this emphasis on showing. You — or preferably the competent agency or scriptwriter you hire — need to prepare rough storyboards as you think through and discuss various ad concepts. A *storyboard* is an easy way to show the key visual images of film, using pictures in sequence. The sketches run down the center of a sheet of paper or poster board in most standard storyboard layouts. On the left, you write notes about how to shoot each image, how to use music and sound effects, and whether to superimpose text on the screen. On the right, you include a rough version of the *script* (the words actors in the scenes or in a voice-over say). See Figure 9-1 for an example storyboard.

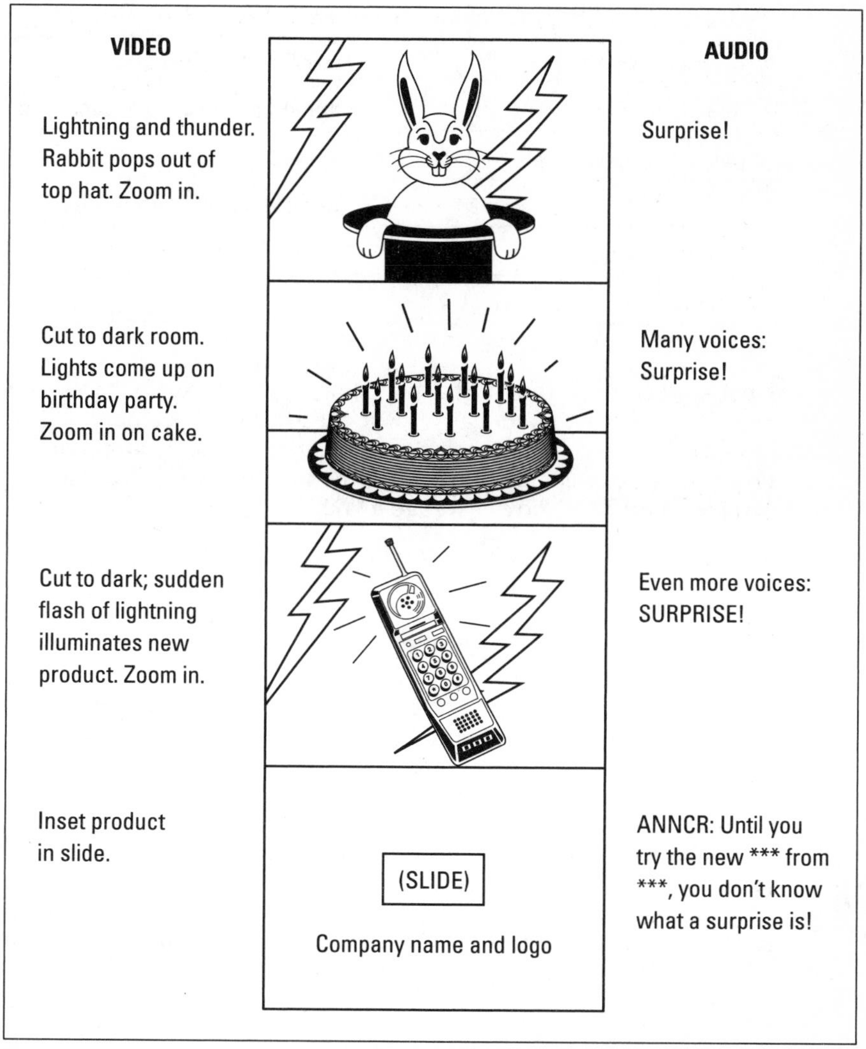

VIDEO		AUDIO
Lightning and thunder. Rabbit pops out of top hat. Zoom in.		Surprise!
Cut to dark room. Lights come up on birthday party. Zoom in on cake.		Many voices: Surprise!
Cut to dark; sudden flash of lightning illuminates new product. Zoom in.		Even more voices: SURPRISE!
Inset product in slide.	(SLIDE) Company name and logo	ANNCR: Until you try the new *** from ***, you don't know what a surprise is!

Figure 9-1: Roughing out a TV ad on a storyboard.

A question of style

You can use a great variety of styles in TV advertising. A celebrity can endorse the product. Claymation fruit can sing and dance about it. Animated animals can chase a user through the jungle in a fanciful exaggeration of a real-life situation. Imagination and videotape know no limits, especially with the recent growing availability of high-quality computerized animation and special effects at a reasonable cost. But some of the common styles work better — on average — than others in tests of ad effectiveness. Table 9-2 shows styles that are more and less effective.

Table 9-2 It Don't Mean a Thing If It Ain't Got That Swing	
More Effective Styles	*Less Effective Styles*
Humorous commercials	Candid-camera style testimonials
Celebrity spokespeople	Expert endorsements
Commercials with children	Song/dance and musical themes
Real-life scenarios	Product demonstrations
Brand comparisons	

Most studies show that both the humor and celebrity endorsement styles work best. So try to find ways to use these styles to communicate your message. On the other hand, making ads that are the exception to the rule may give you an edge, so don't give up hope on other styles. Just make sure that your ad lands well above average if you don't want the rule of averages to apply to it.

Buying ad time on TV

Which television venues work best for your ad? Should you advertise on a network or cable station? Should the ad run in prime time, evening, or late nighttime slots? What programs provide the best audience for your ad?

As in other media, buyers rely on demographic studies to find out about audience size and characteristics. The Simmons Market Research Bureau (www.smrb.com) and Mediamark Research (www.mediamark.com) both provide useful data in publications (which you can get by subscription), and *SRDS's TV and Cable Source* (you can find out more about this publication at `www.srds.com`) gives you an excellent source of data. And the SRDS publication is the only one I've seen that combines data on Asia, Europe, and Latin America, along with U.S. listings. (It's expensive, so try to borrow this publication from an ad agency or the nearest business library.)

But the research firm A.C. Nielsen provides the key data for North American television markets (`www.nielsenmedia.com`). The Nielsen Television Index rates programs based on *sweeps* (or four-times-a-year surveys of viewership in major media markets). The surveys require participants to keep logs of what they watch. And now a high-tech improvement over this approach has appeared online: in-home boxes called *people meters* that record what a household watches and relays that information to Nielsen (or to Arbitron, Nielsen's main competitor in this business). The resulting ratings tell you how many television sets tune in to any particular program in any geographic market. However, advertisers and the television industry argue about the accuracy of the Nielsen ratings constantly because slight differences in ratings make a big difference in the cost of advertising!

Rating surveys provide the following statistics by geographic area:

✔ How many TV sets are in the market in all (*television households* or *TVHHs*)

✔ How many TV sets are turned on at any given time (*households using TV* or *HUTs*)

✔ What percentage of the HUTs are tuned to a specific program (*audience share*)

✔ What percentage of the TVHHs are tuned to a specific program (*rating*)

Say a city has 800,000 TVHHs. If 200,000 (or 25 percent) of these TVHHs are tuned to a particular program, then that program gets a rating of 25. If half of all televisions are on, then HUT equals 400,000 households (or 50 percent), and that program's share of market is $200,000 \div 400,000$, or a 50 percent share.

In general, advertisers pay more attention to ratings than to share of market data, because ratings tell them how big the audience is, and they usually try to reach the largest audience possible with their ads.

A *gross rating point* (GRP) is the total rating points achieved by your *media schedule* (all the times you run an ad over a specific period). When media buyers purchase a series of time blocks on TV for your ad, they add up all the ratings from each of the times/places where your ad runs and give you the total — your campaign's GRPs. The number is big, but it doesn't tell you very much.

The GRP number doesn't distinguish between new exposures *(reach)* and repeat exposures *(frequency)*. Maybe your ad reached ten million television households, but did it reach the same one million households, ten times over — or did it reach ten million households, one time each? The answer probably lies somewhere in between. But how can you find out the exact answer? Obtaining reach and frequency estimates for any TV ad schedule helps you interpret the GRP figure. In some campaigns, you may want ten or twenty repetitions. In others, one or two may be your goal. Let your agency or media buyer know what your goal is. (See www.nielsenmedia.com/terms.htm for more on how reach and frequency are measured and reported.)

More repetitions increase the certainty and usability of the attitudes your ad forms in the viewer's mind. So plan on more repetitions if you need to reinforce these aspects of attitude. But one or a few repetitions can generally form the initial attitude, so you don't need many repetitions when you think the viewer will quickly agree with your ad's message and have no trouble remembering it in purchase situations.

You should add one further refinement to audience data. The statistics for advertisers break down the data into demographic and other categories to help you figure out what percentage of all those households that have tuned into a program are actually the right people — the group that your ad targets. And I recommend always converting overall ratings into a number that represents your own target market — that number is bound to be smaller because your target consists of only a portion of all those households viewing any particular program. And that means the cost per thousand viewers is higher than it looks, if you look at the rating services' CPM figures.

You need to find out how rich in target viewers a television audience is to figure out whether an ad in that space is a good buy or not. Rating points emphasize the size of the program's audience, not the match between the audience and your target market. So be sure to convert — or ask your agency to convert — ratings into figures that represent reach into your target market and exclude those households outside of your target market that you don't need to advertise to. When you look at the TV-buying decision in this way, you often end up advertising on a wider variety of channels and programs than if you relied on straight rating points.

Part IV
Finding Powerful Alternatives to Advertising

The 5th Wave   By Rich Tennant

"IT'S A MACINTYRE PLANK"

In this part . . .

The Japanese poet Matsuo Basho advised us, "Do not seek to follow in the footsteps of the men of old; seek what they sought."

In marketing, the goals never really change. We're no more nor less eager to find new customers and grow our revenues than were last year's or last decade's crop of eager marketers.

But the means of achieving these goals can and do change. We should always look for alternatives and fresh approaches. You especially have to stay on top of your game in today's advertising because entirely new ways of communicating with customers and prospects have emerged in the last couple of decades, and marketers no longer need to feel confined to traditional advertising. Telemarketing, fax machines, direct mail, and now e-mail, Web pages, paid listings on search engines, and many more innovations are transforming marketing.

In addition, I highly recommend that you explore the power of publicity and of events in your marketing area. Sometimes, these approaches can be more effective than anything else in the entire field of marketing, yet marketers traditionally give them too little thought and funding in most businesses.

You can, in fact, design for any business an effective marketing program that completely skips conventional advertising and substitutes one or more of the many alternative media instead.

Chapter 10

Marketing on the Web

In This Chapter

▶ Choosing a Web address that has maximum marketing impact

▶ Creating an effective Web page

▶ Making your site visible on search engines

▶ Connecting to customers with chat rooms and Webcasts

▶ Designing and placing banners

▶ Using e-mail in marketing and sales

▶ Budgeting your Web marketing plan

*T*he World Wide Web creates a wonderfully versatile — and often misused — medium for direct marketing. In this chapter, I share tips and techniques for making the Web a major component of your sales and marketing efforts.

Do you have a Web site? A Web newsletter? A mailing list of e-mail addresses for your customers? Do you track your visibility on search engines? Do you ever do live Webcasts of marketing or sales events to reach a broader audience? You can use the Web to build sales in a lot of exciting ways, whether your budget is $600 or $6,000, and this chapter shows you how. Also check out Chapter 21 for ten tips for boosting Web sales.

The single most important point to remember about Web marketing is that you must invest routinely so that you're always changing and improving your Web presence. Whether you're a do-it-yourself Web marketer or are willing to hire a professional firm (which can be as inexpensive as a couple hundred dollars a month), your Web marketing needs to be a living thing. Don't let parts of your site get old and stale. Don't continue to run a *banner ad* (an ad that appears on a major Web site or service) or bid on a *key term* (a word people use in searching for Web sites, which you can pay to have your message linked to) if you aren't getting results in clicks and sales. Do adapt and change every month. The Web is a dynamic marketing medium. Be dynamic!

Selecting a Web Address

Most Web marketing involves the use of a Web site in one manner or another, so if you don't have one already, you need to create one. To test the availability of a possible Web address (also called a *domain name* or a *URL*), go to `www.register.com` and enter the name into the `Search For a Domain Name` box. The site gives you a detailed analysis of any relevant registrations. For example, you may find out that someone has registered the name you want with the .com extension, but not with a .org or .net extension. If someone has already gotten there first, seek a more unique name because someone could forget your extension and go to the competing site, instead. You can best maintain uniqueness by owning most or all the possible extensions and versions of your Web address.

If consumers may get confused by alternate spellings or misspellings of your domain name, register them, too. Registering a name is cheap, so you shouldn't lose a prospective customer just because they can't spell your name. For example, as an author, I know that people often assume I have a Web site using my name as its address. So I maintain the domain name `www.alexhiam.com`. But I also know that people sometimes reverse the vowels when spelling my last name, so I registered `www.alexhaim.com`, too. How would consumers be most likely to misspell your business name? Make sure you register those misspellings. (If you type either of my registered domain names into your computer, you see that they both go to `www.insightsfortraining.com`, my main business site. It's easy to redirect traffic in this way, so make sure you register any obvious domain names where people may expect to find you, even if you don't want to create separate Web sites for each.)

If you find that some firm has bought your desired address for the purpose of selling domain names and wants you to bid on it, don't. Just go back to the drawing board and find another name that isn't being held hostage. I'm not confident that these domain-hoarding companies are going to handle everything properly and deliver your domain name to you safely, but I do know that most of them process a large fee on your credit card before you can say "marketing mistake."

As you search for potential names, keep the three following criteria in mind to make sure you obtain a good address for your site:

> ✔ **A good address relates to your business or brand.** I can register the domain name `www.lookmanohands.com` if someone else hasn't already. It's catchy. It amuses me. Should I use it for my Web site address? No. It fails my first test. It doesn't relate to my business or brand. My corporate training business is called Insights for Training & Development. So we use the Web address `www.insightsfortraining.com`. It's not clever, but it's clearly relevant to the business.

✔ **A good domain name is memorable.** Someone who wants to remember it can. It doesn't mean that you have to register something stunningly cool or clever — besides, by now, someone else has already registered most of the extremely clever addresses. Using your company or brand name makes the Web site memorable to anyone who knows the name of your business. You can easily remember that Crayola's site is at `www.crayola.com`. Or you can simply combine two or three easy words and make the string into a memorable Web address. A firm selling UV filtering glass and Plexiglas for framing valuable art could choose a sufficiently relevant and memorable Web address like `www.uvprotectionglass.com`.

✔ **Your Web address should be unique.** It needs to be unique to avoid two problems:

- **Misdirecting potential consumers:** If consumers can easily confuse your site with similar addresses, some people go to the wrong site by accident. If your company name is similar to others, add a unique term or word in your Web address to make it more unique. Forexample, The Ford Insurance Agency had to avoid losing Web visitors accidentally to Ford Motor Company's `www.ford.com` address, so the agency uses `www.fordinsurance.net`.

- **Stepping on toes:** You don't want to bump into someone's trademark by accident. My publisher, John Wiley & Sons, owns trademark rights to this book series. Even though nobody has a site on the Web using the address `www.marketingfordummies.com`, I can't use that address without violating the publisher's trademark of the *For Dummies* identity. Where I use that identity (on the Web or somewhere else) doesn't matter. The trademark applies everywhere! So check any Web address against a database of trademarks (in the United States, you can do this search for free by going to `http://patents.uspto.gov/` and clicking **Trademarks Search**). Or ask a lawyer to do a more detailed analysis if you think you may run into an issue. It may be available, meaning you could register it at a site like `www.register.com` because nobody else has yet. But if you begin to use it, the owner of the trademark may sue you.

Designing an Effective Web Page

Designing good Web pages is a key marketing skill, because your Web site is at the center of all you do to market on the Web. Also, increasingly, Web sites are at the heart of marketing programs — businesses put their Web addresses on every marketing communication, from premium items (like company pens) to letterheads and business cards, and also in ads, brochures, and catalogs. Serious shoppers will visit your Web site to find out more about what you offer, so make sure your site is ready to close the sale. Include excellent, clear design, along with plenty of information to answer likely questions and move visitors toward a purchase. Web sites have earned their place in the core of any marketing program.

Finding resources to help with design

If you aren't a do-it-yourselfer, you have a very easy way to create good Web pages: Find an expert who can do it for you under contract. (Just make sure that the contract specifies that you, not they, own the copyright to the contentso that you can switch to another vendor if it doesn't work out.) This section doesn't tell you how to use authoring languages or how to do any of the programming. That would fill an entire book, not a chapter, let alone a section. If you decide to do it yourself, you can find excellent books that do go into all the details, and I keep a current bookshelf of them up and reviewed on the supporting site for this book, www.insightsformarketing.com.

You can use several other books from my publisher as excellent references, and they're kept up to date with regular reprintings and new editions. I recommend, in particular, *Creating Web Pages All-in-One Desk Reference For Dummies* by Emily A. Vander Veer (Wiley). It goes a bit deeper than the also good *Creating Web Pages For Dummies* by Bud E. Smith (also by Wiley). Or, if you really want the light version, check out *CliffsNotes Creating Your First Web Page* by Alan Simpson (you guessed it — Wiley). These three titles cover the range in both price and detail, so take your pick. If you like tinkering, you can certainly build your own Web pages and contract with an Internet Service Provider (ISP) to put them up on the Web.

You can find an Internet service provider to host your site quite easily. Dozens of them may be trying to find you to make a sale. Just pick one that offers the fee structure, services, and flexibility you want — and change providers if they don't satisfy.

Color me rich

I recommend as a monthly feature having some kind of interactive event or contest on your site. Crayola brand crayons used this technique effectively (its Web page is at www.crayola. com). The interactive event targeted households with young children, through a coloring contest in which parents entered their work and kids were the judges. In fact, a contest was held for the judges, too — with kids filling out a written application. The winner of this Big Kid Challenge, as the company called the contest, received $25,000 worth of gold and silver. Not bad for a crayon drawing!

And because the contest was such a big draw, Crayola had a lot of traffic throughout its page. Other options on the site include a section on how they make crayons and, for the practical parent, advice on how to remove stains.

I recommend visiting this site, not to see the promotion described above but to see what they're doing now. You can be sure it's different. Web-based promotions have the advantage of being changeable, and you can change them as often as you like. The development time and cost is low compared to other sorts of events.

Consider using your domain name and *ISP* (internet service provider or Web site host company) to provide your own e-mail addresses, too. Having your e-mail done through your own domain looks so much more professional and gives you more control over the parameters than going through Yahoo!, AOL, or some other public domain does.

Hiring a professional designer

Good Web site design is harder than it looks and you should probably go to a reputable design firm and ask them to do it for you. I recommend a business relationship (spelled out on paper in advance) that specifies that you, not they, own all content at the end, and also specifies an hourly bill rate and an estimate of the site's size and complexity with a cap on the number of billable hours needed to design it.

I asked Wayne Opp, president of MediaPro in San Francisco (www.mediaproof.com), the firm I use for my own Web site work, to give you a quick rundown on what to expect in working with a firm like his and how to get the most out of the process. Here's what he told me:

✔ MediaPro starts by determining the client's goals and budget for their Web site. A site can serve as a simple online brochure, storefront, or dynamic application using a company database. The cost can range from $600 to $20,000 or more, depending on the client's needs.

✔ For a basic site (around five to ten pages), where the client provides a company logo, images, and copy, you should plan to spend around $1,000 to $2,000 for a custom-designed site. This price would include domain name registration and hosting setup. A basic hosting plan costs around $200 to $300 per year.

✔ For a lower budget, you can find many Web site templates available from web authoring programs. Some are quite good, but people often recognize these cookie cutter designs, which lower viewers' opinions of the site design.

✔ MediaPro recommends using a site with a custom look built around your logo, one that contains navigation suited to the service or product that you're offering. Although these customized graphics and stock photography can drive up your costs, your online presence needs a unique, professional Web site that can set you apart from your competitors. (On www.insightsfortraining.com, designed by MediaPro, we purchased the photo at the top of the home page from a stock photography company for hundreds of dollars — but that money is a good investment because that photo helps create an appropriate and appealing look and feel for the site.)

✔ You should also consider an online shopping cart. Many basic hosting plans include a shopping cart (also called a *shopcart*), so you can implement this feature fairly easily by using theirs. Assume that you will be adding products over time, so select a shopping cart that gives you room to grow.

✔ Also consider streaming video, animation, and database management. You can use these technologies as important delivery methods, like showing a speaker in action, demonstrating a new product or providing services, and supporting the consumer online.

Wayne includes stock photography in the budget because sites with relevant images — especially of real people — are graphically more appealing and hold the visitor's attention longer. I highly recommend using photographs in most sites. If you use high-resolution files of the photos, they may be slow to load, which means you could lose some impatient viewers or the few who are still on low-speed phone lines. But stock photography houses sell (at a lower price) low-resolution images that are optimal for the Web and load quickly. These won't slow your site down.

Wayne also recommends having your contractor update your site monthly because these updates give customers good reasons to keep coming back to the site. And he suggests using special promotions or some other monthly feature to add to this evolving appeal. Finally, much of what his firm and others like it do involves optimizing the site to make it more visible in search engines so that traffic goes up. I cover the details of how to do this in the "Getting Your Site Noticed in Search Engines" section later in this chapter because, even if you hire someone to do it, you ought to be involved in the strategizing.

Developing a registration-based site

If you visit www.crayola.com, you may see a new pop-up box that appears as the main site is loading. The pop-up box has a banner that tells you to register now for crayola.com to gain access to activity pages, craft ideas, and more. Registering costs you nothing, and you have much to gain, because of the many extra options that Crayola offers. Why do they give extra content to registered users, and why give away this valuable content? They want to find out who their customers are. The registered users stay in touch and may choose to purchase directly over the site. Crayola uses its Web site to develop direct marketing relationships with registered users. It's a very savvy way to use the Web site as a major marketing tool. You may want to consider this option, too.

Getting Your Site Noticed in Search Engines

Each time someone visits your Web site, he is exhibiting interest in you and your products (or he's lost — which is less likely if your site is aptly named and clearly designed so that no one can confuse it with unrelated types of businesses). And when someone exhibits interest, that makes him interesting to you. So whatever you do, however you go about setting up a site, make sure that you capture information about your visitors in a useful form that gets sent to you regularly.

Ask your ISP what kinds of reports they can offer you — probably more than you imagined possible. With these reports in hand, you can track traffic to your site. You probably notice that you, unlike the giants of the Web, don't have as much traffic as you may want to. Sure, millions of people use Google to do searches or go to eBay to bid on auctioned products. But the average Web site only has a few dozen visitors a day. For an effective site, you need to build up this traffic at least into the thousands of visitors per day. How? By making sure it gets noticed in search engines.

Header and META tag magic

You can make sure that your site is easy to find by tagging it with appropriate terms or words describing its contents for the search engines to pick up.

The first thing you need is a *header block* — that's what your Web site developer calls it — that encodes (in HTML, the language of Web programming) some words to describe your site. Think of it as similar to a headline in an ad, except this one needs to be clean, focused, and simple (search engines don't appreciate creativity). You can incorporate a header tag in this block, which search engines read and pick up for display when someone does a relevant search.

Next, your Web site developer (or you, if you're trying to do Web development on your own) wants to think about what META tags your site has. No need to get too technical about this stuff. *META tags* are simply some additional instructions to Web browsers, and they can sometimes include additional words to signal what you offer and help the Web surfer find your site. You may find *description* and *key word* META NAME tags the most important for what you're trying to do. Both permit you to list information about your content (in the form of terms, and in the form of a short descriptive sentence).

If your Web development software or consultant doesn't bring up the topic, look it up or ask questions to make sure that you address this issue and don't lose any potential visibility as a result. If you don't ask, you can assume that these tags aren't optimal for your site. In fact, developers don't put as much care into most sites' META tags as they should, and the site loses traffic as a result.

Don't try to cover every base by using a laundry list of tags. Search engines are pretty good at noticing and avoiding such ploys, and you don't want everyone coming to your site, anyway. You should make your tags clear and narrowly focused to attract only the best prospects.

Most important, these META tags control when and how (some) search engines describe your site. You can cue the site up for display when someone searches for one of your terms, and then you can determine what sentence that search engine displays to describe the site — essentially, a small, free advertisement for your site. Draft this ad carefully to attract the right prospects with appropriate, accurate information on your content.

Oh, and don't expect that your META tags ensure that people using any of the common search engines get to see your site. Way too many sites are out there these days, and yours may be listed on the 15th page, after 140 other listings, where nobody is ever going to see it. META tags can help put you in the running, but they can't ensure a prominent page-one placement in a search engine's results.

Buying visibility on search engines

Search engines *locate* (or index) billions of sites from user queries each day. A lot of prospective customers are in that statistic somewhere. Google alone indexes more than 3.3 billion Web site pages. So how can relevant queries find their way to your pages rather than to all the others? You're a needle in an immense haystack.

Because the search engines look at traffic when ranking pages, anything you do through direct communication with your customers to build traffic can help. Also, you should use a link to related sites to improve your ranking. You can use the simple but powerful strategy of doing a search, like one your customers may do, and see what sites appear in the top ten listings. Then visit each of them and see if you can find appropriate places and ways to link from your site to theirs (and vice versa, if possible). For example, a company that distributes products for you or vice versa is a natural to link to your site. Also, a professional association in your industry may be a good fit for you to link to, although it may be harder to talk into linking back to your site. Build such links and the higher-ranked sites tend to draw yours up toward them. But make sure that you have great, useful content to justify those links!

Next, to make your site visible to anyone searching for it, optimize your listing by spending some money on it. Sorry, but there's no such thing as a free lunch on the Internet any more! Go to www.google.com and click the Advertise With Us link. They lay out the most recent offerings for us marketers here. I specifically recommend that you look (by clicking on another link) at Google AdWords, a program allowing you to pay per click when people click through to your site. To use this option, do the following:

1. **Designate a short list of highly specific and appropriate key terms that customers may use to search for you.**

2. **Bid by saying how much you'd pay for a click. Starting at $0.10 to $0.15 a click usually gets you into the game. Web advertisers call this offer your *per-click bid.***

   Google allows you to track your results day by day, see your ranking, and see what results (clicks and costs) you get.

3. **If you want more clicks, raise your bid for a higher listing or improve your use of terms or descriptive sentences, and watch to see if your results improve.**

Offering white papers or newsletters

People like to use the Web for research. Often, that research relates to a purchase decision. To be part of that research and purchase process, put useful, noncommercial information on your site. The *white paper,* which is a research-oriented or factual report on a technical topic, gives you the easiest and best way to present this noncommercial information for business-to-business marketing or for consumer durables (because research is important in both types of purchases).

Steelcase, the office equipment manufacturer, has a bunch of useful white papers on its site to help people design and equip offices for optimal comfort and productivity. See www.steelcase.com and click on Knowledge & Design, and then take a look at any of the case studies, survey reports, articles, or papers for good examples of white papers in many of their possible forms.

The Robert Frances Group (www.rfgonline.com) is a consulting firm specializing in information technology trends. It posts news articles and technical reports on its Web site, updating them weekly to help attract regular visits from its customers and others in the industry. It also does some client briefings over the Web — available, of course, only to paying clients and not to the average visitor to the site.

What can you do to inform and educate your prospects on the Web?

I'm not going to tell you more about it because Google presents your advertising options well and simply. Just go have a look at the options — and pick any that seem to fit your site and budget. You don't need to make a long-term commitment; you can experiment with programs at low cost until you find a mix that works.

Yahoo! advertising

Yahoo! uses Overture as its service for buying search engine visibility. Overture uses a bidding system based on the number of clicks your site gets, much like Google's AdWords (see the preceding section for more on Google). You can find Overture by going to www.yahoo.com and finding the Yahoo! Business Services section and then clicking on the button marked Market Online. This link takes you to areas where you can research the Overture options I describe in this book and, if you want, actually make purchases and begin to do your marketing on Yahoo! (Yahoo! likes to rearrange its site, so if you don't see the Market Online option right away, poke around until you find out where they are hiding the information on Overture this week. It is there, I promise!)

A Nielsen audit found that Yahoo! search engine listings reached more than 80 percent of active Internet users. I don't know if that percentage is really true, but Yahoo! certainly has an extensive reach. You may want to buy some visibility in Yahoo! searches, as well as Google. Often, you can use the same key terms in both, which simplifies your work as a marketer. However, you may need to adjust your per-click bids (see the preceding section) differently to get good visibility on Yahoo!. Depending on your industry, one or the other search engine may tend to be more expensive. You just have to see and make appropriate adjustments as you go.

At time of writing, Yahoo! has posted a nice *flash demo* (mini-video that you can watch on your computer) describing how Overture works and how to use it in your marketing. I plan to make sure we keep useful links like this one, and the others I mention earlier in this chapter, updated on this book's supporting site, www.insightsformarketing.com.

Content as a traffic driver

Most Web sites are really just huge, interactive advertisements or sales promotions. After a while, even the most cleverly designed ad gets boring. To increase the length of time users spend with your materials, and to ensure high involvement and return visits, you need to think like a publisher, not just an advertiser. For this reason, I consider Web content to be the hidden factor for increasing site traffic. Unless you have valuable and appealing content, you may have difficulty building up traffic on your site.

Create and deliver fascinating content and refresh it regularly. This content gives your site real appeal, and it can lead to good referrals and word-of-mouth marketing. On the Web, people can easily send each other good links. They can do this word-of-mouth marketing for your site if they like what they see.

Chats and Webcasts: Adding Human Contact and Support

EarthLink is one of a growing number of companies that can set up a live chat center for your Web site visitors to use if they need sales or service support. They use this service on their own site (go to `http://support.earthlink.net/` and click on **Chat** under the **Contact Us** header to see it in action), and the company can set you up to do it, too. But if you decide to go this route, you do need to have someone online to monitor the chat area and answer customer questions. You'll find this option worthwhile only if you build up your Web site's traffic to the point that you almost always have at least one customer in the chat area. For another vendor who can set up a chat-room connection from your Web site to your sales or service personnel, visit `www.providesupport.com`.

Explore the chat-room option after you've built up good basic traffic on your site (as measured by a high number of visitors and clicks). I'd say that you want to be in the thousands a day, unless you have a business in which a small number of customers tend to do high-value orders. In that case, you may be able to financially justify the chat room addition with fewer site visits per day. See the "Interpreting click statistics" sidebar for more information.

You can go even further, if you want, by creating live events on the Web. You can do Web conferencing, virtual sales presentations, and Webcasts of conferences or presentations, with potentially thousands of people watching and listening from the comfort of their office or home computers. I've participated in and used a growing number of these kinds of events in the last few years, and I think they're on the way to becoming an important business-to-business marketing medium. Some day, you may see a *For Dummies* book just about how to stage live events on the Web. But until then, check out vendor solutions, such as those offered by WebTrain (`www.webtrain.com`) and MediaPro (`www.mediaprosf.com`).

If you Webcast a live event to effectively reach viewers, you must face the challenge of lining up an interested audience. I recommend starting with your own in-house list of good customers and offering some kind of seminar or event that they may find interesting. Because marketing's goal is sales, I also recommend keeping it fairly simple by focusing your event on education about your product or service and how to use it. This approach may not attract as big an audience as something exciting like, say, a slight-of-hand demonstration by a magician — but the audience you attract for a product demonstration is more likely to buy that product.

Interpreting click statistics

You may find click-through statistics a useful and easy-to-get indicator of how well an ad or search-engine placement is performing. If you get a lot of people clicking through to your site from an ad or placement, that ad is clearly doing its job of attracting traffic for you. So, all else being equal, more clicks are better.

However, all else isn't equal all the time. Here are a few wrinkles to keep in mind when interpreting click rates:

✔ When a pop-up ad pops up, the companies you buy the ad space through usually report it as a click. But don't believe the numbers because you have no indication that someone actually read or acted on that pop-up. They may have just closed it without looking. Dig deeper into the statistics from whoever sold you that pop-up ad to find out how it actually performed. You can probably get some more detailed data if you ask, but you need more than the simple click count.

✔ Some ads have multiple elements that load in sequence, creating a countable click with each loading so that one ad may generate several click-through counts. This counting method may lead you to think that the more complex ad is better, but the higher number can be an artifact of the way those who sell ad space on the Web count the clicks. (Ask your ISP if it can sell Web ad space to you, or visit any really popular site and look for the section in it that's for advertisers if you want to buy ad space.)

✔ Quality is more important than quantity. Who are these people who clicked to your site? That information is harder to know but more important. On one of my own business's Web sites, insightsfortraining.com, we are seeking the top thousand purchasers of employee and manager training materials and programs in North America. If I get ten thousand clicks in a week, that's nice — but do they include top-tier prospects or not? Only by digging into detailed reports on who goes where and looks at what on my Web site, plus information on what types of e-mailed questions we get and the average order size in that week, can I really begin to evaluate the quality of those clicks.

✔ If you're getting poor quality of traffic clicking through, you need to experiment with putting ads in other places or you need to redesign your ads to specifically focus on your desired target. Keep working on it until you have not the most click-throughs, but the best.

You can evaluate performance of Web advertising every day or week, and you can get statistics on each and every ad that you run. So use this data intelligently to experiment and adjust your approach. Aim to increase both the quantity and the quality of clicks week by week throughout your marketing campaign and track the impact on inquiries and sales.

Designing and Placing a Banner Ad

A *banner ad* (those brightly colored rectangles at the top of popular Web pages) is the Web's answer to display advertising in a print medium or outdoor advertising on a billboard. Viewers don't want to read as much copy as they may in a print ad, so use banners the same way you use a billboard (check out Chapter 8 for a discussion of billboards) — to get across a very simple, clear, and engaging message. Use only a single, brief headline, perhaps supported by a logo and a couple lines of body copy. Or maybe you can use a brand name and an illustration. In either case, the ad must be simple and bold — able to attract the viewer's attention from desired information elsewhere on the screen for long enough to make a simple point. Don't expect too much from a banner ad!

If you decide to use the Web for direct-action advertising, be sure to include a clear call to action in the ad. Typical Web banner ads don't give enough information about the product to stimulate an urge for immediate action. Nor do they make taking action easy. They simply build awareness, at best.

Companies that provide *Web media services* (meaning Web page design) can also design and place banner ads and pop-up ads for you. You can also find plenty of factory-oriented banner ad designers that can make you an ad quickly and economically or sell you a template. See `www.joebanner.com` for an example or check out the following sources:

✔ WebPencil.com (`www.webpencil.com`) offers graphic banner ad design for $60 each and animated banners for $150. It also (for a fee) helps you place them in appropriate locations to reach your target audience.

✔ WowBanners.com (`www.wowbanners.com`) designs *static banners* (nothing moves, like a print ad) and animated ones. It offers many cheap templates that you can use. They also have templates for the more smoothly animated flash banners, in which you can incorporate more movement. The pricing at template-based suppliers like this one is ridiculously low — *any* marketer can afford to use a few banners!

✔ Go to `www.macromediaflash.com` and check out good authoring software for Web page design. Top designers use their Flash MX software to create impressive video and animation for banners and other Web applications.

✔ AdDesigner.com (`www.addesigner.com`) has an extensive library of templates for Web banner ads that you can adapt to your purposes at surprisingly low expense. They have a simple "blinking eyes" design that combines your text with a pair of eyes that blink — I know it sounds silly, but trust me, the eyes draw prospects to this image, and people definitely read the message.

And any competent Web designer or programmer can create custom banners to your specification quite easily because it's such a small ad format.

Focusing on a simple design

I think the best design for starters is a banner that flashes a simple one-line offer or headline statement, shows an image of your logo or product, and then switches to a couple more lines of text explaining what to do and why to do it ("Click here to take advantage of our introductory offer for small business owners and get 20 percent off your first order of . . . "). This ad style delivers a clear marketing message using both print and illustration. Make sure that prospects go directly to a page on your Web site if they click on the banner that supports the product or service with more information and with several easy purchase options.

Placing your banner ads

Designing the banner is just the beginning because you have to buy space to display it from publishers. If you poke around on large sites like www.yahoo.com, you can find sections devoted to advertisers like you, where you can explore ad buying options and rates and ask for help from a salesperson. Alternatively, you can go to a specialty firm, like www.bannerspace.com, and hire them to do the placement. They take a small commission (usually around $0.25 per thousand people reached) but probably more than make up for this loss by negotiating better rates and avoiding some of the inflation of exposure numbers that can happen when you have to rely on the publisher's accounting.

What can it cost you to place a banner ad? On average (at time of publishing), you pay around $2 per thousand viewers — not bad if you have an ad that actually generates some responses. But watch the banner ad closely and pull or modify it, or try running it elsewhere, if the click rate is too low to justify the cost. You may have to make a few tries to get it right, but with the rapid feedback possible on the Web, this experimentation can take place fairly quickly and inexpensively.

Understanding E-mail Etiquette

You can create, or hire your Web site designer to create, an e-mail that looks like a well-designed Web page, with animation and clickable buttons linking to your site. Now, all you have to do is blast it out to millions of e-mail addresses and surely you can make millions overnight.

Not so fast! Okay, so you have this great marketing message or sales pitch, and you want to send it to everyone in the world who has an e-mail address. You can actually do that, but I don't advise it. The more specific and narrow your use of e-mail for marketing, the better. And since President Bush signed the Can Spam Act, U.S. marketers must be careful to avoid violating federal restrictions on *spam,* or junk e-mails. I help you stay on the sunny side of this law in this section.

The best e-mail is a personal communication with a customer you know, sent individually from you with an accurate e-mail return address as well as your name, title, company name, full mailing address, and phone number. It may read as follows:

> Dear so-and-so,
>
> I wanted to follow up after your purchase of (your product) on (date) to see how it's working out for you and to thank you for your continuing business. If you have any concerns or questions, please let me know by return e-mail, or feel free to call my private cell phone number, (xxx) yyy-zzzz. Thanks!
>
> Best,
>
> Your Name

Your customer is going to receive, open, read, and appreciate an e-mail like this one. She may even respond to it, especially if the customer has any current concerns or questions or has another order on its way. Even if she doesn't reply to it, however, she appreciates that e-mail. And that message doesn't bug anyone or look like spam.

Use e-mail as much as you can for legitimate, helpful one-on-one contact and support of customers or prospects.

Sometimes, you can also send out an e-mail to a list rather than an individual, but please make sure that you have a clear purpose that benefits those people on the list. And make sure that your list is as focused as possible to avoid angering people. Good will is a valuable asset, so don't destroy it! The following list has some additional rules of good mass e-mailing that I think marketers should all follow. My inspiration for these rules comes from the Association for Interactive Marketing and the Direct Marketing Association, where they have guidelines for responsible use of e-mail. I've also kept the restrictions in U.S. federal regulations in mind when I put together these guidelines for your bulk e-mailings:

- ✔ **Send e-mails only to those people who ask for them.** Your bulk e-mails should ideally go only to those people who have given you permission. If you're not sure about a particular contact, ask the people who receive the mailing if they mind and give them an option to reply and be taken off the list. It's not (yet) illegal to send e-mails without permission (providing your list is legitimate and not random), but it's not very polite.

You get the most solid form of consent when someone asks you to include him in your mailing. You can get these requests by creating a useful e-newsletter and advertising it on the Web as a free subscription. Those people who sign up really want it, and they're happy to see the next issue arrive.

✔ **Remove addresses from your list immediately when they ask to be removed.** Why? See the rule about not angering your customers, above, and (in the United States) remember that refusing to allow people to opt out is illegal. Also, people have such widespread distrust of Web marketers that you may consider writing the person a brief, individual e-mail from you (identify yourself and your title for credibility), letting them know that you have eliminated them from the list and are sorry if you've inconvenienced them. You shouldn't say any more in the e-mail. Don't try to make a sale — you just make them even madder. You generally make a positive impression by being so responsive to their complaint, so don't be surprised if your special attention to their request leads them to initiate a sale later on.

✔ **If you insist on buying e-mail lists, test them before using them.** Try a very simple, short, nonirritating message to the list, like an offer to send them a catalog or free sample, and ask for a few pieces of qualifying information in return. See what happens. Cull all the many bounce-backs and irritated people from the list. Now your list is a bit better in quality than the raw list was. Save those replies in a separate list — they're significantly better and more qualified and deserve a more elaborate e-mail, mailing, or (if the numbers aren't too high) a personal contact.

✔ **Respect privacy.** People don't want to feel like someone's spying on them. Never send to a list if you'd be embarrassed to admit where you got the names. You can develop an e-mail list in plenty of legitimate ways (from customer data, from Web ads, from inquiries at trade shows, from return postcards included in mailings, and so on), so don't do anything that your neighbors would consider irritating or sleazy.

✔ **Send out your bulk e-mails just like you send an individual one.** Use a real, live, reply-able e-mail address. I hate it when I can't reply to an e-mail — it makes me mad! And — a good rule of marketing — try not to make customers and prospects mad.

✔ **Include your company name and a real mailing address.** If you're in the United States, federal law now requires that you include this contact information. Also give recipients an easy way to opt out of future mailings — another legal requirement in the United States.

✔ **Make sure that the subject line isn't deceptive.** U.S. law now requires that you make the subject line straightforward, and it's just good sense, anyway. In marketing, you want to get to know right away if someone isn't a good prospect, instead of wasting your time or theirs when they have no interest in your offer.

✔ **Keep your e-mail address lists up to date.** When you get a *hard bounce-back* (notice that a message was undeliverable) from an address, remove it and update your e-mail list for the next mailing.

A *soft bounce-back* is an undeliverable message resulting from some kind of temporary problem. Track it to see if the e-mail eventually goes through. If not, eliminate this address from your list, too.

People change their e-mail addresses and switch servers. You can have bounce-backs on your list who may still be good customers or prospects. At least once a year, check these inactive names and try to contact them by phone or mail to update their e-mail addresses. Some of them are still interested and don't need to be cut from your list; they just need their e-mail addresses updated.

If you're e-mailing to an in-house list of people who have bought from you, gone to your seminar, or asked for information in the past, remind them of your relationship in the e-mail. They may have forgotten.

I hate *spam,* junk e-mails that clog up my mailbox. In fact, I change my e-mail address whenever the spam begins to find me. I bet you feel the same way. So don't let your Web marketing make you part of this problem. Use good quality lists, be polite and respectful, and integrate e-mail into your broader Web strategy so that you don't have to rely too heavily on e-mail. Real people live at the end of those e-mail addresses. Treat them as such!

Knowing How Much to Budget for the Web

If you're in a business-to-business marketing situation, I strongly urge you to put at least 10 percent of your marketing budget into the Web, both for maintaining a strong Web site and for doing some Web advertising and search-engine placement purchases. If you add an e-newsletter, Web distribution of press releases, and occasional announcements to your e-mail list, you may need to make the percentage significantly higher.

To put Web advertising (one of the items in your overall Web budget) into perspective, *BtoB Magazine* reports from its extensive company surveys that business-to-business marketers put about 5 percent of their advertising budget into Web ads. (Remember that the ad budget is just one section of your overall marketing budget, and *BtoB Magazine* doesn't ask about the rest.) Five percent of ad spending on the Web is significant, but it's by no means dominant. The biggest category of business-to-business ad spending comes in the good old trade magazine. Ads in business publications make up the biggest part of the typical ad budget; in BtoB's surveys, they get between 40 and 45 percent of the ad budget. (Visit www.btobonline.com for the latest annual update of these statistics.)

But you can find exceptions to every rule, and being the exception often gives you the most profitable and powerful strategy in marketing. If you find that your Web ads, search engine listings, or e-mails are pulling well for you and making a profit, try doubling your effort and spending on them for a month and see what happens. Still working well? Double again. You may find that the Web can do a lot more of your basic marketing work than you think. Many marketers hold Web spending down to a small minority of their budget for no good reason other than tradition and fear of all things new.

If you're a consumer-oriented marketer, you may find that your Web site is even more important (although you can't as easily generalize about the share of budget to give it — that depends on your unique situation and what you find works best). Be sure your Web site does the following:

✔ Engages existing customers, giving them reasons to feel good about their past purchases and connect with your company and other consumers (at least to connect emotionally, if not in actual fact).

✔ Shares interesting and frequently updated information about your products or services and organization on the site, so the consumer can gain useful knowledge by visiting it.

✔ Maintains a section of the site or a dedicated site for business-to-business relationships that matter to your marketing (such as distributors, stores, and sales reps). Almost all consumer marketers also work as business-to-business marketers, and the same advice I gave on BtoB at the beginning of this section should apply to this aspect of consumer marketing, too.

Chapter 11

Publicity, Giveaways, and Word of Mouth

*W*hen people bump into reminders of your company name, brand name, product, or service, they are more likely to buy. And if those exposures to your identity can be good ones that create a strongly positive impression, those exposures can have a big impact on sales. There are many ways to do this, but few ways that avoid looking like out-and-out advertising. If you can work your way into the environment of prospective customers in positive ways that don't have the costs and stridency of advertising, you can make a positive impact in a low-key, and low-cost, manner.

In this chapter, I discuss three complementary ways of winning a right to be visible and liked. Each can make a positive impression in a low-key, polite manner, and can do so (if managed well) for surprisingly low cost.

✔ *Publicity* works you into the editorial part of the media, where exposure to or mention of your company, service, or product can become a part of the news.

✔ *Premiums* are products that people want to use and keep, that are identified with your brand and often with contact information, as well. If people like the premiums, they hold, use, and share them, generating considerable positive exposures for you, again without your having to pay for each exposure.

✔ *Word of mouth* is what people say about you to others. If you give good service and make a friendly, positive impression on people, they will be motivated to share their enthusiasm with others.

In this chapter, I show you how to make effective use of publicity and premiums, which are vastly underrated media. They are ignored or given only minor attention by marketers, but they belong in the front lines of your marketing program because of their ease of use, simplicity, low cost, and potential.

I also cover word of mouth in this chapter, with tips to help you understand it and harness its power. If you make an effort to track and manage word of mouth, it can be your most powerful form of marketing communication, because it holds more sway over purchase decisions than advertising or any other form of marketing. Yet most marketers simply ignore word of mouth on the assumption that they can't affect what customers say. No way. Some marketers combine excellent service and a friendly approach with incentives and encouragement to get those customers to give them referrals, for example. And when this is done right, it can be the best and cheapest source of new customers. Word of mouth needs to be an integral part of your marketing program.

No News Is Bad News: Using Publicity to Your Advantage

Publicity is coverage of your product or business in the editorial portion of any news medium. If, for example, *Consumer Reports* runs an article praising your product as best in a category, that's publicity. Good publicity. If, in contrast, the evening television news programs run a story saying that experts suspect your product caused numerous accidents, that's publicity, too. Bad publicity.

These examples illustrate two common reasons for journalists to cover a product as a story — because the product is better or worse than expected. In both cases, product quality is the key to the publicity. Keep this fact in mind.

Initiate positive publicity by designing and making a truly superior product. If you want to generate negative publicity, just make your product shoddy or do your service poorly. When you use publicity, remember the all-important factor — the quality of your product development and production/delivery. Good publicity starts with a pursuit of quality in your own business!

Public relations (PR) is the active pursuit of publicity for marketing purposes. You use PR to generate good publicity and try to minimize bad publicity (for example, you may send editors a *press release*, which is a letter summarizing a suggested news story). Generally, marketers have the responsibility of generating good publicity. If they create good stories and communicate them to the media effectively, the media pick up the stories and turn those stories into news or entertainment content. Good publicity. Open any *trade magazine* (a publication dedicated to covering an industry and read by those who work in the industry), and I guarantee that 75 percent of the articles were inspired by, or come at least partially from, press releases sent to the magazine's editors.

Marketers or general managers wear the PR hat in smaller organizations, but large companies generally have a PR person or department whose sole job is to generate positive publicity. Also, many businesses hire *publicists* or *PR firms* — experts who do PR on a freelance or consulting basis. A regional or smaller PR firm can often do a decent job for you on a retainer of one to two thousand dollars a month. So don't assume you can't afford PR representation, even if you're a small business. But avoid the cheaper, packaged services that circulate your press release with many others. You need help writing a good press release and placing the story. That assistance makes paying a bit more worth it. You don't get any coverage without it.

A *follow-up call* is a call to the editor a week after a press release is sent, just to double-check that he or she got the press release and to gauge interest and give additional information.

How do you sniff out good stories?

To a journalist, a *good story* is anything that has enough public interest to attract readers, viewers, or listeners and hold their attention. A good story for a journalist covering the plastics industry must hold the attention of people in that industry. I'm sorry to say that most of what you want to communicate to your market doesn't fall into the category of a good story. You need to develop your story (by collecting the right facts and quotes and writing them down clearly and well) to a level that may qualify as good editorial content.

Journalists and editors do *not* want stories about

- Your new product or service and how it differs from competitors or your previous models (unless that's their coverage specialty)

- Why you or your company's senior executive think your products are really great

- Your version of an *old story* — one that they've covered in the same way before

- Anything that seems boring or self-serving to anyone who doesn't work for your firm

Yet reporters often get those kinds of stories because the people handling PR generally aren't skilled journalists (and aren't even trying to think like skilled journalists). You have to give the reporters what they want. Sniff out a story, put together sufficient information to back up the story, and script a version of the story that reporters in your target media can virtually run without doing any work. To generate good positive publicity, you just have to . . . think like a journalist!

What's the hook?

If you don't know how to think like a journalist, use this simple exercise to help you get the idea. Scan today's newspaper (whichever one you like to read) and rank the top five stories based on your interest in them. Now analyze each one in turn to identify the one thing that made that story interesting enough to hold your attention. The *hooks,* the things that made each story interesting to you, differ. But each story has a hook. And these hooks have certain elements in common:

✔ Hooks often give you new information (information you didn't know or weren't sure of).

✔ Hooks make that new information relevant to your activities or interests.

✔ Hooks catch your attention, often by surprising you with something you hadn't expected.

✔ Hooks promise some benefit to you — although the benefit may be indirect — by helping you understand your world better, avoid something undesirable, or simply enjoy yourself as you read the paper.

If you performed the preceding exercise, I think you can write the next paragraph as well as I can.

Looking at the situation logically, you need to design hooks to make your marketing message into stories that appeal to journalists. And your hooks need to be just like the ones that attracted your attention to those newspaper stories, with one exception: You need to somehow tie them to your marketing information. You have to make sure that at least a thin line exists connecting the hook to your brand identity, the news that you've just introduced a new product, or whatever else you want the public to know. That way, when journalists use your hook in their own work, they end up including some of your marketing information in their stories as an almost accidental side effect.

prnewswire.com and businesswire.com

For easy access to a cheap way to distribute releases, check out www.prnewswire.com, where you can click on Small Business Toolkit and see what it currently charges for a 400-page press release. At time of writing, the site offers to create and send a release to all the media in your state, plus trade publications, thousands of news-oriented Web sites, and online services and databases for prices starting at $125. For full U.S. distribution, they charge about $600. Not bad! A similar service is offered at www.businesswire.com.

Journalists don't want to help you communicate with your target market. But journalists happily use any good stories that you're willing to write for them, and if your product gets mentioned or you get quoted as a result, they don't have a problem giving you the reference. So the secret, the key, the essence of good publicity? Develop stories with effective hooks and give those stories away to overworked journalists who eagerly accept a little help from volunteers like you.

How do you communicate a story to the media?

When doing PR training, most training start with the form, not the content. In my experience, content is 90 percent of the battle, form 10 percent. So I've reversed the traditional emphasis. But form does matter. You need to put your story into an appropriate and professional format so that journalists know the subject of the story and find that story easy to work with.

The most important and basic format for communicating a story is the *press release* or *news release;* a short, written document with a clear headline at the top, sufficient facts and quotes to support a short news story, brief supporting background on the company/product involved, a date, and contact information for journalists who want to follow up with a phone call to get more information or to arrange an interview. Just make sure that you include all these elements — and that you have a good hook to start with — and you can write an effective press release.

Figure 11-1 includes all the essential elements of format and style. You can use the release shown in the figure as a template for your own press releases.

May 31, 2004

FOR IMMEDIATE RELEASE

For more information, contact:
Alexander Hiam (413) 253-3658

CRAZY AUTHOR WRITES BOOK FOR DUMMIES

FIRST MARKETING TITLE TO ADDRESS REAL-WORLD NEEDS

AMHERST, Mass. — He's nearly done now. Just a section on public relations. Then the manuscript is off to production and — perhaps — history will be made. This title isn't just another book about business. This book is a redefinition of the marketing field that finally brings it up to speed with the harsh realities of business. And the book is, appropriately, by an author who straddles the boundaries between the ivory tower of business schools and the trenches of marketing management.

"What we teach about marketing on campus is pure fiction," complains Alexander Hiam, author of *Marketing For Dummies,* 2nd Edition (Wiley Publishing, 2004). "It's based on academic research, not on real-world practices and problems." Hiam threw out all his textbooks and visited past clients and other marketing practition-ers before designing his new book. As a result, it . . .

Figure 11-1:
Writing a
killer press
release.

The odds of your release getting picked up by media and receiving any cover-age at all are terribly low. Sorry to disappoint you. Journalists and editors throw away more than 90 percent of the releases they receive. So you need to beat the odds (as in direct marketing, discussed in Chapter 13) by writing a release that stands out from the junk in a journalist's in box.

To beat the odds, pay attention to content (to make sure you have a good story, see the preceding section). And avoid these common press release errors that journalists complain about:

✔ **Don't send inappropriate or late releases.** Target the right media and contacts. The food critic doesn't need a release about a new robotics manufacturing facility. And the business correspondent doesn't either, if the facility opened two months ago, because now it's old news.

You need to build up an accurate database of media contacts and mail your press release first class on occasion to validate it (with first class mail, you get envelopes back if addresses aren't valid). Faxing or e-mailing your release can be sensible because journalists work on tight deadlines, so include fields for fax and e-mail numbers in your database. Think about developing a list identifying authors of stories you like that may be similar to stories related to your business. Now you have a smaller list that's a much tighter match with your content and target audience. You can get commercial lists and directories of journalists from mailing list vendors.

✔ **Don't make any errors.** Typos throw the facts into question. And don't include any inaccurate facts. You want the journalist to trust you to do his research for him, which means he really has to trust you. Prove that you're worthy of his trust.

✔ **Don't give incomplete contact information.** Be sure that you include up-to-date names, addresses, and phone numbers. Let the contacts know when they should be available and what they should say so that the journalist finds them helpful and cooperative. Also, give journalists instructions for how to navigate through the computerized voice mail system. You don't want gatekeeping to prevent a reporter from making that interview!

✔ **Don't ignore the journalists' research needs.** The more support you give them, the easier they can cover your story. You can include photographs of the expert you quote in a mailed release (include the date, name of person, and information about the supplier of the photo on the back or the margin of the photo). Also consider offering plant tours, interview times, sample products, or whatever else may help journalists cover your story.

✔ **Don't bug the reporters.** Journalists don't want to send you clippings of the articles they write, so don't bother asking. Nor do they care to discuss with you why they didn't run a story, or why they cut off part of a quote when they did run a story. They're busy with the next story. Forget about it. You should focus on the next story, too.

✔ **Don't forget that journalists work on a faster clock than you do.** When a journalist calls about your release, return the call (or make sure that somebody returns it) in hours, not days. If you handle her requests slowly, she just finds another source or writes another story by the time you get back to her.

These don'ts can be balanced by a few good do's that help you get pickup (coverage) in the media:

✔ **Do include a list of five tips, rules, or principles.** Include something helpful that the media can quote. (A chiropractor's practice may send out a release that includes five ways to have a healthier back. A management consultant may offer five tips for avoiding cash-flow crises. A home inspection firm may offer five tips to avoid costly surprises when buying a home.)

✔ **Do offer yourself as an expert commentator on industry-related matters, in case they need a quote for another article.** They may just include one sentence from you, but if they mention your company name, you just got some good publicity. For example, an article on how to shop for a used car in the Sunday magazine of a newspaper may quote the owner of a large auto dealership as saying, "If you don't have an independent mechanic evaluate a used car before buying it, I guarantee you will be in for some unpleasant surprises." The article may also mention that this dealership's repair department does free evaluations for car buyers. The combination of a quote and a bit of information about the free service is going to attract many new customers, some of whom will become steady users of the dealership's repair service, and some of whom will become buyers of new or used cars from the dealership.

✔ **Do keep it brief.** Journalists are quick on the uptake and work fast, so let them call or e-mail if they need more information.

✔ **Do post your press releases on your Web site.** Your press releases can do double duty on the Web, providing information for both curious journalists and potential consumers.

✔ **Do send releases to every local editor in your area, no matter how small their publication or station.** You can get local coverage more easily than regional or national coverage, and that local coverage can be surprisingly helpful.

✔ **Do collect examples of good coverage of your type of product or service and build a mailing list of journalists and media that cover your type of business.** Sending your releases to these people makes sense because they've already proven they give similar stories coverage.

Should you consider video and electronic releases?

You can get a story out to the media in ways other than press releases. You can generate a video release, with useful footage that a television producer may decide to run as part of a news story. You can also put a written press release on the PR Newswire or any other such service that distributes hard copy or electronic releases to its media clients — for a fee to the source of the release, of course. You can also pitch your stories to the Associated Press and other newswires (but I recommend hiring a major PR firm before trying to contact a newswire).

Polishing your brilliance

Focus on doing what you do best. If you're the best at something, you're automatically newsworthy. The media wants to talk about and to you. And your customers are wowed by your excellence and want to tell others about you. So don't spread yourself too thin. Know what you do best and keep improving how you do it. Good referrals and publicity come naturally over time if you keep some aspect of your business head and shoulders above the rest.

Premiums (Giveaways): The Most Abused and Misused Medium of All!

A *premium* is any product with a marketing message somewhere on it that you give away. (Okay, maybe you don't always give them away, but you need to at least make getting them easy so as to spread your message as widely as possible.) Classic premiums include T-shirts, coffee mugs, pens, wall calendars, and baseball caps with your company name or logo on them. But you don't have to confine yourself to these choices — businesses have used these classics for years, so you may want to consider something more innovative, too.

You've seen it all before. How many pens with some company's name on them have made their way into your possession over the last five years? If you answered, "Too many to count," you know that one more doesn't get noticed and used unless it's a nice pen that people like the look and feel of. A good rule for all premiums is to select products that people will truly enjoy, even if they cost more than cheap ones. You want your premium to be saved and used, not thrown out.

Brilliant premiums with impact scenarios

As in any marketing initiative, you want a premium to change someone's behavior. And you can't do that very easily with a cheap pen or ugly mug. You have to build an impact scenario to make a premium work. An *impact scenario* is a realistic story about the premium and its user in which the premium somehow affects that user's purchase behavior.

Say that you're marketing a new set of banking services for small businesses, and you want to spread the word about these services to business owners who currently have checking accounts with your bank. Specifically, you want to let these businesses know that you have made a variety of helpful new services available, and you want the business owners to call or visit their branch offices to find out more about these services.

An impact scenario starts with this wish list of what the target customer should understand and do. You finish the scenario by thinking of ways that premium items can accomplish your wish list goals.

What if you have the bank's name and the slogan, "Servicing small businesses better" printed on pens, which you then distribute in the next mailing of checking account statements? This premium item gives you an easy and cheap marketing tactic. But try to imagine the scenario. The small business owner opens his bank statement, and a pen falls out. He grabs the pen and eagerly reads the slogan. Then, curious about what the slogan means, he immediately dials his local branch and waits patiently on hold for a couple of minutes.

When he finally gets someone on the phone, he says, "Hey, I got your pen! Please tell me all about your services for small businesses!"

Somehow this scenario doesn't seem too plausible. In fact, I think that most people would just toss the pen into a drawer, or even into the trash can, without reading the message or thinking about what the slogan means. And if you really look at most premiums, you see that they're a part of equally unlikely scenarios. Sure, they often cost little, and so marketers often fall for them. But they usually don't work too well, so that money largely goes to waste.

But don't give up hope. You can find some impact scenario that works — some way to use a premium so that people actually get the message about your business or product and, as a result, take some action.

A coffee mug may work better than a pen for the bank example. A mug gives you enough room to print more information about the services you offer. You can print a "Did You Know?" headline on the mug, followed by short, bulleted facts about the problems the bank can solve for a small business owner ("Miser National Bank offers automatic bill paying," and so on). A customer, drinking coffee from that mug at the office, sees the information you print on it more often and may become curious enough about one of the services listed to ask for details next time he goes to the bank. But why will he keep it at the office and use it? Because it's an attractive mug, and perhaps because it has something attractive (a nice picture, for example) on the opposite side of your marketing message.

Premiums as profit centers

Speedo, the bathing suit/sports equipment marketer, uses T-shirts very effectively to promote its brand identity. It hires excellent designers to develop truly unique and attractive T-shirts that incorporate the Speedo name and logo within their artwork. And people love these shirts. So much so that quite a few of the shirts retail through sporting goods stores.

Get that? The quality of this premium item is so high that wholesale and retail customers *pay* to use it. Speedo doesn't have to give its shirts away to get people to wear them. People pay for the privilege of advertising the Speedo brand name on their bodies.

Similarly, some companies find their brand names so appealing that they can *license* the name and logo to clothing, bag, and other manufacturers. These manufacturers are willing to pay a percent of their revenues for the name and logo because it helps sell products.

Any popular sports team can make good money from its licensing operations — in essence, getting paid to advertise rather than having to pay for the exposure! And well-known brand names, like Coke and Caterpillar, also generate millions of dollars in licensing revenues.

If you build the strength of your brand, you, too, may find that other marketers want to cash in on your brand's good name — and that you can advertise on their products, just as if those products were premium items!

Or how about this for an out-of-the-box idea? Call up American Slide Chart Corporation (in Wheaton, Illinois, at www.americanslidechart.com or 630-665-3333) to obtain a slide-chart, wheel-chart, or pop-up (when you open it, it unfolds to become a three-dimensional object) to include in that next mailing of checking account statements. I like the idea of a slide or wheel chart because the chart is novel and interactive. You can easily design (or have someone else design) the chart to solve a problem or give access to selected information for the user. The chart may say "How to Solve the Five Most Common Financial Problems of Small Business" on the outside, along with a listing of those five problems. You then print an inner sheet with pointer arrows next to those handy solutions (each solution, of course, involving the use of one of your bank's new services).

To use the chart, the customer slides the inner sheet until a black dot appears in a hole through the outer sheet next to the problem the customer selects. Doing so aligns the appropriate solution in a window on the bottom of the outer sheet. You can also add other pages to the chart, such as a tear-off mailer to sign up for services or request information.

Here's the impact scenario for this slide chart: The customer pulls an odd object out of the envelope, glances at it (unfamiliarity generates curiosity), sees that the object claims to solve financial problems for small businesses, and — at least sometimes — starts fooling around with the chart. Soon the customer selects one of those five financial problems — presumably the most relevant one — and now reads in the display window about how one of your new services solves the problem in a jiffy. Perhaps the customer even picks up a pen (not noticing that the pen has the name of a competing bank imprinted on it), fills in the tear-off postcard, and tosses it in the out box for mailing. Don't forget to put a Web address on the chart, too — and put a virtual version of your problem-solving wheel on your Web page!

Can this premium work? Maybe — at least the scenario is plausible. You need to run the numbers to be sure, of course. If you estimate that one in twenty customers receiving the slide chart will end up trying one of your new services, does this number give you a big enough return to justify the cost of producing and mailing those slide charts? Probably. In fact, that plan sounds very good.

Considering the premium options

As you think about ways of using premiums, consider a wide range of choices (see Table 11-1), ranging from wonderful standards (in the Old Classics column) to innovative options that also work well (in the New Classics column). If I hadn't run across a clever slide chart recently (see the preceding section), I wouldn't know about the American Slide Chart Corporation and what it can do for marketers.

Table 11-1	Finding the Premium Options
Old Classics	*New Classics*
Pens, pencils	Clocks, watches
Calendars	Mouse pads
Key chains	Imprinted computer disks
Note pads	Pocket knives
Rulers	Flashlights
Mugs	Calculators
Caps	Stress-ease balls (try www.promosfast.com)
T-shirts	Frisbees
Thermometers	Leather pad holders and portfolios
Coasters	Children's toys
Balloons	Canvas or nylon tote bags
Umbrellas	Magnetic calendars
Golf balls (call Spalding Sports Worldwide at 413-536-1200 or try try www.logogolfballs.com or www.tsgsports.com	Packaged snacks (popcorn, candy, healthy protein bars)
Lapel pins	Sports/water bottles
Watches	Books with customized covers
	Globe paperweights (a neat design in Lucite is offered by Best Impressions, 800-635-2378 or www.bestimpressions.com)
	Kaleidoscopes (call Van Cort Instruments at 413-665-2000)

The premium industry offers such a wide variety of choices to advertisers that you should think of premiums as a group of specialized media instead of thinking of them as a single medium.

Using the quality strategy

Most marketers think about the *message* (the copy and/or artwork) that they put on the premium. But this focus can lead you to forget that the premium itself communicates a strong message. The premium is a gift from you to your customer. Therefore, the premium tells your customers a great deal about you and what you think of them. A cheap, tacky gift may look good when you run the numbers, but it doesn't look good to the customer who receives it. Yet most premiums are of low or medium quality. Few are as good as, or better than, what we'd buy for ourselves.

You can make your premium stand out by simply selecting an item of higher-than-usual quality. One health spa, for example, orders the nicest terry-cloth robes money can buy, with an elegant embroidered version of its logo on the chest, and sells them at cost to customers, who view them as prized possessions. A customer remembers a better gift more easily, and that gift creates a stronger and more positive image of the marketer. And more customers keep and use the item for a lengthy period of time. Of course, a better gift usually costs more. But you can justify this cost by selecting a gift that makes a greater impact — and reduce the cost by distributing the gift to a better- quality, more selective list. Consider the following example:

- ✔ **Premium A (Cheap gift with direct mail solicitation)**

  - Cost of Premium A = $5 each, or $5,000 for a distribution of 1,000.

  - Response Rate (customer orders within 1 month) = 1.5 percent, or 15 per thousand.

  - If profit from each order is $1,000, *premium gross* = $15,000.

  - Return = gross of $15,000 per thousand minus cost of $5,000 per thousand = $10,000 per thousand.

- ✔ **Premium B (Expensive gift with direct mail solicitation)**

  - Cost of Premium B = $25 each, or $25,000 for a distribution of 1,000.

  - Response Rate (Customer orders within 1 month) = 12 percent, or 120 per thousand.

  - If profit from each order is $1,000, *premium gross* = $120,000.

  - Return = gross of $120,000 per thousand minus cost of $25,000 per thousand = $95,000 per thousand.

And if the $25 gift item is of significantly higher quality, you can expect a more positive impact on your customers — and higher response rates in any direct response program. Thus, the return is often considerably higher on a high-quality premium — provided you target the premium to the right customers (those likely to respond according to your scenario) and don't just blast it out to a poor-quality list.

Most marketers have difficulty bringing themselves to give away an expensive gift. They waver, lose their nerve, and go for a $5 item over a $25 item. Don't assume the cheaper one is more cost-efficient! Run the numbers first. Very often, the quality strategy wins, giving you much higher returns, as well as the far more favorable intangible benefit of improved brand image and customer loyalty. (If you aren't sure about response rates, you can experiment on a small scale before making your final decision.)

I give a contact for each of the more unusual premium items listed in Table 11-1. For example, the kaleidoscopes and other unusual items made by Van Cort Instruments are both unusual and unusually high in quality. Your customers have probably never received premium items such as the ones this company makes! You can get the more common items from many sources and I encourage you to shop around for the best service, prices, and quality.

For a quality take on some classic premiums, plus a broad assortment of high-quality clothing and luggage options, try Lands' End Corporate Sales (visit `www.landsend.com` or call 800-338-2000). They offer everything from aprons to sweaters, canvas bags to beach towels, and they embroider your logo and message neatly. You get a high-quality gift, one that stands out from the average premium item. If you think a high-quality polo shirt with attractive embroidery keeps with your image more than a cheaper silk-screened T-shirt, by all means, call Lands' End.

Making the Most of Word of Mouth

If you survey customers to identify the source of positive attitudes toward new products, you generally find that answers like "my friend told me about it" outnumber answers like "I saw an ad" by ten to one. Word-of-mouth communications about your product don't actually outnumber advertising messages; but when customers talk, other customers listen.

Word of mouth (WOM) gives a consumer (or a marketer) the most credible source of information about products, aside from actual personal experience with those products. What consumers tell each other about your products has a huge impact on your efforts to recruit new customers. Word of mouth also has a secondary, but still significant, impact on your efforts to retain old customers.

Honesty pays

A week after I bought my last new car, I received a surprise in the mail — a note from the saleswoman apologizing for a computational error and a check for a small amount of money to refund the difference.

The amount involved was a tiny fraction of a large purchase price. But I remember the refund most vividly because I was so surprised that the dealership voluntarily found the error and fixed it. This action violated my basic mistrust of car dealerships and salespeople.

I've told this story to many people, and some of them may go to that dealership to buy a car with my story of their thoughtful treatment in mind.

How can you control what people say about your product? You can't very effectively encourage customers to say nice things about and prevent them from slamming your product — many marketers assume that no one can do it. But you can influence word of mouth to some degree, and you have to try. Here are some ideas for how to manage word-of-mouth communications about your product:

- ✔ **Make your product special.** A product that surprises people because of its unexpectedly good quality or service is special enough to talk about. A good product or a well-delivered service wins fans and turns your customers into your sales force.

- ✔ **Do something noteworthy in the name of your product or company.** If no aspect of your product itself is incredibly wonderful and surprising, do some cool activity and associate that activity with your product. Support a neat not-for-profit organization in your neighborhood (see Chapter 12). Stage a fun event for kids. Let your employees take short sabbaticals to volunteer in community services. All these strategies have worked well in the past to generate positive publicity and word of mouth. Get creative. You can think of something worthwhile, some way of helping improve your world that surprises people and makes them take notice of the good you're doing in the name of your product.

- ✔ **Use exciting sales promotions and premiums, not boring ones.** A 24-cent coupon isn't worth talking about. But a sweepstakes contest in which the winners get to spend a day with the celebrity of their choice can get consumers excited. A premium like this sweepstakes generates positive PR and a lot of WOM. Similarly, if you give away notepads and pens that sport your company name, nobody mentions your company to their friends and relations. But if you think of something really unusual to give them, that item becomes a talking point. Especially if they can wear or prominently display the premium in their home or office because people will ask them about it.

✔ **Identify and cultivate decision influencers.** In many markets, some people's opinions matter a lot more than others. These people are *decision influencers,* and if you (hypothetically) diagram the flow of opinions, you find that many of them originate with these people. In business-to-business marketing, the decision influencers are often obvious. A handful of prominent executives, a few editors working for trade magazines, and some of the staff at trade associations probably exert a strong influence over everybody else's opinions. You can find identifiable decision influencers in consumer markets, as well. In the market for soccer equipment, youth coaches, league managers, and the owners of independent sporting goods stores are important decision influencers.

To take advantage of decision influencers, develop a list of who falls into that category for your product or service and then make a plan for cultivating them. Match them with appropriate managers or salespeople who can take them to events or out to lunch, just for fun. You just need to make sure that people associated with your business are in the personal networks of these decision influencers. Consider developing a series of giveaways and informational mailings to send to these decision influencers. If I wanted to sell the shoe to youth players, I'd send free samples of a new soccer cleat to youth coaches. When you know who's talking and who's listening, you can easily focus your efforts on influencing the talkers.

Chapter 12

Special Events, Trade Shows, and Other Face-to-Face Marketing Opportunities

. . . .

In This Chapter

▶ Using face-to-face opportunities

▶ Sponsoring an event

▶ Creating your own events

▶ Marketing at trade shows

▶ Conducting effective demonstrations

▶ Giving gifts to customers and employees

. . . .

*I*n this chapter, I use the term *face-to-face marketing* to describe non-sales-oriented ways of having a personal impact on individuals and groups. When you set up a booth and display your wares at a trade show, this is face-to-face marketing. Many potential buyers walk by that booth, and some will come in to examine and ask questions. That is a powerful opportunity to do good marketing. Face-to-face marketing has a personal, warm, human element to it that gives it special marketing leverage. I should say, however, that sometimes a special event may be a bit less personal than this — perhaps you sponsor a local baseball team, for example, in which case the individuals who play, and their families and fans, do certainly have a high level of involvement — but probably not with you or other representatives of your company. Still, that human contact and sense of bringing people together in some sort of community makes a sports team sponsorship especially effective, so I think it is fair to consider it a form of face-to-face marketing, too.

Face-to-face marketing serves many purposes, and it can take a number of forms. You can sponsor someone else's event or stage your own. You can buy exhibitor space in a trade show — a special kind of face-to-face marketing designed to put you in front of a lot of prospects in a hurry. And with the Web at your command, you can connect people with virtual face-to-face marketing that you don't need to spend a ton of money on to integrate it into your marketing routine.

Whatever the exact nature of the face-to-face marketing, it gives you a temporary way to make a special connection with prospects and customers, putting you face to face with large numbers of customers or prospects. I recommend every marketer consider face-to-face marketing and every marketing plan have a section devoted to it. In this chapter, I show you how to bottle up the face-to-face marketing magic and put it to work in your marketing program.

Harnessing the Power of Face-to-Face Marketing

Face-to-face marketing has to have considerable drawing power. Think of it as theater — a performance that entertains or stimulates people in a satisfying way (and sometimes includes people as participants, not just as an audience). At a trade show, you may need to add interactive activities to your booth or invite a team of massage therapists to do their thing at specified hours to attract your target audience. In a store, appealing to your audience can mean bringing in an expert to give a weekend workshop. For a consulting firm, it may mean offering a special one-hour seminar lead by your principals, accessible to all clients and prospects over the Internet.

Face-to-face marketing is a great example of the real-world marketing principle that you should give away as much as you can. In the competition for consumers' attention, you often have to give them an interesting performance to win that attention. Here are more ideas for face-to-face marketing that you may want to promote:

- A client-appreciation event (what used to be called a party)

- A musical performance

- A weekend at a golf resort for your top customers, along with prizes for the winning golfers — and everyone else, too

- A fundraising dinner for an important charity

- A community event, like a fair or children's workshop

✔ An exhibit or hospitality suite at a major trade show for people in your industry

✔ A community talent show

✔ A workshop in which you share your expertise or solve problems for participants

The possibilities are endless and varied. But they all attract people and hold their attention. And you need that attention to communicate and persuade as a marketer.

Planning it yourself or piggybacking

You have a great deal of choice — not only over the type of face-to-face opportunity you can participate in, but also over the level and nature of your participation. At the highest level of commitment, you can plan and manage your own events. Depending on the scale of the event, that process can be costly and difficult, but sometimes it's the best solution — especially if you want to have enough control to keep any other marketers from using the audience attention that the event generates. But you may also choose an event that others are organizing and sign on as a sponsor. That's easier, and often cheaper, but may be less powerful in terms of marketing impact. It is easier because you piggyback on an existing event and the work others are doing to organize it.

Automaker Volvo has a separate company, Volvo Event Management, which has been working to build excitement for several years in advance of the November 5, 2005, start date for a major event, the Volvo Ocean Race. Beginning in Spain, contestants from dozens of countries will sail around the world with close media coverage the entire way. It is to be the biggest event in sailing in the 2005–2006 season and a major source of media coverage for Volvo. But the coverage started years earlier with a major Web site tracking the progress of the sailing teams as they designed and built special boats for the race, and marketing of subscriptions for the Volvo Ocean Race Magazine. This example shows you event sponsorship on a large, exciting scale.

On a smaller scale, a local Seabrook, Texas, restaurant called Maribelle's sponsors the Clear Lake Racing Association's Wednesday night sailboat races. Featuring exciting action set close to the shore, where spectators can see the boats at local bars and dockside restaurants, these races attract local attention. Some of the sails display Maribelle's company logo prominently, making this advertising an inexpensive, but effective, way to use sailboat race sponsorship in marketing. And Maribelle's uses other events too, such as performances by popular blues bands, to attract customers and pack the house.

Business and industry opportunities

Turn first to your professional groups and industry trade associations for appropriate business-to-business marketing. These venues differ for each industry but have the benefit of collecting your prospective customers in one place in common. Attend conferences and trade shows if your budget is small and do plenty of informal networking. If you can afford to, also rent display space at trade shows, present at conferences, and sponsor industry events. The more visible you are at your own industry events, the more customer attention and credibility you can generate.

Trade shows are great because they draw people who are wearing their business hats, ready to make purchase decisions for their companies. You can also put on special events for your own customers or employees. (In fact, employee events often provide that extra motivating power that you need to get your people fully behind your marketing plan.)

Whatever the business-oriented opportunity, remember that you're still trying to attract and hold the attention of people, not businesses. You're interested in the people in any business who make the purchase decisions. Corporations have only legal lives. They are dead as doornails when it comes to marketing. So, above all, make sure that your business-oriented events interest the people involved.

Getting stuffy and businesslike is very easy, but do people really want to sit through two days of lectures on the impact of new technologies in their industry? You're better off offering them optional, one-hour panel discussions on the topic, with a backbone of outdoor sports and recreation events or a visit to a nearby golf course. (Instead of sponsoring a booth at a February trade show in Minneapolis, go with the one in Florida!). And yes, it's true: Attendance is always high at conferences and other corporate events if you hold them in Las Vegas.

The need for originality

You need to be creative and original in all real-world marketing, but these qualities apply even more in the area of face-to-face marketing. So pay close attention while I tell you the one thing you must never forget about event-based marketing:

It's never as good as the first time!

Be sure to apply this principle when you work with face-to-face marketing. Don't sponsor the same event twice just because it worked well last year. Don't do the same sort of demo, in the same booth, at ten different trade shows in the same year. Always look for something new, different, and fun. Avoid stale reruns. Give people something new and exciting.

I bet you're saying, "But that's obvious!" I know, I know. No performer worth his salt tells the same joke or sings the same song twice in a row. After the audience laughs or applauds, everyone knows that it's time to move on to something new.

But some companies never change. Many — and yours may be one — repeat the same basic events as if they're religious rituals. Employees suffer the most in those awards dinners, holiday gift-giving rituals, or executive motivational speeches because they have to put up with the dull repetition. And think how often companies do the same thing to their customers.

If your company, like most, uses the same basic booth staffed by the same brochure-waving salespeople at every trade show, then it may as well be telling the same joke over and over. And the joke's on you. Similarly, if your company gives to the same charities every year, the repetition has probably long since dulled the impact of those sponsorships.

I don't care what you do — as long as the activity is something new and different that actually has some entertainment value. If face-to-face marketing is a gift to your customers, then why keep giving the same old gift, year after year?

Sponsoring a Special Event

Some people assume that special events are only useful in special circumstances, when you can justify a major effort and expense. Not so. Staging small-scale events or (as I discuss in this section) riding on the coattails of somebody else's event can work, too. (I also think of this as piggybacking on others' investments in events, a helpful term in visualizing the benefits.)

Why create your own event when so many wonderful events already exist? Many companies that sponsor events as a way to expose their names to desirable audiences think that way, at least. But please make sure you get a clear, detailed agreement in writing about where, how, and how often the event identifies your brand name. That identification is the return on your sponsorship investment. Too often, sponsors end up complaining that they didn't get as much good exposure as they expected, so make sure you and the event directors understand the exposure level, up front.

You can find local organizations through local chambers of commerce or by following the events notices in local papers and on local radio stations. Nonprofit organizations can also refer you to other nonprofit organizations. Also consider calling up the local television stations and asking them what local events they expect to cover in the coming year. These events are naturals for your sponsorship because television coverage makes the potential audience bigger.

A number of Web-based companies now help you locate possible events to sponsor. For example, check out www.eventcrazy.com for hundreds of possibilities in everything from sports to the arts, from reenactments and museum shows to auto racing. You can enter your zip code and limit the distance away from your location if you want to find smaller, local events to sponsor through this site. You can find an exciting new event sponsorship out there that fits your budget and customers.

Finding cause-related events

You can attract a lot of positive attention from the media and the community by sponsoring a fundraising event for a charity. This event sponsorship is, for obvious reasons, called *cause-related event sponsorship*. Businesses in North America alone spend an unbelievable $5 billion on cause sponsorship per year. You can generate extremely valuable goodwill by cause sponsorship — at least, if the cause and event are appropriate to your target market.

However, too much of this money is thrown away on events that appeal to somebody at the sponsoring company but don't appeal to its customers. Be careful to pick causes that appeal not only to you and your associates, but also to your target customers. Maybe your CEO really gets excited about those United Way campaigns. But have you checked with your customers to see what charities they're excited about? Many auto dealerships sponsor sporting events that appeal to their male executives, forgetting that the majority of their customers are female. (Yes, the majority of car buyers in the United States, and in some European countries, are women. How about sponsoring a dance performance?)

Donations to controversial causes or to political campaigns are likely to offend people. Stay away from anything controversial. Causes having to do with health, children, preventing diseases and drug abuse, helping animals, and conserving the natural world generally pass the controversy test — unless the particular organization takes an overly controversial approach.

If you don't have the marketing budget to sponsor a local charity, consider donating your time, instead. You can join the board of a charity and offer your energy and business savvy.

Be careful to examine the charity's books and tax-exempt status before sponsoring it or running an event to benefit it. Make sure it has full charitable status (defined as a 501c3 corporation in the United States, for example) and that its audited financial statements show it has relatively low overhead and moderate-looking executive salaries. You don't want to support a charity that turns out to be poorly or dishonestly run. I'm on the board of a charitable foundation that gets hundreds of applications for funding from charities, and I've gone through this due-diligence process many times. It's taught me that some charities are more effective and well run than others and that you never really know until you look. Their records and financials should be available for public inspection, so all you have to do is ask. If an organization hesitates to share this information, don't get involved with it.

Running the numbers on an event

Be careful to pick a cause-related event or other event that reaches your target customers efficiently. Like any marketing communication, an event sponsorship needs to deliver reach at a reasonable cost. So ask yourself how many people will come to the event or hear of your sponsorship of it. Then ask yourself what percentage of this total is likely to be in your target market. That's your *reach*. Divide your cost by this figure, multiply it by 1,000, and you have the cost of your reach per thousand. You can compare this cost with cost figures for other kinds of reach, such as a direct mailing or a print or radio ad (see Chapters 7, 9, and 13 for more information on the costs of these types of reach).

If you think the event sponsorship is more credible and convincing than an ad because of its affiliation with an appealing cause, you can adjust your cost figure to compensate. Doing so is called *weighting the exposure*. For example, say you decide one exposure to your company or brand through a cause sponsorship is twice as powerful as exposure to one of your ads. Then multiply the number of people the event reaches by 2 before calculating the cost. That way, you compare the cost of reaching 2,000 people through the sponsorship to the cost of reaching 1,000 people through advertising, which adjusts for the greater value you attach to the cause-related exposure.

In my experience, the right special event is often many times more effective than an advertisement. But the event has to be appropriate or it's worthless — so keep reading. And make sure you publicize the event well — see Chapter 11 in this book or a longer treatment of this topic in my book *Marketing Kit For Dummies* (Wiley).

Evaluating the options for sponsorship

If you're considering event sponsorship, you're in good company. Worldwide spending is over $12 billion a year for this type of marketing alone, according to the International Events Group, or IEG (www.ieg.com, www.sponsorship.com, or 312-944-1727). This organization provides consulting and information-packed publications to event sponsors, globally. The *IEG Sponsorship Report* shows that North American sponsorship spending is highest for sporting events (68 percent), and that the rest of sponsorship spending is spread over a wide range of other options, including entertainment, tours, attractions, festivals, fairs, and the arts (from 6 to 9 percent each).

If you take these numbers at face value, sporting events are the best place to spend your money, and the arts should get the smallest amount of your sponsorship money. That may be true — but I seriously doubt it. Why? Because these are just the totals, and what's right for your particular firm may be very different. If your product, service, or customer base is related to the arts, or if you happen to be particularly involved in the arts, you may want to ignore sports events and sponsor the arts exclusively. This is an example of letting your own particular interests and talents (your core brilliance) focus how you market.

To decide what is best for you, use the three-step selection process discussed in the three following sections.

By the way, as I go on to examine other forms of events, you find that the same three-step process is useful there, too. That's because you need to design all events through careful examination of your options, by running the numbers, and by screening for relevance.

Step 1: Explore the options

Some businesses are deluged with requests for sponsorships, and so they have plenty of options just sitting in their in baskets. For example, Storybook Vineyards, a small specialty producer of fine California zinfandel wines, receives on average one request every day for donations of wine to special events. But even a company like that may overlook some kinds of events. Most countries have millions of events a year. The more of them you know about, the better.

IEG publishes a sourcebook listing many of the options, including just about every large-scale event. Also, contact chambers of commerce in towns and cities where you want to target your sponsorship dollars. They offer lists of local events that may be the biggest thing in town, even though you've never heard of them. Also, call organizations that seem like a good match with your product and customer to see if they know about or put on appropriate events. For example, if you market sports equipment, educational games, or other products for kids, you may want to call the National Basketball Association to see if you can participate in one of their many events geared toward children (perhaps a Stay-in-School event featuring popular musicians and basketball stars?).

And don't overlook schools and colleges. They usually have a strong base of support in their communities, and some add a broader reach through their alumni, sports teams, prominent faculty, and the like. So try calling their public relations offices to see what kinds of events they have that may benefit from your sponsorship. (For an easy way to search for events locally or nationally in the United States, go to www.eventcrazy.com).

Step 2: Run the numbers

Carefully analyze the marketing impact of each candidate for sponsorship. Cut any from your list if their audiences aren't a good match with your target market. Cut any that may be controversial and likely to generate negative as well as positive attitudes. Cut any that do not seem to have strong positive images — no point sponsoring something unless your customers feel passionate about it! Now compare what's left by calculating your cost per thousand exposures for each one.

And don't be afraid to negotiate. If a sponsorship opportunity appeals to you but is priced too high, show them your comparative numbers and ask if they can cut you a deal!

This process may lead you away from the most popular types of sponsorship. A big, popular event (like a World Cup Soccer match) certainly exposes you to a lot of people — millions, if it is televised. But how many are really in your target market? And what is the cost of reaching them this way? Big sports and entertainment events often charge a premium because of their popularity and size. But they aren't worth that premium if you can buy similar reach for less by sponsoring several smaller events.

Step 3: Screen for relevance

Relevance is how closely the event relates to your product and its usage by customers, and it is the most important, but least considered, factor. Let me give you an example to illustrate the importance of relevance.

Here is an example of a simple, highly relevant, and very successful sponsorship. This one involves a privately owned Italian restaurant called Il Pirata in Amherst, Massachusetts. The restaurant provides free food for an art gallery opening nearby. This early-evening event attracted a large number of local residents interested in the arts. People came. They looked at the pictures, and they ate the food. Then they walked over to the restaurant and stood in line to be seated because their taste test convinced them that Il Pirata was just the place to go for dinner. And many of them became regular customers.

This event sponsorship passes the relevance test with flying colors. Those who appreciate art often appreciate good food, as well. By trying the food, they overcame any uncertainty they may have had about its appeal. What's more relevant than a chance to expose potential customers to your actual product in a pleasing setting?

A chance to use the product, or at least to see the product in use, makes any event highly relevant. And the more relevant the event, the more valuable those exposures.

Putting On a Public Event

Sometimes, you have no alternative but to stage the event yourself. None of the sponsorship options fit your requirements. Or you really need the exclusivity of your own event — a forum in which no competitors' messages can interfere with your own.

Selling sponsorship rights

A good way to make your event pay for itself is to find other companies that want to help sponsor the event. Not your competitors, of course. Many companies often have an interest in the same event as you do, but for different reasons, and these firms make good co-sponsors. Basically, if the event is relevant, novel, and is likely to draw in their target audience, then you have a good pitch. Now you just need to go out and make sales calls on potential sponsors. (Also be sure to publicize the event well by listing it in *Advertising Age* and the trade magazines in your industry and by posting the event on the Web.) Or consider hiring an event management firm (see the following section for a listing). Some of these firms sell sponsorships as well as help to organize and run events.

Getting help managing your event

Some people specialize in managing special events; they work on a consulting basis, from conception through completion, to make sure that everyone comes and everything goes just right. Many such specialists exist, from independent experts (check your city's business-to-business Yellow Pages directory) all the way to major companies, like those listed in the following bullets. I recommend bringing in a specialist of some sort to help you design and manage any event that involves a lot of people, shows, speeches or activities, meals, conference and hotel room reservations, security, transportation, and all those sorts of details that you have to do right in order to avoid disaster.

Here are some examples of event management services to jump-start your research:

- A-S-K (1505 Kasold Dr., Lawrence, KS 66047; phone 800-315-4333; Web site www.askusa.com) offers conference, trade show, and event planning and management.

- BF Golf Tournament Services (101 Thorne Ave., Hempstead, NY 11550; phone 888-333-3479; Web site www.bfgolfservices.com) organizes and runs golf events.

- Carlstrom Productions, Inc. (438 State St., San Mateo, CA 94401; phone 800-388-6395 or 650-401-8881; Web site www.carlstromproductions.com) stages sales meetings, product launch events, entertainment, and other events.

- Centra (430 Bedford St., Lexington, MA 02420; phone 781-861-7000; Web site www.centra.com) has an event management service that can stage Web-based events for your customers or sales associates.

- Designing Events (10910 Reisterstown Rd., Owings Mills, MD 21117; phone 888-417-2589 or 410-654-5525; Web site www.designingevents.com) is a full-service event planner and manager.

- Destination Tour Management (333 Washington Blvd., Suite 360, Marina Del Rey, CA 90292; phone 800-379-4626; Web site www.destination-tour-management.com) handles a wide range of events and can help with everything from planning and travel to marketing the event.

- George Washington University (2121 Eye St., N.W., Washington, DC 20052; phone 202-994-4949; Web site www.gwu.edu/emp/) offers a certificate course in event management, which you can take online.

- PlanetConnect (223 Maple Ave., Red Bank, NJ 07701; phone 732-933-9473; Web site www.planetconnect.com) stages conferences, local road shows, trade shows, and seminars.

Exhibiting at Trade Shows and Exhibitions

Do you need to exhibit at trade shows? If you're in a business-to-business selling situation, I assume that you do. Exhibiting is almost always necessary, even if you only do so to keep competitors from stealing your customers at the show! Business-to-business marketers in the United States devote a fifth of their marketing budgets, on average, to trade shows, and in Europe the figure is even higher — one quarter of the budget goes to trade shows (these figures are from a study in the *Journal of Marketing*).

Other sources suggest that trade shows generate 18 percent of all sales leads, on average. As a way to control your own trade show spending, why not compare percent of budget and percent of leads, adjusting the percent of budget figure until you find the spending level that yields the best return in leads? If you spend 20 percent of your budget on trade shows, you want to try to beat the average and get more than 20 percent of your leads from these shows. That means being a savvy event manager — selecting appropriate shows and staging excellent booths at them.

Some retail or consumer industries also have major shows. Boat manufacturers use boat shows as an important way to expose consumers to their products. County fairs attract exhibitors of arts and crafts, gourmet foods, and gardening supplies. Computer shows showcase new equipment. If your industry has a major show for the public, I highly recommend that you try to exhibit there. Send your in-house list of customers and friends an invitation, too — the more traffic you can get in your booth, the better. (In fact, you should plan to begin direct marketing to announce the event and give people incentives to come, starting at least two months before the show!)

Doing trade shows on the cheap

You may want to consider sharing a booth with a similar (but not closely competing) business if the expenses are too high and you aren't sure you can get a good return on the cost of a booth. We use this money-saving strategy at my firm. We buy half-booths at some regional human-resources meetings by working with our regional affiliates, smaller local training companies. These affiliates show our products, and they also sell themselves and their own services. We both get good leads — at half the regular cost.

Knowing what trade shows can accomplish for you

You can generate leads, find new customers, and maintain or improve your current customers' perceptions of you at trade shows. You can also use trade shows to introduce a new product or launch a new strategy. And they give you great opportunities to introduce back-office people (like the sales support staff or even the president!) to your customers face to face.

Use trade shows to network in your industry. You usually find the best manufacturers' representatives and salespeople by making connections at trade shows. And if you're secretly hoping to find a better employer, a little mingling may yield an offer at the next big trade show. Also, be sure to talk with a lot of attendees and noncompetitive exhibitors in order to find out about the newest trends and what your competitors are doing in the market. The information a good networker gleans from a trade show is often worth more than the price of attendance. Never mind selling — get out there and chat.

In short, you should see trade shows as essential to your marketing program for many reasons. Even if you think you may lose money on the project, a trade show can be worthwhile in the long run. And a well-designed exhibit, well promoted in advance and staffed with people who are prepared to find leads and close sales, usually produces an almost immediate return on investment.

Building the foundations for a good booth

Marketers focus on the booth when they think about how to handle a trade show. But you should consider the booth just a part of your overall marketing strategy for the show. And you don't have a show strategy until you've written something intelligent down to answer each of these questions:

- ✔ How do we attract the right people to the show and to our booth?
- ✔ What do we want visitors to our booth to do at the show and in our booth?
- ✔ How can we communicate with and motivate visitors when they get to the booth?
- ✔ How can we figure out who visitors are and how to handle them in the booth?
- ✔ How can we capture information about them, their interests, and needs?
- ✔ How can we follow up to build or maintain our relationship with them?

The strategy has to start by attracting a lot of prospects and customers, and the easiest way to do so is to just go with the flow by picking a show that potential customers already plan to attend. Ask yourself what shows your customers are going to attend. For example, if you import gift items and your customers include the buyers from retail gift stores, then where do they go to make their purchases? Can the New York Gift Show give you full access to the market in the Eastern half of the United States, for example, or do you need to go to regional shows, like the Boston Gift Show and the Portland Gift Show? You can ask the sponsoring organizations for data on who attended last year's show and who has registered for this year's show, using this information to help you decide. You need to see high numbers of your target customers. Otherwise, the show wastes your company's time and money.

You can also ask a sampling of customers for their opinions about your booth. You may want to use the simplest research method, which researchers call informal qualitative interviews — what ordinary folks refer to as conversations. Just talk to some customers, preferably at the show because their memory of your booth is still clear. See what they think. Or you can do some intercept interviews at the show. You conduct an *intercept interview* when you walk up to people as they pass by your booth and ask them if they will answer a few questions, such as "Do you like the such-and-such booth?" and "How exciting is this booth's design?"

Attractive company seeks compatible trade show for romantic weekend

How do you find out about possible trade shows? I thought you'd never ask! If you subscribe to trade magazines, the shows in your industry find you because the magazines sell their lists to the show sponsors. But don't go just by what comes in your junk mail because you may overlook something important. The Trade Show Exhibitors Association (Springfield, Virginia, 703-941-3725 or www.tsea.org) can provide you with information about shows in your industry. The association also gives a great source of information and training for trade show booth designers and exhibitors.

American Exhibition Services (AES) handles over 300 major shows, so you should check with them, as well (visit www.aesmarketing.com for information on their wide range of services). And www.TSNN.com is a useful clearinghouse of listings for vendors and companies involved in the trade show industry.

For recent listings and press announcements of trade shows and other industry events, visit PR Newswire's trade show area at www.prnewswire.com/prntradeshows/ts_new.shtml. (Or announce your own event using their online distribution of corporate press releases.)

But you do have another source, one that I find much more reliable than any other — your customers. The whole point of exhibiting at a trade show is to reach customers, so why don't you just ask them where you should exhibit? Call or drop by a selection of your best customers and ask them for advice on where and when to exhibit. They know what's hot right now and what's not.

Renting the perfect booth

You need to select a location and booth size. You want to aim for anywhere near a major entrance, the food stands, bathrooms, or any other place that concentrates people. Being on the end of an aisle can help you, too. And bigger is better — in general, you should get the biggest booth you can afford.

But even if you end up with a miniature booth in the middle of an aisle, don't despair. Many shoppers try to walk all the aisles of a show, and these locations can work, too, provided the show draws enough of the right kind of customers for you. In fact, smart buyers often look at the smallest, cheapest booths in the hope of discovering something hot and new from a struggling entrepreneurial supplier.

Setting up other kinds of displays

The firms that make trade show booths also can help with many other kinds of displays, such as lobby, conference room, and tabletop displays. These smaller-scale displays can be effective in the right spot and often cost you less than a trade show booth, so explore all the options before you decide what fits your marketing program and budget best.

Experts can help you design and build your booth or other display, manage the trade show program, and handle the sales leads that result from it. The Freeman Exhibit Co. (8301 Ambassador Row, Dallas, TX 75247; phone 713-681-7722; Web site www.freemanexhibit.com) builds exhibits, manages leads, and coordinates international and domestic trade show programs. And here are a few more established companies in the United States who help with a range of displays and booths, to get you started in your search:

- ✔ Design Marketing Group, Inc., 375 Interstate Blvd., Sarasota, FL 34240; phone 941-377-6709; Web site www.dmgsarasota.com

- ✔ Exhibit Marketing Consultants, Inc., phone 218-365-5596; Web site www.emcplus.com

- ✔ FLEXi Display Marketing Inc., 801 Stephenson Highway, Troy, MI 48083; phone 800-875-1725; Web site www.flexidisplay.com

- ✔ Gilchrist & Associates LLC, 15235 Boones Way, Lake Oswego, OR 97035; phone 503-635-5100; Web site www.gilchristassociates.biz

- ✔ Studio Displays, Inc., 10600 Southern Loop Blvd., Pineville, NC 28134; phone 704-588-6590; Web site www.studiodisplays.com

Many other firms provide booth design services, too — consult business directories at a library or cruise the Internet for leads. And many ad agencies handle trade shows as part of an overall marketing communications program. For example, Dawson Marketing Group (390 Main St., Suite 200, Woburn, Massachusetts 01801; phone 781-933-8855) provides what they call "integrated marketing services" that include trade shows along with many other ad agency services.

I recommend getting opinions and quotes from multiple vendors (and asking for credit references and the contact names of some recent clients) before choosing the right company for your job. I also recommend sharing your budget constraints upfront to find out if the company you're talking to is appropriate for you. Some can do very economical, small-scale projects with ease, and others are more oriented to large-scale corporate accounts.

Don't overlook the drawing power of simple things, like fresh flowers or food. At a recent trade show where we rented a booth, we offered free Mrs. Fields cookies and brought them in fresh each day. A simple gesture, but remarkably effective at drawing traffic to our booth and putting visitors in a positive mood! Other times, we've used comfort as our draw by setting up some cushy seats in the booth. People stand for hours at these shows, so they appreciate a chance to rest — and of course, if someone sits there too long, you can launch into your hard sell and either win an order or politely drive them from the booth to open the seat to someone else. A massage chair or bottles of cold spring water can also draw weary visitors to your booth.

Doing Demonstrations

Seeing is believing. This old saying contains wisdom, and if you think a demonstration is applicable to your goods or services, you should definitely consider giving one. Demonstrations are often the most effective ways of introducing a new product, or even introducing an old product to new customers. When Dummies Press launched *Weddings For Dummies* at a publishing industry trade show, called Book Expo American, the PR staff gave out slices of wedding cake in the Dummies Press booth. Talk about a big hit! Everybody wanted a piece, and everybody became aware of the new book.

You can do a demonstration anywhere. Really. Even when you sponsor someone else's event, if you ask early on, they can often find a time and place for you to stage a demonstration. And when you control the event or a part of it, you have considerable freedom to design demonstrations. Let me show you some specifics.

In a retail store, mall, or other consumer-oriented location, a demonstration is often the most persuasive form of promotion. You see these lame demos used at your local grocery store on occasion: A bored woman handing out teeny-tiny bites of some sloppy new kind of bean dip from a card table at the end of the toilet paper aisle? Give me a break. A proper retail demo should be:

- **Realistic!** Show the product in a natural use context — and that includes normal portions of foods. (*Natural use* means how the customer would normally use it. If you eat a food product for dinner, find a way to demonstrate it on a table with real place settings, for example.)

- **Wonderful!** The event should be worthy of attention, with real entertainment value that adds excitement to the product. Try a cooking demonstration with a lot of action, not just a one-bite taste. Or make the demonstration a taste test in which the new bean dip wins a contest and the tasters get the prizes. Imagine you're creating a skit for a television show — that's the sort of entertainment people pay attention to.

- **A marketing priority!** Here's your chance to sell your product directly to customers. Think of a political candidate going out to shake hands (notice the candidate always wears his or her best suit and biggest smile). Too often, companies put poorly qualified temps in charge of demos. Who do you really want out there selling your product — someone who makes the product look good or someone you wouldn't dare talk to if you sat next to him on the subway?

When you follow these three rules, you create great demos. But note that these demonstrations are more expensive than the lame ones we usually encounter. That's okay because they're more effective. Use them more sparingly, but put more into each one, and they can reward you with a surprisingly high level of customer enthusiasm.

Giving Gifts

Premium items, as the industry calls them, are simply gifts you give to your customers, clients, prospects, or employees. Not bribes; gifts. I recommend that you send your regular customers some kind of premium they will appreciate at least once a year. Another approach is to spread them out in ways that spread the good word about your firm or product, making the premiums, and those who receive them, your ambassadors. A privately owned stationery and office supply store I know does this by offering free pens at its register. The pens are not fancy, but they work well and look nice, and they have the store's name, address, and phone number of them. Thousands of these pens are floating around homes and offices in their market area, helping to keep their store as visible as the new Staples they must compete with.

Giving out a free pen at the register is as simple as putting a FREE PENS sign on a container, but when choosing a gift for your good customers, put more care into the selection and presentation of the premium to make sure it is appreciated. Think of gift giving as a form of theater, as a special option among special events, and you can avoid the standard stupidities. Heck, you may even gain customer attention and goodwill. (See Chapter 11 for more information on premium items and visit www.insightsformarketing.com for my pick of recommendations and links to good vendors who can help you.)

Note that trade show booths usually give away some premium items, and you want to think about what you can give away if you exhibit at a convention or trade show. I recommend that you give a fun or interesting gift (a puzzle, joke book, or toy, for example) as a token of appreciation for filling in a registration form. You want to focus your marketing resources on finding and qualifying leads, so focus everything you do, from advance mailings and e-mailings to booth design and signs, on this goal. Giving everyone who wanders by your booth a gift is silly, and it requires such a large volume of gifts that you can't afford something nice. But there are exceptions to this rule. Free bottles of cold spring water, cookies, or other draws can be offered to all as a way to attract people to your booth. Then add a more durable premium gift as a thank-you when you give out brochures and collect information from serious leads.

If you're selecting premium items for a trade show or other event to which people travel for long distances, stick with easy-to-carry items. Keep gifts small, durable, and suitable for airport security, and also make an effort to keep your marketing materials (brochures, for example) compact and durable enough that they won't be left in the hotel room or ruined in someone's luggage.

As with all face-to-face marketing opportunities, you want to make a positive impact that customers remember down the road, so choose your gifts with this end in mind.

Chapter 13

Direct Marketing: Direct-Response Ads, Direct Mail, and Telemarketing

Doing direct marketing is easy, but doing it well is difficult. You have to master it to the degree that you can beat the odds and obtain higher-than-average response rates. I share multiple ways to achieve this goal in this chapter as I help you review the varied problems and practices of direct marketing. This chapter focuses on conventional media — print ads, conventional mail (versus e-mail, which is covered in Chapter 10), and the telephone. Remember these media can be integrated with (or sometimes replaced with) Web-based marketing, which I discuss in Chapter 10.

Beating the Odds with Your Direct Marketing

Direct marketing, relationship marketing, one-to-one marketing, and interactive marketing: They're all the same thing at heart, so I don't care what term you use. To me, direct marketing occurs whenever you, the marketer, take it upon yourself to create and manage customer transactions through one or more media.

The importance of civility in direct marketing

Many marketers are rushing to direct marketing in the often-mistaken belief that they can handle their customers better than any intermediaries can. But if you aren't accustomed to dealing directly with customers, you're likely to mess up your attempt at direct marketing. The most common way to mess marketing up is to be too direct. If you're in your customers' faces, you're probably getting on their nerves, as well. Direct marketing should build a bridge between you and the customer. No matter what direct marketing you do, always keep it civil and polite, and you get much better results. Avoid impolite calls, errors on labels, and anything else that may offend the average person. Cull lists to eliminate duplications and errors. It costs just a bit more to do it well, but you get far better results.

You have to make a positive impression if you want to achieve high response rates. Here's the most important principle of direct marketing. Please repeat after me: It's better to contact a hundred people well than a thousand people poorly!

The odds of success in direct marketing aren't particularly good. The average direct appeal to consumers or businesses goes unanswered. If you can up the response rate even a little bit over the average, you can make some serious money in direct-response marketing.

Practice makes perfect

Practice makes perfect in direct marketing, if you make sure to keep records of what you do and track the responses. That way, you can tell when a change improves response rates. Even if you have little or no experience in direct marketing, have faith that a small initiative can generate enough information for you to get a grip on how to direct market better and on a larger scale. The best way to become good at direct marketing is to start doing it.

Ease into direct marketing with a modest program to minimize your downside risk and start growing from there. This principle is true, whether you're big or small, a retailer or wholesaler, a for-profit or not-for-profit business. When Levi Strauss & Co. started a direct marketing initiative, they started simply, by including a registration card with each pair of jeans they sold. Equipment marketers know this technique well, but no one in other markets has used it very much. As cards came back, Levi Strauss & Co. built up a database of customers that they could use in their direct marketing.

Developing benchmarks for your campaign

Because your goal is to stimulate consumers to respond to you, your direct-response advertising has a pretty difficult task to accomplish. You need to understand that most of the interactions between your ad and your prospects fail to stimulate the response you want. Failure is the most common outcome of direct-response advertising! So your real goal is to minimize failure. Look at the statistics if you don't believe me:

✔ A full-page magazine ad typically pulls between 0.05 to 0.2 percent of circulation (the *pull rate* is the percentage of readers who respond to the ad by calling or mailing, according to the ad's instructions). So you can expect only two responses per thousand from a decent ad. Pretty bad, huh?

✔ A direct-mail letter, individually addressed, typically pulls between 0.5 and 5 percent of names you mailed to. So you can expect, at most, 50 responses per thousand from a decent letter. Better, but still pretty bad. (By the way, the cost per thousand — CPM — of a letter is often higher, so you don't necessarily get a better deal from direct mail than from magazine ads.)

✔ A direct-mail showing of your product in a portfolio of products, as in a catalog or card deck, pulls far less. Divide that 50 per thousand figure by the number of competing products for a rough idea of the average response rate (prominent placement does improve the rate, and so does any tendency of customers to make multiple purchases from the catalog). For example, if your product is on one postcard in a shrink-wrapped deck of 50 cards, the maximum response may be 1 per thousand. That's really bad, unless you happen to be selling something expensive enough to give you a good return at low numbers.

✔ A telemarketing center making calls to a qualified list can do somewhat better. The center may pull in the 0.75 to 5 percent range for a consumer product, but can get as high as 15 percent for some business-to-business sales efforts. However, telemarketing generates far more failures than successes, and its CPM is often higher than direct mail because it is more labor intensive.

In short, direct marketing doesn't generate very high response rates, and you have to make realistic projections before deciding to pay for a program. However, before you despair, know that good direct-marketing programs beat these odds and can be highly profitable. So don't be discouraged — just be dedicated to doing it better than average.

Using a database

Almost all direct marketers use computerized databases. You should make the transition to this technology eventually if you don't already use it. But you don't absolutely need a computerized database unless you have thousands of names in your database, so if you're a small-time direct marketer who's allergic to computers, you can postpone the transition. In fact, a drawer of customer folders and box of index cards make up the simplest forms of databases, which can do just fine for many smaller businesses. But if your business has a lot of contacts (or a fondness for computers), consider using one of the big-name database management programs: Access, dBase, Paradox, Oracle CRM, DB2 Universal Database, Microsoft CRM, Telemation, Maximizer, and so on.

Programmers have designed Maximizer's CRM (or Customer Relationship Management software) with the smaller business in mind; call 800-804-6299 or check out the Web site www.maximizer.com in North America for more information. Telemation is a CRM program for use in call centers (call 602-265-5968 or see the Web site www.databasesystemscorp.com for more information). If you're unfamiliar with the use of database programs, you may want to take a workshop on database management for marketing. Or consult the *For Dummies* product line, which contains reference books on a wide variety of computer programs at www.dummies.com. And at www.insightsformarketing.com, I've posted products I think may help you.

If you're designing or reviewing a database management system, make a list of the things you want the system to do. Write your list in nontechnical terms. You don't care how the program does its magic, just so long as it does it. For example, although different programs and in-house systems use different techniques to keep track of past customer sales, you just want your system to be able to sort customers by frequency or recency of past sales or give you a sales history on specific customers. Some programs permit this sort of analysis; others may not, so make sure that the program fulfills that list of what you want that program to do before you make a purchase.

The following are some of the most fundamental requirements of any marketing database:

✔ Report on and sort by recency of purchase

✔ Report on and sort by frequency of purchase

✔ Report on and sort by total value of past purchases in a selected period

✔ Support list management (merging and purging functions)

✔ Permit integration of new fields (including data from purchased lists or marketing research)

✔ Support name selection (through *segmentation*, which is dividing the list into similar subgroups; *profiling*, which is describing types of customers based on their characteristics; and *modeling*, which is developing statistical models to predict or explain response rates)

✔ Make sorting, updating, and correcting easy

✔ Make tracking and analyzing individual responses to specific communications easy, in order to test the effectiveness of a letter or script

✔ Allow operators at *call centers* (central collections of equipment and staff for handling incoming and/or outgoing calls more efficiently) to quickly pull up and add to profiles of all customers (or at least customers designated as members of a club or continuity program)

The preceding list shows you that you may want to do a great many things with your database. So please seriously think about what you need from your database and give the software maker or distributor, or the consultant or in-house programmer you work with, a list of requirements. Otherwise, you may spend a great deal of time seeing what your database program can't do, and that's not much fun!

Boosting sales from your offers

Here are a few starting tips to help you get focused on the goal of generating high responses to your direct marketing:

- ✔ Send out a letter, special announcement, small catalog, or brochure by first-class mail once in a while to find out how well your list responds. The U.S. Post Office returns undeliverables if you use first class, so you can remove or update out-of-date addresses.

- ✔ Run a very small display ad because they're the least expensive. Limit yourself to 15 words or less. Describe in a simple headline and one or two brief phrases what you have to sell and then ask people to contact you for more information. (Include a simple black-and-white photo of the product to eliminate the need for wordy description.)

- ✔ Replace your existing advertising copy (your words) with *testimonials* (quotes praising your product or firm) from happy customers or with quotes from news coverage of your firm or product. These comments attract more buyers because they seem more believable than positive things you say about yourself.

- ✔ Give away a simple, useful, or fun gift in exchange for placing an order. People love to receive gifts!

- ✔ Trade customer lists with another business to boost your list size for free.

- ✔ Include an inexpensive premium (giveaway product — see Chapter 11) in your mailing. Nicely decorated pens, pencils, stickers, refrigerator magnets, or anything with utility can boost response rates by making your mailing more interesting and memorable. People love to receive gifts! (How about including copies of local high school, college, or semi-pro game schedules? Use your imagination.)

- ✔ Send a thank-you note or card to customers by mail or e-mail after they place a purchase. This polite gesture often wins a repurchase. It also lets you test your contact information and habituates the customer to reading your messages so that they're more likely to pay attention to a sales-oriented message later on.

✔ Send out birthday or holiday greetings in the form of cards or gifts to your in-house list. If you consider them valuable customers, let them know it. You may be surprised how many contact you afterward to place a new order, even though your mailing to them was noncommercial. (Don't know their birthdays? Send cards on your company's birthday, instead.)

✔ Change the medium or form of your communication every now and then. If you always send out a sales letter, try a color postcard or an e-mailed newsletter. Variations like this can increase customer interest, and you may also find that different customers respond best to different forms of communication.

✔ Use a photograph of a person's face, looking directly at the viewer with a friendly expression. The person should represent a user or an expert on the product, or relate to the product or offer in some other way. A face attracts attention and increases sales for most direct-response ads and direct-mail letters.

✔ Use a clear, appealing photo of the product. Showing what you have to sell attracts appropriate customers simply and effectively. And if some details don't show up in the photo, add close-up photos. Seeing is believing, and believing is a prerequisite for buying! Few businesses use largely visual direct-response ads, though I can't tell you why. Visual direct-response ads can outsell wordy ones by a wide margin.

✔ Try an old-fashioned radio advertisement using a lot of amusing sound effects and asking people to call a toll-free number or visit a Web site. Radio ads can be fun! And people really listen to them when they grab the listener's attention.

✔ Run your direct-response ad in Yellow Pages phone directories. Get a local number for each directory you list your ad in (you can have the calls forwarded to your central office; ask your local phone company for details).

And remember that behind every effective direct marketing program stands a well-managed database of customer and prospect names. If you need some help with yours, see the sidebar, "Using a database," in this chapter.

Designing Direct-Response Ads

Direct-response ads are ads that stimulate people to respond with an inquiry or purchase. (Some marketers call them direct-action ads. Take your pick.) The registration cards that Levi's now includes with each pair of jeans fall into this category, although you see direct-response ads more commonly in print media — magazines and newspapers — and now on the fax machine (I don't recommend this approach) and the Web (a better idea), as well. And the ads and purchased listings on Web search engines give you a new, and often highly effective, form of direct-response advertising. See Chapter 10 for details of how to use these forms of advertising.

When direct-response advertising works, it really works

A modern classic illustrates the ability of some direct-response ads to close the sale without any intermediate steps. You may still find this small, simple, black-and-white ad running in the back pages of the *New York Times Sunday Magazine*. The advertiser is David Morgan of Bothell, Washington, a distributor of the Cattleman, a "traditional Australian Stockman's hat" made by Akbura of Australia. The ad simply shows a photo of a felt hat, along with a body-copy description that includes information such as "Pre-shaped in Akbura's Imperial Quality pure fur felt, fully lined, 3¼-inch brim, ornamental band." And the ad gives an article number and the price (plus shipping and handling). The company lists a toll-free number for ordering, provides an address for those who prefer to write, and gives an e-mail address, as well.

I've seen this ad, without alterations, in dozens of magazines for years. That means it works. And works. And works. Why? Well, the ad stars a product that somebody wants. Men who like unusual hats know about hats like this and want to find a source. The copy is stark and simple —

no stories here — but the ad is engaging to those who can see themselves wearing that hat. The ad also provides an easy way for readers to make contact. David Morgan gives three different options: phone, mail, and e-mail. The ad makes clear that you can call to request a catalog, not just to order the hat, so the ad gives the reader two follow-up options. All this information goes into an inexpensive back-section advertisement.

If you go to www.davidmorgan.com/akubra.html, you can see that the success of this simple print ad has inspired a similar approach on the Web site. The Web page designers use small ad-shaped rectangles on the right side of the page with a layout just like the old print ad: A good, clear photo of the hat fills the top third, with a price and the name of the specific type of hat (plus a reminder of the Akbura brand name) beneath. But, rather than the print-ad information on how to follow up, these Web-page ads just have a clickable BUY NOW icon on the bottom.

The people who respond to such advertising have self-selected as customers or prospects. You need to do two things with them:

✔ Try your best to close the sale by getting them to buy something.

✔ Find out as much as you can about them and put the information in your database for future direct-marketing efforts.

Many businesses build a direct-marketing capacity through this very process. They place ads in front of what they hope is an appropriate target market and wait to see who responds. Then they attempt to build long-term direct-marketing relationships with those who respond (for example, by sending them catalogs or direct-mail letters). Over time, the businesses add respondents to their direct-marketing databases, information about the respondents builds up, and many of those respondents become regular direct purchasers.

You can stimulate responses in ways other than direct-response advertising. I show you how to use direct mail and telemarketing in the same way in the sections "Delivering Direct Mail" and "Tuning in to Telemarketing" later in this chapter (and don't forget the Internet's emerging capabilities in this area, too!). Both print and television advertising also have successful track records in this area — and radio may work, too, but you have to innovate to overcome the problem of people rarely writing down what they hear on the radio. You need to make the otherwise passive radio an action-oriented medium by making your call to action easy to remember. A memorable Web site address may do the trick.

The high failure rates make sense if you consider how much more a direct-response ad must do than the typical image-building or brand-oriented ad. A direct-response ad has to create enough enthusiasm to get people to close the sale, on their own initiative, right now. How do you accomplish this goal? Make sure that your direct-response ad does the following:

- ✔ **Appeals to target readers:** A good story, a character they can identify with and want to be more like — these factors make up the timeless elements of true appeal.

- ✔ **Supports your main claim about the product fully:** Because the ad must not only initiate interest but also close the sale, it has to give sufficient evidence to overcome any reasonable objections on the reader's part. If you think the product's virtues are obvious, show those virtues in a close-up visual of the product. If the appeal isn't so obvious (as in the case of a service), then use testimonials, a compelling story, or statistics from objective product tests — in short, some form of evidence that is logically or emotionally convincing, or better yet, both.

- ✔ **Speaks to readers in conversational, personal language:** Your ad must be natural and comfortable for readers. Don't get fancy! Write well, yes. Polish and condense, yes. Seek better, catchier, clearer expressions, yes. But don't be stiff or formal.

- ✔ **Targets likely readers:** Your ad's readership dramatically affects your response rate. In fact, the same ad, placed in two different publications, can produce response rates at both ends of the range. So the better you define your target consumers, the easier it becomes to find publications relevant to those target consumers, and the better your ad performs.

Highly selective publications work better for direct-response advertising. A special-interest magazine may deliver a readership far richer in targets than a general-interest magazine or newspaper. If you're focusing on women, select a publication read by them. That specification ups your response rate 50 percent right off the bat! *Good Housekeeping,* for example, reaches more than 5 million readers — most of them women.

✔ **Makes responding easy:** If readers can make a purchase easily, ask them to do so. If it's complicated or difficult to buy (because the product is technical, for example), then just ask people to contact you for more information and try to close the sale when they do so. Sometimes, you need an intermediate step. When in doubt, try two versions of your ad — one with an intermediate step and one that tries to make the sale on the spot. Then see which one produces the most sales, in the long run.

Marketers at Cahners, a Boston-based publisher of trade magazines, use direct-response ads to generate inquiries from advertisers interested in buying ad space in its magazines. They use ads, such as a recent four-page insert in *Advertising Age,* to reach the people who influence media buying decisions. Their strategy emphasizes choice. They give readers multiple contact options and multiple things to ask for. The multiple options let a wide range of prospects easily take action by allowing them to select the response they prefer. You can use this good strategy, too. Can you add more options or choices to your ad?

Delivering Direct Mail

Direct mail is the classic form of direct marketing — in fact, the whole field used to be called direct mail until the experts changed the term. *Direct mail* is the use of personalized sales letters, and it has a long tradition all its own. Direct mail is really no more nor less than a form of print advertising. So before you design, or hire someone to design, a direct mail piece, please think about it in this context (and see Chapters 6 and 7).

Actually, a direct-mail piece is not like a print ad. It's like two print ads.

✔ **The first ad is the one the target sees when the mail arrives.** An envelope, usually. And that ad has to accomplish a difficult action goal: to get the viewer to open the envelope rather than recycling it. Most direct mail ends up in the recycling pile without ever getting opened or read! Keep this fact in mind. Devote extra care to making your envelope

- Stand out — it needs to be noticeable and different

- Give readers a reason to open it (sell the benefits or engage their curiosity or, even better, promise a reward!)

Or send a color catalog with a stunning front and back cover they can't resist. Make sure the recipient can see the catalog's exterior. Don't hide it under a dull envelope.

✔ **The second ad goes to work only if the first succeeds.** The second ad is what's inside, and it needs to get the reader to respond with a purchase or inquiry. In that respect, this ad is much the same as any other direct-response ad. The same rules of persuasive communication apply — plus a few unique ones that I discuss in the following section.

Unlocking the secrets of great direct mail

A great many so-called formulas exist for successful direct-mail letters. None of them work. At least, don't make anything about your letter formulaic. Your letter must be creative copywriting and design at its best. It needs to use the secrets of direct-response advertising design (as described in the "Designing Direct-Response Ads" section earlier in this chapter) and to employ the principles of creative marketing and good communications, which you can find in Chapters 5 and 6. However, certain strategies can help you employ these principles of good design in a direct-mail piece.

The most effective direct mail letters generally include several elements, each with its own clear role:

- ✔ **Bait:** You should include some sort of bait that catches the reader's eye and attention, getting him or her to read the letter in the first place.

- ✔ **Argument:** You then need to provide a sound argument — logical, emotional, or both — as to why your great product can solve some specific problem for the reader. Marketers devote the bulk of many letters to making this case as persuasively as possible, and you should keep this sound practice in mind when drafting your direct mail letter.

- ✔ **Call to action:** Finally, you should make an appeal to immediate action, some sort of hook that gets readers to call you, send for a sample, sign up for a contest, place an order — or whatever. As long as they act, you can consider the letter a success. So this hook is really the climax of the letter, and you need to design everything to ensure that this hook works.

These three essential elements can be described in various ways. One favorite of many copywriters is the star, chain, and hook approach. If you can't find and mark all three of these elements in your own letter, it isn't any good:

- ✔ **The star:** A lively opening to your letter. It attracts attention and generates interest.

- ✔ **The chain:** This part of the letter presents your argument — the benefits of the product and your claim about what it can do to make the reader's life better.

- ✔ **The hook:** This part ends your letter, and it asks the reader to do something immediately. If the letter doesn't make a purchase request, then it should offer an incentive for readers to send in their name or call for more information.

These formulas refer specifically to the text of your letter itself. Remember to think hard about what else goes into your mailing, as well. The outside of the envelope needs to entice readers and get them to open the letter in the first place. Following are some techniques to make your envelope enticing enough to open:

✔ **The stealth approach envelope:** You disguise your letter so that it looks like a bill or personal correspondence — or just cannot be identified, at all. Hopefully, the reader opens the envelope just to find out what's inside.

✔ **The benefits approach envelope:** You include a headline, perhaps a little supporting copy, even some artwork, to let people know what the mailing is about and summarize why you think your offer is worthy of their attention. I like this approach best because it's honest and direct — and this is direct marketing, after all! Furthermore, this method ensures that those who do open the envelope have self-selected based on interest in your offer. But this technique only works if you have a clear benefit or point of difference to advertise on your envelope. If you can't say "Open immediately for the lowest price on the XYZ product ranked highest in *Consumer Reports,*" then this ploy may not work.

✔ **The special offer envelope:** This envelope entices with your hook — never mind your offer. By letting consumers know that they can enter a sweepstakes to win a billion dollars, or get free samples, or find valuable coupons or a dollar bill enclosed, this envelope gives them a reason to read the letter inside. But the envelope doesn't try to sell the product — it leaves that to the carefully crafted letter inside.

✔ **The creative envelope:** If your mailing is unique enough, everyone wants to open it just to find out who you are and what you're up to. Consider an oversized package in an unexpected color, an envelope with a very funny cartoon or quote on the back, or a window teasing readers with a view of something interesting inside. Or how about an envelope that says, "Don't open this envelope!" You can make your envelope the most exciting thing in someone's mailbox by using any number of creative ideas. Yet this strategy is the least common, probably because creative envelopes cost more. But don't be penny wise and pound foolish. If you spend 25 percent more to double or triple the response rate, then you've saved your company a great deal of money on the mailing by spending more on the envelope!

What else should go into your mailing? In general, a letter combined with a *circular* — a simple catalog-style description of your product(s) — pulls more strongly than a letter alone. Circulars don't work for all products (don't bother for magazine subscriptions), but do work well for any product or service the consumer sees as expensive or complex. And make the circular more elaborate, involving, glossy, colorful, and large where involvement should be higher. Big circulars for big-ticket items, little ones for simple items.

Also include reply forms. Allow readers to easily get in touch with you in multiple ways. Give readers some choices about what offers they want to respond to, if possible. Postage-free (or prepaid) reply forms generally ensure a higher response rate and thus justify their cost many times over. Don't skimp on the form because, after all, getting that response is the whole point of your mailing.

The final design issue is how to send the letter. Third class versus first class via the U.S. Postal Service? Should you use an overnight air service for an offer to business customers? Or maybe send the letter by e-mail or fax? In general, the postal service is still best. And, on average, third class pulls as well as first class, so save your money, unless timeliness is important or you want to check your list (first-class postage means the envelope comes back to you if the address is no good).

Do these principles apply to e-mail? Yes, but think screens, not pages, when writing the body copy of an e-mail sales letter. It takes as much effort (and involvement) to click on the next screen as it does to turn the page, yet a screen holds less than a page. So be more precise and less wordy, or your e-mail can't pull as well as the same letter in printed form.

Getting your letter mailed

One little detail often puzzles first-time direct mailers — how to actually get your mailing printed, folded, stuffed, and mailed. If you don't know, you should probably hire someone who does. Your local telephone directory lists some companies that do this kind of work under "mailing" or "marketing" headings, and commercial printers often do this type of work, as well. Printers can often handle anything from a small envelope to a major catalog. Talk to various printers to get an idea of the range of services and prices.

If you're planning small-scale mailings — say, less than 2,000 at a pop — then you may find doing the work in-house offers you a cheaper and quicker route. Many local businesses and not-for-profits do small-scale mailings, and they'd be throwing away money by hiring printers. If you want to set up this in-house capability, talk to your local post office to find out how to handle metered or permit mail. And consider purchasing mailing equipment, such as the following (all these items can process standard-format mailings): feeders, sealers, scales to weigh the mailings, and meters. Combine this equipment with your local photocopy shop's ability to produce, fold, and stuff a mailing, and you have an efficient small-scale direct-mail center. Table 13-1 shows several equipment sources to get you started, and I post and update a longer list at www.brilliancemarketing.com.

Table 13-1	Mailing Equipment Sources
Company/Web Address	**Phone Number**
Hasler, www.haslerinc.com (manufacturer)	203-926-1087
A-1 Business Systems, a-1businesssystems.com (used and rebuilt equipment from leading makers)	850-668-7935
Pitney Bowes, www.pb.com (manufacturer)	800-672-6937 or 203-356-5000

Purchasing mailing lists

I cover this topic in more depth in my book *Marketing Kit For Dummies* (Wiley), but I cover the basics here, in case you want to use purchased lists to prospect for leads. Don't expect the purchased lists to work very well — response rates can be low, and you may get high returns or undeliverables. But that's okay because you're using them just to build up your own higher-quality in-house list of purchasers. So, plan to send out relatively inexpensive mailings with easy-to-say-yes-to offers, and then focus on the replies. If you get any calls, faxes, or postcards from these purchased lists, qualify them as leads or customers, and move them to your own list.

I recommend buying one-time rights to mailing lists, with phone numbers (plus e-mail, if it's offered) to make replying to a response easier for you. One-time use means that you don't own the list, just rent it. But you do own the replies. As soon as someone contacts you from that mailing and you begin to interact with them and gather information about them, you can add them to your own list.

Buy lists from list brokers or other vendors; you can find hundreds (I have some links posted at insightsformarketing.com). List suppliers usually have minimums. I recommend buying the minimum (it comes on sticky mailing labels or in a database, depending on what's easiest and cheapest for you to use in your business). Then test the list with a mailing and see what happens. If you get some good customers out of it, go back and buy a larger number of names, excluding the ones you already used. Or if you're disappointed in the response, buy a different list next time. (And if your mailing is too expensive to test on the minimum — which is often 1,000 names — just mail to the first 250. That's enough to find out how the list performs.)

You have so many lists to choose from that you can keep shopping until you find one that works for you. But remember the basic principle of list-buying:

> The best indicator of future purchase is past purchase.

So try to find lists of people who have purchased something similar to what you're selling, preferably through the mail, rather than people who fit your customer profile in other ways.

If you're new at the list-buying game, be prepared for some list sellers to refuse to send their names to you. They worry that they'll rent a one-time use of a list, but users won't honor this, so they sometimes want to work through a pro they trust, like a graphics designer, ad agency, or printer in your area. You probably use the services of someone they do trust, so if you run into this roadblock, network around until you find someone the list-seller will send the lists to.

Establishing and Running a Call Center

A *call center* is the place where telephone calls from your customers are answered. It can be a real, physical place — a big room full of phones staffed by your employees. It can also be a virtual place, a telephone number that rings to whatever subcontractor you're currently using to handle telemarketing for you.

Every business is a call center, but most don't realize it. If you have telephones and people calling in and out on them, you need to manage this point of customer contact very carefully. Small businesses may not operate on a big enough scale to hire or build a dedicated call center, but they still must manage this function wisely if they want to win customers, rather than lose them, on the phone. So please, read and apply the principles of this section, no matter how large or small your business may be!

Being accessible to desirable customers when they want to call you

If you service businesses, then you can use business hours to answer business calls (but make sure that you cover business hours in the business's time zones, not just your own). If you service consumers, however, be prepared to take calls at odd hours. Some of the best customers for clothing catalogs do their shopping late at night — just before bed, for example.

And remember, being accessible means more than just having staff by the phones. You need to make sure that nobody gets a busy signal (your local phone company has a variety of services to help solve this problem — ask them for details). If you answer your phone faster than the competition does, you can gain some market share from them.

You need to measure and minimize customer wait time. Don't leave people sitting on hold for more than what they perceive to be a moderate amount of time. Depending upon the nature of your product and customer, that time limit is probably less than two perceived minutes. A *perceived minute* is the time period a customer on hold thinks he has waited for a minute — and that time typically comes out to be more like 40 seconds when you measure it on the clock. You have to convert actual wait times to perceived wait times in order to appreciate the customer's perspective.

A hidden advantage of keeping the control center in-house is that managers can keep an eye on the accessibility issue and add more lines and staff quickly, if a problem arises.

Capturing useful information about each call and caller

One of the most important functions for your call center is to field inquiries or orders from new customers as they respond to your various direct-response advertisements — such as magazine ads, letters to purchased lists, and your Web page. These callers are hot leads. You don't want their order as much as you want their data. Don't let them escape from your call center. Make sure that your operators ask every caller for her full name and address, how she heard of your company, and perhaps a few other qualifying questions, as well.

The best way to capture call-ins for your customer database is to have your operators online, so that they can enter the data directly into your database as they obtain it. At the very least, give them a printed information form they can fill in — or, if you're the one answering those customer calls, make yourself a form so you don't forget to capture useful information about the prospects, their needs, and how they found your number.

Recognizing — and taking care of — repeat customers

Putting your operators online also solves the related problem of recognizing repeat customers. Repeat customers' names pop up on-screen for the operator's reference. That way, the operators don't have to ask stupid questions, and they can surprise customers with their knowledge.

Gathering data on the effectiveness of direct-response ads and direct mail

I'm often amazed by how little information marketers gather about the effectiveness of their own work. What you don't know does hurt you in marketing! You can easily find out which direct-response ads, call scripts, or mailings pull the best. And by doing so, you make your direct-marketing program more effective, over time. You only need to tell your operators to ask every caller where they heard about you (or ask repeat customers what prompted this latest call).

You can also use this more rigorous way to track the effectiveness of each marketing effort: Use a unique code number on each mailing to help trace each call or other customer response. You can broaden this technique to include all written promotions, if you want — even ones on the Web. An identifying code links calls and sales to specific ads, allowing easy analysis of their effectiveness.

You can also use codes for each ad to support customized sales promotions. For example, one mailing may offer a special two-for-one price over a two-month period — with the code, your operator can quickly display the terms of this offer on screen. And because you have associated an offer with this code, you motivate the customer to give you this information.

If you don't want to set up a call center yourself, you can hire a consultant to design a call center for you or simply use a service firm to perform the function for you. One leading service provider is 24-7 INtouch, 230 N. Kenwood St., Suite 118, Burbank, CA 91505; phone 800-530-1121; Web site www.24-7intouch.com, which provides in-bound and outbound call handling, voice mail services, and also a new e-mail response service (you have to provide a menu of standard e-mail replies for their operators to select from, so you can use this service best for a high volume of repetitive questions or requests over the Web). Another top call center service provider is Televista, headquartered in Dallas, Texas, www.televista.com, which describes itself as a contact center solutions provider and also innovates in the integration of telephones with computers, e-mail, and other tools for handling customer contacts. And if you want to get a good feel for the current pulse of this industry, consider subscribing to the Call Center News Service from Silver Lake Publishing, LLC (Los Angeles, CA), which you can find at www.callcenternews.com.

Tuning In to Telemarketing

In the United States, three-fourths of all consumers use a toll-free number at least once each year. And more than $500 billion in sales take place over the phone. Telemarketing has emerged in the last 15 years as a major medium for direct marketing.

Although telemarketing requires nothing but a telephone, combining it with toll-free, inbound calling usually makes it most effective. In the United States, you can offer free calling to your customers and prospects with all 800-numbers since their introduction in 1967 and now for 888-numbers and other sequences. And toll-free numbers are becoming increasingly available in similar forms in other countries, as well. You, the marketer, get to pick up the cost of the customer's telephone call so that you can remove a possible objection to calling. Of course, a local phone number is just as good, if not better (many people prefer to do business locally), but marketers currently prefer the toll-free number because it can route all calls to one centralized *call center* (an office dedicated to handling incoming calls).

By the way, you can also arrange for most phone companies to list a local number in each local market you sell to, and then have the phone company bill you the added cost of transferring that call to your non-local office. That way, people pay only for their local call and feel that they're dialing a local business rather than an impersonal national business. List the local number in the local Yellow Pages or other phone directories for effective local advertising! Fewer marketers know about this alternative to the toll-free number, but it may be more effective for you if you're in a business that values local relationships, like pest control, lawn care, or computer repair.

The toll-free number is useful in only one form of telemarketing: *inbound telemarketing,* in which customers call you in response to direct-response advertising. And every direct-response ad should have a phone number as one of the contact options — with a trained telemarketing sales force or an eager entrepreneur at the other end. (I recommend posting a toll-free phone number prominently on your Web site and printing it on packaging, brochures, business cards, and so on, in case someone prefers to talk rather than e-mail or mail you. Add a toll-free fax number, if customers in your industry like to fax in orders, too.)

Actually, everything you send out that could have your phone number and Web address on it should have it. It's amazing how often I find myself staring at a catalog page, package, product, Web site, or memo, trying to find a phone number that just isn't there. Then what? I may just call the competition instead. The solution? Audit and order!

- First, *audit* your mailings and other customer communications to find those holes where you've accidentally left out contact information.

- Next, *order* up some simple contact information stickers with your brand or business name, phone numbers, address(es), and Web site and e-mail information. Pop those stickers on folders, boxes, cards, products, scribbled notes, or anywhere else anyone may conceivably look when thinking of calling you with a question or order.

The other form of telemarketing is *outbound telemarketing,* in which salespeople make calls to try to get prospects on the phone — and then pitch them to try to make a sale; see Chapter 17 for how to design a good sales presentation. You can do a little bit of outbound telemarketing informally as part of a broader routine of contacting customers and following up on leads, or you may have a full-blown outbound telemarketing program set up in a call center that you either run yourself or contract with. One way or the other, though, every marketer makes some calls to customers and prospects and must be prepared for the reality that outbound telemarketing yields plenty of rejections. In fact, I don't generally recommend outbound telemarketing for "cold call" lists, or lists of strangers who have never done business with you before. You can buy such lists from *list brokers* easily, but expect lower response rates than from lists you build yourself.

Navigating the do-not-call list

You can feel a growing momentum behind legal restrictions over telemarketing. In the United States, consumers can put themselves on a do-not-call list to block inbound telemarketing. When buying lists, ask whether the broker or supplier is up-to-date and has pulled any names that are illegal to call. And if you get any complaints from people who say they ought to be on the do-not-call list when you use a purchased list, stop and recontact the list supplier to find out what went wrong. In business-to-business marketing, fewer restrictions apply, but the need for respect and courtesy remains.

A lot of telemarketers just hire a bunch of college kids at hourly rates to make random calls in the hopes of finding a few good prospects for each hundred calls made. That type of marketing isn't smart and may not be legal any more (see the "Navigating the do-not-call list" sidebar). Please, don't waste your time and consumers' goodwill by dialing numbers from the phone book!

You can improve the success rate of outbound telemarketing dramatically by developing a good list before you start calling. Preferably, this list is of people who have had some contact with you before (they've purchased, returned an inquiry card, tried a sample, or responded to a print ad or Web banner ad.) With a good list, you can afford to put competent salespeople on the phones so that your company puts its best face forward. I don't know why most telemarketers haven't figured out that the first contact between their company and a prospective customer should not be in the hands of a temp worker who can't even pronounce the name of the product correctly. To avoid such problems, you need to develop lists and a script that gives your callers at least a 15 percent success rate — more than ten times the average for typical bottom-feeder consumer telemarketing operations. By the way, I don't even discuss those darn computers, not humans, that make outbound telemarketing calls. What an awful idea! If you decide to use one, just make sure that you don't give it my number.

The Benchmarking Network, which has a variety of projects in the telemarketing field, provides you with an intriguing resource. You can work through them to find out how leading telemarketing operations work, and benefit from their experiences. Contact them through the phone number 281-440-5044 or at the Web site www.iccbc.org/tba.html. And see the section on call centers later in this chapter for more referrals.

"Hello, sir; I'm calling from (company name), which has been retained by (prestigious economics magazine publisher) to see if you are receiving your copy of (magazine name) on time and in good condition." So said the female caller when I picked up the telephone at my office the other day. And my "abusive marketing antennae" immediately sounded a warning.

When I pointed out that I thought she was really calling for some other purpose, she admitted that she wanted to offer me "an opportunity" to extend my subscription because "prices are going up," but she could give me a multiple-year subscription at the price I currently pay.

When I then pointed out that her opening line gave a good example of an illegal sales call — it was designed to deceive me into thinking the call had another, more altruistic purpose — she quickly hung up. And so she denied me the opportunity to point out another potentially illegal aspect of the call. The assertion that prices are going up was probably not true. When I checked my records, I found out that the company's price for subscriptions had actually dropped slightly in recent years, not gone up. And since I received the call, the prices have gone down, not up.

The bottom line is that this kind of telemarketing script is improper and can lead to legal complications. But a lot of telemarketing scripts can land you in hot legal water, these days. Why? Because the pressure is on. Selling anything over the phone is much harder than it used to be — whether it's a magazine or a long-distance telephone service. People are getting sick of these sales calls and adding their names to "don't call lists" by the millions, and businesses are setting up impenetrable phone systems to duck telemarketing calls. So, marketers are experimenting with stealth techniques, and these techniques lead them into dangerous ethical and legal territory.

A formerly new distribution channel, the telephone, has matured. Desirable consumers became jaded to junk mail, print ads, billboards, and radio and television ads decades ago. But the rise of telemarketing in the '80s gave marketers something new and different to experiment with. It was great fun — for a while. But now, most prospects have received hundreds, if not thousands, of telemarketing calls. I get them at my office, which is why you don't get me in person, if you call. I consider paying someone to answer my phone and weed out salespeople worth the money; otherwise, I couldn't run a business (or write this book).

So today's telemarketers have only two choices. One, they can go on doing what they've always done, which can only lead to increasingly desperate and shady practices as their medium matures and their industry shakes out. Or two, they can wake up and smell the coffee and realize that it's a new dawn. Telemarketers need to find new strategies for their newly mature medium. Some of these strategies include:

> ✔ **Use the phone to follow up on leads, not to find them.** Whenever possible, use your Web marketing activities (see Chapter 10), events (check out Chapter 12), and advertising (see "Beating the Odds with Your Direct Marketing," earlier in this chapter, plus all of Part III in this book), to generate telephone or personal sales call leads. When you generate inquiries about your product or service, you have permission to call. The prospect takes your call gladly in 99 percent of these cases, and you close a sale in many of them.

✔ **Don't overuse the phone.** Save calls for issues that really deserve personal contact from the prospect's perspective, and try to call people who actually know you or your firm or will welcome the call for some other good reason. If you have something truly important to talk about, then you don't need a misleading hook to keep people on the phone. Remember that every marketing program should use a balanced mix of media and methods. You can't do all jobs with one tool. And also remember that even where telephoning is appropriate, your customers and prospects don't want you to call constantly. Give them a little breathing room.

✔ **Be respectful.** Remember that you're interrupting anyone you reach by phone.

✔ **Compensate telemarketers for building relationships, not frying them.** If telemarketers are paid only by the *kill* (commission on sales), then they can get frustrated and start berating and hanging up on your prospects and customers. Note that this rule means that you should not use *subcontractors* (specialized companies that telemarket for you) if they pay by the kill — and most of them do!

✔ **Guard existing customers from bad telemarketing.** After the call I received from the economics magazine, I wrote to complain and cancel my subscription — even though I had been paying for two subscriptions (one went to my Dad) for many years. Deceptive, high-pressure, or irritating phone sales tactics may produce a good-looking end-of-day sales report, but they are guaranteed to increase customer turnover. Why? They bring in deal-prone customers, who can be taken away by the next telemarketer, and they irritate your loyal customers, rather than reward them. At the very least, use two different strategies and scripts: one for existing customers and one for deal-prone prospects. At best, focus your telemarketing on building existing customer loyalty; for example, by really calling to see if you can improve the product or service quality.

✔ **Gaining insight from other media.** Holding someone's attention long enough to deliver a marketing message is a major problem in every medium, not just telemarketing. And marketers have developed clever solutions in other media. Why not try some of them in telemarketing? You can write a script that includes entertainment — a very short story, a good joke, a warm and pleasant manner, or another engaging opener may build interest far better than a deceptive claim about the purpose of the call. Similarly, a sales promotion tie-in can hold attention. For example, your script can start with the offer of a contest or free sample giveaway and then go on to a pitch for the product. Get creative!

Profiling telemarketing programs

Let me illustrate the uses of outbound telemarketing with two very different examples of telemarketing programs.

Example #1: The first company (I dare not name names) sells what they claim to be a highly superior vacuum cleaner. The machine sells for a highly superior price as well — one that includes a much higher margin than typically appears in the product category — and you can only get it through their direct marketing.

Its marketing program focuses on outbound telemarketing, using names from local phone books in order to generate prospects who are interested in the product. A salesperson then visits these prospects for a full-blown sales presentation and closing effort.

The telemarketers are by-and-large young women with pleasant telephone manners. They're paid (in cash) at $5 per hour, making 200 calls per five-hour shift. Most people hang up right away, but about 25 out of these 200 prospects are interested enough to listen to the telephone pitch. Of these prospects, about five qualify financially (they must have full-time work, a credit card, and own their own home).

Out of this pool, several actually end up receiving an in-home demonstration, and one or two ultimately make the purchase. Thus, the closure rate falls at about 1 percent. However, the (illegal) use of cheap, cash-only labor keeps the calling costs so low that the company can sustain the operation — at least until somebody from the Department of Labor or the IRS busts them for back payroll taxes.

Example #2: The second is a story more to my liking because its approaches telemarketing more responsibly and sustainably. The Steppenwolf Theatre in Chicago prefers to sell subscriptions. Doing so guarantees an audience (or at least a box office take) for each show in its season.

Theatre marketers discovered that a 16-week phone campaign to its *in-house list* (a list of current and past customers and qualified leads), supplemented with any other appropriate names they could find, was very effective at selling subscriptions. The telemarketing effort happens in-house by properly trained, knowledgeable staff and has a fairly high hit rate.

Note that this telemarketing program successfully generates sales, and it doesn't risk legal and financial liability or expose prospects to incompetent — and possibly rude — telemarketers.

Furthermore, this program actually completes the sale, instead of requiring a follow-up sales visit. This approach is, therefore, far better than the first example. Outbound telemarketing covers a wide range. Plan to be at the top of that range, not at the bottom!

Part V

Selling Great Products to Anyone, Anytime, Anywhere

In this part . . .

If you can design a great product, give it an appropriate brand name, package it well, and then turn it over to a good salesperson, you may be able to dispense with everything else discussed in this book. The combination of an appealing product or brand, plus good sales and service, can make a business successful, all on its own. And so it seems fitting to devote an entire part to these topics.

I once was hired to consult to the chief executive of a specialty chemicals company. They wanted me to evaluate his overall business plan and suggest ways of making the business grow. After poking around the premises for a few hours and interviewing a bunch of his people, I discovered a startling thing: They apparently did no marketing at all. They had no marketing department, and the company had no brochures, no ads, no publicity, and no Web site. So, how had they gotten this far, and where in the world did their customers come from?

In this part, I explain the secrets of companies like this one. I show you how to maximize the impact of your product and its packaging, tell you how to price your products and services, keep you from underselling yourself by making common mistakes associated with distribution and pricing, and help you approach sales and service like an old pro.

Chapter 14

Branding, Managing, and Packaging a Product

The product is the heart and soul of any marketing program. If the product is good — if the target customer is really pleased with it — then that marketing program has a decent chance of success. But if the product is not good, or nothing special in the customer's eyes, then no marketing program can make that product a winner in the long run. Many people in the field of marketing and in business, in general, don't catch this point. They underestimate their customers and overestimate the persuasive power of marketing. Something of real value has to be at the core of any marketing program. The product, whether a good or a service, had better have some notable advantages from the consumer's perspective.

Keep in mind that I used the term "product" as an umbrella term that means a product, a service, or anything else your company wants to sell.

Finding Simple Ways to Leverage Your Product

This chapter shows you how to conceive and develop such winning products, how to manage them as part of a product line, and how to select your products' names to amplify their natural strengths and communicate those strengths to the target customer. However, those activities are done infrequently and have fairly long-term planning horizons. But you can take small steps to keep a product fresh and vital and boost its visibility and appeal. Product management is a lot like gardening. You occasionally plant a whole new crop, and you tend the existing plants routinely, too.

Here is a list of simple and quick things you can do to build customer loyalty and grow sales by working on your product:

- ✔ **Update the appearance.** Many companies present good products to the world in poorly designed exteriors that don't dress those products for success. Look at the product itself (colors, attractiveness, and visibility of brand names).

- ✔ **Update the packaging.** A consumer product that sits on a shelf waiting for someone to pick it up should be highly visible and appealing. Can you add a brighter color to the packaging to attract the eye? Can you mention key features on the outside? Or maybe you can add a clear window to show the actual product.

- ✔ **Make sure the product is attractive and easy to use.** Your product should also feel nice — smooth, polished, soft, or whatever texture is appropriate to the product's use. Even very minor changes in its look, feel, and function can improve customer satisfaction and product appeal.

- ✔ **Improve any printed materials that come with the product.** Can you improve their appearance? Dress them up? Make them clearer or more useful? Please make sure they instill pride of ownership in the product. I have a 1994 Jaguar XJS convertible, and the manuals for it are stored inside a beautiful black leather pocket folder with the Jaguar logo on the outside. If I ever have to sell that car, I'm keeping the binder!

- ✔ **Choose your product's best quality.** (See brilliance-based marketing in Chapter 1 or visit www.insightsformarketing.com to find out more about doing a Brilliance Audit if you're not sure how to figure out your product's best quality.) Then coin a short phrase to communicate this best quality to the consumer and put that phrase on the product, its packaging, and its literature in prominent places. Have simple (but attractive) color-printed stickers made up for this purpose, if you want — that's the quickest and cheapest way to add a marketing message.

- ✔ **Eliminate confusion about which product does what for whom.** Clarify the differences and uses of your products if you have more than one, by pricing and naming them distinctly (to make them obviously different). You'd be amazed how confusing most product lines look to the average buyer.

✔ **Make your logo beautiful.** Apple switched from a somewhat dated-looking rainbow-colored version of their distinctive apple-shaped logo to a beautiful, sophisticated version made of a clear plastic panel backlit with diffused white light. This logo sits on the top of all their newer laptops, giving those computers a more sophisticated appeal. Can you upgrade your image by improving the appearance of your logo on your products?

✔ **Pick up a related but non-competing product from another company and repackage and distribute it as part of your product line.** Adding another good product your customers like can increase the average purchase size significantly. And I recommend that you use distributor-style arrangements that eliminate the investment of product development, giving you a good way to expand your product line in a hurry, if you want to. Selling a new (or new to you) product to an existing customer is often easier than finding a new customer for an existing product.

I hope this list of simple ideas for action has your marketing blood circulating! You can do a lot with and for your products, even if you don't have the cash or time right now to develop and introduce an entirely new product.

But, in the long run, you're only as good as your products, so you do also need to try to update, upgrade, or perhaps even replace your current line of products. It's a long-term but vital activity that most marketing plans need to include, just as gardeners have to remember to plan the next planting along with their more routine weeding and watering duties.

Identifying When and How to Introduce a New Product

I wish I could say that you don't need to worry about new product development very often. But if your market is like most, innovations give you a major source of competitive advantage. A competitor's major new product introduction probably changes the face of your market — and upsets your sales projections and profit margins — at least once every few years. So you can't afford to ignore new product development. Ever. You should, therefore, introduce new products as often as you can afford to develop them.

One product strategy or multiple strategies?

One market or more? How you answer this determines whether you need to have one product line and one strategy or multiple lines and strategies. Many businesses sell into multiple markets. PepsiCo sells into the beverage and snack markets. Car manufacturers sell to consumers and to fleet buyers. Small companies do this, too: A local cleaning service may have both home-owners and businesses as customers, and the marketing (and specifically the product offering) needs to be different for each.

Okay, you think you need a hot new product. But where do you get the idea? First, check out the basic creativity skills covered in Chapter 5 That chapter offers a host of brainstorming and idea-generating techniques that you can use. If you and your fellow marketers are stale, bring in salespeople from the field, production, repair, or service call center. Try bringing in some customers for a brainstorming session. Your approach hardly matters, as long as it's new and different. New ideas come from new thought processes, which come from new approaches to thinking. Do something new to produce something new!

Also consider two cheap sources of new product ideas that the product development specialists at Rosenau Consulting (based in Houston, Texas, and Santa Monica, California) report as valuable: old ideas and other people's ideas. Oh, and don't forget to ask your customers for ideas (they're people too!).

In with the old

Old ideas are any product concepts that you or another company have previously abandoned. They may have been considered but rejected without being marketed, or they could even be old products that have fallen out of use but could be revived with a new twist. Because people have been struggling to develop new product concepts for decades in most markets, a great many abandoned ideas and old products are around. Often, companies fail even to keep good records, so you have to interview old-timers and poke through faded files or archived catalogs to discover those old ideas. But old ideas may be a treasure trove, because technological or marketing developments may have made the original objections less serious than when marketers originally scrapped the idea. Technical advances or changing customer taste may make yesterday's wild ideas practical today. Even if you can't use any of the old ideas you find, they may lead you to fresh ways of thinking about the problem — perhaps they suggest a customer need that you hadn't thought of before.

Also note that old products in one market may be new products in another. Old-fashioned hand-cranked cash registers sell well in some countries, even though they have been replaced by electronic cash registers in others. The use of electronic cash registers depends upon the nature of the local economy and the availability and reliability of local electrical service. You may be able to turn your dead products from the United States or Europe into winners in other countries, if you can partner with local distributors.

Stealing — er, borrowing — ideas

You can often pursue the second source, other people's ideas, through licenses. A private inventor may have a great new product concept and a patent for it, but she may lack the marketing muscle and capital to introduce the product. You can provide that missing muscle and pay the inventor 5 or 10 percent of your net revenues as reward for her inspiration.

Many companies generate inventions that fall outside of their marketing focus. These companies are often willing to license to someone specializing in the target market.

That's the official way to use other people's ideas; however, an unofficial way exists that's probably more common and certainly more important for most marketers. You simply steal ideas. Now, by steal, I don't mean to take anything that isn't yours. A *patent* protects a design, a *trademark* protects a name or logo, and a *copyright* protects writing, artwork, performances, and software. You must respect these legal rights that protect other people's expressions of their ideas. But you can't legally protect the underlying ideas to anything in most countries where you're likely to do business.

If the ideas make it to your ears or eyes through a legitimate public channel of communication, then you can use them. (Just don't bug your competitor's headquarters, go through their dumpster, or get their engineers drunk — doing so may violate *trade secrecy laws* — ask your lawyer before planning any questionable research.)

Although a competitor may be upset to see you knocking off or improving upon its latest idea, nothing can stop you as long as your source was public (not secret) and you aren't violating a patent, trademark, or copyright. In most markets, competitors steal ideas as a matter of routine. And look at other industries for inspirations that you can apply in your industry. The good idea thief has to be open-minded — you never know where you may find something worth stealing!

Note that you're less likely to violate these legal protections if you just take a public idea and develop it all on your own, but you may still want to have a qualified attorney (preferably one who specializes in intellectual property law) review what you've done before going public with it.

By the way, I call this activity "stealing" in humor. It isn't really, if you do it legally. Some people call it *benchmarking;* others call it being inspired by others. Whatever you call it, try to be aware of new concepts and keep your product offerings up to date with them. For example, in my employee training business, we develop and sell assessments, or simple paper-based tests to evaluate behaviors in the workplace. The trend now is for such tests to be computerized so that the administration and analysis of them is easier. I didn't invent that idea, but my firm, like most in my industry, is introducing computerized versions of our assessment products, because this is where the market is headed.

Picking your customers' brains

A final source of new product ideas comes from your customer. Customers are the best source, but they don't know it. Ask a customer to describe a brilliant new product you should provide for him or her, and you get a blank stare or worse. Yet frustrations with the existing products and all sorts of dissatisfactions, needs, and wants lurk in the back of every customer's mind. And you may be able to help them with these gripes.

How do you mine this treasure trove of needs, many of them latent or unrecognized? Collecting the customers' words helps you gain insight into how they think — so talk to them and take notes that use quotes or tape-record their comments. Get them talking, and let them wander a bit, so that you have a chance to encounter the unexpected. Also watch customers as they buy and use your product. Observation may reveal wasted time and effort, inefficiencies, or other problems that the customer takes for granted — problems that the customer may happily say good-bye to if you point them out and remove them.

Using the significant difference strategy

New product development has a downside: Almost all new products fail. Between 75 percent and 95 percent of tangible products fail according to research on the topic, and while new services tend to have a better track record, they can fail, too. (My definition of failure consists of not providing a decent financial return on investment and not gaining a significant following among customers.) Given high failure rates, you need to make sure your new product beats the odds — that it proves much better than the typical new product. How?

Common sense and a large pile of research reports say that new products do better — make more money, for a longer amount of time — when customers see something strikingly new about them. Walk down the aisle of your supermarket and notice the number of packages proclaiming something new. Without the word splashed across them, you may never have been able to tell they were new. Same with services: I have the same trouble seeing what's really new in the financial services industry, for example. Take a look at the brochures and posters in your bank and see whether the "new" services really seem more like repackaged old services with fancy new names and pricing.

To achieve real success, you have to introduce something that's not only new, but that looks new and different to the market. The product needs a radical distinction, a clear point of difference. Innovations that consumers recognize more quickly and easily provide the marketer with a greater   return. Researchers who study new product success use the term *intensity* to describe this phenomenon — the more intense the difference between your new product and old products, the more likely the new product can succeed.

You should also know about the Product Development & Management Association (PDMA), 17000 Commerce Parkway, Suite C, Mount Laurel, NJ 08054; phone 856-439-9052; Web site `pdma.org`. Their Web site posts reviews of good new books on product development, and they offer conferences, certification training, and other services to their members.

Branding and Naming Your Product

What do you call your new product? Should you launch it under an existing brand identity or give it a new one? Should you attempt to add value (and raise the price) by creating a positive brand identity, or should you save your marketing dollars and just get the product out to point of purchase? You have to make all these tough decisions. Let me show you how to make them well.

Designing a product line

A *product line* is any logical grouping of products offered to customers. (Remember products can be goods, services, ideas, or even people — such as political candidates or stars.) You usually identify product lines by an umbrella brand name with individual brand identities falling under that umbrella.

A beer by any other name . . .

The Boston Beer Company recently went public. Famed for its upstart products sold under the Samuel Adams brand name, the Boston-based company is an example of a local brewer that made it to the national market. But the company may be in danger of losing its specialty image as it grows ever bigger. Something about drinking a beer that other people haven't tried adds to the appeal of the specialty market — and now most beer drinkers have at least heard of, if not tried, Samuel Adams.

To avoid losing the company's association with small, specialty brewing, it introduced an additional brand name: LongShot. The LongShot name applies to the winners of a World Homebrew Contest — home-brewers make fine beers in their basements. You can find a LongShot Black Lager, a LongShot American Ale, and a LongShot Hazelnut Brown Ale — each a winner at the professionally judged contest. The event itself and the new LongShot brand name both reinforce the company's small-time roots. The LongShot name and the "1,680 entries, three winners" slogan capture the excitement of an amateur's brew making it to the big time. Somebody was wearing a marketing cap at the Boston Beer Company when he or she came up with the idea for this new brand name.

The Macintosh computer line includes many different products, but they all bear the same Macintosh brand name (a trademarked asset of Apple Computers), and the company has made each product distinct enough that together they give the customer a wide range of choices. You can think of product lines like this one as families of products — and, like families, their relationship needs to be close and clear.

You have two key issues to consider when designing your product lines:

✔ **Depth:** How many alternatives should you give the customer within any single category? For example, should you make a single T-shirt design in a range of sizes? How about offering the design in a variety of colors? All these options increase depth because they give a customer more options. Depth gives you an advantage because it increases the likelihood of a good fit between an interested customer and your product. You don't want to miss a sale because somebody was too big to wear a size large.

Increase depth when you're losing customers because you don't have a product for them. Increasing your depth of choice reduces the chance of disappointing a prospective customer.

✔ **Breadth:** This option allows you to generate new sales. For example, if you sell one popular T-shirt design, you can increase breadth by offering more T-shirt designs in your product line. When you add anything that the customer views as a separate choice, not a variant of the same choice, you're adding breadth to the product line. A broad line of T-shirts includes dozens and dozens of different designs. A broad and deep product line offers each of those designs in many sizes and on many different colors and forms of T-shirts.

Increase breadth whenever you can think of a new product that seems to fit in the line. By *fit,* I mean that customers can see the new product's obvious relationship to the line. Don't mix unrelated products — that's not a product line, because it doesn't have a clear, logical identity to customers. But keep stretching a successful line as much as you can. Doing so makes sense for one simple reason: You sell new products to old customers. Of course, the line may also reach new customers, which is great. But you can sell to your old customers more easily (read that: more cheaply), so you definitely want to do more business with them in the future, and offering them products is a great way to do this.

Maintaining your product line: When to change

The secret to good product management is the motto, "Don't leave well enough alone." But if you keep growing your lines, you can obviously bump into some practical limits after a while. How do you know when the pendulum is going to swing the other way — when it's time to do some spring-cleaning?

You should decrease your depth or breadth (or both) if your distribution channels can't display the full product line to customers. Often, distribution becomes a bottleneck, imposing practical limits on how big a product line you can bring to the customer's attention.

When I consulted for the Kellogg Brush Company some years ago, I was amazed to find out that they made many hundreds of different items. Yet the grocery and hardware stores selling their products never displayed more than a couple dozen items. Obviously, their product line was far broader and deeper than their end customers ever realized. I recommended that they either develop a direct, catalog-based distribution channel in order to bring these choices to customers, or that they cut the product line back to the top 20 or 30 items purchased by retailers and try to make those items better and cheaper. (They chose the latter option.)

You should also cut back your product line if customers don't understand it. Procter & Gamble chopped its product offerings roughly in half for this very reason. Surveys showed that all the variety confused their customers: customers didn't have a clear idea of what the company offered or why. Too many choices frustrate customers and lead to confusion between products. Brand identities start to overlap, and you make customer decisions harder rather than easier.

Always calibrate your product line to your distribution channels and your customers. Don't overwhelm. Don't underwhelm. Keep talking to all your customers and watching how they behave with your product to see if you need to shrink or grow your product line.

Naming a product or product line

Naming a new product isn't simple, but you can use a number of effective methods. You can choose a word, or combination of words, that tells people about the exact character of your product — like LongShot (see the nearby sidebar "A beer by any other name . . . "). This approach is kind of like giving a new puppy a name. You want to get a feel for its personality first and then give it a name that fits. A stand-offish poodle can be Fifi, but that name doesn't fit a playful mutt!

The Ford Mustang, an extremely successful brand name, used this strategy. Marketers presented the car as simply having the personality of the small, hardy horse of the American plains from which the car took its name. And those marketers hoped that the driver saw himself as a modern-day cowboy, akin to the real cowboys who broke and used the mustangs for their work. This strategy has a powerful effect because it uses existing terms whose meaning marketers apply to their product.

You can also name your product by making up a brand-new word that has no prior meaning. This approach gives you something you can more easily protect in a court of law. But it isn't necessarily effective at communicating the character of your product. You have to invest considerable time and money in creating a meaning for the new name in consumers' minds.

When you use meaningful components for your made-up names, they are called *morphemes,* which NameLab Inc. (a leading developer of such names) defines as the semantic kernels of words. For example, NameLab started with the word "accurate" (from the Latin word *accuratus*) and extracted a morpheme from it to use as a new car brand: Acura. They also developed Compaq, Autozone, Lumina, and Zapmail in the same manner. Each is a new word to the language, but each communicates something about the product because of meanings the consumers associate with that word's components. Word mavens call this technique *constructional linguistics*. (NameLab is based in Honolulu, HI, and San Francisco, CA; phone 808-927-4931; Web site www. namelab.com.)

Legally protecting your product's name and identity

You can gain legal protection by using, and getting legal recognition for, a unique identifier for your product, a line of products, or even for your entire company. This protection can apply to names, short verbal descriptions, and visual symbols. All these forms of identification are marks that can represent the identity of the thing you apply them to. A tangible product's name and/or visual symbol is a *trademark*. A service name is termed a *service mark* — U.S. law treats a service mark similarly to a trademark. A business name is a *trade name* — again, with similar protection under the law.

In the United States, you establish and protect your rights to exclusive use of any unique trademark by using it. Yes, you should register it (with the U.S. Patent and Trademark Office — contact any law firm handling "intellectual property" to find out how). But registering the trademark isn't nearly as important as using the trademark. In other countries, usage and registration also matter, but sometimes governments reverse the emphasis — without registration, usage gives you no protection. So check with local authorities in each country where you plan to use a trademark.

Registering trademarks in the United States

If you want to register a trademark of any kind in the United States, contact the United States Patent and Trademark Office (USPTO), Crystal Plaza 3, Room 2C02, P.O. Box 1450, Alexandria, VA 22313; phone 800-786-9199 or 703-308-4357; Web site teas.uspto.gov/. The Web site now has an electronic application system. You can also telephone the Trademark Assistance Center at 703-308-9000, and the USPTO will send you the appropriate form, along with an instruction booklet. To do your own search and check to find out whether a trademark is available before you apply, visit the USPTO Web Trademark database at http://tess2.uspto.gov/bin/ gate.exe?f=tess&state=t4horv.1.1. (If this Web address is out of date by the time you try it, and you can't find the right page, check www.insightsformarketing.com where I keep the link updated for you.)

You need to contact a lawyer who specializes in intellectual property to help you register your trademark in other countries. Most of the countries in which you may want to do business subscribe to the Berne Convention (as does the United States), which means your legal protection for a published work (including a label or ad) in one country is honored in other countries, too.

For more information on establishing and strengthening trademarks, contact your lawyer, any experienced ad agency that does brand marketing, or a name lab. More detailed coverage of the topic can be found in *Patents, Copyrights & Trademarks For Dummies,* by Henri Charmasson (Wiley).

Packaging and Labeling: Dressing Products for Success

At some point in every marketing program, the product has to take over and market itself. You reach that point when the customer and product meet and the customer makes a purchase decision — for or against your product. A customer enters a grocery store, glances over the shelves, pulls a package down, and carries it to the register. A customer opens a catalog or brochure, flips through its pages, selects an item, and dials the toll-free number. A customer goes online to purchase airplane tickets and make a hotel reservation. At all these points of purchase, the marketer is out of the picture. The product must sell itself. But to do so, the product must be noticeable. It must be enticing. It must appear to be better than (and a better value than) the competition.

To prepare your product for its solo role at this vital point-of-purchase stage, you need to give careful thought to how you display and present the product. You can't play this all-important role for your product, but you can select the stage and design the set and costume. The *stage* is made up of the store, catalog, or other meeting place; the *set* includes the shelving, signs, display, or other point-of-purchase designs; the *costume* is the exterior package you give your product. Together, they make up what marketers refer to as the *packaging*.

Every product has a package!

If you work in banking or real estate, sell windshield gaskets to auto manufacturers, or distribute your products by mail order rather than in a store, you may be wondering if you can skip this chapter. But, sorry, you can't. Remember, the package is the product as the customer first sees it. Taken broadly, this definition means that every product has a package, whether it fits your traditional notion of packaging or not. And, therefore, marketers must give careful thought to package design, regardless of the product. Services, ideas, and even people (like musicians, job seekers, and political candidates) are included because they can all be products in the right context.

Can your packaging make the sale?

The packaging makes the sale in the majority of purchase decisions (along with any additional point-of-purchase influences to draw attention to the product — but you can look at those eye-catchers in Chapter 16. That means your packaging may well be the most important part of your marketing plan.

Yes, it's true! In spite of the vast sums of money and attention lavished elsewhere — on advertising, marketing research, and other activities — it all comes down to the package. Does the prospective customer see the package and choose it over others? Studies of the purchase process reveal that people rarely know just what they will buy before the *point of purchase* (POP) — the time and place at which they actually make their purchase. The majority of consumers are ready and willing for your product to sway them at point of purchase, as the findings in Table 14-1 (from a study by the Point-of-Purchase Advertising Institute) reveal.

Table 14-1	The Point of Purchase Decision-Making Process	
Nature of Consumer's Purchase Decision	*Percent of Purchases, Supermarket*	*Percent of Purchases, Mass Merchandise Stores*
Unplanned	60%	53%
Substitute	4%	3%
Generally planned	6%	18%
Total = Product selection made at point of purchase	70%	74%

As Table 14-1 shows, unplanned purchases make up the biggest category. Furthermore, specifically planned purchases (those purchases not included in the table) are less than a third of all purchases — all the rest can be influenced at least partially by the package and other point-of-purchase communications. (The study is for packaged goods in stores, but I find that service purchases can also be strongly influenced by the brochure, sales presentation, or Web site that packages the service.)

And if more than half of final decisions about what to buy are made at point of purchase — where the customer is interacting with the product and its packaging — then the package may be more important than any other element of the marketing program. Wow! In fact, you may want to stop and ask yourself whether you can dispense with all other forms of marketing communication, and invest only in packaging and point-of-purchase promotions and displays. If your target customer is open to a point-of-purchase decision, then this extreme is at least a possibility. And by focusing 90-100 percent of your marketing attention on the point of purchase, you can handle the point of purchase better than less focused competitors. You may want to at least think about this option, if for no other reason than its radical nature means your competition probably won't think of it.

See Chapter 16 for more on point-of-purchase sales. In addition, here are some ways to make sure your packaging makes the sale:

- ✓ **Bump up the visibility of the package.** Increasing the size of the brand name, the brightness or boldness of the colors and layout, or the size of the package itself helps make it more visible, as does arranging (or paying) to have stores display it more prominently. Look at the cover of this book for a good example. The *For Dummies* series is an amazing marketing success, partly because you can easily find the books in a bookstore due to their bold, clear cover designs. The books are colorful, flashy, and highly visible, which makes finding them easy when you need one.

- ✓ **Choose a color that contrasts with competitors.** Nabisco chose green when they introduced their SnackWells brand of healthy but delicious cookies a few years ago. Green isn't typically used on the cookie aisle of the grocery store, so their products really stand out.

- ✓ **Improve the information on the package.** Less is more when it comes to clarity, so can you cut down on the number of words you use? Also, ask yourself if the shopper may find any additional information useful when making a purchase decision.

- ✓ **Use the Web to package a product in information.** If you go to www. bhphotovideo.com and shop for SLR cameras, you find that each product has a detail page on which you can click on one of four tabs labeled Accessories, Features, Specifications, and Item Includes. A clear, detailed listing or table of information about the product, what comes with it, and so on appears under each tab. The site gives you enough information to compare options and actually make a purchase decision without having to go into a store and look at the product. In this case, the Web page provides *virtual packaging* for the product.

- ✓ **Let the packaging sell the replacement, too.** Make some aspect of your packaging (if only a label on the bottom) be so permanent that it sends the user to your Web page or phone number for a reorder when the time comes.

- ✓ **Give your package or label emotional appeal.** Warm colors, a friendly message, a smiling person, and a photo of children playing are all ways to make the product feel good when someone looks at it. Purchases are about feelings, not just logic, so give your packaging a winning personality.

✔ **Add some excitement to the package.** The Nike swish symbol is exciting — it symbolizes smooth, rapid movement. Do you have a symbol of movement, achievement, or excitement somewhere in your packaging? If not, try to make your packaging more dynamic. A wave is exciting. A box is not. Put a wave on your box! My firm publishes a booklet for use in training workplace teams. One cover my firm tried had a team working around a table, with a zap of lightning bolting down from the top of the cover to touch and electrify the team's work. This image worked as a great symbol of the exciting benefits our product offers. Later, we changed the cover to a more conservative, static image in an effort to make our products more consistent in appearance. Big mistake! The version without the lightening bolt didn't sell as well, and we are switching back next time we reprint.

✔ **Increase the functionality or workability of the package.** Can you make your packaging protect the product better? Can you make it easier to open, useful for storage, or easier to recycle? Packages have functional roles, and improving functionality can help increase the product's appeal.

These ideas and tips all fall into a popular framework for designing packaging, called VIEW (for Visibility, Information, Emotion, and Workability). Use my ideas or your own to improve the VIEW by upgrading your packaging. Also, make sure you comply with any regulations that govern packaging in your industry. See www.insightsformarketing.com for more on this topic and seek appropriate legal advice if you have any doubt.

Other packaging ideas and resources

I can't do full justice to packaging in this book. That subject is big enough to justify its own book. So I've put a lot more information about packaging design on the book's supporting Web site, www.insightsformarketing.com, and I can also refer you to some of the many other useful resources for readers seeking to make their packaging work harder in the marketing mix:

✔ **Institute of Packaging Professionals** (1601 N. Bond St., Suite 1601, Naperville, IL 60563; phone 630-544-5050; Web site www.iopp.org).

The Institute of Packaging Professionals has a searchable directory at www.packagingconsultants.org.

✔ **Advanced Packaging Magazine** (98 Spit Brook Rd., Nashua, New Hampshire 03062; phone 603-891-0123; Web site www.apmag.com).

✔ **Packaging Magazine** (Sovereign Way, Tonbridge, Kent TN9 1RW, UK; phone +44 (0)1732 377361; Web site www.dotpackaging.com).

Modifying an Existing Product: When and How

Some products are so perfect that they fit naturally with their customers, and you should just leave them alone. For example . . . well, I can't actually think of an example right now. Which tells you something important about product management: You'd better modify your products to improve performance, value, and quality with each new season and each new marketing plan.

You're competing on a changing playing field. Your competitors are trying hard to make their products better, and you have to do the same. Always seek insights into how to improve your product. Always look for early indicators of improvements your competitors plan to make and be prepared to go one step farther in your response. And always go to your marketing oracle — the customer — for insights into how you can improve your product.

The following two sections describe tests that a product must pass to remain viable. If your product doesn't pass, you need to improve or alter your product somehow.

When it's no longer special

At the point of purchase — that place or time when customers make their actual purchase decisions — your product needs to have something special. It has to reach out to at least a portion of the market. Your product needs to be better than its competition on certain criteria because of inherent design features. Or it needs to be about as good as the rest, but a better value, which gives you a sustainable cost advantage. (Do you have such a cost advantage? Marketers generally underestimate the rarity of those cost advantages!) Or the product needs to be the best option by virtue of a lack of other options.

For example, if you sell sewing needles, your product may be about as good as most of the competition — but not noticeably better. But if you happen to be the company that a major grocery store chain uses to single-source needles for its small sewing section, then you have a distribution advantage at point of sale.

Don't assume your lack of special features means that your product isn't special. You can be special just by being there when customers need the product. You can justify keeping a product alive just by having a way of maintaining your distribution advantage. But a product at point of sale has to have at least something special about it if you expect it to generate a good return in the future. Otherwise, it gets lost in the shuffle.

If your customers don't think your product is unique in any way, then you may need to kill that product. But don't set up the noose too quickly. First, see if you can work to differentiate it in some important way.

When it lacks champions

Champions are those customers who really love your product, who insist on buying it over others, and who tell their friends or associates to do the same. But such loyal champions are rare. Does your product have champions?

The championship test is tougher than the differentiation test. Many products lack champions. But when a product does achieve this special status — when some customers anywhere in the distribution channel really love it — then that product is assured an unusually long and profitable life. Such high customer commitment should be your constant goal as you manage the life cycle of your product.

Products with champions get great word of mouth, and their sales and market shares grow because of that word of mouth. Even better, champions faithfully repurchase the products they rave about. And this repeat business provides your company with high-profit sales, compared with the higher costs associated with finding new customers. Check out the principles of good marketing in Chapter 1.

The hook? The repeat buyer must want to repeat the purchase. They need to be converts, true believers — what Ken Blanchard of The Blanchard Companies in San Diego, California, calls *raving fans* (see www.insightsformarketing.com for details or buy his book by that name if you're interested). Otherwise, you need to think of each sale as a new sale, and the sale costs you almost as much as selling to someone who's never used the product before.

How do you know if you have champions rather than regular, ordinary customers? Because when you ask them about the product, they sound excited and enthusiastic. "I'd never drive anything but a Volvo. They're comfortable and safe, they don't break down, and they last longer than American cars." Some U.S. customers say just that when asked about their Volvos, so Volvo has an excellent base of repeat buyers. For that reason, it doesn't vary its models as much from year to year as other car companies do. The existence of customer champions gives Volvo the luxury of selling virtually the same car to people time after time, while competitors are madly retooling their factories every year or two.

Killing a Product

Unlike people and companies, products don't die on their own. They never had a pulse anyway, and product bankruptcy just doesn't exist. Consequently, the marketer needs to have the good sense to know when an old product has no more life in it and keeping it going just wastes resources that ought to go to new products, instead.

Yet often you see weak products hanging around. Companies keep them on the market despite gradually declining sales because everybody, from manufacturer to retailer, hates to face reality. Even worse, you sometimes see marketers investing treasured resources in trying to boost sales of declining brands through renewed advertising or sales promotions. If the product has one foot in the grave, anyway, you should put those resources into introducing a radically improved version or a replacement product.

When to kill a product

You need to face facts: Many products would be better put out of their misery and replaced with something fresh and innovative. "But," you rightly object, "how do we know when our particular product reaches that point of no return?"

In the following sections, I discuss the warning signs that you're due to replace a product.

The market is saturated and you have a weak/falling share

Saturation means that you and your competitors are selling replacement products. You don't have many new customers around to convert. Growth slows, limited by the replacement rate for the product, plus whatever basic growth occurs in the size of the target market.

Saturation alone is no reason to give up on a product — many markets are saturated. An obvious one is the U.S. automobile market. You find very few adults who don't already own a car if they have the means to buy one and the need for one. So manufacturers and dealerships fight for replacement sales and first-time sales to young drivers, which can still be profitable for some of the competitors — but usually not all of them. If you have a product that has a share of less than, say, 75 percent of the leading product's market share, and if your share is falling relative to the leader, then you're on a long, slow, downward slide. (Market share means the percentage of all product sales, in units such as dollars or pounds, that one company captures for itself.)

Better to introduce a replacement and kill the old product than to wait it out. You have to replace the product eventually, and the sooner you do, the less your share and reputation suffer. Whatever else happens, you can't afford for customers to see you as a has-been in a saturated market!

I use the term *product* in the marketing sense, to include whatever you're offering, whether a good, service, idea, or person. Remember, too, that services, ideas, and even people sometimes need to be withdrawn from the market, just as goods do.

A series of improvements fails to create momentum

Often, companies try a series of "new and improved" versions, new packages, fancy coupon schemes, contests, and point-of-purchase promotions to breathe life into products after they stop generating year-to-year sales growth. Sometimes these ploys work and help to renew growth. Sometimes they don't. I borrow my own personal rule from baseball, but it seems to work: Three strikes and you're out. Don't bother trying for a fourth time. Time for a new player to approach the plate.

Something is wrong with your product

All too often, marketers discover some flaw in a product that threatens to hurt their company's reputation or puts its customers at risk. If your engineers think that the gas tank in one of your pickup trucks can explode during accidents, should you pull the model immediately and introduce a safer version or keep selling it and put the technical report in your paper shredder? A major auto company chose the second option. In the long run, the faulty gas tank killed some of its customers, and the company had to stage an extremely unprofitable recall, along with a repair-the-damage publicity campaign, topped by several lawsuits.

Brand equity and profits take a licking whenever your customers do. But many marketers lack the stomach or the internal political clout to kill a bad product, even when the product may kill customers.

I don't know exactly why some marketers keep making these mistakes, but I hope that you don't. Pull the product if you find out it may cause cancer, give people electrical shocks, choke a baby, or even just not work as well as you say it does. Pull the product immediately. Ask questions later. And write a press release announcing that you're acting on behalf of your customers, just in case the rumors are true. By taking this decisive step immediately, you let the market know that you have a great deal more integrity than most. And that can only make your brand equity stronger, not weaker. Trust me — pulling a product takes courage, but it's the best option, when the dust settles. And if you follow my advice and always invest creative energy and funds in your product development efforts — you should have something better to offer as a replacement.

How to kill or replace a product

Actually, getting rid of old products is the least of your troubles, because *liquidators* are happy to sell your inventory below cost to various vendors. Contact some of your distributors or your trade association for referrals.

But you may want to use a more elegant strategy — one that avoids the negativity of customers seeing your old products offered for a tenth of their normal price: Stage some kind of sales promotion to move the old inventory to customers through your normal distribution channels. I much prefer this option, especially if it also introduces consumers to the new product. But this method only works if you get started before the old product loses its appeal. So you have to aggressively replace your products. Don't wait for the market to kill your product; do the deed yourself. The following sections discuss more strategies that help you bow out gracefully.

The coattails strategy

The *coattails strategy* uses the old product to introduce the new. The variety of ways to put this strategy to use are limited only by your imagination. You can offer a free sample coupon for the new product to buyers of the old product. You can package the two together in a special two-for-one promotion. You can do special mailings or make personal or telephone sales calls to the old customers. If the two products are reasonably similar from a functional perspective, you can call the new product by the old product's name and try to merge it into the old identity as if you wanted to introduce an upgrade rather than something brand new.

In other words, you can dress the new product in the old product's coat instead of just attaching it to the coattails. You need to be able to defend this stealth strategy from a common-sense perspective, or your customers get angry. If you can make the argument that customers are getting a "more and better" version of the same product, then the strategy should work.

The coattails strategy is a great promotional device for replacing an old product with a new one. Use it whenever you want to kill an old product in order to make room for a new one. *Room* can mean room in the customer's mind, room on the store shelf, room in the distributor's catalog, or room in your own product line. Products take up space, and physical or mental space can give you an important resource. But you do take a risk — and it's a big one. When you make room for your new product, competing products can try to take that space, instead. Why? Any customers still faithful to the old product have to reconsider their purchase patterns, and they may choose a competitor over your new option. Similarly, retailers, distributors, or other channel members may give your space to another product. So you need to hold on to your space, even as you eliminate your product. Avoid any gaps in the availability of your products.

The product line placeholding strategy

You can use *product lines* to create clear product niches and hold them for replacement products. You should keep pricing consistent with product positions in your product line, as well — a practice called *price lining.*

For example, a bank may offer a selection of different savings options to its retail customers — a mix of straight savings accounts, savings with checking, mutual fund accounts, and certificates of deposit of varying lengths. If the bank organizes these options into a coherent range of named products and lists them in a single brochure in order from lowest-risk/lowest-return to highest-risk/highest-return, then it creates a clear product line with well-defined places for these products. (The bank must be sure that each product sits in a unique place on that spectrum — no overlaps, please!)

Now, when the bank wants to introduce a new product, it can substitute the new one for an old one, and consumers accept that this new product fills the same spot in the product line. The bank can also extend the product line in either direction or fill gaps in it with new products. Whatever the bank does, the product line can act as a placeholder to ease the entry of new products. (See the "Branding and Naming Your Product" section, earlier in this chapter, for more information on product lines.)

But I bet that your bank doesn't use this strategy — few do. As a result, you're always confused when you try to get your mind around their offerings, and they therefore lose some business that they should have won. Make sure your offerings fall into a clear product line with an obvious logic to it and clear points of difference anyone can understand at a glance. Product lines are a very important part of any marketing strategy, yet marketers often neglect them. What can you do, right now, to clarify the options you give your customers and make sure your branding and product offerings make good sense to everyone?

Chapter 15

Pricing and Price-Based Promotions

. . . .

In This Chapter

▶ Uncovering useful facts about pricing

▶ Establishing or modifying your list price

▶ Using price-based special offers

▶ Staying out of legal hot water

. . . .

Some marketers believe that businesses fail most often for two simple reasons: their prices are too high, or their prices are too low! Getting the price just right is the hardest task marketers face, but finding the right pricing approach, makes success a lot easier to achieve.

The bottom line of all marketing activities is that the customer needs to pay — willingly and, you hope, rapidly — for your products or services. But how much will they pay? Should you drop your prices to grow your market? Or would raising the price and maximizing profits be better? What about discounts and special promotional pricing? Getting the price part of your marketing plan right is hard . . . but the coming pages help you through it.

Understanding the Facts of Pricing

Most companies fall prey to the myth that customers only choose a product based on its list price. They set their list prices lower than they need to. Or when they need to boost sales, they do so by offering discounts or free units. If you insist on selling on the basis of price, your customers buy on the basis of price.

But alternatives always exist. To raise your price and still sell more, you can:

- **Build brand equity:** Better-known brands command a premium price.

- **Increase quality:** People talk up a good product, and that word of mouth earns it a 5 to 10 percent higher price than the competition.

- **Use prestige pricing** (see the "Discounts and Other Special Offers" section, later in this chapter): Giving your product a high-class image can boost your price 20 to 100 percent.

- **Create extra value through time and place advantages:** Customers consider the available product worth a lot more than one you can't get when you need it. (That's why a cup of coffee costs twice as much at the airport — are you really going to leave the terminal, get in a taxi, and go somewhere else to save a couple of bucks?)

Sure, price is important, but it doesn't have to be the only thing — unless the marketer doesn't know this price fact.

Avoiding underpricing

You're always going to have an easier time lowering a price than raising it. In general, you want to set price a bit high and see what happens. You can take back any price increase with a subsequent price cut. You can take back price increases much more easily (if they don't work) than price decreases.

Customers may not be as price sensitive as you fear. They may tolerate an increase better than you think, and they may not respond to a decrease in price as enthusiastically as you need them to in order to make that decrease profitable. They may even assume that price correlates with quality — in which case, they don't buy your product unless the price is high enough. Instead of assuming that you need a price cut whenever you want to boost profits, start by experimenting with a price increase. Be a contrarian. They usually succeed!

Exploring the impact of pricing on customers' purchases

Price sensitivity is the degree to which purchases are affected by price level. You need to estimate how price-sensitive your customers are.

How in the world can you estimate the price sensitivity of customers when you lack good data? The following checklist lists a series of *qualitative indicators* (clues we can guess from) of price sensitivity. You have to ask yourself a bunch of questions about your customer, product, and market, checking the box next to each question that you answer with "yes." Then you add up the number of checked boxes and see which way they lean. This study isn't scientific, but it's better than ignoring the problem altogether!

❑ **Does the customer view the price as reasonable?** If you're operating within an expected price range, customers aren't very price sensitive. Outside of the expected price range, they become more sensitized to price.

❑ **Is the product valuable at (almost) any price?** Some products are unique, and customers know that they can have a hard time finding a cheaper substitute. That fact lowers price sensitivity.

❑ **Is the product desperately needed?** I don't care how much fixing a broken arm at the emergency ward of a hospital costs — at least, I don't care if my arm is broken! And I'm not too price sensitive about roadside repair and towing services if my car has broken down on the highway at night. These products meet essential needs. But if your product is a *nonessential* (something that customers want but don't have to have right now), the customer is more price sensitive.

❑ **Are substitutes unavailable?** If the customer purchases in a context where substitute products aren't readily available, price sensitivity is lower. Shopping for price requires that substitutes at different prices be available. (For example, if you're the only company offering emergency plumbing repairs on weekends in your town, your customers will pay a high price for your services.)

❑ **Is the customer unaware of substitutes?** What the customer doesn't know costs him. And shopping is a complex, information-dependent behavior. I live in a small New England college town where not many substitutes for consumer products exist. Prices are high, as a result. But I keep a Manhattan Yellow Pages phone directory in my office and often shop in New York City by phone in order to get better prices. If more of the consumers in our local market knew how easily they could use this method of shopping, they would be more price sensitive, too — but they don't know about the option.

❑ **Does the customer find comparing options difficult?** Even where options exist, the consumer can have a lot of difficulty comparing products in some product categories. What makes one doctor better than another? I don't know — I have no idea which doctor is better able to treat me. The technical complexity of their work, plus the fact that you can't consume medical care until after you make the purchase decision, makes comparing options hard. And that difficulty makes health care consumers less price sensitive — and doctors richer.

❑ **Does the product seem inexpensive to customers?** Customers don't worry too much about price when they feel like they're getting a good value. However, if customers feel the pinch on their pocketbooks when they make the purchases, they pay close attention to prices. That's why you negotiate so hard when you buy a car or a house. Even products that cost far less can seem expensive if they're at the high end of a price range. For example, you're more price sensitive if you shop for a fancy, high-performance laptop computer than for a simple, basic desktop unit because the former probably costs 50 to 100 percent more than the latter, making the laptop expensive by comparison.

The more boxes you checked, the less price sensitive your customer is. If you checked multiple boxes, you probably can raise prices without hurting sales significantly. And that's great news!

You can supplement your estimate of price sensitivity (from the checklist) with actual tests. For example, if you think a 5 percent increase in prices won't affect sales, try that increase in a test market or for a short period of time, holding the rest of your marketing constant. Were you right? If so, roll out the increase nationwide (or townwide, for you small-business folks).

Finding profits without raising prices

When you think about profits, you may assume that your focus should be on the price. But many factors drive your company's cash flows and profits, not just the list price of your products. If your manager tells you to figure out how to raise prices because profits are too low, don't assume she's going at it from the right angle. Here are some ways to boost profits without raising prices:

✔ Check to see how quickly you're making collections — are vendors paying in 65 days? If so, cutting that time by 25 days may make up the needed profits without any price increase.

✔ All the discounts and allowances your company offers affect its revenues and profits, so you need to look at these factors, too, before you assume that price is the culprit. Are customers taking advantage of quantity discounts to stock up inexpensively and then not buying between the discount periods? If so, you have a problem with your sales promotions, not your list prices.

✔ Or perhaps you're in a service business that charges a base price, plus fees for special services and extras. If so, look hard at the way in which you assess fees. Perhaps your company is failing to collect the appropriate fees, in some cases.

✔ Or maybe your fee structure is out of date and doesn't reflect your cost structure accurately. For example, a bank that charges a low price for standard checking accounts, plus a per-check processing fee, may well find its profits slumping as customers switch to automated checking over the bank's computers — because banks often set the introductory fees for this service low or waive them to stimulate trials. If so, the problem isn't with the base price of a checking account, it's with the nature of the fee structure.

Setting or Changing Your List Price

If you need to establish a price, you're stuck with one of the toughest things anybody does in business. Surveys of managers indicate they suffer from a high degree of price anxiety. So let me take you through it logically, step by step. Price setting doesn't have to be a high-anxiety task if you do it right! (Figure 15-1 illustrates the process that I describe in the following sections.)

Step 1: Figure out who sets prices

This step isn't obvious. You, as the marketer, can set a list price. But the consumer may not ultimately pay your price. You may encounter a distributor or wholesaler and a retailer, all of whom take their markups. Furthermore, the manufacturer generally doesn't have the legal right to dictate the ultimate selling price. The retailer gets that job. So your list price is really just a suggestion, not an order. If the retailer doesn't like the suggested price, the product sells for another price.

And so you need to start by determining who else may be setting prices along with you. Involve these parties in your decision-making by asking some of them what they think about pricing your product. They may tell you that you have constraints to consider. Know what those constraints are before you start.

For example, if you're setting the price for a new book, you find that the big bookstore chains in the United States expect a 60 percent discount off the list price. Knowing that, you can set a high enough list price to give you some profit, even at a 60 percent discount rate. But if you don't realize that these chains expect much higher discounts than other bookstores, you may be blind-sided by their requirement.

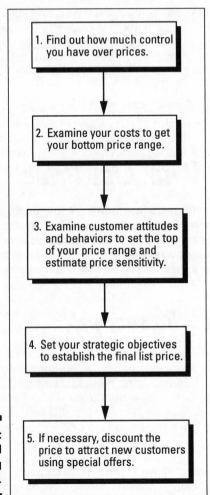

1. Find out how much control you have over prices.

2. Examine your costs to get your bottom price range.

3. Examine customer attitudes and behaviors to set the top of your price range and estimate price sensitivity.

4. Set your strategic objectives to establish the final list price.

5. If necessary, discount the price to attract new customers using special offers.

Figure 15-1: A helpful pricing process.

Marketers who operate in or through a *multilevel distribution channel* (meaning that they have distributors, wholesalers, rack jobbers (companies that keep retail racks stocked), retailers, agents, or other sorts of intermediaries) need to establish the *trade discount structure*. Trade discounts (also called *functional discounts*) are what you give these intermediaries. These discounts are a form of cost to the marketer, so make sure that you know the discount structure for your product before you move on. Usually, marketers state the discount structure as a series of numbers, representing what each of the intermediaries get as a discount. But you take each discount off the price left over from the discount before it, not off the list price.

Step 2: Examine your costs

How do you know your costs? That's easy — in theory. In theory, your company's excellent cost accounting system captures all your costs, and some guy in a green eyeshade can simply give you the figure.

In practice, you may not have good, accurate information on the true costs of a specific product or service. Take some time to try to estimate what you're actually spending, and remember to include some value for expensive inventories if they sit around for a month or more (assume you're paying interest on the money tied up in those products to account for the loss of capital wasting away in inventory).

After you examine your costs carefully, you should have a fairly accurate idea of the least amount you can charge. That charge is, at a bare minimum, your actual costs. (Okay, maybe sometimes you want to give away a product for less than cost in order to introduce people to it — but don't use this ploy to take customers from competitors or you could be sued for dumping. See the section "Staying Out of Trouble with the Law" later in this chapter for the dirt on dumping.) More often, you need a price that includes the cost plus a profit margin — say, 20 or 30 percent. So that means you have to treat your cost as 70 or 80 percent of the price, adding in that 20 or 30 percent margin your company requires.

This cost-plus-profit figure is the bottom of your pricing range (see Figure 15-2). Now you need to see if customers permit you to charge this price — or perhaps even allow you to charge a higher price!

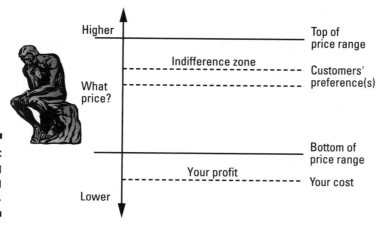

Figure 15-2:
Defining
your pricing
range.

Step 3: Evaluate customer perception of price

Your costs and profit requirements impose a lower limit on price. But your customers' perceptions impose an upper limit. You need to define both of these limits to know your possible price range. So you need to figure out what price customers are willing to pay.

In Figure 15-2, I show the price that customers favor as *customers' preference*. Note that customer preference may not be the upper limit. If customers aren't too price sensitive, they may not notice or care if you set your price somewhat higher than their preferred price. (See the section "Understanding how customers perceive and remember prices" earlier in this chapter.)

Pricing experts sometimes call the difference between the customer's desired price and a noticeably higher price the *indifference zone*. Within the indifference zone, customers are indifferent to both price increases and price decreases. However, the zone gets smaller (on a percent basis) as the price of a product increases. How big or small is the zone of indifference in your product's case? Go back to the price sensitivity checklist. The zone is small if your customers are highly price sensitive, and the zone is large if they aren't that price sensitive. Just make some assumptions that seem reasonable for now — I know this process involves some guesswork, but still, breaking down the pricing decision into a series of smaller, educated guesses is better than plucking a number out of thin air! At worst, your errors on all those little guesses may be random, in which case they cancel each other out.

You can also get at customer preference by looking at the current pricing structure in your market. What are people paying for comparable products? Does a downward trend exist in the prices of comparable products? An upward trend? Or are they stable? Go shopping to figure out the existing price structure; you get excellent clues as to how customers may react to different prices for your product.

Through these sorts of activities, I assume you have at least back-of-the-envelope figures for the customers' preferred price and how much higher you can price without drawing attention. That means you have established the top of your price range.

The simplest approach to pricing is to set your price at the top of the range. As long as the price range is above the bottom limit (as long as your preferred price plus the indifference zone is equal to or greater than your cost plus your required profit), you're okay.

But you can't always set your price at the top of the range. In the next step of the pricing process, I show you how to figure out what your final price should be.

Step 4: Examine secondary influences on price

You need to have your costs and the customers' upper limits as the two primary considerations. They set a price range. But you need to consider many other factors, too. These factors may influence your decision by forcing you to price in the middle or bottom of the price range rather than at the top, for example.

Consider competitive issues. Do you need to gain market share from a close competitor? If so, either keep price at parity and do aggressive marketing, or adjust your price to be slightly (but noticeably) below the competitor's price. Also consider likely future price trends. Are prices trending downward in this market? Then you need to adjust your figures down a bit to stay in synch with your market. Similarly, currency fluctuations may affect your costs and, thus, your pricing options. If you're concerned that you may take a hit from the exchange rate, better to be safe and price at the high end of the range. Finally, product line management may dictate a slightly lower or higher price. For example, you may need to price a top-of-the-line product significantly higher than others in its line just to make it clear to the customer that this product is a step above its competition.

Step 5: Set your strategic objectives

You may have objectives other than revenues and profit maximization. Many marketers price near the bottom of their price range to increase their market share. (They price so low because a high market share later on will probably give them more profits — so it's an investment strategy. See Chapter 2 for details.)

This low-price strategy only makes sense if the customer is fairly price sensitive! If not, you're throwing away possible revenues without any real gain in market share. You should be pricing at the top of the range and using the extra revenues to invest in quality and brand-building marketing promotions in order to increase market share (see Chapter 2 for details on these and other strategy options).

In other cases, marketers have certain volume goals they need to reach — like when they need to run a factory near its capacity level. So they may price in the low end of the range in order to maximize unit sales, even if doing so doesn't maximize net profits per unit (the increase in sales for a given decrease in price depends upon the level of price sensitivity).

Sometimes marketers even want to minimize unit volume — for example, when introducing a new product. They may not have the capacity to sell the product to a mass market and so decide to *skim the market* by selling the product at such a high price that only the very wealthy or least price-sensitive customers can buy it. Then they lower prices later on, when they have made maximum profits from the high-end customers and have added production capacity. CD players, fax machines, and satellite dishes for receiving TV programming all entered U.S. and European markets at high prices, using the skimming strategy.

Don't use a skimming strategy unless you're sure that you're safe from aggressive competition in the short term.

Understanding how customers perceive and remember prices

If the top of your price range for a new child's toy is $10, you probably want to drop it down to $9.99 or $9.89 for the simple reason that this price seems much cheaper to most consumers. Assuming they're price sensitive at all, they buy considerably more of the lower-priced product, even though the price difference amounts to only pennies. Why? Because people perceive prices ending in 9 as cheaper — generally 3 to 6 percent cheaper in their memories than the rounded-up price. It's just something about the way your customers see your price, and you can take advantage of it.

The only hook to using prices ending in 9 — which is called *odd-even pricing* — is that customers sometimes associate this pricing with cheap products that have worse quality. So don't use odd-even pricing when your customers are more quality sensitive than price sensitive. For example, odd-even pricing may cheapen the image of an original work of art for sale in an art gallery. But, in general, the strategy seems to work.

You may also want to adjust your price to make it fit into your product line, or into the range of products sold by your retailers or distributors. The idea is to fit your product into a range of alternatives, giving the product a logical spot in customers' minds. Marketers know this common and generally effective strategy as *price lining*.

You may want to price relative to an important competitor or set of competitors. Marketers call this practice *competitive pricing,* for obvious reasons. If you're in a highly competitive market, you should exercise competitive pricing. Decide which competing products the customers may view as closest to yours and then make your price sufficiently higher or lower to differentiate your product. How much difference is enough difference depends upon the size of the customers' indifference zone (see the section "Step 3: Evaluate customer perception of price" earlier in this chapter to find out about the indifference zone).

Should you price above or below that tough competitor? That decision depends on whether you offer more or fewer benefits and higher or lower quality. If you offer your customer less or about the same, you need to make your price significantly lower so that you look like a better value. If you offer greater benefits, you can make your price a little higher to signal this fact — but not too high because you want to be sure that your product seems like a better value than the competition.

If you want to appear significantly superior to the competition, make sure that your prices are significantly higher. If Tiffany & Company priced its jewelry too low, the jewelry would lose its prestigious image. In fact, this loss of image is just what happened when Avon bought Tiffany — Avon tried to mass-market the Tiffany name by putting it on inexpensive jewelry. Millions of dollars of losses later, Avon sold out and Tiffany went back to success — by going back to exclusively high prices.

Sometimes you should just price exactly at the competitor's price. You may want to match prices if you plan to differentiate your product on the basis of some subtle difference because this way, customers focus their attention on the difference rather than on price.

Finally, some competitors try to convince customers that their product is better but costs less than the competitors' products. Nobody believes this claim — unless you present evidence. If you do, customers will love you — we all hope to get more for less, after all! For example, a personal computer with a new, faster chip may really be better but cost less. A new anti-wrinkle cream may work better but cost less if you've discovered a new formula. And a retailer may be able to sell the same brands for a cheaper price because it has larger stores that do more volume of business. As long as you have — and can communicate to the customer — a plausible argument, you can undercut the competitor's price at the same time that you claim superior benefits. But make sure that you back up the claim, or the customer assumes that your lower price means the product is inferior.

Figuring discount structures

Confused? Let me show you how to compute prices and discounts in a complex distribution channel. Say that you discover the typical discount structure in the market where you want to introduce your product is 30/10/5. What does that mean? If you start with a $100 list price, the retailer pays at a discount of 30 percent off the list price (0.30 × $100 = $70). The retailer, who pays $70 for the product, marks it up to (approximately) $100 and makes about $30 in gross profit.

Now, the discount structure figures tell you that other intermediaries exist — one for each discount listed. The distributor, who sells the product to the retailer, has a discount of 10 percent off the price that she charges the retailer (that's 0.10 × $70 = $7 of gross profit for the distributor).

And this distributor must have paid $70 − $7, or $63, for the product to another intermediary (probably a manufacturer's representative or wholesaler). The marketer sells to this intermediary. And the 30/10/5 formula shows that this intermediary receives a 5 percent discount: 0.05 × $63 = $3.15 in profit for him.

Subtracting again, you can also determine that the marketer must sell the product to this first intermediary at $63 − $3.15, or $59.85. You, as the marketer, must give away more than 40 percent of that $100 list price to intermediaries if you use this 30/10/5 discount structure. And so you have to calculate any profit you make from a $100 list price as costs subtracted from your net of $59.85. That's all you ever see of that $100!

In pricing services, set a price that's consistent with your quality. Don't accidentally cheapen the perceived quality of your service by setting your price too low.

Discounts and Other Special Offers

Special offers are temporary inducements to make customers buy on the basis of price or price-related factors. Special offers play with the price, giving consumers (or intermediaries) a way to get the product for less — at least while the offer lasts.

Why play with the price? If you think the price should be lower, why not just cut the price permanently?

A price cut is easy to do, but it's hard to undo. A special offer allows you to temporarily discount the price while still maintaining the list price at its old level. When the offer ends, the list price is the same — you haven't given anything away permanently. Here are some cases in which maintaining your list price can be important:

✔ When your reason for wanting to cut the price is a short-term one, like wanting to counter a competitor's special offer or respond to a new product introduction

✔ When you want to experiment with the price (to find out about customer price sensitivity) without committing to a permanent price cut until you see the data

✔ When you want to stimulate consumers to try your product, and you believe that after they try it, they may like the product well enough to buy it again at full price

✔ When your list price needs to stay high in order to signal quality *(prestige pricing)* or be consistent with other prices in your product line *(price lining strategy)*

✔ When your competitors are all offering special lower prices and you think you have no choice because consumers have come to expect special offers

This last reason makes me mad as all get-out that so many marketers have trained their customers to expect special offers and only buy in response to them. I'm serious. Very serious. This mistake is the biggest and dumbest one that marketers make, and they've been making it over and over for many years. Consequently, customers purchase many product categories on the basis of price more than on the basis of quality and benefits. As a result, the rates of coupon redemptions keep climbing in the United States, Canada, and many European countries. Ultimately, special offers take up a bigger and bigger share of marketing budgets every year and often eat unnecessarily into profits.

What happens when competitors get too focused on making and matching each other's special offers? They flood the customers with price-based promotions. Discounts and other freebies begin to outweigh brand-building marketing messages, focusing consumer attention on price over brand and benefit considerations. Special promotions can and do increase customer sensitivity to price. They attract *price switchers,* people who aren't loyal to any brand but just shop on the basis of price. And these promotions encourage people to become price switchers, thus reducing the size of the core customer base and increasing the number of fringe customers. So special offers have the potential to erode brand equity, reduce customer loyalty, and cut your profits. This slope is slippery, and you can easily lose your footing on it!

Procter & Gamble's marketing managers recently came to the same conclusion and decided to stop using price-based promotions entirely. No more coupons and discounts. Period. But they couldn't make the change stick. Retailers complained. The U.S. government thought this move was tantamount to price fixing because Procter & Gamble wanted competitors to stop price-based promotions, too (see the section "Staying Out of Trouble with the Law" later in the chapter for an explanation of price fixing), and that, of course, violates antitrust laws. So Procter & Gamble is still sliding down the special offers slope, in spite of its desire to stop.

Okay, I've warned you about what General Foods executives like to call *coupon fever*. But you still may have legitimate reasons to use special offers (see the preceding bulleted list). Or you may not have the power to change practices in your market — after all, Procter & Gamble couldn't — and so you have to go with the flow. So, if you have good reason to use discounts and deals, the following sections explain some options available to you.

Designing coupons and other special offers

You can offer coupons, refunds, *premiums* (or gifts), extra products for free, free trial-sized samples, sweepstakes and other event-oriented premium plans, and any other special offer you can think up — just check with your lawyers to make sure that the promotion is legal. (Legal constraints do exist. You can't mislead consumers about what they get. And a sweepstakes or contest has to be open to all, not tied to product purchase. See "Staying Out of Trouble with the Law" later in this chapter for more on marketing legal no-nos.)

If you're promoting to *the trade,* as marketers collectively term intermediaries like wholesalers and retailers, then you can also offer your intermediaries things like free-goods deals, buy-back allowances, display and advertising allowances, and help with their advertising costs (called *cooperative,* or *co-op, advertising*).

A large (and growing) majority of all special offers takes the form of *coupons,* and so I focus on them in explaining how to design special offers.

Any certificate entitling the holder to a reduced price is a coupon, which gives a pretty broad definition — and that means you have a lot of room for creativity in this field. To get a good feel for the options and approaches to coupons, just collect a bunch of recent coupons from your own and other industries.

How much to offer?

How much of a deal should you offer customers in a coupon or other special offer? The answer depends on how much attention you want. Most offers fail to motivate the vast majority of customers, so keep in mind that the typical special offer in your industry probably isn't particularly effective. A good ad campaign probably reaches more customers.

But you can greatly increase the reach of your special offer simply by making the offer more generous (the higher the price sensitivity, the more notice you generate, of course). In consumer nondurables, whether toothpaste or canned soup, research shows that you have to offer at least 50 cents off your list price to attract much attention. All but the most dedicated coupon clippers ignore the smaller offers —less than 10 percent of consumers in surveys find these small offers attractive. But when offers get over the 50-cent level, attractiveness grows rapidly — sometimes even reaching the 80-percent level! You can find within this larger percentage of interested consumers many brand-loyal, core customers — both yours and your competitors. And you should find these core customers far more attractive than the knee-jerk coupon clippers who flock to smaller offers.

So I think (and I disagree with many marketers on this point) that you do better to use fewer, bigger offers than to run endless two-bit coupons. Too much noise exists already, so why add to the clutter of messages when you can focus your efforts into fewer, more effective coupons?

Forecasting redemption rates (good luck — you'll need it!)

Designing a coupon isn't the hard part. The hard part comes when you try to guess the *redemption rate* (or percentage of people who use the coupon). And you raise the stakes when you use those big offers I advocate, which makes them riskier to forecast.

I can tell you that, on average in North America, customers redeem a little over 3 percent of coupons (and the average coupon offers a bit under 40 cents off list price). So you can use that as a good starting point for your estimate. But the range is wide — some offers are so appealing, and so easy to use, that customers redeem 50 percent of those coupons. For others, the redemption rate can be close to zero. So how do you find out if your coupon will have a high or low redemption rate?

You can refine your redemption estimate by looking at your offer compared to others. Are you offering something more generous or easy to redeem than you have in the past? Than your competitors do? If so, you can expect significantly higher than average redemption rates — maybe twice as high or higher.

Also, look at your past data for excellent clues. If you have ever used coupons before, your company should have rich information about response rates. Just be sure that you examine past offers carefully to pick ones that truly match the current offer before assuming the same response rate can be repeated.

Think about price sensitivity. Again. Yes, go use the price elasticity formula in the sidebar "Price sensitivity mathematics" earlier in this chapter (if you have data) and the qualitative evaluation of price sensitivity in the earlier section "Fact 2: A lower price isn't always better." Your offer really just shifts the price on a temporary basis — at some cost to the customer because of the trouble they need to go to in order to redeem the coupon. So the real new price is something less than the discount you offer on the coupon — adjust it a little to reflect how much the customer thinks it costs him to redeem the coupon. Now ask yourself if this real price is lower enough than the list price to alter demand. Does the price fall outside of most customers' indifference zones or not?

Many coupons do not shift the price very far beyond the indifference zone — that's why they generally attract those fringe customers who buy on price but don't attract the core customers of other brands. And that's why redemption rates are only a few percent, on average. However, if your coupon does shift the price well beyond the indifference zone, you're likely to see a much higher redemption rate than usual. Coupon deals gone wild is the most common reason for marketers to lose their jobs. So always check the offer against what you know of customer perception and price sensitivity to make sure that you aren't accidentally shifting the price so far that everyone and her brother wants to redeem coupons.

Forecasting the cost of special offers

Okay, after you've thought about the redemption rate, say you believe that 4 percent of customers will redeem a coupon offering a 10 percent discount on your product. To estimate the cost of your coupon program, you must first decide whether this 4 percent of consumers accounts for just 4 percent of your products' sales over the period in which the coupon applies. Probably not. They may stock up in order to take advantage of the special offer. And so you have to estimate how much more than usual consumers will buy.

If you think they'll buy twice as much as usual (that's a pretty high figure, but it makes for a simple illustration), just double the average purchase size. Four percent of customers, buying twice what they usually do in a month (if that's the term of the offer), can produce how much in sales? Now, apply the discount rate to that sales figure to find out how much the special offer may cost you. Can you afford it? Is the promotion worth the money? That's for you to decide — and it's a judgment call; the math can't tell you.

Some marketers have their cake and eat it too when it comes to special offers. They use what they call self-liquidating premiums, which don't cost them any money at all in the long run. A *premium* is any product that you give away to customers or sell at a discount as a reward for doing business with you (see Chapter 11 for a lot of ideas on how to use premiums). A *self-liquidating premium* is one that customers end up paying for — at least, they cover your costs on that product. Say you run a contest in which some of the customers who open your packaging are instant winners, able to send away for a special premium by enclosing their winning ticket plus $4.95. If your direct costs for the premium you send them are $4.95, you don't have to pay out of pocket for what the customer may see as a fun and valuable benefit.

Staying Out of Trouble with the Law

You don't have to be a legal whiz to know when pricing is illegal. Whenever a customer or competitor can make a good case for unfair or deceptive pricing, you're as good as busted. However, just to keep legal eagles happy, I'm providing a short list of some of the more common and serious illegal pricing practices. (And, of course, because you want to run an ethical business.) Make sure that you read this correctly — these are things you should not do!

- **Price fixing:** Don't agree to (or even talk about) prices with other companies. The exception is a company you sell to, of course — but note that you cannot force them to resell your product at a specific price.

- **Price fixing in disguise:** Shady marketers have tried a lot of ideas. Those ideas don't work. If your competitors want you to require the same amount of down payment, start your negotiations from the same list prices as theirs, or use a standardized contract for extending credit or form a joint venture to distribute all your products (at the same price), you better realize that these friendly suggestions are all forms of price fixing. Just say no. And in the future, refuse even to take phone calls from marketers who offer you such deals.

- **Price fixing by purchasers:** Believe it or not, you shouldn't even treat marketers unfairly. If purchasers join together in order to dictate prices from their suppliers, this can very well be price fixing. Have a skilled lawyer review any such plans.

- **Exchanging price information:** You can't talk to your competitors about prices. Ever. Okay? If it ever comes to light that anyone in your company gives out information about pricing and receives some in return, you're in big trouble, even if you don't feel you acted on that information. Take this warning seriously. (By the way, *price signaling* — announcing a planned price increase — is sometimes seen as an unfair exchange of price information, because competitors may use such announcements to signal to others that everyone should make a price increase.)

- **Bid rigging:** If you're bidding for a contract, the preceding point applies. Don't share any information with anyone. Don't compare notes with another bidder. Don't agree to make an identical bid. Don't *split* by agreeing not to bid on one job if the competitor doesn't bid on another. Don't mess with the bidding process in any manner, or you're guilty of *bid rigging.*

- ✔ **Parallel pricing:** In some cases, the U.S. government can charge you with price fixing, even if you didn't talk to competitors — just because you have similar price structures. After all, the result may be the same — to boost prices unfairly. In other cases, the law considers similar prices as natural. Here's a good-sense rule to keep in mind: Don't mirror competitors' prices, unless everyone and her uncle can see that you selected those prices on your own — especially if your price change involves a price increase.

- ✔ **Price squeezes, predatory pricing, limit pricing, and dumping:** To the average marketer, these illegal acts are effectively the same (although they are tested under different U.S. regulations). They involve using prices to push a competitor out of business, or to push or keep them out of a particular market. For example, the classic *squeeze* involves setting wholesale prices too high for small-sized orders. Doing so drives the independent or small retailer out of business, giving unfair advantage to the big chain buyers that can qualify for a volume discount. At the retail level, *predatory pricing* involves setting prices so low that local competitors can't keep up. Predatory pricing is also used by chains and multinationals to drive locals out of business. If you're pricing at or below cost, you're probably doing predatory pricing. Similarly, if your prices are so aggressive that they lock other competitors out of a market (even if you price above cost), then you're probably guilty of *limit pricing.* A variant is *dumping,* in which you try to buy your way into a new market by dumping a lot of product into that market at artificially low prices. Don't.

Some people throw up their hands in despair because so many pricing techniques are illegal. They say, "What can I do?" Let me just add that trying to influence prices in certain ways is okay. You can offer volume discounts to encourage larger purchases, as long as those discounts don't force anybody out of the market. And although you, as a marketer, can't force a retailer to charge a certain price for your product, you can encourage them to by advertising the suggested retail price and by listing it as such on your product.

Also, you can always offer an effective price cut to consumers through a consumer coupon or other special offer. Retailers usually agree to honor such offers (check with an ad agency, the retailer, or a lawyer to find out how to form such contracts). However, if you offer a discount to your retailers, you can't force them to pass that discount on to your customers. They may just put the money in the bank and continue to charge customers full price.

Chapter 16

Distribution, Retail, and Point of Purchase

*T*he companies with the widest distribution are often the most successful, because that distribution system gives them access to so many potential customers.

Of course, reaching out into the world of your customers with your distribution does not guarantee success, it only makes success possible. The customers still have to know and like your product (which, I ought to remind you, can be a service as well as a tangible good). And customers have to view your product as affordable, too. So distribution is not the only important matter in marketing, but it is a big one. In fact, in developing a marketing program (see Chapter 1), I encourage you to treat distribution as one of the five key factors, or five Ps, of marketing. I have to use a synonym for distribution, the term placement, to fit it into this list of marketing Ps along with product, promotion, pricing and people, but the idea is the same. What you're doing in distribution is placing your offering when, where, and how prospective customers need and want it.

Think of this book's distribution as a simple example. It receives good placement on the shelves of bookstores, especially the increasingly important major chain stores like Barnes & Noble and Borders, where it is placed in the marketing area of the business section, making it easy to find. It is also placed conveniently by topic, title, and author on searchable Internet bookstores like Amazon.com (www.amazon.com). These two main distribution channels provide broad reach into the market of people who are looking for helpful advice and information about how to market their businesses and sell their products or services. Without this broad distribution, you may never have encountered this book, regardless of how well written, packaged, or priced it may be.

Can you add distributors or expand your distribution network? If so, your product many become available to more people, and sales may rise as a result. (If not, consider the Web, direct-response marketing, and events as three alternatives, because they bypass distributors and reach out directly to customers. See Chapters 10, 12, and 13, respectively.)

Can you improve the visibility of your product within its current distribution channel, for example by making sure it is better displayed (if it's a product) or better communicated (if it's service)? That's another way marketers use distribution strategies to boost sales. Or perhaps you can find a way to shift your distribution slightly so as to give you access to more desirable or larger customers. A consultant I know who helps small businesses with their hiring and employment issues is beginning to visit the human resources directors of large businesses in her area to explore what she can do for them. One contract with a big firm may be as valuable to her as 10 or 20 smaller clients, so this new effort to reach out to the largest companies in her area may grow her business significantly.

Increasing the availability of products in your distribution channel can also help boost sales and profits. Can you find ways to get more inventory out there? Or can you speed the movement of products out to customers so that they feel that they can more easily find your product when they need it? These sorts of improvements can have a dramatic impact on sales by making finding what they want easier for more customers, when and where they want it.

Also, I urge you to make a list of every company that has a hand of any sort in making your sales and servicing your customers, and then to think about ways to strengthen your business relationship with them. Think about doing something simple, like sending them a gift basket at the holidays. Do something to invest in these relationships — they're very important to most businesses but too easily taken for granted.

And drop everything and go find a new distributor right now! Almost every business can sell through distributors if you're open minded and creative about cutting deals. You may already sell through distributors, in which case, you should go find some more. In my business, we try to either add a new distributor or talk an old distributor into selling a new product each month. It's a low-cost way to keep expanding. Even if we have to give a distributor a deeper discount than we want so that we motivate them, we often do because we believe that our business hasn't achieved its potential until our products are readily available everywhere within our industry.

Getting Distributors on Your Side

Distributors want items that are easy to sell because customers want to buy them. It's that simple. So the first step in getting customers on your side is making sure your product is appealing. A brilliant product and a clear way of presenting that product so its brilliance shines through, is a great investment for growing any distribution system. You may still have to go out and tell distributors about it and work to support them and make them, but if you start with a product whose unique qualities shine through, it will be a lot easier to expand your distribution.

After you're confident that you have something worth selling, ask yourself what distributors may be successful at selling it. Who's willing and able to distribute for you? Are wholesalers or other intermediaries going to be helpful? If so, who are they and how many of them can you locate? Phone companies publish business-to-business telephone directories by region for most of the United States (call the business office of your local phone company to order them), and these directories often reference the category of intermediary you're looking for in their Yellow Pages sections. You can also find several helpful trade associations and trade shows specializing in distributors in specific industries. For example, the International Food Distributors Forum puts on an annual conference for food distributors. A couple of days at an event like that, and you know more than you want to about the structure and trends of the distribution channel you're studying.

Major conventions in your industry are the best places to find distributors. Hop on a plane, bring product samples and literature, put on comfortable shoes, and walk around the convention hall until you find the right distributors!

You may also want to contact the American Wholesale Marketers Association (AWMA), 1128 16th Street NW, Washington, DC 20036; phone 202-463-2124; Web site www.awmanet.org. The AWMA publishes a directory of intermediaries that marketers see as a useful resource. And to easily find distributors, go onto Google.com (or any other search engine) and search for products like yours. Who's selling them? Maybe they'd sell yours, too!

Who are the retailers that may help you sell? You can much more easily identify retail stores for the simple reason that they're in the business of being easy to find. The Yellow Pages phone directories in any U.S. metropolitan areas of interest to you list retail stores. These stores also have their own trade associations, such as the International Council of Shopping Centers, 1221 Avenue of the Americas, 41st Floor, New York, NY 10020; phone 212-421-8181; Web site `www.icsc.org`. Consult any directory of associations for extensive listings (available in the reference sections of most libraries). Finally, consider wearing out a little shoe leather and tire rubber to find out who the leading retailers are in any specific geographic market. Just visit high-traffic areas and see what stores are prominent and successful to identify the leading retailers in the area.

Understanding Marketing Channel Structure and Design

Efficiency is the driving principle behind *distribution channel* design. (*Channel* refers to the pathways you create to get your product out there and into customers' hands.) Traditionally, channels have evolved to minimize the number of transactions, because the fewer the transactions, the more efficient the channel.

As Figure 16-1 shows, a channel in which four producers and four customers do business directly has 16 (4 x 4) possible transactions. In reality, the numbers get much higher when you have markets with dozens or hundreds of producers and thousands or millions of customers.

You lower the number of transactions greatly when you introduce an intermediary because now you only have to do simple addition rather than multiplication. In the example shown in Figure 16-1, you only need 8 (4 + 4) transactions to connect all four customers with all four producers through the intermediary. Each producer or customer has only to deal with the intermediary, who links him to all the producers or customers he may want to do business with.

Although intermediaries add their markup to the price, they often reduce overall costs of distribution because of their effect on the number of transactions. Adding a level of intermediaries to a channel reduces the total number of transactions that all producers and customers need to do business with each other.

This example is simplistic, but you can see how the logic applies to more complex and larger distribution channels. Introduce a lot of customers and producers, link them through multiple intermediaries (perhaps adding a second or third layer of intermediaries), and you have a classic indirect marketing channel. Odds are that you have some channels like this in your industry.

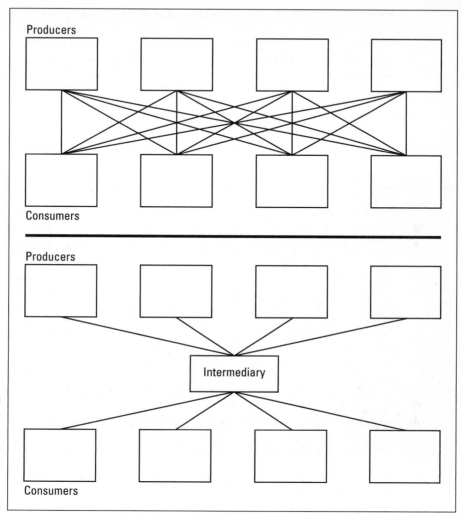

Figure 16-1:
Reducing
transactions
through
interme-
diaries.

I have to warn you that I'm suspicious of these traditional, multi-level channels. The longer and more complex they grow, the more types of intermediaries they have. The more times a product is handed from intermediary to intermediary, the less I like the channel. I prefer to see only one layer between you and your customers, if possible.

How come? I don't like traditional, many-layered channels because they separate you too much from the end consumer. I think that improved transportation; computerized links between channel members (through *electronic data interchange* or *EDI*); the creation of just-in-time inventory systems in which suppliers bring only what's needed, when it's needed; and the emergence of direct marketing technologies and practices all make running lean and mean channels much easier. Just as big companies are de-layering to become more efficient and get closer to their customers, the big distribution channels in many industries are trying to do the same thing.

The trend is toward simpler and more direct channels, and marketers need to be prepared to handle a large number of customer transactions on their own without as much help from intermediaries. Database management techniques alone do much to make this future possible.

So think hard about how to get closer to your customer. Can you reduce the layers in your channel or begin to develop direct channels (by mail, phone, or Internet) to supplement your traditional indirect channels? If so, balance the advantages of being close to the end customer with the benefits of broad reach from having many distributors. One way to do this is to add more distributors in the horizontal direction, where each new distributor buys directly from you, not through another distributor who then bundles their purchase with others and sends it on to you. Think broad distribution, not deep, if you want modern reach without traditional layers and all of the complexities and costs of those layers.

What the heck do intermediaries do to earn their cut?

In deciding how to distribute your product, I recommend that you draw up a list of tasks you want distributors to do. For example, you may want distributors to find you more customers than you can find on your own. That's just one of the functions distributors may be able to perform. Decide what you'd like them to do, and then seek out distributors who say they want to do those things for you. That way, you will be more likely to get a good match. Here's a starting list of functions you may want your intermediaries to perform. One or more of these functions may be important to you as you look for distributors:

✔ Finding more customers for your product than you can on your own

✔ Researching customer attitudes and desires

✔ Buying and selling

✔ Breaking down bulk shipments for resale

✔ Setting prices

✔ Managing point-of-purchase promotions

✔ Advertising at the local level (*pull advertising,* which is designed to bring people to a store or other business)

✔ Transporting products

✔ Inventorying products

✔ Financing purchases

✔ Separating poor-quality leads from serious customers (marketers call this *qualifying sales leads*)

✔ Providing customer service and support

✔ Sharing the risks of doing business

✔ Combining your products with others to offer appropriate assortments

Channel design considerations

Yes, your intermediaries can do several useful things for you, as the preceding section indicates. You need to decide who can do which of these things. But, in addition to thinking about those various functions and who should perform them, you may want to consider the following strategic issues. How you set up and manage your distribution channel or channels affects each issue.

✔ **Market coverage:** How well does your channel reach your target customers? If you go direct, doing everything yourself, you may be unable to cover the market as intensely as you want to. By adding even one layer of intermediaries, you suddenly have many more warm bodies or storefronts out there. As you add more layers to the channel, the bottom of the channel grows ever larger, allowing you to achieve increasingly good market coverage.

In short, market coverage increases as you add layers and members to your distribution channel. As you increase market coverage, you increase your availability to customers, which in turn maximizes your sales and market share. You can't fight that. So sometimes building a channel, rather than de-layering it, makes sense. Just make sure that you really do get better coverage and that the coverage translates into increased sales. Otherwise, those intermediaries aren't pulling their weight.

✔ **Level of intensity:** Thinking about the issue of market coverage in terms of *intensity,* defined as the extent of your geographic coverage of the market, can help you figure out how many and what types of distributors to use. Conventional wisdom says that three practical strategies exist. An *intensive distribution strategy* attempts to put every customer within reach of your products by using as many intermediaries and layers as needed to create maximum coverage. You should use this strategy in mature markets where your competitors are trying to do the same thing, or in markets where the customer makes a convenience purchase — because intensive distribution makes your product convenient. Keep in mind that this strategy costs you a lot, and you may not need it in other circumstances.

The second alternative is *selective distribution strategy,* in which you target the most desirable areas or members of your market. For example, the business-to-business marketer may decide to target a geographic region where many users of her technology are headquartered. The consumer products marketer may decide to market to zip code areas or counties where he finds heavy users of his product.

The third alternative is *exclusive distribution,* in which you cherry pick to find the best intermediaries and customers. This strategy is appropriate when you don't have any really serious competition and you have a specialty product that you want to keep providing at the same profitable level. This method doesn't grow your market or boost share significantly, but it does maximize profit margins, and that's not bad!

Exclusive distribution is also appropriate as you introduce an innovative new product, whether a good or service. You find a limited number of early adopters in any market, so a massive effort to mass-market a new innovative product usually fails. Start with exclusive distribution to those customers most interested in trying new ideas and then work up to selective distribution as competition builds and the product goes mainstream. Finally, push toward intensive distribution as the market matures and your emphasis shifts from finding first-time users to fighting over repeat business.

✔ **Speed to market:** The longer the channel, the slower the product's trip from producer to customer. A relay team can never beat an individual runner in a sprint. If your customers need or want faster delivery and service, you have to prune the distribution channel until it's fast enough to satisfy the consumers. You may even need to replace physical distributors with a Web site where everything can be ordered immediately, for next-day delivery.

Think about the trend toward catalog direct shopping in the clothing industry. Customers can obtain their choice of style and size from a large assortment within a few days, if the shipper uses UPS, and the next day, if the shipper uses an overnight air service. You may think that you can shop in a department store even more quickly because you can walk out with your purchase. But the busy consumer may not have time to visit a department store for days or weeks, whereas she can take care of a late-night call to Lands' End today. And you may need to visit several stores to find what you want, which eats up more days and more lunch hours. However, you can look through a stack of catalogs in a flash. Catalog clothing sales are gaining over retail sales, in part, because many consumers perceive catalog shopping as the quicker and easier alternative.

Reviewing Retail Strategies and Tactics

If you decide to improve sales at a retail store and you bring in a specialized retail consultant, you may soon be drawing *planograms* of your shelves (diagrams showing how to lay out and display a store's merchandise) and counting *SKUs* (stock-keeping units — a unique inventory code for each item you stock). You may also examine the statistics on sales volume from end-of-aisle displays (higher sales) versus middle of the aisle (lower sales), and from eye-level displays (higher sales) versus bottom or top of the shelf (lower sales). Great. Go for it. However, I have to warn you that, although a technical approach has its place, you can't use this method to create a retail success story.

The real winners in retail are the result of creative thinking and good site selection, in that order. Those points are the two big-picture issues that determine whether your store has low or high performance. A creative, appealing store concept. In a spot that has the right sort of traffic, and a lot of it.

Traffic is a flow of target customers near enough to the store for its external displays and local advertising to draw them in. You want a great deal of traffic, whether it's foot traffic on a sidewalk, automobile traffic on a road or highway, or virtual traffic at a Web site. Retailers need to have people walking, driving, or surfing into their stores (and "virtual" stores on Web sites need to have traffic in the form of lots of clicks and visitors; see Chapter 10). Customers don't come into a store or onto a site in big numbers unless you have plenty of people to draw from, so you need to figure out where high traffic is and find a way to get some of it into your store.

An old joke about retailing goes like this: "The retail business has three secrets of success — location, location, and location." Not very funny, really, unless you've ever tried to market a store in a poor location. And then you laugh pretty hard over the joke, but with a certain hysteria! Pick a location carefully, making sure that you have an excess of the right sort of traffic nearby. Think of designing a retail store like digging a pond. You wouldn't dig a pond unless running water was nearby to fill it. Yet people dig their retail ponds in deserts or up steep hills, far from the nearest flow of traffic, all the time.

You also wouldn't dig a huge reservoir beside a small stream. You must suit your store to the amount and kind of traffic in its area, or move to find more appropriate traffic. My small town, Amherst, Massachusetts, has a three-block downtown shopping district. The district has dozens of storefronts, and at any one time, a handful of them are available for rent because the stores in them have gone belly up like fish without water. The stores usually stay vacant for a few months, and then another brave soul comes along to try his luck. Sometimes the person is a hapless entrepreneur who is the next to fail. Sometimes the next failure is a big company that should have known better (McDonald's came and went at one point, unable to generate enough sales from a store to keep it open).

I make something of a game of guessing who fails and who makes good. Doing so isn't hard, really. Downtown Amherst doesn't have heavy traffic. The town is small, and even with two colleges on either side of the downtown area, not enough people are around most of the time to make the sidewalks crowded.

Any retailer has to find a way to appeal to a broad cross section of that traffic or has to find something so compelling to sell that people flock from out of town to visit the store. This attraction power is termed *pull* or *draw,* and few retail concepts are so unique that they can draw traffic from beyond their immediate area. But some do.

For example, a jewelry store in town has such a good selection of merchandise that it draws far more traffic than the surrounding stores. And its owner carefully stimulates this traffic through a direct mail program and by giving the store a unique and highly visible appearance — the store is in a huge, ornate, yellow Victorian house with lots of ground-floor windows displaying interesting gifts. The store's strategy focuses on the one thing that old joke about retailing leaves out — the store concept. The *concept* is a creative mix of merchandising strategy and atmosphere that you can use to give your store higher-than-average drawing power. An exciting concept, well executed, makes shopping an enjoyable event and can boost traffic and sales tenfold.

Developing merchandising strategies

Whether you retail services or goods, you need to think about your merchandising strategy. You do have one, whether you know it or not — and if you don't know it, then your strategy is based on conventions in your industry and needs a kick in the seat of the pants to make it more distinctive. *Merchandising strategy,* the selection and assortment of products offered, tends to be the most important source of competitive advantage or disadvantage for retailers.

What's your merchandising strategy? To answer this question, you need to recognize your own brilliance — what makes you especially notable — and make sure you translate that brilliance into visible, attractive aspects of both exterior and interior store design.

I want to encourage a creative approach to merchandising. The majority of success stories in retailing come about because of innovations in merchandising. So you should be thinking of new merchandising options daily — and trying out the most promising ones as often as you can afford to. The following sections describe some existing strategies, which may give you ideas for your business. Perhaps no one has tried them in your industry or region, or perhaps they suggest novel variations to you.

General merchandise retailing

This strategy works because it brings together a wide and deep assortment of products, thus allowing customers to easily find what they want — regardless of what the product may be. Department stores and variety stores fall into this category. *Hypermarkets,* the European expansion of the grocery store that includes some department store product lines, are another example of the general merchandise strategy. In the United States, Wal-Mart is a leader because it offers more variety (and often better prices) than nearby competitors. The warehouse store (like Home Depot or Staples) gives you another example of general merchandise retailing. And as this varied list of examples suggests, you can implement this strategy in many ways.

Limited-line retailing

This strategy emphasizes depth over variety. In New England, the Bread & Circus chain of grocery stores specializes in natural and organic food products; as a result, the chain can offer far greater choice in this specialized area than the average grocery store. Similarly, a bakery can offer more and better varieties of baked goods because a bakery sells only those baked goods.

Limited-line retailing is especially common in professional and personal services. Most accounting firms just do accounting. Most chiropractic offices just offer chiropractic services. Most law firms just practice law. For some reason, I've seen little innovation in the marketing of services.

Perhaps you can combine several complementary services into a less limited line than your competitors. If you can expand your line without sacrificing quality or depth of offerings, you can give customers greater convenience — and that convenience should make you a winner.

After all, the limited-line strategy only makes sense to customers if they gain something in quality or selection in exchange for the lack of convenience. Regrettably, many limited-line retailers fail to make good on this implied promise — and they're easily run over when a business introduces a less-limited line nearby. What makes, say, the local stationery or shoe store's selection better than what a Staples or Wal-Mart offers in a more convenient setting? If you're a small businessperson, you should make sure that you have plenty of good answers to that question! Know what makes your merchandise selection, concept, or location different and better than that of your monster competitors.

Mixing and matching

Can you think of the perfect new combination of stores? How about a gym and a laundromat, so people can work out while washing their clothes? Or a connections store that offers the combined services of a flower shop, jewelry and gift store, card and stationery store, e-mail/Internet access service, gift-wrapping and shipping service, and a computerized dating/introduction service? With all these services under one roof, the store can serve any and all needs having to do with making or maintaining personal relationships. See? Coming up with novel combinations isn't hard — give it a try!

Scrambled merchandising

Consumers have preconceived notions about what product lines and categories belong together. Looking for fresh produce in a grocery store makes sense these days because dry goods and fresh produce have been combined by so many retailers. But 50 years ago, the idea would seem radical because specialized limited-line retailers used to sell fresh produce. When grocery stores combined these two categories, they were using a *scrambled merchandising* strategy, in which the merchant uses unconventional combinations of product lines. Today, the meat department, bakery, deli section, seafood department, and many other sections combine naturally in a modern grocery store. And many are adding other products and services, such as a coffee bar, bank, bookshop, dry cleaners, shoe repair, hair salon, photographer, flower shop, post office, and so on! In the same way, gas stations combine with fast food restaurants and convenience stores to offer pit stops for both car and driver. These scrambled merchandising concepts are now widely accepted.

You can use scrambling as a great way to innovate. It gets at the essence of creativity because many people define creativity as the search for unexpected but pleasing combinations of things or ideas. I hope that you pursue this strategy. But I want to warn you that you should never employ this strategy just for your convenience as a marketer. Too often, retailers add a novel product line just because doing so is easy. They know someone in another industry who can handle the line for them, or they have a chance to buy a failed business for peanuts. Those reasons are the wrong sort to justify scrambling. Scrambling only works if you approach it from the customer's point of view by seeking new combinations that may have special customer appeal.

For example, several innovators around the United States have stumbled independently upon the concept of combining a coffee shop and an Internet access service into one retail store. The result is a natural — a coffee shop where you can enjoy your espresso while cruising the Internet or flirting with another customer online. This new combination adds up to more than the sum of its parts, giving customers a pleasurable new retail experience.

Creating atmosphere

A store's *atmosphere* is the image that it projects based on how you decorate and design it. Atmosphere is an intangible — you can't easily measure or define it. But you can feel it. And when the atmosphere feels comforting, exciting, or enticing, this feeling draws people into the store and enhances their shopping experience. So you need to pay close attention to atmosphere.

Sophisticated retailers hire architects and designers to create the right atmosphere and then spend far too much on fancy lighting, new carpets, and racks to implement their plans. Sometimes this approach works, but sometimes it doesn't. And at any point in time, most of the professional designers agree about what stores should look and feel like. And that means your store looks like everyone else's.

Instead, I think you should develop the concept for your store yourself. If you think a virtual tropical forest gives the right atmosphere, then hire some crazy artists and designers to turn your store into a tropical forest! Rainforest Cafe did so a few years ago, creating a fantasy environment they call "a wild place to shop and eat." Their first store, in the Mall of America in Minnesota, was so successful that they plan to open others around the country.

Maybe you really like old-fashioned steam engines. Great. Make that the theme of your children's toy store or men's clothing boutique. Run model train tracks around the store, put up huge posters of oncoming steam engines, and incorporate the occasional train whistle into your background music. Some people will love it; others will think you're nuts. But nobody will ever forget your store.

Atmospherics are important because consumers increasingly seek more from retail shopping than just finding specific products. In consumer societies, shopping is an important activity in its own right. Surveys suggest that less than a quarter of shoppers in malls went there in search of a specific item. Consumers often use shopping to alleviate boredom and loneliness, avoid dealing with chores or problems in their lives, seek fulfillment of their fantasies, or simply to entertain themselves. If that's what motivates many shoppers, you need to take such motivations into consideration when you design your store.

Perhaps you can honestly and simply provide some entertainment for your customers. Just as a humorous ad entertains people and, thereby, attracts their attention long enough to communicate a message, a store can entertain for long enough to expose shoppers to its merchandise.

Examples of entertaining retail concepts include The Rainforest Cafe and the Hard Rock Cafe, two ways of combining a restaurant with entertaining extras. Likewise, Sharper Image mall stores display lots of interesting gadgets, including massage chairs people can try out — a form of entertainment. And some Barnes & Noble bookstores create comfortable, enclosed children's book sections with places to play and read or be read to, so that families with young children can linger and enjoy the experience.

Building price and quality strategies

Retail stores generally have a distinct place in the range of possible price and quality combinations. Some stores are obviously upscale boutiques, specializing in the finest merchandise — for the highest prices. Others are middle class in their positioning, and still others offer the worst junk from liquidators but sell it for so little that almost anybody can afford it. In this way, retailing still maintains the old distinctions of social class, even though those class distinctions are less visible in other aspects of modern U.S. and European society.

As a retailer, this distinction means that customers get confused about who you are unless you let them know where you stand on the class scale. Does your store have an upper-class pedigree, or is it upper-middle, middle, or lower-middle class? Do you see your customers as white collar or blue collar? And so on.

After you make a decision about how to place your store, you're ready to decide what price strategy to pursue. In general, the higher class the store's image, the higher the prices that the store can charge. But the real secret to success is to price just a step below your image. That way, customers feel like they're buying first-class products for second-class prices. And that makes them very happy, indeed!

Pursuing retail sales

Many retailers take a passive approach. They put the products on the shelves or display racks and wait for customers to pick them up and bring them to the counter. Other retailers are a bit more proactive. They have staff walking the aisles or floors, looking for customers who may need some help. But few retailers go all the way and actually put trained salespeople on the floor to work the customers.

Industry members throw around various numbers, but the numbers I've heard suggest that less than 20 percent of retailers make active efforts to close a sale. The actual number is probably much lower. Even approaching customers to ask whether they need help is rare these days.

Sometimes that hands-off approach makes sense, I guess. But in general, if people walk into a store, they're considering making a purchase, which makes them likely prospects. To me, that means that somebody should find out what their wants or needs are and try to meet them! The effort doesn't need to be pushy — in fact, the effort shouldn't be pushy or you reduce return visits — but you should make a friendly effort to be helpful. Find out what customers are looking for, offer them whatever you have that seems relevant, and ask them if they want to make a purchase. The last part, asking them for the purchase, is especially important. In selling, you call that the *close,* and when you attempt to close sales, you usually up the sales rate. See Chapter 17 for more details.

If you want to get plugged into a wide variety of publications, conferences, and other events of interest to U.S. retailers, get in touch with the National Retail Federation, 325 7th St. NW, 1100,Washington, DC 20004; phone 800-673-4692; Web site www.nrf.com. You can also contact the International Council of Shopping Centers, 1221 Avenue of the Americas, 41st Floor, New York, NY 10020; phone 646-728-3800; Web site www.icsc.org. And if you need to find out more about store planning or track down experienced store planners, try The Institute of Store Planners, 25 North Broadway, Tarrytown, NY 10591; phone 800-379-9912; Web site www.ispo.org. You can find the Institute's Directory of Store Planning and Design Firms link near the bottom of its Web site. And don't overlook the useful book, *Retail Business Kit For Dummies,* by Rick Segal (Wiley), which goes into the topic in far more depth than I can here.

POP! Stimulating Sales at Point of Purchase

Point of purchase, or *POP,* is the place where customer meets product. It may be in the aisles of a store, or even on a catalog page or computer monitor, but wherever this encounter takes place, the principles of POP advertising apply. Table 16-1 gives you percentage figures relevant to retail design and point-of-purchase marketing, according to the Point of Purchase Advertising Institute (whose members are professionals working on POP displays and advertising, so the Institute does a fair amount of research on shopping patterns and how to affect those patterns at points of purchase).

Table 16-1	Nature of Consumer's Purchase Decision	
	Supermarkets Percent of Purchases	*Mass Merchandise Stores Percent of Purchases*
Unplanned	60%	53%
Substitute	4%	3%
Generally planned	6%	18%
Specifically planned	30%	26%

Getting more fizz for your POP

For more information about POP, a directory of POP designers and manufacturers, or a calendar of trade shows and events for the industry, contact the Point of Purchase Advertising Institute, 1660 L Street NW, 10th Floor, Washington, DC 20036; phone 202-530-3000; fax 202-530-3030; Web site www.popai.com. I also recommend POPAI's *Point of Purchase Design Annual* (Watson Guptill Publications), a book offering color photos and plans of hundreds of displays. You can come up with your own winning POP or retail concepts by perusing the latest winners of merchandising awards. Finally, don't overlook the interactions between package design and labeling and POP (see Chapter 14). Also check out Chapter 8 for details on how to design and use signs and banners.

Customers plan some purchases outside of the store — 30 percent of supermarket purchases and 26 percent of mass merchandise purchases fall into this category. In these cases, customers make a rational decision about what stores to go to in order to buy what they want. Because they have a clear idea of what they want to purchase, their purchases aren't highly subject to marketing influence. Even so, the right merchandise selection, location, atmosphere, and price strategy can help get customers to choose your store for their planned purchases rather than a competing store. And the right store layout and point-of-purchase displays help customers find what they want quickly and easily. So even with so-called specifically planned purchases, you do have an influence over what happens.

Furthermore (and this news is really good for marketers), you have a far greater influence over the majority of purchases than you probably realize. All the studies that I've seen, including the one from which I took those statistics in Table 16-1 (and also the statistic saying that three-fourths of people visiting malls aren't looking for a specific item), all add up to the startling conclusion that . . .

Shoppers are remarkably aimless and suggestible!

The fact that customers don't plan between a half and three-fourths of all retail purchases is really incredible. What happened to the venerable shopping list? How do consumers get their checkbooks to balance with all that impulse buying? And why do they wander aimlessly through stores, in the first place — don't they have jobs, families, or hobbies to keep them busy? Evidently not.

I don't pretend to understand our consumer society, I just write about it. Although I can't explain the fact that the modern retail shopper is in some sort of zombie-like state much of the time, I can tell you that this fact makes point-of-purchase marketing incredibly important to all marketers of consumer goods and services. Whether you're a retailer, wholesaler, or producer, you need to recognize that customers make an impulse decision —to buy your product or not to buy it — in the majority of cases. And that suggests you should do what you can to sway that decision your way at point of purchase. Otherwise, the sale goes to the competitor who does.

Designing POP displays

You can boost sales by designing appealing displays from which consumers can pick your products. Free-standing floor displays have the biggest effect, but retailers don't often use them. They take up too much floor space. Rack, shelf, and counter-based signs and displays aren't quite as powerful, but stores use these kinds of displays more often than free-standing displays. Customers are likely to use any really exciting and unusual display, which means that display works very well because it has a general impact on store traffic and sales, as well as boosting sales of the products it's designed to promote. Exciting displays add to the store's atmosphere or entertainment value, and store managers like that addition.

Because creativity is one of the keys to successful store concepts, creativity also drives POP success. Let me show you what I mean through an example that worked well to boost retail sales and won design awards for its originality.

When Procter & Gamble introduced a new formulation of the Vicks 44 cough syrup, they created a point-of-purchase display (that store owners could use as a freestanding display or as a wall rack) that featured a rotating frame in which two clear bottles were on display. Each had some red syrup in it — one with Vicks 44, the other with a competing cough syrup. When customers rotated the frame to turn the bottles over, they could see that the Vicks 44 coated the inside of the bottle and the competition's syrup sloshed to the bottom. This interactive display was supposed to prove the unique selling proposition that Vicks 44 coats your throat better than the competition. I like this display because it's interactive — giving customers something interesting to do to build their involvement — and because it demonstrates the product's *USP* (its unique selling proposition — what makes it brilliantly different from all competitors). Like a good advertisement, this POP display attracts attention, builds involvement, and then communicates a single, powerful point about the product.

Too often, POP displays don't do everything the Vicks 44 display does. They don't work well unless they

- ✔ **Attract attention.** Make them novel, entertaining, or puzzling to draw people to them.

- ✔ **Build involvement.** Give people something to think about or do in order to build their involvement in the display.

- ✔ **Sell the product.** Make sure that the display tells viewers what's so great about the product. The display must communicate the positioning and USP (you better hope you have one!). Simply putting the product on display isn't enough. You have to sell the product, too, or the retailer doesn't see the point. Retailers can put products on display without marketers' help. Retailers want help in selling those products.

You may have noticed that I keep worrying about whether retailers like and use POPs. This concern is a major issue for marketers because between 50 and 60 percent of marketers' POPs never reach the sales floor. If you're a product marketer who's trying to get a POP display into retail stores, you face an uphill battle. The stats say that your display or sign needs to be twice as good as average, or the retailer simply tosses it into the nearest dumpster.

Answering questions about POP

The following sections give you some facts to help you develop and implement your own POP program.

Who should design and pay for POP — marketers or retailers?

In some cases, marketers design POPs and offer them to retailers as part of their marketing programs. In other cases, retailers develop their own POPs. The Point-of-Purchase Advertising Institute (POPAI) reports that the industry is about equally divided. In other words, retailers directly purchase half of all POP displays, and marketers who offer their materials to retailers make up the other half. So the answer is a bit of both.

What kinds of POPs do marketers use?

The Point-of-Purchase Advertising Institute is a helpful source of data (see contact information for the POPAI in the sidebar "Getting more fizz for your POP" earlier in this chapter). Their surveys reveal that salespeople spend the most on POPs for permanent displays (generally, retailers make these purchases). Next in popularity (based on spending) are in-store media and sign options. And temporary displays come in third. Yet marketers generally think about temporary displays first when talking about POP. Maybe marketers need to rethink their approach and redesign their programs to emphasize permanent displays and signs first and temporary displays second.

How much can POP lift your sales?

Lift is the increase in sales of a product attributable to POP marketing. Researchers compare sales with and without POP to calculate lift (it's the difference between the two). You need to estimate lift in order to figure out what return you can get for any particular investment in POP. First, I can tell you that, in general, accessories and routine repurchases have the highest lifts. Also, significantly new products have high lifts if their POPs effectively educate consumers about their benefits. I give you a range of lift statistics (shown in Table 16-2), based on a detailed study of the question by the Point of Purchase Advertising Institute.

Table 16-2	Lift Statistics
POP Displays/Signs For	*Typical Lift (Percent)*
Film/photo-finishing	48 percent
Socks/underwear/pantyhose	29 percent
Dishwashing soaps	22 percent
Cookies and crackers	18 percent
Videos	12 percent
Butter/margarine	6 percent
Pet supplies	6 percent
Stationery	5 percent
Salty snacks	4 percent
Salad dressing	3 percent

How much of your marketing budget should you allocate to POP?

I can't answer this question with any certainty because every program has to be shaped by its unique circumstances. But I can tell you that POP advertising ranks third in spending among measured media in the United States, which surprised the heck out of me because I had expected it to be much smaller. (Television is first at around $30 billion, print second at about $25 billion, and POP third at $12 billion.) And that means most marketers don't realize the large size of the POP medium. Yet, partly because retailers, distributors and wholesalers, and producers spread this spending out broadly between them, POP doesn't get the attention that other media do in most marketing programs and plans. Big mistake. Try to identify who in your distribution channel is involved in POPs that affect your sales and work toward an integrated strategy and plan so that you can bring this hidden medium into the spotlight and make it work more effectively for your plan.

POP is just one example of what I consider to be proactive marketing. It's not enough just to get a distributor to agree to sell your product, or to write a sale to a retailer. Now you have to get to work making sure that your product moves faster than others so that you win the enthusiastic reorders and loyalty that make for durable, profitable distribution channels. Channel management is an important part of most marketers' jobs and requires attention and a generous share of marketing imagination. One good way to do this is to offer a varying selection of good point-of-purchase options to help your distributors succeed in selling your product.

Chapter 17

Sales and Service Essentials

· ·

In This Chapter

▶ Improving sales effectiveness with a strategic focus

▶ Looking at personal selling and your sales performance

▶ Managing the sales and service process

▶ Organizing and compensating a sales force and finding sales representative

▶ Practicing great service recovery to retain unhappy customers

· ·

*I*n marketing, the whole point is to make a sale. In fact, in business, the whole point is to make a sale. Nothing else can happen without that. But do you need to be doing personal sales and service, in which you interact with people directly as part of your marketing? The answer is always yes. Whether you have a formal sales role or not, selling should be a natural, everyday part of business life, and something you do whether you're interacting with clients, ringing sales at a register, meeting other professionals, or taking a phone call. So this chapter may be the most important one in the book

Providing Strategic Leadership in Sales

The sales process is a journey for the buyer. Sometimes, he just takes a quick trip down the block, but he often has to make a difficult, even lengthy, journey — and then he needs the leadership of a good salesperson.

I teach and write about leadership, as well as sales and marketing, and some people think that those topics are unrelated. Not at all! When I teach leadership skills, I am often struck by the similarities between great leadership and great salesmanship. As a salesperson (or an entrepreneur, consultant, or other professional who needs to wear a sales hat sometimes), you need to be prepared to help and guide your prospects toward purchase. You can't force it, but you can guide and facilitate their journey. To paraphrase the old saying, you can lead your customers to water, but you can't make them drink. You can't close their sales. Instead, they have to be prepared to close them with you, and that won't happen until they arrive at the end of their purchase journeys.

Every purchase of any consequence involves the whole human being — and that means his thoughts and feelings. You need to address the prospect's cognitive and rational thoughts, but you also need to address his irrational, emotional feelings. Think about buying a car, for example. You don't buy a car if you think it's ugly. It has to appeal aesthetically, part of the emotional side of the purchase journey. But most people don't buy a car if they think it's poorly designed or in poor repair and likely to break down. Those considerations involve the rational side of the purchase journey. Advertising needs to appeal to both the rational and the emotional dimensions of this journey, as I point out in Chapter 6, and so does selling. But doing this multidimensional appeal well, and at the appropriate times, can be hard without some special training and practice.

Most people tend to focus on one or the other appeal when they sell — they orient their sales pitch more toward information and logical argument (I call this factor the *X dimension* in my sales workshops), or they focus it on relational and emotional elements in their approach (the *Y dimension*).

Are you an intuitive, feelings-oriented salesperson?

The classic example of the feelings-oriented or intuitive approach is the super-friendly salesperson who knows everyone well, remembers their birthdays, entertains them, and brings them considerate gifts. This strong relationship builder may do reasonably well in sales but he's, in essence, just a well-connected order taker. He leaves the logical side of the purchase process to the prospect and often doesn't give enough information and problem-solving support.

Are you a logical, fact-oriented salesperson?

Some people naturally tend to emphasize the cognitive side of selling. They prepare by researching the prospect's needs, they present a lot of factual information, and they anticipate and refute objections. They can be effective at selling, too. But sometimes their prospects balk — they refuse to complete the journey, even though it seems like all the evidence points that way.

Why do people sometimes fail to purchase when the purchase seems like a natural for them? Maybe the problems aren't rational or cognitive, but emotional. For example, you don't make a major purchase if you're feeling uncomfortable or uncertain — you postpone it or back out entirely.

Are you a coaching, multidimensional salesperson?

Perhaps you're one of the rare people who naturally combines both facts and feelings in their efforts to help a prospect move toward purchase. (I call this approach *combining the X and Y dimensions* in my sales workshops.) When the prospect has both factual and feelings-oriented issues or barriers, you need to use this strategy by encouraging the prospect to take small steps with plenty of support from you. For example, you may break the purchase decision down to make saying "yes" to a small thing possible today. Positive results from a trial or test purchase or a small use of a service can reinforce both the factual and emotional dimensions of the prospect's journey, allowing her to reach the next level.

Think about selling like being a coach, patiently improving the performance of an athlete. What can you get the prospect to do today to increase her comfort and move her closer to a major commitment? Try to do something with her each time you interact, even if you're only warming her up to the big purchase. Salespeople have the most success using the coaching-oriented style, especially with complex purchases, so if you don't use this style already, make a point of practicing it in the future.

Are you a delegating salesperson who knows when the prospect is ready to take the lead?

Many people overuse this delegate strategy. They assume that, if the customer needs something, he asks for it. Delegating means trusting the prospect to take initiative and make the purchase. Delegators set up the opportunity for a purchase, and then step back and wait to see who buys. That's not necessarily a good way to approach sales, because many prospects don't complete their purchase journeys without more help than that.

Normally, you want to check on your prospects and assess their level of factual and feelings-based readiness for purchase — and then step in, using one of the three strategies listed in the previous sections. Otherwise, if you delegate and leave it up to the prospect, he may not make it to the end of his purchase journey. However, you can use the delegate sales strategy effectively at certain times.

If your prospect is really committed and ready on the emotional dimension, and also has all the information needed to decide what to do, then you should delegate the purchase journey to him. Try a simple closing strategy, like asking him if he wants to place an order or what kind of purchase he wants to make. When the time is right, you need to trust your prospect to make a sound decision that's to his (and thus your) benefit. Try to close in several low-key ways until you secure the sale. Then make a flow of business occur easily by providing continuing access and service support.

I call the support you do after the initial sale the *Z dimension* in my workshops, to make sure that the business people I'm talking to don't forget this all-important element of maintaining a flow of business through good customer support. If you ignore the customer after the order comes in, you probably lose the customer and have to start all over again with another customer — a much harder task than retaining a good customer would have been. Put all three of these dimensions together and you have what I call the *XYZ method* of selling, where you attend to the facts (X) and feelings (Y) of the sale and then support with ongoing service to retain the customer (Z).

I've just taken you through the heart of a strategic sales workshop. Treat the four sales strategies and the three-dimensional sales process as the basic framework for all your sales challenges. Remember to ask yourself (or the prospect) what emotional (feelings) and informational (facts) barriers exist, and then choose a strategy to fit the strategic context. A great salesperson has (and uses) this core skill.

Knowing When to Emphasize Personal Selling

Sometimes you need *personal selling* — that is, selling face to face — as a part of the marketing process. In that case, you need to make sales the main focus of marketing plans and activities. Any advertising, direct mail, telemarketing, event sponsorships, public relations — or anything else you may think of — has to take a back seat to sales. To find out if your business should rely on sales, take the following sales-needs quiz.

Are Personal Sales and Service the Key to Your Marketing Program?

❏ yes ❏ no		Our typical customer makes many small purchases and/or at least a few very large ones in a year.
❏ yes ❏ no		Our typical customer usually needs help figuring out what to buy and/or how to use the product.
❏ yes ❏ no		Our typical customer's business is highly complex and imposes unique requirements on our products/services.
❏ yes ❏ no		Our products/services are an important part of the customer's overall business process.
❏ yes ❏ no		Our customer is accustomed to working with salespeople and expects personal attention and assistance.
❏ yes ❏ no		Our competitors make regular sales calls on our customers and/or prospects.
❏ yes ❏ no		We have to provide customized service to retain a customer.

If you gave multiple "yes" answers to the questions in the previous table, then you can probably use personal sales (one-on-one with prospects) effectively, and you should make them an important part of your marketing plan and budget. You should focus your marketing program on personal selling and good follow-up service. Although you certainly also want to do many other marketing methods, be sure to think of the rest of your marketing effort as support for the personal sales process. That personal sales process is going to be the key to your success — or failure. And that means you need to give careful thought to how you hire, manage, organize, support, and motivate salespeople. Their performance determines whether your marketing succeeds or fails.

Figuring Out Whether You Have What It Takes

Some people seem born to sell, and others are doomed to fail. But most of the population muddles along, struggling to improve their sales ability and wondering if they really have the right stuff. You can't categorize most people as either sales stars or duds. They sit somewhere in the middle — capable of great performances but not so gifted that the performances come naturally. These potential salespeople can figure out how to do better, by practicing the strategic approach that I outline with the XYZ method in the preceding section. You probably fall in this middle range and can increase your performance, too.

I recommend that you check your sales talent in order to decide whether you should find someone else to do this challenging task for you, whether you're a natural sales star, or whether you're somewhere in between and can easily improve with study and practice.

The following table gives you a simple version of a test of sales ability. Take five minutes to answer the questions and then another couple minutes to score them. At the end, you have some useful feedback about your overall sales ability right now, plus an idea about the areas you need to focus on if you want to improve your overall score in the future.

Employers take note. Tests like this one don't guarantee someone's success — your management and the rest of your marketing program affect her performance as much as her sales ability does. Also, ability alone doesn't give you much without appropriate training and technique. But anyone who you think ranks low on this test probably shouldn't take over an important sales territory.

Measure Your Sales Ability

Check any statements that describe you well. If a statement doesn't fit you, leave it blank.

❏   1. I feel good about myself much of the time.

❏   2. I usually say the right thing at the right time.

❏   3. People seek out my company.

❏   4. I don't get discouraged, even if I fail repeatedly.

❏   5. I'm an excellent listener.

❏   6. I can read people's moods and body language with ease.

❏   7. I project warmth and enthusiasm when I first meet people.

❏   8. I'm good at sensing and bringing out the real reasons behind a negative answer.

❏   9. I can see many ways to define a problem and understand its causes.

❏ 10. I'm skilled at drawing out other people's concerns and problems.

❏ 11. I know enough about business to help others solve their problems with ease.

❏ 12. I'm so trustworthy and helpful that I quickly convince people to work with me in true collaborations.

❏ 13. I manage my time so well that I'm able to get to everything that's important in a workday.

❏ 14. I focus on the big picture goals that matter most to me and my company instead of always reacting to the latest crisis or chore.

❑ 15. I can balance the need for finding new customers with the demands of maintaining and strengthening all existing customer relationships.

❑ 16. I keep looking for and finding ways to be more effective and efficient.

❑ 17. I find that, for me, a sense of accomplishment is even more rewarding than money.

❑ 18. My internal standards and expectations are higher than any imposed on me by others.

❑ 19. I don't care how long it takes to succeed at a task — I know I can succeed, in the end.

❑ 20. I feel I deserve the respect and admiration of my customers and associates.

Scoring:

A. Positive Personality?

Total number of checks on statements 1 through 4:

Less than three checks means that you need improvement on personal attitude, emotional resiliency, and self-confidence.

B. Interpersonal Skills?

Total number of checks on statements 5 through 8:

Less than three checks means that you need improvement on communication and listening skills, including your ability to control your own nonverbal communications and read others' body language.

C. Solution-Finding Skills?

Total number of checks on statements 9 through 12:

Less than three checks means that you need improvement on problem-finding, creative problem-solving, and collaborative negotiating skills.

D. Self-Management Skills?

Total number of checks on statements 13 through 16:

Less than three checks means that you need improvement on organization, strategy, and focus skills.

E. Self-Motivation?

Total number of checks on statements 17 through 20:

Less than three checks means that you need to build your personal motivation and figure out how to find rewards in the pleasures of doing a job well and accomplishing a goal.

F. Overall Level of Sales Ability?

Total number of checks, all statements (1 through 20):

Total Number of Checks	Score
0–5	Guaranteed to fail. Sorry, but you should let somebody else do the selling!
6–9	Low sales ability. Not likely to succeed.
10–12	Low sales ability, but with practice and study, may become moderately capable.
13–15	Moderate sales ability. Capable of good improvement.
16–18	High sales ability. Capable of rapid improvement.
19–20	Guaranteed to succeed. Superstar potential!

If you checked a total of 13 or more, you have enough ability to be out there on the road making sales calls right now. However, this score doesn't mean that you're perfect. If you checked less than 19 or 20 boxes, you should work on your weak areas — and when you do, your sales success rate should go up. (But be aware that rating yourself on such tests can be difficult and inaccurate. What do you think your customers would rate you on each item? Finding out may be useful!)

Technique can and often does trump natural ability. The salesperson who starts with high-quality prospects and then uses the right strategy at the right time with them, doesn't have as tough a sales task as the one who starts with less. You can close a sale far more easily when you start with good-quality leads and use the right strategy. These factors can make even someone with little natural talent perform like a star!

Making the Sale

The sales process can sometimes be painful. If you think of sales in this way, you can divide and conquer. You can divide sales into multiple steps and then focus on one step at a time as you prepare a sales plan or look for ways to improve your sales effectiveness. As with any complex process, a weak link always exists. When you look at the steps in your own sales process, try to find the one you perform most poorly at right now. And focus on that one!

Figure 17-1 displays the sales and service process as a flow chart. Note that the chart doesn't flow automatically from beginning to end. You may be forced to cycle back to an earlier stage if things go wrong. But, ideally, you never lose a prospect or customer forever — they just recycle into sales leads, and you can mount a new effort to win them over. (By the way, the strategies I describe in the "Identifying Strategic Leadership for Sales" section earlier in this chapter can apply at multiple stages of this flowchart. The strategy gives you an overall approach and the steps give you a narrow tactical focus.)

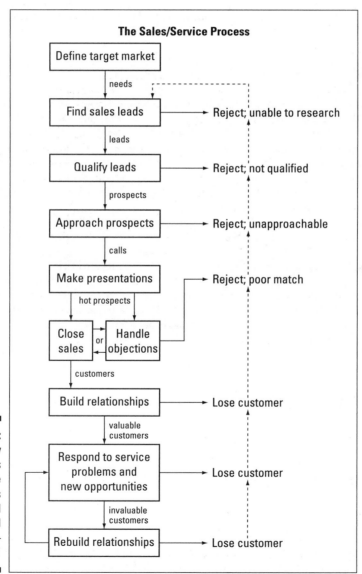

Figure 17-1:
This flow chart shows you the process behind sales and service — try it!

I use Figure 17-1 for some workshops where I emphasize the need to integrate the sales and service processes. Why? Because that's real-world selling. You can't stop when you close a sale and write the order. Your competitors certainly don't stop trying to win that client or account. So you need to think of a completed sale as the *beginning* of a relationship-building process. More sales calls, further presentations, and efforts to find new ways to serve the customer — you should focus on these points after you close a sale.

You also have to anticipate problems. You always do have a problem at some point — something goes wrong that upsets, disappoints, or even angers your customer. Trust me — it happens, no matter how good your company is.

Therefore, the sales process has to include a *service recovery* step. You have to figure out how to detect a service problem — how good is your communication with that customer? Make sure that the customer knows to call his salesperson when that problem occurs. If you think that you can use even more help in the customer service arena, start with the section "Retaining Customers through Great Service" later in this chapter and then consider *Customer Service For Dummies* by Karen Leland and Keith Bailey (Wiley), my additional coverage of the topic in *The Marketing Kit For Dummies* (also from Wiley), and the free content I've put up for you at www.insightsformarketing.com.

How well can the salesperson respond to a problem? If the salesperson finds himself overscheduled with sales calls, he can't take the time to solve problems. So budget, say, one in ten sales calls as *service recovery time* to prepare for this contingency. (Over time, you should be able to drive down the need for recoveries; perhaps you only need to budget 1 in 20 calls next year, if you make a point of trying to eliminate the most common root causes of these problems.) And keep in mind that the salesperson needs some resources, in addition to time, to solve customer problems and rebuild relationships. Give the salesperson some spending authority so that he can make the customer whole and turn her anger into satisfaction (or, if you're a small business, budget some funds for yourself to use on service recovery).

The most faithful customers are the ones who have had a big problem that you managed to solve in a fair and generous manner, so anything that you invest in service recovery is time and money well spent!

Generating sales leads

In many companies, the most important steps in the sales and service process are those steps in which you find and qualify sales leads because — as in any process — the *garbage in, garbage out* rule applies. *Qualifying* means gathering enough information about someone (or some business, if that's what you sell to) to make sure he or she is appropriate. By appropriate, I mean that the prospective customer fits a profile of a good customer. What is this profile? You need to decide, based on criteria like wealth, age, and interests (for a consumer sale), or size, industry, and location (for a business sale).

Don't throw garbage leads into your sales and service process. Make sure that you feed your sales process with a constant flow of quality sales leads. Know what your customer profile is and seek out qualified prospects with questions or screening criteria that allow you to sift through and eliminate poor-quality prospects quickly.

Sales leads can come from any of the other marketing activities I describe in this book. In fact, I recommend that you try using as many alternatives as possible so that you can find out which works best for you. Your Web site may produce the best leads (see Chapter 10 for a discussion of Web site design). Or joining a professional group or association may help you network and meet potential clients. Perhaps a direct-mail campaign produces leads. And many marketers use direct-response advertising to find their sales leads. (Chapter 13 talks about both direct mail and direct-response ads.) Then you can consider telemarketing (Chapter 13), trade shows, event sponsorship (both discussed in Chapter 12), and so on.

You get the idea. You can use almost any kind of marketing to produce leads. You just have to find a good way to communicate with people who seem like good prospects for you and ask whether they're interested in your product or service. You also need to begin to ask for factual information: who they are, how to contact them, what they've bought or used in the past, and what their current needs are. Getting even a bit of information and an indication that someone is interested means that you have yourself a lead!

Here is a very, very simple way to generate leads:

1. **Select a magazine, newsletter, e-newsletter, or newspaper that the kind of people who should be interested in what you sell or do are likely to read.**

2. **Find the smallest, cheapest display ad in that publication and buy that ad space for the shortest possible time — one insertion, if you can.**

3. **Write a very simple, short description of what you do or sell, keeping it clear and factual.**

   Include a clear, simple photo, if you have a relevant one (you can show the product, if you're in a product business), or use your name and logo to illustrate the ad.

4. **End the ad with the following sentence: Please contact us to find out more about our offerings by calling 800-xxx-yyyy, or by using the inquiry form on our Web site at www.mywebsite.com.**

You run a no-nonsense direct-response ad if you use the preceding method. This ad is designed to generate some sales leads. It may or may not work well — you always have to experiment to get your lead-producing formulas down — but it certainly gives you a good start. (If you already use some good lead-generation techniques, why not test something simple in a new medium? Everyone should be experimenting in marketing or they can't improve.)

Purchasing lists for lead generation

You can, of course, buy names from list brokers. You can find mailing and call lists widely available (I try to maintain some links to the better vendors of U.S. lists on this book's site at www.insightsformarketing.com). You may find these links useful in your quest for leads, but don't make the mistake of thinking that they're leads in and of themselves. Nobody can sell you leads; you have to make them for yourself. Write a letter describing your offer and what you do and make sure your brilliance — what you're especially good at and want to be known for — is clearly and persuasively described in this letter. Send it out to a purchased list and ask recipients to contact you if they want more information.

To increase the response rate, try including a special short-term offer and a prepaid postcard or fax form for recipients' replies. Or try following up on the letter with a telephone call to the recipient. You may have to make two or more contacts to sort out the real leads from the rest of the list (see the following section).

After you get some responses and capture their names and other information, you can call them leads. You own these leads and have the opportunity to follow up on them and see how many actually turn into customers. Good luck!

Doing multi-step lead generation

Lynden Air Freight in Seattle, Washington used a new multi-step system to generate qualified sales leads for its 60 salespeople. The close ratio for sales calls improved by 70 percent after they instituted the new system. Here's how it works:

1. **Start by pulling the names of potential prospects from a CD database of U.S. companies called *Dun & Bradstreet's MarketPlace.***

   This source groups companies by *SIC code* (a U.S. government designation based on product type), location, and size (as indicated by annual sales), so that you can target companies by industry and city and eliminate any that seem too small.

   Dunn & Bradstreet recently migrated and expanded this database on its Web site, www.dnb.com. Click on Small Business to find the Small Business Services division, which sells sales and marketing lists and offers services and support for your research efforts. It's a great site; take a look. You find that you can get (for a small fee) reports on firms of interest to you that give you telephone numbers, addresses, the name of at least one top executive, and some financial information (like annual sales) to help you decide whether a company makes a good prospect. Anyone doing business-to-business sales finds this resource valuable for lead generation.

2. **Call the names yourself, use a telemarketing firm, or hire a temp telemarketer to call each of these companies.**

    You make this first call to find the appropriate decision-maker and ask her some basic informational or qualifying questions to see if she uses or may have a need for what you sell.

3. **Analyze the responses you get to identify prospects who should be interested in the kind of services or products that you provide.**

    These leads, now qualified by the telemarketing, now just need salespeople who can use them to set up personal meetings with the decision-makers.

One thing about many companies' lead-generation systems troubles me: Many companies these days give telemarketers a *survey script* for those calls that they make to qualify the leads. People answer a survey more often than they talk to a salesperson. But this practice is deceptive. As a card-carrying member of the American Marketing Association, I happen to recall that its code of ethics prohibits selling or fundraising under the guise of conducting research. Why? I can give you a couple of reasons:

- ✔ The practice abuses the respondent's trust. (And deception in sales can run afoul of *fraud laws* — so it may be illegal, as well as unethical.)

- ✔ Deceptive prospecting irritates respondents so that, if it's widely done, people stop participating in legitimate marketing research. That consequence, which is beginning to happen, poses a big problem for marketers.

You can use the multistep process without deceiving people just by making your sources good, your script short and honest, and your telemarketers polite and well trained. As long as you keep your questions short, to the point, and clear, the majority of decision-makers take the time to answer you. You can get the full benefits without any dishonesty. The multi-step information gathering and screening makes this method a success.

And remember, telemarketers are the first people from your company to talk with decision-makers at these prospects, so make sure that they're well spoken and polite. Better yet, have your salespeople select and train your telemarketers (or do it yourself, if you have a smaller business) so that you have plenty of control over that vital first impression.

Forgetting cold calling on households

The classic retail salesperson walks a residential block, ringing doorbells to pitch brooms, encyclopedias, aluminum siding, or other household products.

Forget that approach. This method no longer works in most North American and European countries. Nobody's home at most houses in the daytime anymore, and the few people who do stay home are afraid to admit a stranger carrying a large suitcase — or should be. Some nonprofit organizations (like Greenpeace) canvas door-to-door at dinnertime with moderate success — if they pick neighborhoods where their name is well known and their cause popular. But this tactic doesn't work for most salespeople. Cold calling door-to-door is dead.

So how do you use personal selling to reach households? At *Encyclopedia Britannica*, which eliminated its traditional sales force 20 years ago, they generate leads through advertising and referrals. They then do follow-up by telemarketing, or in person, if absolutely necessary. To eliminate cold calling, you need to get really good at generating sales leads — and to use many other marketing program components for the purpose of getting leads.

You can also use a Web page or online newsletter to reach out for prospects and generate visits and inquiries that you can turn into leads. See Chapter 10 for more ideas on how to use the Web to supply your salespeople with better leads. Another idea is to ask your current customers to supply you with referrals and to thank them for this or even to reward them with gifts or discounts for it. Current customers often can find you good-quality leads through their personal networks.

If you do consumer marketing, also consider following the lead of a couple of the most successful cosmetics companies. At Avon, they reach households by *networking,* using personal and professional contacts, in order to set up appointments — usually after working hours. This strategy gets through people's natural suspicions and busy schedules. In North America alone, Avon has about half a million salespeople — evidence that person-to-person selling isn't dead in the retail industry. You just have to do it differently, and with a bit more finesse, than in days of old. Mary Kay uses a similar strategy with success, as well. Its salespeople typically schedule a personal showing or a neighborhood event through their network of contacts, allowing sales representatives to sell cosmetic products in the home with success.

Developing great sales presentations and consultations

At the sales presentation, the salesperson must convince the prospect to become a customer, which can be a challenge. Only the truly great sales presentation can persuade prospects to become customers at a high rate of success.

What makes a sales presentation great? Success. Any presentation that works, that gets customers to say "yes" quickly and often, is an exceptional presentation. Be prepared to experiment and think creatively about this task. And make sure that you've designed the presentation to cover both basic fact needs and basic feelings needs. Your presentation needs to inform while also making the prospect comfortable (see the "Identifying Strategic Leadership for Sales" section earlier in this chapter for details). Sometimes, the right approach to sales presentations is to be consultative, meaning that you should first ask a lot of questions to figure out what the customer needs, and then propose a somewhat customized solution, not just a generic purchase. This is good in some cases — especially if you sell complex services. But consultative selling may not be right for your company. Maybe you can't see any obvious ways to sell customized services along with your product. You just want to deliver an excellent product and let the customer worry about what to do with it. If so, the last thing that you want your salespeople to do is to pretend that they're consultants.

Or — and this problem is increasingly common — perhaps you have the ability solve customers' problems, but customers don't give you the time. Bringing a salesperson up to speed about a business so that she can solve the company's problems takes considerable time. In many markets, the buyers can't be bothered, in which case you can forget consultative selling. In that case, you need a good old-fashioned *canned approach*. That's when you write a detailed, specific, script that you (or your sales force if you have one), follow every time you give a sales presentation.

You can use a simple, canned approach as effectively as a sophisticated consultative approach, if the customer just wants an easy way to evaluate your offering. Be sure to tailor your sales style to accommodate your customers' needs, purchase preferences, and habits.

Organizing Your Sales Force

If you have a large enough sales operation that you need to think about bigger-picture sales force management issues, you should look over this section.

Who does what, when, and where? Such organizational questions plague many sales or marketing managers, and those questions can make a big difference to sales force productivity. Should your salespeople work out of local, regional, or national offices? Should you base them in offices where staff provides daily support and their boss can supervise their activities closely? Or should you set them free to operate on the road, maximizing the number of calls they can make — and communicating with the company through high-tech laptop computers rather than through regional offices? Or — if you have a small business — should the owner do all the selling, or does bringing in a sales-person on commission make sense? I don't know. Honestly. These decisions depend on your situation. But I can help you decide by giving you an idea of the options available — several exist — and by sharing some of the conventional wisdom that helps you assess your particular situation.

Determining how many salespeople you need

If you have an existing sales force, you can examine the performance of each territory to decide whether more salespeople can help, or if perhaps you can do with less. Are some territories rich in prospects that salespeople just don't get to? Then consider splitting those territories. Also consider splitting, or adding a second person to create a sales team, if you're experiencing high customer turnover in a territory. Turnover probably indicates a lack of service and follow-up visits. Alternatively, if you see some territories that have little potential (I cover how to estimate sales potential in Chapter 4, you may be able to merge those territories with other territories. (Similarly, the small business owner should consider adding commissioned salespeople if she can't cover all prospects adequately because of time or travel constraints.)

You can also use another, more systematic approach — which you really need when you have to design a sales force from scratch. Study your market to decide how many sales calls you want to make over a year-long period. The process isn't very complicated, and I explain it in detail in the sidebar "How many salespeople does it take to sell a light bulb?"

Hiring your own or using reps?

You have to make the most basic choice of whether to do it yourself or subcontract. Good sales companies exist in most industries that take on the job of hiring and managing salespeople for you. Called *sales representatives* (or reps), they usually work for a straight commission of between 10 and 20 percent, depending on the industry and how much room you have in your pricing structure for their commission. Also, in areas where you need more work done — customer support through consultative selling and customized service —reps earn, and deserve, a higher commission.

If you have a small company or a short product line, I recommend using sales reps. They're the best option whenever you have *scale problems* that make justifying the cost of hiring your own dedicated salespeople somewhat difficult. Scale problems arise when you have a too-short product line, which means that salespeople don't have very much to sell to customers. Each sales call produces such small total orders, so those sales don't cover the cost of the call. Reps usually handle many companies' product lines so that they have more products to show prospects when they call than your own independent salesperson would. Many product lines spread the cost of that sales call over more products, which may make the sales call more valuable for the buyer, as well. If you sell too few products, a busy buyer may not be willing to take the time to listen to your salesperson's presentation — so again, the rep has a scale advantage.

However, if you can possibly justify hiring and running your own dedicated salespeople, by all means do! You have much more control, better feedback from the market, and you find that a dedicated sales force generally outsells a sales rep by between two and ten times as much. Why? The dedicated salesperson is focused and dependent on your product. Often, the rep doesn't care what he or she sells, as long as the client buys something. And so reps tend to make the easy sales, which may not be yours!

How many salespeople does it take to sell a light bulb?

One to hold it and ten to convince it to turn? I can't really tell you the best answer to this question, but I do know how you can determine the number of salespeople you need to sell your product or service. To find your personal answer to this burning question, follow these steps:

1. **Count how many potential customers you have in your entire market.**

2. **Decide what proportion or how many of those customers you want to call on.**

3. **Decide how many calls you want to make over the next year for each customer, on average (for example, 2 per month or 24 per year).**

4. **Multiply Step 2 by Step 3.**

   Doing so gives you the total sales calls you need for the entire year.

5. **Decide how many calls one person can reasonably make in a day.**

The answer depends on the nature of the call and the travel time between customers.

6. **Multiply this daily figure (in Step 5) by the number of working days in your company's calendar.**

7. **Divide the total number of calls needed per year (from Step 4) by the number of calls one salesperson can make per year (from Step 6).**

   Doing so gives you the number of salespeople needed to make all those calls.

For example, 10,000 sales calls needed next year, divided by 1,000 calls per salesperson per year, means that you need a sales force of ten people to execute your plan. If you only have five on staff, you'd better hire five more or bring on some sales reps to help your staff — if you can't get authority for or raise funding for either plan, scale back your sales goals by half. You can never sell that light bulb to 10,000 customers with only five salespeople.

Finding good sales reps

How do you find sales reps? The obvious doesn't work — you can't find them listed in any telephone directory. I don't know why, but rep firms prefer that you find them by networking. Doing so may avoid a lot of requests from companies that don't know the industry and don't have decent products. But if you want to find reps, you have to do it on the reps' terms, which means getting word-of-mouth referrals or meeting them at a trade show or industry conference. Or, even simpler, ask the buyers of products such as the one you sell for names of reps who currently call on them.

As far as word-of-mouth referrals go, I recommend asking the companies that reps sell to for their opinions about the best rep firms. After all, you need the reps to sell your product to these customers, so their opinions are the most important! You can also get referrals from other companies that sell (non-competing) products through the same kinds of reps. And if you have some reps already, they can tell you about firms that cover other territories.

I also highly recommend networking for reps at trade shows in your industry. Reps attend the trade shows, and many of them rent booths to represent their products. You can find them just by wandering the exhibition hall, using your eyes and nose, and asking occasional questions.

Managing your reps — with an iron glove!

After you have reps lined up for each territory, your work has only just begun. You must, absolutely must, monitor their sales efforts on a regular basis. Which rep firms sell the best (and worst)? Usually 10 or 15 percent of the reps make almost all your sales. If you notice such a pattern developing, you can quickly put the others on notice. And if they don't heat up in a hurry, you can replace them.

Renting a salesperson

Many businesses have made temps popular these days, so why not temporary salespeople? Temp agencies have been providing telemarketers on a temporary basis for years. Businesses often use those temporary telemarketers for a few weeks in conjunction with any special project that requires telephone prospecting or follow-up — such as generating leads for a new product or new territory.

Temp agencies can fill a short-term need for experienced telemarketers, salespeople, trade show staff, and other marketing people. Look under *Employment Contractors — Temporary Help* in your local Yellow Pages telephone directory (or try *Employment Agencies,* if your book doesn't have this listing). One of the big, national temp agencies probably has an office nearby, as well, so you can also check your directory for Kelly Services (www.kelly services.com) or Manpower Temporary Services (www.manpower.com).

Both also have local offices across most of North America and in dozens of countries around the world. Kelly even has a marketing division that offers staff for trade shows, sales promotions, telemarketing, sampling, demonstrations, and other marketing and sales functions (see its U.S. Web site at `www.kellyservices.us` for details).

Businesses don't use temporary salespeople that often, but I think they provide you with a great alternative because they allow you to put a lot of salespeople on the street quickly without making a long-term financial commitment. Use them to help you open up a new territory, introduce a new product, or follow up on a backlog of sales leads from that big trade show you exhibited at last month. You probably want to hire these sorts of temps on a monthly basis to give them time to develop some continuity. And consider teaming them with your full-time salespeople (if you have any) to ease the transition for new accounts when the temporary service period ends.

Compensating Your Sales Force

You face one of the toughest and most important management decisions in marketing when you have to figure out how to compensate salespeople. Compensation has a significant impact on the sales staff's motivation and performance, and (of course) salespeople's performance has a big effect on sales. The issue becomes difficult because compensation's effect on motivation isn't always obvious.

Check out this resource if you want to dive deeper into this topic: World at Work, 14040 N. Northsight Blvd., Scottsdale, AZ 85260; phone 877-951-9191; Web site `www.worldatwork.org`. This professional association offers an introductory course on Sales Compensation Design and also publishes reports on compensation practices to compare against yours. I can also recommend the books *The Sales Compensation Handbook* by Stockton B. Colt (AMACOM), and *Compensating New Sales Roles: How to Design Rewards That Work in Today's Selling Environment*, by Jerome A. Colletti (AMACOM). Jerome Colletti gets into an important issue worth thinking about: How to make sure that you have relationship-oriented salespeople, not folks who just shoot for the maximum number of transactions. Make sure that you aim your commissions and also your non-financial incentives (recognition, praise, and so on) at both finding and *keeping* good customers, not just writing the most new business.

If you want to recruit special salespeople, you may need to offer them a special compensation plan. You want to do something sufficiently different from the norm in your industry to make your job openings really stand out. For example, what if you want to make sure that your salespeople take a highly consultative, service-oriented approach, with long-term support and relationship building? You need people with patience and dedication, people who are looking for a stable situation and can build business over the long term. So try offering them less commission than they would earn elsewhere. Make your compensation salary based. If you give them sales incentives, consider bonuses linked to long-term customer retention or to building sales with existing customers. Your compensation plan stands out from your competitors and sends a clear signal about the kind of sales behavior you expect.

Similarly, if you want the hottest, most self-motivated salespeople, offer more commission than the competition. Realty Executives, a Phoenix-based real estate firm, did just that. In an industry in which commissions from home sales typically get split between the agent and their realty firm, Realty Executives gives 100 percent of the sales commission to its realtors. And rather than offer a base salary, it charges its agents a monthly fee for use of the firm's name and facilities. This unusual approach attracts top salespeople who can earn more than the average broker would. And it weeds out low performers who would otherwise slide by on their base salaries and an occasional commission at a more conventional firm.

Retaining Customers through Great Service

Sales and service go hand in hand. When your business relies on personal selling — like in many business-to-business markets and a variety of consumer markets, as well — you can bet that you also need great customer service. Why? Although personal selling produces new customers, personal service keeps them. If you don't know how to keep new customers, you shouldn't waste your time seeking new customers. You will just lose them.

Measuring the quality of customer service

Do you know your *customer turnover rate* (the percent of customers who leave each year)? If your turnover goes over 5 percent in most industries, you need to build retention to lower that percentage. You probably have a customer service problem. If you don't already calculate *customer turnover (churn rate)*, I tell you how in the following steps. Find out by comparing customer lists from two consecutive years — or asking your salespeople (if you have any) to gather the data if you can't do so easily from your central customer database or billing records.

Sometimes companies define a lost customer as one whose business has fallen by more than half, which gives you a more conservative measure than one based only on customers who have stopped ordering entirely.

To figure your churn rate or rate of customer turnover, follow these steps:

1. **Compare last year's and this year's customer lists to find out how many customers you lost during the year.**

   Ignore new customers for this calculation.

2. **Count the total number of customers on the first of the two lists, the list from the previous year.**

   That gives you your *base,* or where you started.

3. **Divide the number of lost customers (from Step 1) by the total number of customers (from Step 2) to get your turnover or *churn rate.***

If you started the year with 1,500 customers and lost 250, your turnover rate is 250 ÷ 1,500, or nearly 17 percent. If you find yourself in that situation, you fail my 5 percent test and need to figure out the problem with your customer service!

Practicing service recovery

Service recovery starts with recognizing when service isn't going well. What makes your customer unhappy? Which customers are stressed or frustrated? Talking and thinking about these questions can lead to a list of the five top warning signs of an unhappy customer. I'm not going to write your list for you because every company has a different one. Whatever your top warning signs, educate everyone to recognize them and to leap into action whenever they see one of them.

Service recovery needs empathy and polite sensitivity. You should make the starting point just paying polite attention to someone. In fact, sometimes that can be enough to turn the customer around.

You can practice service strategically, in the same way as sales (like I describe in the section "Identifying Strategic Leadership for Sales" earlier in this chapter), with the goal of winning back the customer by solving her problem or helping her feel better. Usually, you have to start with the feelings of the unhappy customer. Use your emotional intelligence to empathize with her. Let her vent or complain, and don't argue with her. The unhappy customer is always right.

After she has calmed down a bit and is ready to listen to you and look to you for help, you can ask factual questions and give her information in return. But remember, every service recovery starts with working on the (hurt) feelings of the disgruntled customer, not on the facts. That important insight can save a lot of customer relationships and help you build a reputation as a great company to buy from.

Part VI
The Part of Tens

The 5th Wave   By Rich Tennant

KNOB BROS.
• Paint Drying Equip.
• TV Test Pattern Design
• Sap Buckets

"Maybe it would help our Web site if we showed our products in action."

In this part . . .

I'd give you ten good reasons to read this part, but why bother — it already contains more than 40.

I bet you want to save as much money as you can on marketing. Believe me, almost every marketer shares this wish. But few accomplish it, at least without ruining next year's revenues and profits and sending customers away angry. So please consult this part of the book to find out how to save money by being an economical marketer. Given unlimited funds, any idiot can sell something, but doing it for less is a true art form.

Next, I've rounded up some great tips and ideas for making more sales because, after all, that's usually the foremost objective of anyone picking up a book on marketing.

In this part, I also warn you how to avoid many of the common mistakes and causes of failure that have torpedoed other marketers and their programs in the past. Personally, I try to reread this section once a month, just to make sure that my marketing inoculations are up-to-date. It's easy to fall into bad habits if you don't pay attention!

FYI, if you finish this part and still want more, feel free to have a look around www.insightsformarketing.com, where I post more tips and lists of what to do (and what *not* to do) to succeed in marketing!

Chapter 18

Ten Common Marketing Mistakes to Avoid

*Y*ou don't want to reinvent the wheel. Especially if you invent a square wheel. Try to avoid making any of the all-too-common marketing mistakes that so often derail sales and marketing efforts. (And I post more good examples of bad mistakes at www.insightsformarketing.com in the hope that nobody has to repeat any of them.)

Don't Sell to the Wrong People

I don't want to have to throw away any more business magazines for professions other than my own. Why do we keep getting free subscriptions to *CFO Magazine?* We don't even have a Chief Financial Officer at this office — we're all trainers, consultants, and marketers. And why do I keep getting spam e-mails about breast enlargement, while my female assistant has to delete spam e-mails about penis enlargement? You can sort people by profession or gender pretty easily, thus eliminating the obvious mismatches. Face it, most people are the wrong people — meaning that they probably don't want to buy from you — and if you pull out the obvious mismatches, you can eliminate lost-cause prospects and not waste your money on them.

Don't Give Away Money

Many marketers devote half or more of their budgets to price-oriented promotions, and I can't tell you the number of times I've heard managers say things like, "Sales seem to be off this month. Why don't we cut prices and see if that helps?" Discounts and price cuts have their role, to be sure — but you should never use them unless you have clear evidence that the net result can be profitable. And it usually isn't, as I demonstrate in Chapter 13. Sometimes, customers are highly price sensitive, competitors undercut you, and you have no choice but to slash your prices, too. But, in general, you don't want to compete on price. You'll find making a profit (and staying in business) far easier when you compete on your *brilliance*: the elements that make you different and better.

Don't Forget to Edit Before You Print

If your letter, e-mail, Web page, print ad, sign, or billboard has a typo in it, people remember that goof from the communication. I often see signs outside of businesses or on vehicles that have obvious typos, and a fair number of business cards have typos, too. Boy, talk about making a bad first impression!

Don't Keep Repeating Yourself

If you send someone a mailing or e-mail once, they can chuck it or act on it quickly, no harm done either way. But what if they get the same communication two or three more times in rapid succession? Now they're going to respond in a third way — by getting mad at you for bothering them.

Avoiding this error can be difficult. Check every list before you use it, looking for redundancies that may slip by and end up causing irritation at the other end. I don't need to get three copies of a sales letter addressed to me with three different misspellings of my name — but I often do (and you probably do, too).

Don't Offer Things You Can't Deliver

BellSouth marketed its long-distance telephone service in a mailing sent to some states where it didn't have regulatory approval to do so. Aside from confusing and angering some customers, they got in trouble with the U.S. Federal Communications Commission, and the media had a field day writing about how stupid they were. You may not have regulatory limits on what you can do and sell, but you certainly have many practical limits. Don't advertise a new service or product until you're sure that it works and you can deliver it promptly. And if you're a service business, avoid getting sucked into the temptation of bidding on work that you don't have enough expertise to do well. Wandering from your core brilliance always hurts the bottom line in the long run (see Chapters 1 and 2 for more on marketing strategy).

Avoid the Wish-We-Could Trap

Every business has its core specialty and does best when it stays close to it. Sometimes you should expand into a new market area or try a new kind of product or service — but do this expansion with a careful, well-researched and funded strategic thrust (see Part I of this book). Otherwise, trying to play in someone else's back yard is a big mistake. To fool around in an area that you aren't expert in just invites disaster. The grass may look greener on the other side of the fence, but someone put the fence there for a good reason. Make sure that you're prepared to fight with the dog that lives next door before you jump over that fence.

Watch Out for Impersonal Treatment

Every one of your customers is a person, and they like to be treated as such. Yet sometimes, businesses send out generic bills or mailings that have misspellings of customers' names. And perhaps the person who answers the phone doesn't know that the caller is an old customer. You can make these easy, casual mistakes often without even noticing that you make them. But put yourself in the customer's shoes and take a hard look at all your customer interactions. Are they as personal as they should be? If not, invest in better list-checking, a central list or software database of customers, training in how to pronounce customer names, and whatever else it takes to allow your business to treat good customers like important individuals.

Don't Blame the Customer

We recently received a past-due notice on a bill from a cleaning and maintenance company that we'd used many months ago. Our bookkeeper was puzzled because she thought that she remembered paying the bill when it first came in. Reviewing her records, she called the company and gave them the check number, date, and amount of our payment and asked them to correct their records. This company met her polite efforts to correct this error with sullen irritation on the other end of the phone. A manager at the company chewed her out for "sending a misleading check" and "not making it completely clear which account it applied to" (even though she had returned their invoice with the check). In short, instead of apologizing for the confusion, this contractor blamed us for the error. He may have felt better after venting on the phone, but he just lost a customer forever. Don't make the same mistake with your customers, please!

Don't Avoid Upset Customers

You naturally want to avoid someone who's irritated with you — but don't. Customers can get unpleasant or abusive if they feel that they've been poorly treated — even if you don't think they really have been. Treat the unhappy customer as your top marketing priority. And don't stop working on him until he's happy again. If you win him back, he's especially loyal and brings you new business. If you let him walk away mad, he becomes an anti-marketer, actively trying to drive others away from your business. The choice is yours.

Don't Stop Marketing

When things go well, you may be tempted to relax and let marketing costs slip down while you enjoy higher margin sales. If you have a loyal following and a recognized brand name, you can probably stop active marketing for a while without noticing any significant drop in sales. But whether you notice it right away or not, this slip undermines sales and erodes your customer base. Keep up your marketing momentum at all times!

In the United States, a candy called Kitts used to be very popular. Made by a manufacturer in Kentucky, every candy store throughout the Midwestern states carried it at one time. But the company didn't promote its brand, and more aggressive marketers gradually elbowed it aside. Now, even finding the candy is almost impossible. Too bad — but entirely predictable because the marketers failed to support their product, therefore gradually turning it from a winner to a loser.

Chapter 19

Ten Ways to Save Money in Marketing

In This Chapter

▶ Cutting costs and being creative

▶ Staying close to home

▶ Taking advantage of free marketing opportunities

*E*veryone wants to know how to do marketing on the cheap. In general, you can only find worthless advice on this topic out there. Sure, you can place photocopied fliers under people's windshields for pretty cheap (although some towns have made this form of advertising illegal). But when you compare the impact of a cheap flier under the windshield wiper with a well-produced TV spot, you can easily justify the difference in price. In general, you get what you pay for in marketing. The cheapest consultants, designers, and researchers may be good professionals on their way up — but they usually aren't. And free exposures usually don't reach your target market or, if they do, don't make a favorable impression on that market. You may find it hard to do good marketing cheaply.

However, you can find good ways to save money in marketing. Real money. A lot of it. The real money-saving techniques aren't as obvious or easy as some people try to tell you, but these techniques can really work. In general, they involve doing real marketing, rather than substituting some cheap alternative. If you want an approach that really saves money, do the right things — better. This chapter gives you 10 — er, 19 — good ways to save money without reducing your effectiveness or embarrassing yourself.

Planning on Planning

I'd estimate that businesses don't plan half of their marketing expenses, meaning they spend the money without thinking about how it fits into the big picture of the marketing program. Companies often reprint their four-color brochures, renew their sales reps' contracts, buy expensive display ads in phone directories and trade magazines, inventory large quantities of poor-selling products, or spend money on fancy packaging without any idea of whether they're making good marketing investments. If you and your organization make a commitment to spend nothing on marketing without knowing why — and considering alternatives — then you can avoid wasting money on marketing activities that don't have much impact on sales. The more time you spend on developing strategy and designing your program, the more cost-effective and economical your marketing becomes.

Targeting Your Audience Narrowly

Most marketing programs waste much of their effort on people or organizations who can never become good customers because they aren't in the target market — or shouldn't be. Think about the waste involved in running an ad that thousands or millions view, when only a small fraction of that audience is your target. And think of the waste involved in direct marketing to a list that generates a 1 percent response rate. Look for the narrowest, most specific, way to talk to your customers and prospects. If you switch from a list with 75 percent wasted names to a list with only 25 percent wasted names, you can have the same impact with a mailing that costs half as much but still reaches the same number of prospects!

Thinking Small

Sometimes, you can make a big impact in marketing media by being smaller than anybody else. A little print ad sometimes out-pulls a big one. Not on average, to be sure. But sometimes. And that means you should be able to develop a great small ad of your own if you work at it hard enough.

The same holds true in other media, especially media where they measure the size of an ad in time. Most radio spots run 30 seconds. And most of the time, radio ad writers struggle to hold the listener's attention for the full 30 seconds. Why not give up that battle and just make a ten-second radio ad?

More recently, the think-small strategy hit the Internet with a number of advertisers creating *micro sites* that have nothing more than animated product ads. Banner ads bring consumers to these fun pages. And in the future, ten-second commercials may become common on e-billboards displayed at checkout counters, elevators, and other public sites.

Narrowing Your Territory

You can also think small by focusing on a smaller market area to concentrate your resources. In essence, you become a bigger fish in a smaller pond. Many entrepreneurs use this strategy successfully by marketing (at first) in a single metropolitan area. After they gain significant market share in a small area, they can afford to roll out to other areas.

The trick to this strategy is understanding the effects of *scale* in your business. Most industries have a minimum profitable market size, and that size varies dramatically. So, do some quick calculations. Can a 10-percent or 20-percent share of the market in a single region, state, or city cover your fixed costs as well as variable costs and get you significantly above your break-even point? If your fixed costs aren't too high for that market, it can. Businesses with high fixed costs — a factory, for example — usually have to think bigger when choosing a market. Consultants can think very small because they have minimal overhead. Consultants can best boost consulting sales by focusing a local marketing effort on the members of just one chamber of commerce.

Rolling Out Sequentially

You can concentrate your resources by rolling out sequentially. Even the biggest consumer marketers often use this strategy to concentrate their resources. Introduce your new product in one market at a time, and make a big impact in that market before going to the next one. This strategy works for more than just new product introductions. You can roll out an expensive advertising campaign in one or two markets and then wait for your returns from this investment before funding the program in additional markets. If you're patient, you can fund a much higher level of advertising and achieve far higher impact than you may think your annual budget permits.

Integrating Your Efforts

In the Japanese approach to total quality management, you sometimes hear the expression "too many rabbits" to describe the situation in which a business has a lot of initiatives under way without sufficient coordination. Marketing programs usually have too many rabbits when they really want one big rabbit. To solve the "too many rabbits" problem, you need to integrate all your marketing communications by doing the following:

1. **Identify all the channels of communication with your market.**

2. **Design an overall message strategy that says what your organization should communicate through any and all channels and defines a general feel or style for all communications.**

You communicate far more effectively using integrated marketing communications, and you may find that you can cut back your budget and still get your point across. Have one (just one!) way to display your name and logo, plus one (just one!) key point you want to make to sell people on your benefits. Then be consistent in all your communications.

Cutting Your Fixed Costs

Consider cutting your *fixed costs* (those costs that you incur regularly, like rent, regardless of what you do or don't sell). Although this advice sounds more like accounting or operations management than marketing, you can use it as an incredibly powerful marketing strategy!

Apply your marketing imagination to cost management for a change, and see if you can find a smaller-scale way to produce that product or perform that business process. If so, you can do small-scale and local marketing activities that your competitors can't profit from — but you can. If you're trying to figure out how to introduce a new product on a shoestring budget, consider searching for a low-cost supplier who can make the product for you in small batches. Even if you end up with slightly higher total costs, you have much lower fixed costs because you don't have to advance order in quantity and then inventory extra units. And so you can *bootstrap* (or grow on your own cash flow) by making and marketing a small batch in a small market and then plowing your profits into a slightly bigger second batch.

Cutting Back Where Customers Can't See

To a customer, many of the line items in a company's budget seem unimportant. Yet nobody asks the customer what they think about the company's budget. Customers may tell you to cut back on many expenses that don't affect the product's quality or availability in ways that matter to them. From the customer's perspective, the landscaping outside the headquarters building doesn't matter (and many people inside that building feel the same way!). Most customers couldn't care less whether you print the department's letterhead in two colors or one, or whether salespeople drive new or used cars. Put money where customers will see it, not where they won't.

Concentrating Your Resources

Don't spread yourself too thin. Concentrate your salespeople, your stores, your direct marketing, or whatever you do in your program into certain areas or periods of time so that you can cash in on economies of scale. *Economies of scale* means that your costs per ad or other marketing task go down as you do more of that task. Make sure that you do each marketing activity on a large enough scale to make it economical. Take advantage of discounts from printers, mailing list houses, and the media that sell ad time and space. If you print and mail 50,000 copies of your catalog rather than 5,000 copies, your costs fall to less than half per copy. However, apply this advice only to aspects of your marketing that you know will work well enough to pay their own way, like mailing a catalog that you have already tested and found to be profitable. Otherwise, be careful of overcommitting — see the "Cutting Your Fixed Costs" and "Thinking Small" sections earlier in the chapter.

Focusing on Your Bottleneck

Many marketers spend their money on raising awareness of their brands when they don't actually have a problem in that area. If consumers already know about the brand, exposing them to it more often may not help sales — or, at least, not very much. Marketing more likely needs to work on the brand's image so that more of those people who do know about the brand decide that they *like* it.

Or you may have the problem that a lot of people try it, but too many of those people give up on the product without becoming regular users. Then the problem may lie in the product itself, and marketing money should go to an upgrade rather than to expensive sales or advertising. A weak distribution system poses another common problem that makes finding your product when a person wants it difficult. If you don't know where your bottleneck is, you aren't spending your money wisely. Make sure that you focus hard on the most important bottleneck. Spend your marketing money there, and you'll see the biggest return on your marketing investment, in the form of increasing sales and profits.

Being Creative

All things being equal, the more you spend on marketing, the more you sell. Competitors with the largest marketing programs get more attention and sales. It's no wonder that winning the marketing war can get pretty expensive.

However, one of the wonderful things about marketing is that you can escape this spending war — by being more creative than your competitors. Every year, one or two of the most effective ad campaigns works on a shoestring budget but succeeds because of its great creative concept.

When the California Raisins TV commercials using Claymation singers first aired, it rose to the top of the ad industry's charts in spite of having a far smaller budget than other top-ten ads. Similarly, a creative new product concept or package design, a clever approach to point-of-purchase advertising, a pop-up color brochure with a musical chip — any such innovations can help you achieve big-money returns from small-time investments. You can get big results on a shoestring budget, but it's gonna take some creativity!

Recognizing Your Own Brilliance

The one thing customers find most attractive about you is . . .?

If you don't know how to finish this sentence in your sleep, you need to invest in understanding, polishing, and communicating your brilliance before doing any more marketing. You can't be all things to all people, and trying to be spreads your money and effort way too thin.

So, tell me, what *is* your most appealing quality? If you don't know, your marketing budget is poorly spent. Figure it out, and then show and tell the story of what makes you special everywhere you do marketing.

Spending Money (Wisely)

This advice may seem out of place in a chapter on how to save money, but remember that well-designed marketing programs are an investment in future sales. You can most obviously save money on marketing by cutting the marketing budget, but across-the-board cuts rarely work. They save money this year but hurt sales and profits disproportionately next year. If you don't reach out to customers, they don't reach out to you! So remember to view marketing as an investment in future revenues and profits. You save money by making smarter investments, not by stopping the investments entirely. Take a look at your results from the past year (or month, or even week, if you're looking at Web marketing, where you can get reports immediately) and figure out which investments are working the best. Then, simply cut low-return investments and shift the spending into the best-performing marketing activities. If you keep a vigilant eye on your activities, your returns keep growing from your marketing spending. Benefiting from experience in this way is surprisingly rare in marketing.

Giving Your Product or Service Away

I like to make money as much as the next guy, but if you visit my company's Web site, you find a surprising amount of free material on it. You can even download whole copies of some of my publications. Why give this content away when my competitors don't? Because I believe in the quality of my products and services and know that they can make the sale for me after people have a chance to experience them. Often, when I give someone one of my products or some free time on the phone, I win a happy new customer who may buy more and who also tells others about me and my company.

Let your product find you more customers. Give some of it away!

Using Free Placements for Your Name, Logo, and Tag Line

The vast majority of company-owned vehicles and vehicles of company employees don't have any signs on them, yet these same companies pay good money to buy expensive advertising space elsewhere. Don't overlook free advertising space. Use any vehicles, buildings, windows, packaging, and envelopes or mailers to spread the good word about your brand or company. Pass out window-sticker and bumper-sticker versions of your logo and company name (with Web address). Give out premium items (pens, mugs, caps, shirts, notepads, or whatever — but make sure that you've made them nice enough that people use them). This way, your customers and the people in their extended networks can all begin to promote your business for you.

Never pass up free marketing opportunities and always think about ways to create them. Handing out a business card and shaking someone's hand costs almost nothing — yet done in the right context, it can be the most effective marketing activity in the known universe.

Rewarding Your Customers

Give your customers a treat as a reward for their business. Send them a tin of home-baked cookies, a cake, a bouquet of flowers, or some other treat you think they may like, along with a personal thank-you note. This tip is very simple, but it does a lot to let people know that you care about their business. It's worth its weight in gold because customers who feel you've treated them well always send new customers your way.

Using New Channels and Media

You can do direct marketing on the Internet cheaper than doing it on the telephone. Take advantage of that fact by shifting your efforts to this new and better medium. Or be one of the first in your industry to switch from mailings to faxes for new product announcements. Or be one of the first to experiment with direct marketing as a replacement for the traditional intermediaries in your industry. Also, when selecting media, favor new magazines with growing readership because the cost of advertising in these magazines always lags behind their circulation and gives you more exposures for your money.

How about a radio ad, accompanied by a text message appearing on the digital control of the car radio? Not many marketers have used that emerging medium yet.

Whenever possible, find the up-and-coming thing and hop on for the ride. Or better yet, create the new thing yourself. (Can you use an exciting new event with associated publicity instead of using advertising?) Your marketing money goes much farther when you do something novel for three reasons:

- ✔ New means unproven and advertisers charge you lower prices as a result.

- ✔ New means smaller, so you can be a big fish in a little pond. You have much higher visibility in a new medium than in an overcrowded mature medium. I like to advertise where no competitor advertisements distract the consumer from mine. That way, I get to be the star cheaply and easily.

- ✔ Your originality catches eyes and impresses customers. Be a market leader, not a follower!

Giving Solid Guarantees

If you really think that you have a good product or service, why not take the risk out of trying it? A money-back guarantee, without a lot of small print to qualify it, tends to get customer attention. And what's the cost? If you're right and they love it, the offer costs you nothing at all. If you're wrong occasionally, then you still have a pretty low cost and it isn't cash out of pocket. You can't lose on a guarantee unless you're selling a bad product — in which case, you need to upgrade it right away because nothing is more expensive to market than a bad product!

Joining and Participating

I call this approach the *J and P strategy,* and many entrepreneurs say that it's the foundation of their success.

The average marketer goes home in the evening and watches two hours of television. Well, you're not average, and you can use those ten perfectly good hours each week (plus some weekend time) for more productive activities. Join community and professional groups, sponsor or coach youth sports teams, volunteer at a local community service agency, help raise funds for a local museum, or go to educational and cultural events (especially those events at which you can mingle with other professionals, like art gallery openings and ribbon-cutting ceremonies). Get out there and participate in these many fun and rewarding activities, and you find that your network grows quite naturally. Although your participation in such activities is its own best reward, you may also be pleasantly surprised at how often you bump into leads for your sales and marketing or discover that prospective customers have heard about your good works and call you up to introduce themselves.

Chapter 20

Ten Quick Ways to Make More Sales

In This Chapter

▶ Rewarding customers in a variety of ways

▶ Finding ways to sell more to existing customers

▶ Intervening to salvage upset or angry customers

You have lots of simple ways to make your product or company more appealing, draw more prospects, and ease the customer's purchase decision. Using the ten tips (plus one bonus tip) in this chapter, see what you can do right now to bring in more or bigger sales. You can always find growth potential!

Keeping Your Place Clean

Hemingway wrote years ago about a "clean, well-lighted place for books." Well, a clean, well-lighted place gives you the best area for selling just about anything, not just books. A dirty window, worn-out paint, or shoddy, second-rate marketing materials send the wrong message to a company's customers. Show you care! Be meticulous about everything that the customer sees and interacts with. An airline that can't keep its bathrooms clean and in good repair doesn't inspire confidence in its ability to maintain its engines. And a management-consulting firm that can't keep its lobby plants fresh and healthy doesn't inspire confidence in its ability to help clients thrive. To present the best possible face to the world, you and your employees need to have pride in the company and its products. Invest in building morale and enthusiasm within your firm, and everyone can contribute to the cause and help you project a clean, well-lighted appearance to customers and prospects.

Installing a Friendly Telephone System

You may have found doing business with most companies by phone difficult. Common errors include having

- No instant way to opt out of the computerized phone answering system and get a human being on the line
- Overly lengthy on-hold messages and preliminaries
- Extension-based dialing without an easy way to find the extension of the person you want
- No quick way to leave a voice mail
- Poor or no follow-up on voice mails

I could go on. If your customers have to go through hoops and over hurdles to call you, they just don't. You don't even know how much business you miss. And if you can't make a fancy telephone system friendly and easy to use, turn it off and go back to the old standby: When a phone rings, whoever can get to it scrambles to answer it within three rings. And if you miss it, make sure that you have a very quick and simple option for leaving a message — that you return within the hour. These standards make a phone system friendly and win you both new and repeat business.

Smiling More Often

Even if you have to take a little "me time" to get back into a good mood, do it. If you and those you work with can maintain and project a positive attitude, customers take notice and enjoy working with you or buying from you. Smiles really do attract more and better business.

Complimenting Your Customers

People like to feel noticed and appreciated. So when a natural opportunity arises, compliment your customers by sharing your respect or praise for what they do. I meet a lot of really impressive, highly skilled people through my work, and sometimes I'm amazed by the clever ways they find to use my products and incorporate them into their own good work. And I tell them so. You should, too. The positive feelings tend to strengthen the customer relationship, and when you're not stingy with your praise, customers aren't, either — which means they may compliment you to others who may become future customers.

Throwing a Party

Treat your customers and employees to a party at least once a quarter. Entertain to celebrate a holiday or local event, or just for the heck of it. Or how about a customer appreciation party? Any excuse works, really. Parties bring people together in a fun, low-stress way, building goodwill and strengthening relationships that turn into future business.

Inviting a Customer to Lunch

You should eat lunch with a customer at least once a week. You can use this great way to stay in touch to keep your ears open for input and ideas. It also generates repeat or expanded business, in many cases. (If you don't know your customers or how to reach them because you distribute through intermediaries, take those intermediaries to lunch, instead. They're your immediate customers, and they deserve the same royal treatment that you want them to lavish on your end customers.)

Offering a Community Service Award

Accept nominations for a community service award throughout the year and announce your winner at an award ceremony. Use *PSAs* (public service announcements — which give you free advertising) and press releases to publicize your event in advance. Send special VIP invitations to your good customers. The visibility you receive from this award may astound you, but be prepared to take the project seriously and do it with sincerity or it doesn't work.

Revisiting Existing Customers or Accounts

You can focus so hard on new customer acquisition that you ignore your old customers. Don't! Revisit them, re-research their needs, and network to meet new contacts (if the customer is a business, you need to meet as many of its employees as possible). Communicate often with existing customers — they're the backbone of your business and without some attention, they may eventually wander off to the competition.

Accessorizing Your Product Line

My customers at Insights buy training materials and programs for their companies — infrequent, expensive purchases, in many cases. But these same individuals go elsewhere to buy disposable or consumable items. We're finally getting smart and starting to distribute related accessories to our customers. It's a win-win situation because they can benefit from the convenience of one-stop shopping and we find that we get add-ons to our orders plus more frequent small orders to keep us in regular touch with our customers. It's not necessarily as profitable as our core business, but we're happy to see the order size and frequency go up even a little bit — it all adds to the bottom line! What can *you* add to your product line to bump up the size or frequency of a sale?

Conducting a Survey and Publicizing the Results

What's the latest trend in your industry? If you knew the answer to this question before the rest of us, you could get a lot of publicity and attention by sending out press releases and sharing your findings. You can use an *omnibus survey* (look the term up on google.com to find out how) in which you buy a few question slots in a large consumer survey, an economical way to do it. Or conduct your own by finding 100 people willing to respond to your questions. Your sweat equity doesn't show up on the expense ledger, so you can do a survey in this way for almost nothing. Then see Chapter 11 or visit www.insightsformarketing.com for more details on how to generate media interest in your results.

Converting Anger to Purchases

When my company sends out e-mails to customer lists, someone inevitably fires back an angry "Don't bother me, you jerks" reply, asking us to remove her from the mailing list. Because I know that people who have purchased or inquired about our products or services in the past make up our in-house lists, I figure that these angry people may still be good prospects who just happen to be in a bad mood. They probably get too much spam and junk mail from other marketers, or maybe they had a rough commute to work that day. Rather than give up on them, try to contact such responses personally by phone, letter, or card to offer an apology and see if you can turn them around. They're usually pleasantly surprised to receive a personal and polite response — and somewhat embarrassed about the angry e-mail that they dashed off in a thoughtless moment. Often, they end up responding in a friendly manner and becoming a good customer. Be an optimistic marketer — see most complaints as openings!

Chapter 21

Ten Tips for Boosting Web Sales

H ere are 10 (okay, really 12) quick ideas to kick-start your marketing imagination.

For several ideas in this chapter, I spoke to Wayne Opp, President of Media Pro (3739 Balboa St., San Francisco, CA 92141; phone 415-751-8323; Web site www.mediaprosf.com). I use Wayne's firm to design my Web sites, so I called on him to contribute to this chapter and to Chapter 10.

Generating Great Content

With any Web marketing success, you need to develop a site with compelling, informative content. You may want to invest in such content because it gives prospective and current customers good reason to come to the site. And unless you give them a good reason, they don't come and you don't win their business.

Including Useful Information

My personal favorite strategy for building traffic (and getting that all-valuable repeat traffic) involves giving away useful information for your customers on your site. Even if you just collect and cue up surveys, technical specifications, links, or other information they want, do it! When people find a site useful, they bookmark it and go there regularly. Guess which site gets the most business? Right. The one people go to regularly.

Offering Variety for Frequent Users

The best thing that can happen to your site is to have customers come often and use it as a regular resource. To encourage people to become frequent visitors, vary the content from time to time. Offer a weekly tip or showcase a different featured product each month. Put up a quote of the day. Ideas like these help avoid boredom and reward frequent visitors with fresh content.

Designing a Clean, Uncluttered Site

Cramming too much into your opening page turns potential customers off. Make it simple enough to take in at a glance. You may have to focus your content better than you have in the past. Figure out your most important content and cue that content up front and center, putting other content behind tabs or clickable buttons.

Offering Straightforward Site Navigation

Don't let the navigation get too complicated. A prospect should be able to easily move around. Avoid dead ends and long winding pathways. Keep the links logical and don't give the site too many layers. Many sites lose traffic when visitors get confused, lost, or frustrated with the navigation.

Making a Full-Purchase Site

Support the entire purchase process. Some people want to research their product options on the Web. Others want to buy. Still others want to track their order or ask about service and support. If you have customers who want to do such things easily and conveniently on the Web, please allow them to! Otherwise, they search for another site where they can do their business more easily.

Using Streaming Video, When Appropriate

Use streaming video on your site if it's at all relevant and useful because it adds interest. Make the video an option that visitors can click on if interested (rather than something they have to watch before the site finishes loading). Use the video to entertain or inform if you're in a consumer business, but stick to good solid information if you're in business-to-business sales. A short talk by an expert (you or a principal of your firm, if possible) gives you a simple and appropriate way to jazz up your site.

Linking Up with Other Sites

Offer a links page as a service to your customers. Cue up good links to useful services, vendors, and sources of information, and maintain these links so that they all work. This simple service for your target customers earns you their regular traffic. Then when they want to buy, they probably begin their search on your site.

Using Promotional Offers on Your Home Page

Are you willing to offer a special discount, a free sample of a new product, or a nice premium item (gift for customers) if people make a purchase through your site before the end of the next month? If so, put this offer up in a prominent place on your main (home) page and see what happens. A simple offer like this may increase sales and inquiries from a Web site.

Placing Your Banner Ad on Other Sites

Run banner ads on major sites where you can find your customers. Banners have a short (sometimes animated) marketing message, and prospects can click on your banners to take them directly to your Web site. Marketers design these ads along the same principles as outdoor ads and billboards, but you can get more fancy because these ads are on the computer and near the viewer's eyes and ears. Many firms offer design and placement of banners, along with tracking of the results (for example, go to `www.worldata.com` and click on the `Online Advertising` link for information on banner ads and examples of reports from their ICS Tracking System, which is a system for getting reports about your Web traffic).

Putting Your Web Address Everywhere

Most marketers overlook this no-brainer: Make sure that you use your own communications to promote your Web site! Every e-mail that your firm sends out should have an attractive, clickable logo linking to your site, as well as your address and phone number(s) for follow-up. Also, put your Web address on everything you print, including business cards, envelopes, brochures, bills, packaging, and letters. Make it easy for people to find you!

Soliciting Feedback

Let users tell you which parts of your site to expand and contract. Your *Internet Service Provider* (where your Web site is hosted) can provide you with information on the usage of your site, breaking it down right to the page level. Study this information to figure out where people are going. What parts of your site are most popular? Study them to figure out their appeal, and use this feedback to make your site even more useful. Your visitors tell you the secret of boosting your site's appeal, if you only listen to them!

You can also use a rating system for your products (if you sell a variety of retail products) and let customers do the rating. According to Angela Pablo of Media Pro (www.mediaprosf.com), this simple device helps people make a selection and adds value to the site. She also recommends adding a special offer, like free shipping or a discount, as an incentive for visitors to purchase your products. (In direct response advertising and direct mail, marketers call this technique the *call to action,* which I discuss in Chapter 13. The call to action is an important element of Web marketing, too.)

Index

Notes

Notes

FOR DUMMIES®

The easy way to get more done and have more fun

FOR DUMMIES®

Plain-English solutions for everyday challenges

FOR DUMMIES®

The advice and explanations you need to succeed

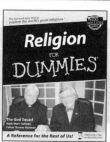
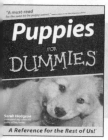

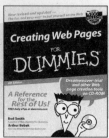

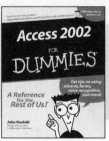